Rancheros in Chicagoacán

MARCIA FARR

Rancheros in Chicagoacán

Language and Identity in a Transnational Community

University of Texas Press *Austin*

Printed in the United States of America
First edition, 2006

Requests for permission to reproduce material from this work should be sent to:
Permissions
University of Texas Press
P.O. Box 7819
Austin, TX 78713-7819
www.utexas.edu/utpress/about/bpermission.html

♾ The paper used in this book meets the minimum requirements of ANSI/NISO Z39.48-1992 (R1997) (Permanence of Paper).

Library of Congress Cataloging-in-Publication Data

Farr, Marcia.
Rancheros in Chicagoacán : language and identity in a transnational community / Marcia Farr.— 1st ed.
p. cm.
Includes bibliographical references and index.

ISBN-13: 978-0-292-71483-0

1. Anthropological linguistics—Mexico. 2. Anthropological linguistics—United States. 3. Mexican Americans—Languages. 4. Spanish language—Social aspects—Mexico. 5. Group identity. I. Title.
P35.5.M6F37 2006
306.44089′68—dc22

2006016888

This book is in memory of my mother,
from whom I learned empathy for others,
and for my father,
from whom I learned an uncompromising sense of fairness.

Contents

Illustrations

Figures

Tables

Transcription Conventions

—	dash indicates a sudden stop in speech (e.g., "Look—")
[ ]	square brackets surround nonverbal communication (e.g., "[*laughter*]") and comments to aid interpretation
italics	Spanish
CAPS	all capitals indicate increased stress or loudness
:	colon after a vowel indicates increased length (e.g., "hello:")
" "	quotation marks indicate reported speech

Preface

In the autumn of 1997 I was experiencing considerable angst in the writing of this book. I was ambivalent about whether or not I had the right to represent the people I had become so close to over the course of my study by writing a book about them, and I worried about whether or not the very process of writing about people necessarily made them into objects of my ethnographic gaze. The task had become difficult partly due to an increasing critique of ethnographic research that questioned whether or not "outsiders" could ever really understand "insider" meanings and whether or not studying other people was even ethical because it turned them into "objects." I also realized at that time that I was resisting my own drive to finish this book, partly because developing an academic voice for my writing seemed to require a distancing from the human element in my participant-observation.

These concerns were laid to rest one Saturday evening that autumn. During that evening, we ate *pozole,* talking alternately in English and Spanish and laughing in a warm, fragrant, happy, and fully packed small apartment in Pilsen, the traditional port-of-entry Mexican neighborhood in Chicago. By this date I had known this large extended *familia* for almost a decade, and I'd eaten many meals in their homes both in Chicago and in the rancho in northwest Michoacán, Mexico, the two ends of this particular social network's "transnational migrant circuit."

After dinner, I was introduced to María, a close friend of the family said to have spiritual "gifts." During my time with her, and in front of the others, this woman quite accurately diagnosed my angst and ambivalence. She urged me to finish the book as a way to "give voice" to people who had little voice in Chicago, to counteract those people who blamed Mexicans themselves for problems in the Mexican neighborhoods. She told me that, even though I was anxious about writing the book, out of fear of being criticized (touché!), I nevertheless must do so. She insisted, "It is important that you do this; you must do this!" Before I left for home that evening, one of the women in the family, Esther Pulido, came to speak to me, to thank me for "helping us in this country" and especially for "taking us into account." How much pain must be behind gratitude to an ethnographer for thinking them important enough to be written about in a book! Her remarks further reinforced the support that I had already felt that evening from María and others, enabling me to move ahead in the difficult but important task of finishing this project. Their expressed desire for this book decisively pushed me past angst and ambivalence and forced me to recognize that this was my crisis, not theirs.

Ethnographic research, done with respect and care, can be an excellent way for the world to "take notice," in Esther's words, of people normally ignored or even denigrated. This book, then, presents with respect what I have learned from my remarkable involvement with this *familia* for almost two decades. I profoundly thank them for supporting me in writing this book, even obligating me to write it.

Acknowledgments

The research that forms the basis for this book was initiated with a grant from the National Science Foundation (Linguistics Program). I thank Frances Karttunen for her support in funding me and Lucía Elías-Olivares during the first year of this long-term project. I continued my work after this first year with multiple research grants from the Spencer Foundation, and I am extremely grateful to the foundation (and especially to the late Rebecca Barr and to Catherine Lacey) for their substantial support. One of these grants, along with a Fulbright Foundation Scholar Award, allowed me to spend most of a year in Mexico. Spencer grants also allowed me to hire as research assistants a wonderful sequence of undergraduate (María Tristán, Susana Bañuelos, and Mayra Nava) and graduate (Juan Guerra, Raul Ybarra, and Elías Domínguez Barajas) students from the University of Illinois at Chicago (UIC), as well as a number of young women from the families themselves (Verónica and Dalia Castillo, María Esther Heredia, Rosario Pulido, Beatriz Leonor, and Judith Carabez) over the course of the project. In addition, I was able to hire Elizabeth Juárez of the Colegio de Michoacán, when she was a graduate student, to gather data for me in Mexico while I was in Chicago. Finally, a Spencer Mentor Network award allowed me to hire Teresa Fernández Aceves and Abel Mercado, while they were graduate students at UIC, to search Mexican archives to construct the history of the rancho presented in Chapter 3. Janise Hurtig also worked on this project, thanks to Spencer grants, while writing her own dissertation for the University of Michigan. I thank all of these people from the bottom of my heart for working with me to reach the understandings that I present in this book.

Because of the long-term nature of this study, we accumulated a large corpus of data, notably 130 ninety-minute audiotapes which were first transcribed by undergraduates at UIC and by some family members (acknowledged above) and then laboriously revised according to discourse analytic methods by Elías Domínguez Barajas. I am grateful to Elías as well for continuing to advise me on difficult translations (the translations throughout the book are my own). When I moved to the Ohio State University in the fall of 2002, my graduate assistant Juyoung Song carried out many tasks necessary to the completion of this book: she digitized all the tape-recorded data, prepared the references section and subject and author indices, and formatted all chapters. My Ethnography of Communication seminar during winter of 2003 at OSU gave me helpful responses to draft chapters (I thank Haivan Hoang for especially detailed responses), as did the Culture Workshop of the Sociology Department at Northwestern University in the spring of 2005 (I thank Michael McCoyer in particular for a helpful question). Finally, just as this book was going to press, Kenneth Varner, a graduate student at OSU, worked with me to do final checks on Spanish transcriptions. I am happy to be able to thank graduate students from both UIC and OSU for their contributions to this study.

My friends and colleagues both in Mexico and in the United States who supported me in various ways during the course of this project know who they are. I thank Robert Gundlach of Northwestern University for lunches throughout the last two decades, at which he peppered me with questions about my research, forcing me to clarify, and sometimes realize, understandings. I deeply thank the many Mexican-origin colleagues who approached me after conference and other presentations to affirm my research. In this regard, I especially want to thank Otto Santa Ana and an anonymous reviewer of this manuscript for their support of the work. I am also grateful to colleagues at the Colegio de Michoacán: Andrew Roth for very helpful comments on particular chapters and Alvaro Ochoa for important historical references to rancheros in Mexico.

Finally, I am deeply grateful to two families. The first is the family featured in this book, without whom the book could not be and without whom I would not have experienced the personal transformations that came about during the ethnographic process. The second, and most important, is my own family, who supported me throughout this long period even when I had my own doubts. My husband, Michael Maltz, has never failed to believe in me, and neither has my daughter, Julianna Whiteman. In addition, my husband constructed all the figures for this book, creating maps, charts, and a family tree (that looks more like a cholla cactus), and read drafts of all chapters. He even accompanied me on a trip to Asturias, Spain, in July 2004 to locate the natal village (three centuries ago) of the families I write about here. Finally, I thank my stepson Bob, who speaks fluent Spanish, and my stepson David and his wife, Antje, for their interest in this project. With varying degrees of skill, we all have made Spanish the second language in our family (with Antje's German a third!). Nothing of importance is ever accomplished by one person alone in the world, and this project proves it.

Rancheros in Chicagoacán

ONE

Introduction

> One says Mexico: one means, after all, one little town away South in the Republic: and in this little town, one rather crumbly adobe house built round two sides of a garden *patio:* and of this house, one spot on the deep, shady veranda facing inwards to the trees, where there are an onyx table and three rocking-chairs and one little wooden chair, a pot with carnations, and a person with a pen. We talk so grandly, in capital letters, about Morning in Mexico. All it amounts to is one little individual looking at a bit of sky and trees, then looking down at the page of his exercise book.
>
> It is a pity we don't always remember this. When books come out with grand titles, like *The Future of America,* or *The European Situation,* it's a pity we don't immediately visualize a thin or a fat person, in a chair or in bed, dictating to a bob-haired stenographer or making little marks on paper with a fountain pen.
>
> D. H. LAWRENCE, *MORNINGS IN MEXICO*

D. H. Lawrence's words caution against generalizing experiences or phenomena which in reality are always grounded in particular historical and social contexts. Lawrence himself may have become aware of such grounding, and the cultural variation that it implies, by living in Mexico and thereby coming to perceive a (not the) Mexican view of reality which differed substantially from that of the (particular) English world in which he had been socialized. I pointedly use the indefinite article "a" rather than the definite article "the" in modifying "Mexican view of reality," since what I have primarily learned over the dozen plus years of this ethnographic study is the truth of that now-classic phrase "There are many Mexicos." And if there are many Mexicos, then there are many (different) Mexicans.

Such cross-cultural experiences can be revelations: one begins to see that the very same behavior (e.g., a particular utterance) can hold entirely different meanings for different people or for different groups of people. In addition to developing a sense of cultural relativity, in which understandings of behavior shift from one "culture" to another, we can draw another meaning: because meaning is so tied to context, and because contexts vary across time and space, variation is at the heart of social life. That is, variation is at the core of groups that are often referred to as though they were relatively homogeneous and unchanging (e.g., national "cultures" such as French, German, or in this case Mexican, or ethnic "cultures" within the United States such as African American and Puerto Rican).

This understanding of variation as central contrasts sharply with traditional views of culture, which have been critically examined in recent decades by anthropologists and other scholars. The critique of a now-outmoded concept of culture as a homogeneous, static, bounded—and apolitical—entity attempts to correct, among other things, the imposition of a perceived homogeneous culture onto entire groups, a way of thinking that stereotypes and marginalizes ethnic minorities within Western countries and non-Western peoples (Kuper 1999). By assuming variation to be at the heart of culture, as it is of language, however, we can salvage valuable aspects of the concept of culture without including aspects that essentialize entire populations. Sociolinguistic research that has amply documented the regional and social variation that inevitably accompanies language use (see, e.g., Eckert 2000; Labov 1972a, 1972b, 1994; Wolfram and Schilling-Estes 1998) serves as a model in this regard (Keesing 1974). The variation that is at the heart of language, then, is also at the heart of culture.

Alessandro Duranti (1997) reviews the debate over theories of culture. He argues that although culture as a notion has been and can still be used in colonialist ways, it is nevertheless a concept worth refining and using, in order to "help us understand similarities and differences in the ways in which people around the world constitute themselves in aggregates of various sorts" (Duranti 1997, 23). While being mindful of the ways in which ethnographic, and ethnolinguistic (Farr 2004, 2005), research can be misused, I agree with Duranti that it would be worse to ignore linguistic and cultural differences, which, in any case, are very real. Moreover, as Richard Bauman (1997) has argued, much of the critique of ethnography by James Clifford (1988) and others has not given sufficient attention to the ways in which the ethnographer, rather than dominating the ethnographic encounter, is effectively guided, even controlled, by those studied to achieve their own communicative goals. Viewing ethnographers as dominating, in fact, underestimates and denigrates the people ethnographers work with and attempt to understand. As I have explained in the Preface, writing this book has been a commitment and even an obligation for me, since a number of individuals from the families in this study, on different occasions, have urged me to do so. Inasmuch as Mexicans have been misunderstood, and stereotyped and marginalized, in the United States (Santa Ana 2002), I hope that this book can shed some light in dark corners.

I should note that, like the larger Mexican society, rancheros as a group and the social network in this study cannot be ascribed a single identity.[1] Variation is everywhere. Although members of the network share orientations about the ways of speaking focused on here, they use these language styles in different ways for different purposes. This community, then, illustrates David Warren Sabean's proposed constraints on the concept of culture:

> What is common in community is not shared values or common understanding so much as the fact that members of a community are engaged in the same argument, the same *raisonnement*, the same *Rede*, the same discourse, in which alternative strategies, misunderstandings, conflicting goals and values are threshed out. Insofar as the individuals in a community may all be caught up in different webs of connection to the outside, no one is bounded in his [or her] relations by the community, and boundedness is not helpful in describing what community is. What makes community is the discourse. (Sabean 1984, 29–30)

As I describe this transnational community, I attempt both to articulate identities expressed in speech and at the same time to show the variation, even tension, within the community over these identities. Differences abound from individual to individual, even though the ways in which these differences are communicated are shared. In terms of gender, for example, many women do not entirely accept male linguistic claims to authority; nor do younger men refrain from challenging older men. But the language practices in which these challenges are fashioned are part of the shared knowledge that makes this community a community.

What I write here should be understood, then, not as a reification of a particular Mexican subculture but as an attempt to build toward generalizations both inductively and cautiously, with a constant search for exceptions to these generalizations and for what these exceptions mean to various people. Moreover, this book represents my own understandings of this community, based on much shared time and interaction. This web of understandings is the result of a personal journey lasting more than a decade. Heeding Lawrence's advice, the reader should remember that I am one person sitting at her computer table, typing away (or sitting and thinking, and struggling, between typing spurts), in a small, pleasant study with a skylight and large windows looking out on lush greenery in Evanston, Illinois. I am writing about a specific group of families, especially the adult women in these families, from a particular village in Mexico, many of whom have lived or now live in Chicago.[2] I especially direct this book to those people, whether researchers, educators, or community workers, who are in a position to benefit from this ethnolinguistic portrait and to use the insights they gain to serve Mexican-origin students and families better.

The verbal portrait of Mexicans presented in this book has evolved out of much shared time and lived experience with one social network of families in Chicagoacán—that is, in the transnational spaces in which they live, both in Chicago and in their rancho (hamlet) in Michoacán, Mexico. The historical trajectory of these families as rancheros (people from rural ranchos) is part of what has been called *la sociedad ranchera* (ranchero society), which developed in postconquest Mexico (see Chapter 2). Ranchero societies, formed of lower-status Spaniards who mixed with Indians and Africans, emerged on the moving frontiers of a colonizing state (first Spain and then Mexico). As such, these rancheros and rancheras share some characteristics (e.g., a stance of toughness and independence) with United States frontiersmen and frontierswomen (think western cowboy/rancher); in other ways, of course, these two identities are quite distinct from each other.

The portrait of rancheros and rancheras that I provide in this book focuses primarily on the adults in this network (sometimes referred to as the Mexican generation), those twenty-five and older. Given the importance of gender for organizing interpersonal relations in ranchero societies, it emphasizes the viewpoints of women, because I am female and follow local rules for interaction that restrict my closest relationships to women. Most ethnographies written by men are similarly restricted (i.e., they actually are based on primarily male perspectives), although they often do not acknowledge that, so this ethnography is no more limited than others. Because this book focuses primarily on adults, it necessarily deemphasizes, although it does not entirely omit, the perspectives of those second- and third-generation youths (the so-called American generations) who are being schooled at least partially in Chicago. The issues around identity and language that are central to these succeeding generations I leave for a future study. First, I want to provide a deeper understanding of who their parents are, where they have come from in

Mexico, and what ideologies and cultural practices are intertwined with their ways of using language. Many of these cultural and linguistic practices are being continued into the second generation and beyond; others are being modified and changed as succeeding generations confront new cultural contexts, a new language, and changing (usually improving) material conditions.

Overview of the Study

Since 1989 I have carried out a long-term ethnographic study of one social network of Mexican families, first in Chicago and then in their village of origin in Michoacán, Mexico. A social network—a unit of analysis developed within anthropology and put to use in the study of naturally occurring language (Milroy 1987)—is a group of individuals who are in close interaction on a frequent basis. Here it refers to a group of families organized around nine siblings (now grandparents) who began to migrate to Chicago in 1964 from their village of origin in northwestern Michoacán, a state in western Mexico (see Chapter 3). These families constitute part of what has been called a transnational community (Schiller et al. 1992), which lives on both sides of a nation-state border and maintains social, economic, political, and emotional ties that extend across that border (in this case between Mexico and the United States).

I would add another aspect to this definition, however: the discourse of people on both sides of the border is filled with references to those on the other side, a concrete indication that this is indeed a single transnational community. Moreover, this discourse is replete with indexical references to both physical settings, the rancho and its microregion and Chicago. For example, a young woman in the network told me about the arrival in Chicago of another young woman from the rancho. When I tried to place this recently arrived young woman in my memory, my friend coaxed me with, "You know, she lives right across from Teyo." Then I knew who she was; her house is situated at one end of the rancho across the main (unpaved) road from one of several "Teyos" (a nickname for Esther) in this social network. I could then respond, "Oh, yeah, we went to Los Bukis [a musical group] together." My young friend had no need to specify which Teyo or which physical setting, which I easily inferred from shared knowledge of network members and their homes both in Chicago and in Michoacán.

Having been fortunate enough to be welcomed into this network within weeks of beginning the study, I was repeatedly urged by both men and women to visit the rancho from which they had emigrated. Over the last decade I have stayed in the rancho (a rural hamlet of about four hundred people) numerous times for periods of several weeks to months, beginning with a month in January 1991 and including a year, 1995–1996, spent in the region as a Fulbright Scholar at El Colegio de Michoacán. All this lived experience has personally transformed me (Mexicanizing me to a surprising extent); but, more importantly, it has enabled me to understand better who these families are, where they have come from, and their place within the larger Mexican and U.S. societies. Although Mexicans are often generalized into stereotypes in the United States, I have learned that rancheros (including the families that I now know so well) are a very important subgroup of the larger Mexican society, constituting perhaps 20 percent of the Mexican population and many Mexican migrants to the United States (Barragán 1997). Even a brief visit to Chicago's Mexican neighborhoods reveals that rancheros, identifiable through clothing and musical styles, certainly constitute large numbers of Mexicans in Chicago and probably other major U.S. cities.

Lo ranchero (all that is ranchero), what it means to be ranchero and ranchera, and what particular cultural and language practices distinguish this group are more fully discussed in succeeding chapters. Here I want to emphasize how a tendency to generalize, both in the general public and in the academic literature on Mexico, has by and large left these rancheros out of the picture. With this book I hope to amend the picture with an ethnographic portrait of one social network of families, a portrait that is grounded in their own speech. That is, the cultural analysis presented here is based on analyses of language practices among these families, in the hope that a careful consideration of their own discourse will provide deeper insights into their identities, values, attitudes, and beliefs—ultimately, into their distinctiveness as a particular group of rancheros and rancheras.

After a year or so of fieldwork, primarily within the homes of these families in Chicago, I became increasingly uncomfortable with extant academic studies of Mexicans. Having searched the ethnographic literature, especially concentrating on studies based in Michoacán, I was disconcerted. Certainly the people I was coming to know were Mexican, but they did not entirely fit the descriptions of Mexicans provided by anthropologists and linguists publishing either in the United States or in Mexico. Fortunately, my search ultimately led me to work by an eminent Mexican historian (González 1974) and to recently published work by a Mexican ethnographer (Barragán 1990b). Eureka! In the work of these scholars the people I knew were accurately described. I was, in fact, astonished by the similarities between Esteban Barragán's study and my own fieldwork experiences.

Among Mexicans, *ranchero* (or the female version *ranchera*) is a polyvalent term, with both positive and negative connotations. Neutrally it usually refers to those who work their own land (often relatively small plots) in small rural communities (ranchos). In some Chicago-area Mexican communities, the abbreviated term *'chero* is used derisively to index the lack of modernity and sophistication of recent rural migrants (Cintron 1997). In urban Mexico, rancheros, as rural Mexican "hillbillies," also are stereotyped as backward (not "modern"), uncouth, uncultured, and uneducated. Bradley Levinson (2001, 178–179) reports that secondary school youths in a Michoacán town denigrate young ranchero men who come into the town from the hills, with their big hats, boots, and rough macho ways, although it is interesting that the students show some ambivalence in their disdain (would they themselves be considered somewhat ranchero by the elite of larger cities?). Claudio Lomnitz-Adler (1992, 196) notes this kind of condescension even toward relatively wealthy rancheros in the Huasteca region of Mexico, whom the nearby urban elite in San Luis Potosí ridicule "for 'not wearing socks' and not knowing how to read." Reflecting this widespread attitude, urban upper-class Mexican mothers chide their daughters, *¡No seas ranchera!* (Don't be so backward!—i.e., lacking in social skills).[3]

Yet there is also an extensive tradition in Mexico which valorizes *lo ranchero* as "the real Mexican" (and male) identity. Just as cowboys have been idealized in the United States, Mexican rancheros have been used, especially in films, to promote postrevolutionary nationalism by creating "an idealized, romanticized, and imaginary Mexico that illuminated the movie screens of Latin America" (Berg 1992, 15). In the popular imagination in Mexico, during the golden age of Mexican cinema from the mid-1930s through the mid-1950s, rancheros (as *charros* or elegantly outfitted Mexican cowboys) were valorized in the popular *comedia ranchera* (ranch comedy) film genre as epitomizing *mexicanidad* (Mexicanness) in an idealized agrarian society. Such films and popular music during this time featured, among others, Jorge Negrete and Pedro Infante, two well-known ranchero idols, representing men of honor. Ranchero images are also evoked when Vicente Fernández and Lola Beltrán croon heartfelt ranchero ballads, and when mariachi bands in form-fitting highly decorative suits and wide sombreros play "GuadalaJARA! GuadalaJARA!" as a central icon of *la música ranchera.* These representations fill the airwaves in Chicago on Spanish-language radio stations and are part of various community events such as *jaripeos* (rodeos), at one of which the late Pedro Infante's son, Armando, made an appearance.

Some scholars critique this use of rancheros as reflective of a "powerful conservative tendency in the society" in its promotion of traditional Catholic values and a hierarchical agrarian social order (Mora 1982, 47; see also Berg 1992; de la Vega Alfaro 1995), suggesting that this conservatism was a reaction against modernizing, progressive moves on the part of the revolutionary government. Certainly these films portray an idealized hierarchical social order based on rural aristocratic control, with their *charro* heroes, socially below the hacendados (hacienda owners) but above the rural masses, exhibiting admirable (masculine) moral qualities that end up saving the day and winning the beautiful but humble (and powerless) woman. The representations in this idealized world nonetheless greatly appeal to many contemporary, real-life rancheros because they symbolize the values, demeanor, and status that they hold dear.

In spite of very specific ranchero identities within the larger Mexican society, however, U.S. representations of Mexicans in popular culture and media (e.g., newspaper articles) continue to generalize and essentialize them as monolithic Others (Santa Ana 2002). A few of these representations positively present Mexicans as "hardworking," although this is often linked to "submissive." Others, often generalized to all "Hispanics," characterize them negatively, linking them to the inner city, crime, welfare, "broken" families, gangs, and illiteracy—a far cry from the film world of Pedro Infante and Jorge Negrete that valorizes a stable agrarian social order maintained by men of honor.

Neither extreme, of course, accurately represents contemporary real-life rancheros. This book intends to provide just such a real-life portrait based on a particular group of contemporary ranchero Mexicans, the transnational spaces they inhabit, and the language practices which both constitute and express their identities, as constructed by themselves, not by outside media. It is the strength of ethnography, of course, to gather multiple "insider" perspectives and to collate these perspectives into meaningful interpretations of cultural practice. Given the importance of such populations in understanding globalization processes in which many people are on the move worldwide, as well as the importance of this subgroup of Mexicans both in Mexico and in the United States, I hope that this description will contribute to discussions of a variety of social issues, including migration, ethnicity, and gender. In particular, however, because of the increasing numbers of Mexican-origin students in classrooms across the United States, and because language is so central to education, I hope that the detailed treatment here of ranchero and ranchera identities as constructed by their own language practices will be useful to discussions involving educational and other policy issues.

Rationale of the Study

This ethnographic project originally was undertaken to develop understandings of the communicative competence (Hymes 1972) of Mexican-origin students: how language is used in culturally appropriate ways within Mexican families. These students, like others from nondominant U.S. cultures, frequently use communicative styles that differ from those favored by formal educational institutions (see Heath 1983). That is, their communicative competence consists of a repertoire of complex verbal styles that have cultural and linguistic value in themselves and yet differ from the academic register of English favored in U.S. schools and universities. This register is characterized by explicitness and objectivity, and it is typified in composition instruction; that is, it is largely what we teach when we teach expository writing in the United States (Farr 1993). Composition classes, of course, are notorious for being gatekeeping mechanisms within colleges and universities. Not performing well in this register of language can handicap an individual in terms of future aspirations, educational achievement, time, money, and self-esteem.

Yet we have very little understanding of the discourse styles that are natural to many U.S. populations for whom such academic English is unfamiliar. Such an understanding provides a crucial foundation for improving language and literacy instruction to an increasingly diverse population. In order to teach academic language genres, we should understand what students already know—what styles of discourse they already have learned through socialization in their homes and communities, and how these discourse styles, in both form and function, may complement or differ from those required for success in educational institutions. Equally important as differences themselves are the social meanings of the differences, especially as they impact identity. That is, students may have trouble with differences in styles of discourse not only because they might be initially unfamiliar but because adopting them might signify a change in identity (Lindquist 1999).

Mexican professors with whom I have worked have commented on the highly developed oral skills of many Mexican students (they can eloquently *echar rollo:* generate a long oral discourse on a topic), adding that these same students have difficulty learning to write clear and concise academic Spanish. Such highly developed oral language abilities are indicative of the high value placed on them in Mexican society, as well as the emphasis on oral performance in Mexican schools (Levinson 2001; Rockwell 1991). All students, of course, are faced with new ways of using language in schools and universities, either in Mexico or in the United States. In the United States, however, Spanish-speaking students not only must confront new academic language genres and their associated identities but, in addition, must learn them in a new language, English. Moreover, while academic English and academic Spanish certainly share characteristics, they are also distinct in some ways (Spicer-Escalante 2005).

Language, then, is of central importance in education in myriad ways. As Courtney Cazden (1988) notes, education not only involves the teaching of language but occurs through language. Crucial to such teaching is a receptiveness and sensitivity to the discourse styles and identities that students bring with them to the classroom. Although sociolinguistic studies have analyzed the verbal styles favored by some U.S. groups (see Farr and Ball 1999 for a review), little research has focused on language use among Mexican-origin groups, in spite of the fact that Mexicans are one of the fastest-growing segments of the U.S. population. Hispanics/Latinos now constitute 26 percent of the population in the city of Chicago and 17 percent of the Chicago Metropolitan Statistical Area; Mexicans alone constitute 18.3 percent of Chicago's total population and 12.7 percent of the Chicago MSA (Northeastern Illinois Planning Commission 2005). In addition to the scarcity of research in this area, most of what exists (e.g., Briggs 1988; Elías-Olivares 1979; Galindo 1992; Galindo and Gonzales 1999) has been carried out in the Southwest. Little research has illuminated the language capabilities of Mexican-origin people in the Midwest. The Midwest, after all, is different from the Southwest for Mexican populations, in that its history does not include conquest and colonization of Mexican territory. Moreover, Chicago's heavily immigrant history and ambiance provides a somewhat more tolerant milieu for attitudes toward immigrants in general and toward non-English languages in particular (see Farr 2004, 2005). Chicago, then, is an important site for broadening our understandings of language use among Mexican-origin populations.

Research has begun to provide these understandings. A number of publications have focused on literacy practices among the families of this study (Farr 1994a, 1994c, 2000; Farr and Guerra 1995; Guerra and Farr 2002). Other publications have focused on oral genres, especially what is called *echando relajo* (see Chapter 8 and Farr 1994b, 1998). Juan Guerra (1998) analyzes both oral genres and literacy practices, especially "self-fashioning" in oral narratives and the writing of letters and autobiographies. Finally, the present study focuses entirely on oral discourse styles and how they construct a ranchero identity. Three "ways of speaking" (Hymes 1974b) in particular construct various facets of this identity. These three ways of speaking emerged as significant during the course of my fieldwork; they both complement and contradict each other. Each way of speaking constructs an aspect of ranchero personhood, and together they provide a fuller verbal portrait of rancheros than is provided by any one of them alone. Before giving an overview of these three verbal styles and their place in ranchero culture, I describe below the theoretical frameworks and methods that I have used in this study to gather, select, and analyze these oral language practices.

An Ethnography of Language

Dell Hymes's original conceptualization of the ethnography of communication (1974a) stimulated the ethnography of literacy (Street 1984, 1993; Szwed 1981).[4] Much work in the ethnography of literacy tradition has been advanced by social concerns regarding inequities in education and literacy. Unfortunately, important though such studies are, they increasingly ignore the relevance of oral language practices. Understandings of literacy are deepened and enriched by attention to oral practices among populations learning or using literacy (Farr 1993), especially as these practices are so central to identity construction. Although Shirley Brice Heath's (1983) seminal research relies heavily on oral language practices to illuminate educational and literacy issues, much subsequent work has not been as grounded in a deep understanding of language as the base from which both literacy and identity spring. Ruth Finnegan (1988) and Brian Street (1984), however, use ethnographic evidence to critique the assumed "special" attributes and effects of literacy (that supposedly detach it from orality) posited by Jack Goody (1968, 1977), Walter J. Ong (1982), and David Olson (1977, 1994). More recently, James Collins and Richard Blot (2003) use both ethnographic and historical evidence to undermine the dichotomous thinking that divides orality and literacy in the first place.

This study takes a holistic ethnographic approach to the study of language and its constitutive role in social and cultural life; that is, it divides neither orality from literacy nor language (oral or written) from its social context. The larger project of which this study is a part was conceptualized to include both orality and literacy. Although particular publications have focused either on literacy practices (Farr 1994a, 1994c, 2000) or on oral traditions (Farr 1994b, 1998), both modes of using language are perceived in relation to each other and in relation to the social contexts which they partially constitute.

In this book I analyze three common ways of speaking in order to achieve a deeper understanding of various aspects of ranchero identity. As Guerra (1998) notes, informal conversation (*echando plática*) has a central place in these families' lives. Societies vary in the importance they give to talk, and Mexican cultures are known for being highly verbal and for creatively using a wide variety of expressive genres (Herrera-Sobek 1990, 1993; Limón 1992, 1994; López 1995; Paredes 1993). These families revel in talk. Those who excel in weaving oral language genres such as jokes, proverbs (Domínguez Barajas 2002, 2005), and humorous narratives into their conversation are esteemed and respected by their relatives and friends: skill in language is skill in life. I had the good fortune to be included in many communicative events over the years in which such performances emerged spontaneously. Out of the many which occurred, I have selected, presented, and analyzed representative examples throughout this book.

Methods

Over the course of a decade or so, I collected an abundant variety of data for this study's components on history, fieldwork, sociolinguistic interviews, and language use. Regional and familial history was documented by Teresa Fernández Aceves and myself. This history synthesizes archival data collected in Mexico, published sources, oral history interviews of local people, and life history interviews of older persons in the rancho.

The fieldwork component consists of my own participant-observation. This means, of course, that I not only observed but participated actively in this social network (can you imagine people putting up with a researcher for so many years who did not?), interacting with a wide variety of friends and kin. Because of the long-term nature of my involvement, which is both personal and research-related, some children grew up seeing me "around." This long-term personal involvement enabled the building of *confianza* (trust), so that I was allowed to tape-record conversations for many years. With the Spencer Foundation funding of the project I was able to hire a number of young women from these families to assist me in my research. They taped when I was not present (both in Chicago and in Mexico), helped with transcription of the tapes, interviewed people on occasion,[5] explained things to me when I was uncertain of my own interpretations (or affirmed them when I had intuitively understood things as they did), and drew a large map of the rancho from memory for the wall of my research office in Chicago. In that sense, this has been a very collaborative project.

My participant-observation resulted in extensive field notes as well as some "head notes": those events and comments that the researcher remembers vividly but somehow did not write down. My copious field notes over a decade or so were first written in WordPerfect then transported into Ethnograph, a database management program formulated especially for ethnographic studies. In Ethnograph, I coded my field notes with thematic labels (gender, reading, morality, etc.) then worked with a research assistant, Elías Domínguez Barajas, to refine them and organize them into hierarchical (parent-child) groupings of related themes. The process of grouping themes not only allowed another pair of culturally aware eyes on my field notes but also illuminated thematic connections not otherwise obvious to either of us. The resulting map of codes permitted me to run searches of particular themes or combinations of themes, identifying and pulling out relevant stretches of my field notes, which I used in developing analyses and writing chapters.

Both my participant-observation and the audiotaping of oral language data (for the sociolinguistic interview and language use components) took place within families on their own turf, whether in Mexico or in Chicago. Informal sociolinguistic interviews were carried out by Lucía Elías-Olivares and Juan Guerra, with whom I collaborated during the early phases of the larger project. These interviews were conducted with the adults in the network, in pairs, and included ten modules on oral and written language practices and histories, language attitudes, schooling experiences and attitudes toward education, mass media usage and preferences, and marketing practices. All these interviews, almost entirely in Spanish, were transcribed and then used on relevant occasions in analysis. Although I have made heavy use of these interviews for particular publications (e.g., Farr 1993), in this book I rely more on my field notes and on the second audiotaped data set that constituted the language use component of the project.

A corpus of 130 ninety-minute audiotapes of naturally occurring conversation was accumulated for the language use component of the project simply by turning on the tape recorder in the kitchen or other area of the home in which we gathered and talked.[6] These tapes were indexed for content and laboriously transcribed (see the Acknowledgments) over a ten-year period. After transcription, all 130 tapes were examined for instances of conversations which illustrated identified themes (akin to the coded themes that developed out of an analysis of my field notes). Templates containing these instances could then be pulled from the larger data set to facilitate analysis of particular themes. This subset of transcriptions provided the instances of recorded oral language analyzed throughout this book and, along with my field notes, constitutes the primary data relied on for this study. In the next section I describe the primary conceptual frameworks that I used to analyze this oral language.

Discourse, Performance, and Ideology

Joel Sherzer (1983, 295), quoting Franz Boas (1911), points out that "language patterns are unconscious and provide access to unconscious cultural patterning otherwise inaccessible to researchers." Some aspects of social and cultural life cannot be understood simply by asking people about them, as Charles Briggs (1986) has shown, although this is how most social science (including most anthropology) proceeds. Sherzer (1983, 296) shows how discourse—which he defines as language use, oral or written, brief (like a greeting) or lengthy (like a novel or oral narrative)—is "the nexus, the actual and concrete expression of the language-culture-society relationship." Thus through microlevel discourse analysis researchers can illuminate larger social and cultural processes. John Lucy (1993, 24), citing Boas (1911), notes the unconscious quality of discourse relative to other cultural practices, making discourse analysis a productive source for grounding ethnographic interpretation. Discourse, in fact, constructs social reality. Both culture and language are created, re-created, and changed through language use. Furthermore, particular kinds of discourse are especially fertile sites for this:

> . . . it is especially in verbally artistic discourse such as poetry, magic, verbal dueling, and political rhetoric that the potentials and resources provided by grammar, as well as cultural meanings and symbols, are exploited to the fullest and the essence of language-culture relationships becomes salient. (Sherzer 1983, 296)

This study, then, looks at especially aesthetic instances of discourse, some of which involve speech play, but all of which are performative (Bauman 1984 [1977]; Hymes 1981; Sherzer 2002; Tannen 1989). Special empirically discoverable qualities make performative discourse stand out from surrounding "everyday" discourse (Bauman 1984 [1977]):

- beginnings of performances (e.g., jokes, stories) are signaled by the reframing of ordinary language (e.g., with a code-switch or unusual intonation);

- poetic devices (notably parallelism and repetition with variation) intensify the importance of the form of the language, beyond its communicative value;
- someone takes responsibility for performing, knowing that it will be evaluated with shared standards;
- participants who become "audience" reorient to the performer (e.g., bodies and faces turn toward the performer, other talking ceases).

Verbal performance can occur in formal, scheduled, public events (in which primarily males perform in most cultures), or it can emerge spontaneously in everyday conversation (a frequent province of female performers). All instances of discourse in this book occurred in private settings in people's homes or vehicles, either in Chicago or in Mexico (or traveling from one to the other).

Performance makes particular "pieces" of language stand out from "ordinary" language as "text"; that is, it entextualizes them (Briggs and Bauman 1992; Silverstein and Urban 1996). Such texts are highly noticeable, which facilitates reflexivity and critique on the part of participants:

> . . . performances move the use of heterogeneous stylistic resources, context-sensitive meanings, and conflicting ideologies into a reflexive arena where they can be examined critically. . . . Performance . . . provides a frame that invites critical reflection on communicative processes. (Bauman and Briggs 1990, 60)

Performances of verbal art are not just interesting aesthetically but are particularly salient sites for the creation, re-creation, and transformation of language, culture, and society. Joking in particular, in its microlevel creation of carnivalesque disorder (i.e., fiesta or carnival at the level of language), allows people to turn the existing social order upside down, at least for the moment (see Chapter 8). Such "play frames . . . provide settings in which speech and society can be questioned and transformed" (Bauman and Briggs 1990, 63) and thus have ramifications for reconfiguring social relations.

Recently developed conceptualizations of language ideology (Kroskrity 2000; Schieffelin et al. 1998) link beliefs about language to broader sociocultural and political processes. Thus particular styles of using language, including verbal performances, are the expected way to speak in specific contexts and simultaneously to construct oneself as a culturally valued person. As Kathryn Woolard (1998, 3) has noted, language ideologies are never just about language but are also about "the very notion of the person and the social group, as well as such fundamental social institutions as religious ritual, child socialization, gender relations, the nation-state, schooling, and law." Language ideologies, then, mediate between "social structures and forms of talk" (Kroskrity 2000, 21). As people use language in conventional ways, they simultaneously organize relations among people and define "us," as opposed to "them," in terms of specific moral, aesthetic, epistemological, and other qualities. The rancheros who are the focus of this book distinguish themselves from other groups, primarily Indian Mexicans, with language ideologies constructed in particular ways of speaking or styles of language use (Hymes 1974b). In Chapters 5 through 8 I analyze verbal performances that occurred in informal conversation in both Chicago and Mexico; these verbal performances represent particular language styles, and language ideologies, that construct ranchero identities vis-à-vis their Others.

Language Styles, Language Ideologies, and Ranchero Identity

Hymes (1974b, 434) proposed "style," in its "root sense of a way or mode of doing something," as an alternative to traditional grammar as a starting point for language analysis.[7] Defining a speech community as an organized set of diverse speech styles, he argued that such styles, as parts of words and utterances, express social meanings in contradistinction to referential or "literal" meanings. That is, people choose among conventional uses of verbal means (e.g., intonation) to voice a particular attitude (e.g., irony) toward a topic, hearers, or situation. When these conventional means are grouped into "significant speech styles" in a community, they constitute more global "ways of speaking" that represent "community attitudes and beliefs with regard to language and speech" (Hymes 1974b, 445). In other words, ways of speaking are conventionally agreed upon speech styles that, with their associated contexts, implicate language ideologies and thus larger social and political processes, including social relations.

This book focuses on three significant ways of speaking among ranchero Mexicans: *franqueza* (frankness, directness, or candor), *respeto* (respect), and *relajo* (a carnivalesque communicative event in which people "joke or fool around"). These three ways of speaking construct ranchero language (and other) ideologies, as well as identities. The speech style in which a ranchero identity is most evident is *franqueza,* which emphasizes the characteristics of self-assertiveness and independence, which may have evolved in ranchero frontier societies (see Chapters 2 and 6). Honest, candid, direct talk is highly valued among rancheros: it constructs a person who is trustworthy and admirable, whose *palabra de honor* (word of honor) can be relied upon. Instances of *franqueza* from many hours of tape-recorded speech, both in Chicago and in Mexico, illustrate this language ideology. As a way of speaking, it is linked to an egalitarian, liberal individualist ideology which values *el progreso* (progress) through hard work and individual entrepreneurial effort, key qualities of ranchero identity. This identity is contrasted with that of Indian Mexicans, who, in the ranchero view, are communally oriented. Thus ranchero men, women, and even children construct themselves as authoritative, independent, and self-assertive in their interactions with others, peppering their speech with frequent imperatives. For example, an eight-year-old girl ordered her ten-year-old brother "¡Aguántase, si es hombre!" (Handle it, if you're a man!) as he winced in pain when she applied lime to the *granitos* (little bumps) that appeared on his arm after *juntando aguacate* (gathering avocados) with his father in their orchard.

Respeto (respect), a second way of speaking, enacts another ranchero language ideology (see Chapter 7). *Respeto* calls for deference to authority, according to age and gender hierarchies, as well as respect for individual dignity. To talk with respect (for example, to parents or teachers) calls for particular linguistic and nonlinguistic behaviors that support the dignity or public face of both parties. *Respeto,* then, maintains traditional boundaries (e.g., between men and women, parents and children, the old and the young), with rules for interaction. These interactional rules are important both within the family (because they buttress family roles such as father, mother, brother, and sister) and beyond it, in the larger community. Such nuances of politeness are culturally specific and can easily be misunderstood or ignored in the United States, where people interacting in public often move quickly to informality and the familiarity of first names (the equivalent of using informal *tú* rather than formal *usted* for "you" in Spanish). Many students who descend from ranchero Mexican backgrounds thus might enact themselves as deferential in classrooms yet as self-assertive and independent at home and in other contexts.

A third way of speaking, *el relajo* (see Chapter 8), stands in apparent opposition to the first two. Whereas *franqueza* and *respeto* are seen as affirming social order (things as they "should" be), *relajo* (a joking style) is acknowledged as the designated space for disorder, for violating boundaries and normal rules for behavior and interaction. *Relajo* within this social network occurs primarily in intimate, informal contexts, but it can also occur at school, at work, or in other public contexts, as a subversive response to discipline and constraints. This way of speaking is recognizable out of context, which affirms its status within this speech community as a significant speech style (Hymes 1974b, 440). As a language ideology, *relajo* constructs individual people as creative and clever verbal performers who challenge the status quo while entertaining and delighting their immediate audiences. It also promotes a democratic leveling of participants while building solidarity and, particularly among women, consensus. *Relajo* disrupts the social order established through both *respeto* (in its respect for familial and societal roles) and *franqueza* (in its serious, straightforward representation of everyday reality as well as of candid and egalitarian relations between individuals). *Relajo* allows a carnivalesque inversion of the normal social order by providing a space for humorous critique.

It is arguable whether *relajo* thus affirms the status quo (and the existing social order), by allowing people to "let off steam" in verbally sanctioned ways, or facilitates change, by allowing people to initiate new ways of speaking and being and even assert challenges in a relatively safe, face-saving context. Either way, however, *relajo* is specifically about disorder. Significantly, it is humorous disorder, since much of what is humorous during *echando relajo* (joking or fooling around) would not be amusing or entertaining without a presumed background of solid social order. For example, although a respectable woman is not supposed to swear, it amuses people when she does so fluently, even eloquently, during *relajo.*

Order and Disorder in Ranchero Society

The three ways of speaking that form the focus of this book relate to order and disorder, work and play, being serious and nonserious, in contrasting ways. *Franqueza* and *respeto* are primarily tied to the first members of these pairs: they are about order, work, and seriousness. Both of these ways of speaking organize social relations, either egalitarian (*franqueza*) or hierarchical (*respeto* but also *franqueza* at times). Tying them together in this way, a Mexican friend once said to me that *franqueza* is *respeto.* This kind of *franqueza* indexes egalitarian relations between people: if all persons respect one another and are candid and honest with one another, violence is avoided and social order is affirmed. But *franqueza* also can index authority speaking "down" to a subordinate. In either context, however, *franqueza* is the style of language used for serious talk—for work, not for play—so is predominantly referential in terms of language functions (Jakobson 1960).

Respeto is explicitly tied to order by organizing social relations. As one man in the network explained to me, "Respeto es vivir en paz" (Respect is to live in peace). His words echo, but do not exactly quote, the famous utterance of Benito Juárez, the late-nineteenth-century Mexican president: "Entre los individuos, como entre las naciones, el respeto al derecho ajeno es la paz" (Among individuals, as among nations, respecting the rights of others is peace; http://usuarios.lycos.es/Aime/manifiesto.html). Many other members of the social network in this study expanded upon this definition of *respeto,* adding (the same) specific rules for living in peace (don't take what is not yours and don't run around with someone else's husband or wife). At the level of linguistic interaction, *respeto* regulates the use of informal or formal "you" (*tú* or *usted*) according to social roles organized by age and gender, thus affirming the traditional hierarchical social order. The difference between *franqueza* and *respeto* as language ideologies, however, is that, whereas *franqueza* often presumes egalitarian relations between equals (as noted above, it can also presume top-down authoritative speech), *respeto* always presumes hierarchical relations organized according to gender and family roles, including a respect for elders.

Finally, as I have noted above, *echando relajo* is an occasion for disorder, for undermining seriousness, a time for verbal play. As such, it is a rich communicative event for the poetic and metacommunicative functions of language, as is evidenced in much speech play, poetic language devices, and reported speech in humorous narratives (Sherzer 2002). *Relajo* both undermines order in the present moment and provides a discursive space for trying out new identities, behaviors, and attitudes that can ultimately transform social relations. Its humor, however, is dependent on the existence of a stable order for its effect. Paradoxically, although *franqueza* usually connotes stability and order, as bold self-assertion it also can threaten stable order in the same way that *relajo* can. In fact, such *franqueza* in the midst of *echando relajo* can yield instances of tension that are often resolved with face-saving humor (see Chapter 8).

Ranchero societies have a particular relation to order, and orderliness is an important part of ranchero social life. Originally established by lower-status Spaniards and *castas* (varying mixtures of Spanish/Indian/African), these societies always existed on the margins of elite Spanish colonial and Mexican society (see Chapter 2). Rancheros were used by the Mexican government to impose order on the frontiers of the republic, that is, to colonize along the moving margins of the nation (Barragán and Linck 1994). As government-sponsored colonizers, they were given land in exchange for bringing frontier areas of the nation under state control, either by fighting nomadic Indians (Alonso 1995) or by developing settlements of *gente de razón* (civilized people of reason) who would provide a model for "uncivilized" Indians (Barragán 1997). Although *mestizaje* (racial mixture) is acknowledged among rancheros in this study and others, the Spanish side of their heritage is culturally predominant; and in many families in this study it is genetically predominant as well (see Chapter 4).

As *civilizados* (civilized people), rancheros in frontier societies worked their own land. In fact, working one's own land was (and is) an important index of both civilization (i.e., nonindigenous identity) and masculinity (Nugent and Alonso 1994). In Ana María Alonso's study of Namiquipa (1995), going to the *labor* (field) to which one held *derechos de posesión* (rights of possession) illustrated both a civilized, nonindigenous identity, since the indigenous Apache were nomadic and did not work to domesticate nature, and a "fully socialized masculinity," in which men who were *muy trabajador* (hard-working) were actualized as men of honor who supported their families (Nugent and Alonso 1994, 234). For the ranchero identity presented in this book, the association of "masculine identity, power, and autonomy" (Nugent and Alonso 1994, 234) is key.

Although Nugent and Alonso distinguish such a desire for autonomy from (capitalistic) individualism, they also acknowledge that the communal rights to land (*derechos de posesión*) that Namiquipan peasants held were the same in practice as private property and that individual titles were originally promised but never delivered. Moreover, Namiquipans claimed that "[t]hey were all willing to pay taxes as long as their lands were respected as private properties" (Nugent and Alonso 1994, 233, note 50). Other studies of rancheros, including this one, similarly emphasize the importance of autonomy and land ownership, but they also indicate an entrepreneurial spirit that is consonant with an ideology of liberal individualism. As I argue in Chapter 6, ranchero values include both individualism and familism. These need not be viewed as dichotomous opposites, as is often assumed by researchers implicitly or explicitly contrasting U.S. (capitalistic) "individualism" with Latin American "communalism." In fact, the rancheros in this study see themselves as entrepreneurial, self-assertive, and individualistic in contrast to Indians, whom they perceive as communal.[8] Emphasizing communal over individualist values may reflect a romanticized view of Indian Others as more "authentic" than mestizos, especially those mestizos who actively reject an indigenous identity (see Chapter 5). It may also reflect a particular theoretical stance on historical political processes. I argue in this study, however, that ranchero discourse is replete with an emphasis on individualism in the context of familism but not communalism.

As frontiersmen and frontierswomen, rancheros were continually faced with mobility and with creating order out of the "disorder" of nature and "uncivilized" Indians; but the order they were intent on creating was their own. Tom Sullivan's (1990) study of frontier narratives in the United States and in Latin America emphasizes the importance of both order and individualism in Spanish and Latin American culture. He claims that a conflict between these two desires was often resolved in *caudillaje,* the rule of a powerful man in a "large area, a state, or a nation" (Sullivan 1990, 7). Sullivan (1990, 37) notes that "the hierarchical structure of Hispanic society reinforces the centralist concept of government which the *caudillo* epitomizes." Although rancheros, existing far from the central powers of government (and regional or national caudillos), formed basically egalitarian societies (Barragán 1997), they mirrored the larger society's hierarchy in their patriarchal family structures. Order within ranchero society was established by (extended) family units. Clusters of these family units developed in isolated ranchos distant from colonial Spanish, then Mexican, government (see Chapter 2). The valuing of autonomy described above is directly related to this frontier history: "No había ley" (There was no law), as an elderly man said in an interview, even early in the twentieth century in the rancho in this study.

According to Barragán (1997), after constructing provisional housing for protection from the elements, rancheros who formed a sufficient nucleus next constructed a chapel in which a traveling priest could officiate the mass. In central western Mexico especially, ranchero societies were and are intensely Catholic, as evidenced by the counterrevolutionary Cristero Rebellion (Meyer 1976) that erupted in this area in the mid-1920s, following the Mexican Revolution of 1910–1920. In addition to supporting the *cristero* fight against an anticlerical revolutionary government, most rancheros in this area were and are fervently opposed to government-led agrarian reform. This is not to say that there were no *agraristas* (agrarian reformers) among rancheros, many (but not all) of whom used agrarian reform instrumentally, as a way to get land. Ann Craig (1983), for example, explores agrarian reform in the cradle of ranchero society, Los Altos of Jalisco. Even here, however, as in the microregion in this study, the dominant ideology was *anti-agrarista.* Daniel Nugent and Ana María Alonso (1994) attribute this *anti-agrarista* attitude in Namiquipa to a resistance to state control, a stance prevalent as well among rancheros in western Mexico both historically and currently. Traditionally averse to and distrustful of any government, rancheros prefer to make their own way, to create their own social order based on the family and, in western Mexico, the church. (Rancheros in studies of other regions of Mexico are not necessarily religious and are sometimes actively anticlerical.)

The Catholic Church in Mexico has promoted a "civilized" (and hierarchical) social order. As Spanish priests argued upon their arrival in New Spain in order to convert indigenous Mexicans to Catholicism, to be Catholic was to be "civilized," and this civilized order provided very clear rules regarding right and wrong as well as appropriate relations between people. Marjorie Becker (1995, 9) argues that Catholicism in northwestern Michoacán affirmed a hierarchical class order through a symbolic system based on gender:

> It was a symbolic system largely based on gender that called for a self-denial that the priests referred to as purity. That is, Catholic elites had developed a symbolic system that depended on an understanding and acceptance both of women's actual abnegation and of that abnegation as a metaphor designed to restrain the potential nonconformity of Indians, peasants, workers, all subordinate groups. In return, priests held out an infinite array of consolations.

Centered on "*La Purísima,* the Virgin Mary in her most chaste aspect" (Becker 1995, 16), the conservative Catholicism that developed in this region emphasized the submissiveness of women in all classes and, by extension, a hierarchical class order in which peons were submissive toward elite hacendados. Although acknowledging the existence of minute differentiations among peasants, Becker does not distinguish rancheros from other mestizo campesinos. Instead, she assumes that, "even in a world where agrarian capitalism was so old that it felt habitual, the Michoacán majority also experienced traditions of conviviality and noncapitalist social relationships" (Becker 1995, 21). Unfortunately, as is prevalent throughout the literature, peasants ("the Michoacán majority") seem to be generalized here as "communal" and "noncapitalist." The rancheros in this study, however, did and do embrace agrarian capitalism and, in fact, often imagine themselves as larger landowners.[9] Becker (1995, 26) did interview people who evidenced "a certain acceptance of the sanctified private property relations that peons knew"; but she explains this with one of the "consolations" provided in priestly sermons: "in order to emulate the *hacendado* or to safely express frustrations based on their landless plight, peons required subordinates" (i.e., their wives, in a gender order in which women must at least publicly be submissive to their husbands). Omitted in this account (and in much other research) is the status order in which rancheros consider Indians to be subordinate.

Clearly, however, the religiosity of this region affirmed both a class order and a gender order. Within their own marginal societies rancheros in this area created their own social order along hierarchies of age and gender and according to church-reinforced rules of morality with disciplined enforcement within families. Such order itself both is significant in rancheros' daily lives and has a historical trajectory for them. Usually living on land left over from that taken by haciendas (large relatively flat expanses of land easily worked as part of large estates), rancheros generally are accustomed to "making do" with smaller pieces of land (often on the slopes of mountains and other undulating terrain) and to creating provisional homes and chapels in an effort to establish a "civilized" order. As frontiersmen and frontierswomen, they colonized vast areas of Mexico throughout four centuries (Barragán 1997) and during the twentieth century continued a tradition of mobility by migrating in large numbers to cities both in Mexico (Cabrales Barajas 1994; González de la Vara 1994) and in the United States.

Ranchero Mobility and Transnationalism

Migrating to the United States, according to Barragán (1997), is only the latest move in a long tradition of mobility among rancheros. The extension of such movement across nation-state borders, however, makes migration qualitatively different from moves within Mexico (even more so in comparison to moves within one region or microregion of Mexico). For example, issues of cultural reproduction, including the reproduction of ranchero ways of being and speaking, are complicated by the territorial spread of families and the difficulty of movement across borders that require legal documents. Intrafamilial communication, essential to the socialization of children (Schieffelin and Ochs 1986), is constrained both over time and across space. Moreover, such communicative socialization processes, as well as family relations themselves, are increasingly vulnerable to the disjuncture in ideas, images, and "imagined worlds" characteristic of a "chaotic" global system with people and cultural material on the move worldwide (Appadurai 1996). Concretely, both intergenerational and marital conflict can ensue from such disruptions to the traditional social order in many of these communities as both women and children, increasingly aware of new ways of being in the world, begin to question the traditional authority of husbands and parents.

Key to the question of cultural reproduction and/or transformation is the nature of the relationship that the community sustains with both home and host societies. The social network under study here is part of a transnational community because a continuing circulation between

Mexico and Chicago enables them to "forge and sustain multi-stranded social relations that link together their societies of origin and settlement." These "multi-stranded social relations" constitute the "networks of relationships" in which these "transmigrants take actions, make decisions, and develop subjectivities and identities" (Basch et al. 1994, 7). Although such transnational communities are often described as deterritorialized (Basch et al. 1994), or cut off from the geopolitical locus of their ethnic origins, the tightness and constancy of the links between the rancho and Chicago mitigate this deterritorialization, especially for those with legal papers, who move across the border more easily and frequently than those without papers.[10]

In this established transnational community (see Chapter 3), someone is virtually always on the move between the rancho and Chicago. Every few months people retired in Mexico visit Chicago, young people make it across the border to join friends and family there, families in Chicago decide to return to Mexico to retire, to start businesses, or to raise children in the safer context of the rancho, and other families reluctantly decide to return to Chicago because the continuing economic crisis in Mexico constrains their abilities to support their families. Communication by telephone, and for some by e-mail (formerly letters), is now a regular part of their lives. Money, of course, passes from Chicago to Mexico with even greater regularity, from unmarried adult children to their parents and from relatives of all ages (young cousins, aunts, and uncles) to particular people on special occasions (e.g., to a young girl for her *quinceañera* [fifteenth-birthday] celebration in the rancho).

Ties to "home" are especially strong for the adults, most of whom work, socialize, and live with others from the rancho. They live, at least initially, in Chicago neighborhoods that are virtually entirely Mexican-origin (see Chapter 3). As Guerra (1998) argues persuasively, although much is made of cross-cultural "contact zones," the reality for most in this social network is that they live most of their Chicago lives in a Mexican "home front." There is little interaction with non-Hispanic whites or blacks or even with other Spanish-speaking groups such as Puerto Ricans. This is especially true of adults who work, live, and socialize together; but it is also true for many children, who attend schools with predominantly, even entirely, Mexican populations. Moreover, these populations are often from similar ranchero backgrounds, since the migration from Mexico to Chicago has been predominantly from heavily ranchero western states such as Michoacán, Jalisco, and Guanajuato (Kerr 1984). The relative lack of daily interaction with culturally different populations constrains the development of hybrid identities, another aspect of globalization that some researchers have emphasized (Appadurai 1996).

Thus the transnational nature of the social network under study and the segregated communities in which they live in Chicago mediate and cushion the effects of deterritorialization as well as its concomitant disruption of traditional social order. This is not to say that migration to the United States has not motivated changes in this social network. Such changes are evident at both ends of the "migrant circuit" (Rouse 1991), especially in gender relations (see Chapters 7 and 8). Such changes, however, have been less extensive than many transnational and globalization theorists have predicted, due both to the contiguity of Mexico and the United States (possibly allowing more and more frequent back-and-forth movement) and to ethnically separate neighborhoods in Chicago. Moreover, these families actively work to counter the estrangement of deterritorialization by keeping the rancho and its environs as the orienting center of their transnational lives (e.g., ritual social events as well as living and work arrangements are centered around connections in Mexico) and by reuniting families (moving wives and children to Chicago or entire families back to Mexico) as soon as is practically possible. These efforts augment the effects of continuous transnational circulation and segregated Chicago neighborhoods to reinforce the ranchero identity explored in this book and facilitate cross-generational socialization of traditional ranchero ways of being and speaking.

Organization of Chapters

To conclude this chapter, I describe the chapters that follow, so that readers with specific interests can approach them individually. There is a flow to the chapters, however, that lends a front-to-back reading of them a certain logic and clarity not as easily grasped when they are read separately.

In Chapter 2, "Of Ranchos and Rancheros: The Historical Context," I explore the multiple popular meanings of the word *ranchero*, building from the etymology of the word *rancho* and examining the historical contexts in which these words have accumulated their meanings in Mexico. Then I describe rancheros as a significant subpopulation within the larger Mexican society, synthesizing various published studies of rancheros in different regions of Mexico. Finally, I detail the history of rancheros in western Mexico, focusing on northwestern Michoacán when possible. In this history I begin with the sixteenth-century conquest of Mexico by the Spanish and end with the mid- to late-twentieth-century massive migration of rancheros to cities within Mexico and to the United States. This history includes attention to incipient ranchero societies on the moving frontiers of both colonial and independent Mexico, and it discusses the implications of these material historical conditions for the development of characteristically ranchero identities and ways of speaking.

Chapter 3, "The Spatial Context: San Juanico, Illinois, and Chicago, Michoacán," describes physical locations on both ends of the "migrant circuit" (Rouse 1991). I include maps of (1) the much-traveled route between the Michoacán rancho and Chicago, (2) the region within which the rancho is located in northwest Michoacán, (3) the rancho itself, and (4) the Chicago neighborhoods in which the families live. I also include a history of the rancho and the social network and a history of Mexicans in the Midwest and Chicago. Chapter 4, "The Social Context of *La Familia:* Work, Education, Religion, and Language," describes the social network of families in terms of key aspects of their lives, including their notable work ethic, binational schooling, their intense Catholicism, and their lively use of ranchero dialect. I provide photographs of people and their homes in Mexico and Chicago and a family tree that details the relationships of social network members. Although people in the photographs gave permission for their use, I sometimes obscure identities throughout the book in order to protect privacy, even though some individuals preferred to be identified. Such decisions are always a balancing act, but as author I had to make them, sometimes in consultation with members of the network. These two chapters provide the backdrop against which readers can imagine more clearly the scenes from which I draw instances of discourse for analysis in later chapters.

Chapter 5, "Rethinking *Mestizaje:* Racial Discourse among Rancheros," introduces the cultural (and, for some families, genetic) predominance of the Spanish side of their "mixed" heritage with one family's oral tradition regarding its origins in a village in northern Spain. To place ranchero racial ideology in context I review the history of *mestizaje* (racial mixing) in Mexico, arguing that although Mexico is widely perceived as a thoroughly "mixed" country (more so than many other Latin American countries), this homogenized mixture has been erroneously generalized. This is especially true of rural western Mexico, with its pockets of isolated, Spanish-dominant ranchos, some of which are even nestled right up against the Meseta Tarasca, the northwestern Michoacán "tableland" in which indigenous P'urhepecha (Tarascan) villages predominate.

Using my field notes and tape-recorded discourse, I detail the racial ideology of these rancheros, placing them in the middle of a local status order, with indigenous P'urhepecha below them and elite urban Mexicans above them. (From the perspective of many of those "above," however, all campesinos or rural peasants are "Indianized"—that is, seen as Indian or as having acculturated to Spanish ways from a primarily Indian base.) I show how rancheros construct their Spanish-dominant identities primarily in contrast to indigenous Indians but also in contrast to "effete" urban dwellers. These identities are then maintained via various sign systems, including language. I explore racial discourse in both Mexico and Chicago, showing how these rancheros and rancheras place themselves ambiguously within, and thus disrupt, both the U.S. and Mexican traditional racial hierarchies. Finally, I analyze a transcript of tape-recorded joking in a van traveling from Chicago to the rancho for the Christmas holidays one year, demonstrating how the women on this tape play with, and thus reveal the illogic of, the racial order in both countries. As they play verbally with race and identity, they are and are not "Indian," depending upon whose perspective (their own or that of the dominant U.S. or Mexican classes) is taken.

Chapter 6, "*Franqueza* and the Individualist Ideology of Progress," describes this predominant ranchero way of speaking as direct, candid, even blunt speech, linking it to an ideology of liberal individualism which valorizes capitalist entrepreneurial attitudes and practices. I argue here that such individualism has been wrongly dichotomized with communalism or familism and that individualistic and familistic orientations complement each other in ranchero societies. People thus construct themselves as hard-working, enterprising, and distinctive individuals who, by virtue of their qualities, are valuable and desirable members of the group. Using sociolinguistic politeness theory (Brown and Levinson 1987) I analyze several instances of *franqueza* in this chapter, showing how the linguistic devices that constitute a "grammar of self-assertion" construct men, women, and even children as self-assertive, authoritative individuals. I end the chapter with an analysis of two instances of *franqueza* constructed in narrative performances of self-presentation. In the first instance, an older male recounts a personal experience in which he confronted an immigration officer on behalf of a younger male relative. In the second instance, an older woman narrates how she confronted her husband (and a colluding female relative) with his infidelities. These narratives show how both legal status and gender are implicated in struggles over power and how *franqueza* can be used to challenge dominance.

Chapter 7, "Social Order among Rancheros: Equality and Reciprocity, Hierarchy and *Respeto*," describes the implicit rules for social order in traditional ranchero society, organizing the discussion around two primary codes for interaction: reciprocity and *respeto.* Unlike the larger Mexican society, which is decidedly hierarchical, ranchero societies practice largely egalitarian relations between, if not within, families. Patriarchy prevails within families, although there are cracks in the system (and women work to widen these cracks). Relations between families or between individuals deemed "equal" by virtue of gender or age (e.g., adult male to adult male or adult female to adult female) are guided by a principle of reciprocity. A pattern of egalitarianism and reciprocity developed historically in frontier ranchero societies because people had to rely on each other to survive. Reciprocity, however, in sharp contrast to a communal orientation in which everything is owned jointly by the community, presumes independence and autonomy. That is, reciprocity implies the cooperation of separate individuals or families in particular endeavors, such as the borrowing and lending of help or money when needed. Such relations construct and affirm the community as a community, even as they are based on the distinct autonomy of community members.

Finally, this chapter explores the norms for personal (primarily verbal) interaction, *respeto,* an attitude of respect toward the dignity of individuals and the roles they play. Linguistically this requires the careful use of informal and formal "you" pronouns (*tú* and *usted*), according to the relative status levels and closeness of the interlocutors. Interactions that evidence *respeto* protect the face of both interlocutors. That is, the positive public self-image of each person is protected. Pronoun choices guided by age and gender hierarchies, within families and between them, construct both an egalitarian (between equals) and hierarchical (by age and gender) social order. Since gender is so central to ranchero social order, I discuss gender ideologies and how they are linked to "house" (women and order) and "street" (men and disorder) and to *respeto* and *relajo.*

Chapter 8, "*Relajo* as (Framed) Disorder: The Carnivalesque in Talk," explores "permitted" disorder that is framed as verbal play. *El relajo* is the sanctioned site for humorous diversion, lack of discipline, and even immorality. Kept within its verbal bounds (specific linguistic devices are used to signal or "frame" a stretch of talk as *relajo* and so to be taken "nonseriously"), *relajo* affirms social bonds among participants while simultaneously providing opportunity for face-saving resolution of tensions and for critical evaluation of the status quo. Thus *relajo* is comical verbal play, but it is more than that. This chapter explores both the poetics and the politics of *relajo:* the aesthetic gratification and entertainment derived from rhetorically pleasing language play as well as the critiques of power relations implicit (and sometimes not so implicit) in the joking. Arguing that *relajo* is really a microfiesta at the level of language, I draw out the parallels between *relajo* and fiesta or carnival, emphasizing their shared emphasis on disorder and resistance. Finally, this chapter examines gender ideologies in the context of *relajo*, analyzing tape-recorded instances of all-male and all-female *relajo*. These analyses illustrate how the men in this network often recount stories of challenges to patriarchy that end by affirming it, whereas the women often recount stories that challenge it.

Chapter 9, "Conclusion," sums up the major understandings of the study. I recapitulate three overarching themes that emerged: first, the lack of scholarly awareness of rancheros as a distinct subgroup of rural Mexicans; second, the importance of both individualism and familism among rancheros, undermining the commonly perceived dichotomy between these two values; and third, tensions around and changes in gender relations. I follow this discussion of themes with reflections on the research process itself, including reflexivity (my own presence in the scenes in which I gathered data) and the influence of these families on me as a person. Finally, I consider the implications of the study for broader social concerns, including education and literacy for multicultural populations.

TWO

Of Ranchos and Rancheros

The Historical Context

The term *ranchero,* like its literal English translation, "rancher," conjures up images of rural frontier spaces, horses and cows, and rugged, leathery men (and sometimes women) who take no guff from man or beast. Hollywood cowboy films, featuring John Wayne and others, are replete with these images (Tompkins 1992; Wexman 1993). As Richard Slatta (1990, 191) notes in *Cowboys of the Americas,* "Literary and symbolic evocations of cowboys often show strong transnational similarities. Cowboys are viewed as representing rugged individualism, unbending principle, frontier spirit, and manly courage."

Arguing the Spanish origins of cowboy culture, Slatta (1990) compares and contrasts similar figures across North and South America: the gaucho of Argentina (Slatta 1992 [1983]), the *huaso* of Chile, the *llanero* of Venezuela, the vaquero of Mexico, the cowboy of the United States and Canada, and even the *paniolo* of Hawai'i. In all of these places except Canada, cowboy culture developed in the transition from wild cattle hunting to cattle ranching: "We can properly speak of a Western Hemisphere 'cowboy culture,' bound together by Hispanic influences, shared values, and similar types of work and play" (Slatta 1990, 223). In Mexico, an elite equestrian tradition imported from Spain, *charreada* (Chávez 1993), occurred alongside the developing culture of lower-class vaqueros, the lower-status Spaniards, mestizos, and other *castas* (various categories of mixed races) who were hired by the Spanish elite to manage their cattle ranches (Barragán 1997). Over time many of the vaqueros' maneuvers found their way into the more elite *charreada* (Slatta 1990).

This way of life and its attendant values and practices continue to exist in the public imagination, nourished especially by popular arts such as film, recorded song, and literature. Although Mexican film has fewer examples of this genre than does U.S. film, the ranchero, as the inheritor of cowboy culture in Mexico, is represented in a few famous ones (e.g., *Allá en el Rancho Grande, ¡Ay Jalisco, no te rajes!*) which feature ranchero heroes exhibiting the moral qualities associated with cowboys: individualism, fair play, honesty, integrity, and clean living (Slatta 1990, 215). Although U.S. cowboys have an equally notable presence in literature as in film, Mexican vaqueros and rancheros are only present in a handful of novels, notably including those by Agustín Yáñez and Juan Rulfo (González 1991, 3). Instead, much Mexican literature emphasizes oppressed, deferential, and primarily Indian peasants, as in the classic novel of the Mexican Revolution, *Los de abajo* (The Underdogs) (Slatta 1990, 209). Thus there has been less public awareness of vaqueros in Mexico than of cowboys in the United States, a lacuna that is paralleled by a similar lack of recognition of rancheros as a distinct rural population.

Technically, those who identify as rancheros in Mexico today are simply those who live in (or come from) ranchos; but contemporary meanings of *ranchero* are much more complex than this (as suggested in Chapter 1). Moreover, a rancho is not simply a small hamlet with any type of rural inhabitants. Historically, the words *rancho* and *ranchero* have accumulated a range of meanings, rich in connotations as well as visual and musical images from film and popular songs. Central to this set of images and meanings is the frontier and its effect on the developing culture of first vaqueros and then rancheros.

Frontiers and Frontier People

Frederick Jackson Turner's classic 1893 essay (reprinted in Weber and Rausch 1994) argued that the frontier had permanent effects on the American character:

> From the conditions of frontier life came intellectual traits of profound importance. . . . That coarseness and strength combined with acuteness and inquisitiveness; that practical, inventive turn of mind, quick to find expedients; that masterful grasp of material things, lacking in the artistic but powerful to effect great ends; that restless, nervous energy; that dominant individualism, working for good and for evil, and withal that buoyancy and exuberance which comes with freedom—these are traits of the frontier, or traits called out elsewhere because of the frontier. (Turner 1994 [1893], 18)

The traits that Turner claimed grew out of frontier conditions parallel those attributed to rancheros in various studies (Barragán 1990a, 1997; González 1974). These traits surface in common *dichos* (sayings) in Mexico, such as references to *el ingenioso ranchero* (the ingenious ranchero) who comes up with expedient, practical solutions to various material problems.

Turner's claims, however, have been fiercely debated, especially in their unilateral reliance on one set of factors: the frontier itself created more egalitarian relations, individualism, and even a more direct, unaffected rhetoric (Turner 1994 [1893], 14). This direct, unaffected rhetoric is described here as *franqueza* (see Chapter 6). Scholars have countered Turner's sole reliance on frontier conditions by stressing the role of cultural backgrounds in creating differences among various frontiers across the Americas (e.g., Spanish versus Anglo-Saxon). Slatta (1990), for example, argues that indigenous cultures influenced the developing cowboy culture, though not as much as did Spanish culture, which spread from (Mexican) Texas and California to U.S., Canadian, and even Hawai'ian cowboys. Others have contrasted the (elite) Spanish disdain for manual labor (traced to medieval Catholic Spanish culture: Slatta 1990, 226), which in Latin America they relegated to more plebeian Spaniards and *castas,* with the valuing of one's own labor as part of the Protestant work ethic in British North America (Slatta 1990; Weber and Rausch 1994). Also, frontiers in Latin America have been seen as inclusive, incorporating various ethnic groups into a hierarchical society, whereas frontiers in the United States and Canada have been seen as exclusive, enforcing ethnic and racial separateness (Weber and Rausch 1994).

In spite of all the criticisms, both Arthur Aiton (1994 [1940]) and Silvio Zavala (1994 [1965]) affirm Turner's claims, at least for some frontiers in Latin America and, notably, for Mexico. While granting the staying power of Turner's argument, David Weber and Jane Rausch (1994, xviii) note that the frontier in Latin America, unlike in the United States, also engendered some negative perceptions, especially on the part of elite Latin American intellectuals, who saw the frontier as uncivilized and primitive. This attitude can be found today in the disdain of many urban, elite Mexicans for rancheros, whom they see as ignorant, uncultured, and rudely direct in their language. Thus frontier peoples, like rancheros, have been "both romanticized and demonized" (Weber and Rausch 1994, xxviii).

The material conditions of the frontier in Mexico, populated first with vaqueros and then with rancheros, no doubt have had some influence on contemporary ranchero culture and on the attitudes of elite Mexicans toward rancheros. These material conditions developed historically across Mexico with moving frontiers, resulting in ranchero societies that had common characteristics: the valuing of independence, individualism, practicality, ingenuity, and directness or candor in primarily egalitarian social relations. In addition to material frontier conditions, the structural position of rancheros had a seminal influence on their developing culture, in spite of regional differences that yielded rancheros of varying socioeconomic levels. Frans Schryer (1980), for example, presents a case study of rancheros in the Sierra Alta of Hidalgo who formed a local upper class (given the absence of haciendas there), a peasant bourgeoisie of small and medium-sized landowners. Schryer (1980, 6) also notes variation in rancheros across Mexico, from "farmers of predominantly Spanish descent in the state of Jalisco, to traditional landowners occupying very modest estates in more isolated regions in other parts of central and southern Mexico, or to pioneer cattle ranchers in the more sparsely populated northern frontier." What all these rancheros have in common, however, is "their 'middle class' status in rural Mexican society, or their intermediate position between the mass of landless peons or sharecroppers and a small elite of hacendados" (Schryer 1980, 6).

Although the rancheros in Schryer's study owned land and were materially richer than the peasants who depended on them, they "shared the dress, the deportment, and speech of their economic subordinates" (Schryer 1980, 7). In other words, these landowners were relatively indistinguishable culturally and linguistically from those who were landless and lived, like the landless, a peasant or rustic life. This, of course, gave all of them (upper and lower strata alike) low status in the eyes of the urban elite. Schryer's study reminds us of the economic variation among rancheros; but it also reminds us of their similarities in terms of values and lifestyle (Brading 1994). If language indexes identity, as numerous studies have shown (e.g., Farr 2004), then the fact that Schryer's "upper"-class rancheros speak just like his "lower"-class rancheros probably indicates that they identify in some sense as members of "the same" group. Their shared speech does distinguish them from urban, professional, and otherwise elite Mexicans, both in terms of its characteristics as a rural dialect with archaisms and in terms of its rhetorical style (as I discuss in Chapter 6).

In addition to shared cultural characteristics, Schryer's rancheros shared ties of kinship and *compadrazgo* (fictive kinship akin to godparenthood) as well as common origins. In other areas of Mexico (including the microregion of the present study) rancheros seem to be, if not an established "peasant bourgeoisie," then an "incipient" middle class, even though the amount of land they own is generally relatively small. They are higher in status than other local peasants (McBride 1923), especially those who are either Indians or "de-Indianized" (acculturated) mestizos, with whom the rancheros do not share dress, deportment, speech, or ties of kinship or *compadrazgo.*

The sameness of cultural and linguistic practices, in spite of varying levels of wealth, points to common historical (frontier) conditions, and to a common status position, that engendered these shared cultural practices across different groups of rancheros. What specifically were these conditions? How did the term *ranchero,* or *rancho* for that matter, come to refer to these particular groups and the settlements in which they lived (and still live)? In what follows, I first trace the etymology of these words, moving from Europe to New Spain, and then explore the conflicting meanings of *ranchero* in the public imagination. Finally, I describe the formative historical conditions in western Mexico, from the Spanish conquest to the late twentieth century, in which the words *rancho* and *ranchero* accumulated their meanings and in which ranchero societies developed. This chapter thus provides the foundation for understanding the emergence of ranchero identity and ways of speaking in a specific historical context.

Dictionary Definitions and Word Origins

The *Diccionario del español usual en México* defines *ranchero* as:

> 1) a person who is owner of a rancho or who lives in it and is dedicated to work in the fields, 2) what belongs to the rancho or its inhabitants or is related to them: ranchero boots, ranchero salsa, ranchero life, ranchero songs, 3) what is timid or extremely shy: a young girl very "ranchera," as in the expression, "Don't be ranchera: greet the others!" (Lara Ramos 1996)

Thus the overall frame of reference for *ranchero* is what in the United States would be called "country" or "country western" (as opposed to urban and cultivated); indeed, there is some similarity between *ranchero* and what is called "cowboy" in the United States. A fuller understanding of what people mean by *ranchero* is illuminated through an exploration of the history of the word itself.

Herón Pérez (1994) traces the word *rancho* to its origins in old northern European languages, specifically the Germanic family. Originally the word *hring* meant ring or crown, signifying royalty, but it soon came to mean meeting or assembly (a circular assembly of people). Then German *Ring* moved into French and became *harangue,* an open conversation, a harangue, a sermon, or any discourse. Later the French *rang* emerged, meaning stroll or walk, post or encampment, order or command, line or military rank. Even later two loan words, both verbs, moved into Spanish from French, two centuries apart: *derranchar,* a military word meaning to distinguish oneself, excel, break rank, or go beyond limits (break out of the ring?), which had appeared by the twelfth century in Spain; and *ranchar* or *ranchear,* meaning to shift for oneself, install oneself provisionally in a place, which appeared in the fourteenth century. This second loanword, like the first, and along with related derivative words, had a military connotation, which continued into the sixteenth century, among soldiers and other Spaniards in the Americas.

The derivation of the word *rancho,* then, is associated with soldiers, a group known for its mobility; so it is not surprising that rancheros as well are characterized by mobility (Barragán 1997). Rancheros have been on the move throughout Mexican history, and their contemporary range of mobility includes the entire United States, beyond what was formerly part of Mexico.

By the fifteenth century in Spain, the verb *rancharse* had changed in use, coming to mean to provide food for a large group of people, then provisional lodging, and then a hut. By the end of the fifteenth century, when expeditions to the Americas began, the noun *rancho,* formed from the verb *rancharse,* was a part of Spanish vocabulary; and the first manifestations of the word all connote provisionality, be it military or some other kind. This connotation, like mobility, also is tied closely to contemporary meanings associated with rancheros, primarily in reference to their styles of housing and living, traceable to the use of *rancho* for "various types of dwellings, residential installations, and, at the end of the sixteenth century, to 'rustic haciendas' which emerged out of the heat of necessity" (Pérez 1994, 37). Although situations in which the word *rancho* was used were plentiful in sixteenth-century America, it was mostly used in *el habla vulgar* (folk language), not by the educated and literate, since it can be found in few literary sources. Those literary uses that do exist, however, indicate that this word meant improvised housing, midway between more stable dwellings and more transient ones. Moreover, several such ranchos constituted a pueblo or small village. Finally, *rancho* also (without eliminating other current meanings) came to mean a part of land that is farmed (e.g., a lime ranch).

Today *rancho* retains the old meaning of a rural dwelling, with military vestiges. It also means a small independent exploitation of the land and a residence attached to or annexed by an hacienda. Noting that the word *rancho* has evolved not by substituting one meaning for another but by accumulating meanings, Pérez (1994) adds that another contemporary meaning of the word is also old: food that is made for many, like that given to soldiers.

In Mexican Spanish, then, *rancho* now primarily refers to (1) a quite modest rural dwelling, (2) a small property that is worked primarily by one family, or (3) a small community of rancheros who are mostly if not entirely small property owners (*pequeño propietarios*). Although it can sometimes refer to properties that are in effect small haciendas, that meaning does not pertain in the present study. Rather, the rancho in Mexico from which the families in this study migrated to Chicago is a small rural hamlet in which most families own small pieces of land that they work themselves, sometimes with the help of one or two hired workers.

Additionally, the word *rancho* in this region of Mexico can also refer to small rural communities centered around an *ejido,* a communal plot of land given by the government to people as part of agrarian reform. Often workers from a former hacienda were given shares in *ejidos* created from the dismantling of the hacienda. Such agrarian reform occurred primarily in the years following the Mexican Revolution of 1910–1920, especially during the Lázaro Cárdenas presidency from 1934 to 1940. This meaning of the word *rancho,* however, does not apply in the present study, since this community fiercely opposes agrarian reform. *Ejidal*-centered ranchos are often composed of former hacienda workers (*peones acasillados* or in-house peons) and their descendants and are located around former haciendas. They are distinct from the rancheros in this study, a distinctness possibly grounded in a different historical position in relation to haciendas and the ruling classes. Differences emerge in both verbal and nonverbal communication styles: whereas people who are referred to as *peones* show deference in body language (lowered gaze, hat in hand) and discourse (the formal *usted* rather than the informal, egalitarian *tú* for "you"), the rancheros of this study stand erect, gaze directly into others' eyes, and rarely use asymmetrical politeness terms: *usted* to the superordinate other, who uses *tú* in return (see Chapter 7).

Such cultural and historical distinctness among people who might appear to be otherwise similar corrects against the unfortunate tendency, in the United States and elsewhere, to generalize into one category all Mexicans, all Mexican migrants, or, as is common in Mexico, all campesinos. In spite of the diversity attached to the word *rancho,* however, contemporary meanings attached to the word *ranchero,* to which I now turn, do fit the community under study. That is, while there is some variety among referents of the word *rancho* in Mexican Spanish, the word *ran-*

chero is much more specific and very much fits the people presented in this book and their discourse. Moreover, as rancheros are a very important subgroup within the larger Mexican population, perhaps 20 percent according to Luis González (1991) and possibly even more within Mexican migrants in the United States (Barragán 1997), ranchero culture is important to understand.

Before moving to a consideration of the meanings of *ranchero* and ranchero culture, I quote the following verbal portrait of a rancho, which accurately describes the rancho in this study.

> The "rancho" to which I refer is a rural village, without design, whose houses, generally of adobe, have a corral for the chickens and/or pigs, fencing walls at times of drab adobe, at times of tree branches, at times of shrubs, stones or large buried logs. The richer rancheros formerly had a horse for transport and a cow for the daily milk: today they go around on bicycles or in legalized vans, "made in USA." Moreover, in the houses of the rancho, there never fail to be dogs. The houses of the rancho group themselves in the center or at the head of a series of small pieces of cultivated land. . . . The inhabitants of our ranchos live in general by a series of economic practices that are complementary among themselves: agriculture, the raising of chickens and pigs, some have their cows; and, now, the "bracereada" [migrants going as braceros or workers to the United States]. (Pérez 1994, 47–48)

Ranchos, as opposed to larger villages and towns in Mexico, have no planned design. Houses have been constructed here and there, usually near the cultivated fields of the residents. The rancho has no *zócalo* (central plaza), as is so characteristic of planned Mexican towns. Often there is a chapel but not a church. Roads are unpaved, although sometimes parts of roads may be filled in with paving stones, to minimize the dust that is stirred up each time someone rides by on a horse or (now more frequently) drives by in a pickup truck or van. Ranchos are pure "country," as are their inhabitants, rancheros.

From Rancho to Ranchero

As a word, *ranchero* has two dominant uses: one is pejorative and the other simply classificatory. The pejorative use proceeds from the urban elite, who often view rancheros as uncultured peasants (Pérez 1994, 51). Certainly the admonition *¡No seas ranchero!* (Don't be ranchero!) fits this more pejorative meaning. This phrase is used to refer to both (male) rancheros and (female) rancheras, who are presumed to be shy or lacking in verbal social skills to the point of being antisocial. In fact some rancheros not on their own "turf" (e.g., when they are in what might be called "urbane contexts") can be somewhat reticent, though not deferential. As my fieldwork attests, however, when they are on their own turf (whether within their own homes and neighborhoods in Chicago or in the rancho in Mexico) they are most certainly not shy or awkward—quite the contrary, in fact. In this context they could be described as extremely forthright and authoritative, even arrogant or proud; depending on the context, this is true of both men and women.

The other, simply classificatory meaning of *ranchero/a* allows room for this pride and directness. *Pueblo en vilo* (published in English as *San José de Gracia: Mexican Village in Transition*), a microhistory of rancheros and ranchero life by Luis González, a leading Mexican historian, led the way for the study of rancheros as a distinct subgroup of Mexicans. Like Slatta and others, González links Mexican rancheros with their counterparts in other countries of the Americas: the *llaneros* of Venezuela, the gauchos of Argentina, the *huasos* of Chile, and the cowboys of the western United States and Canada. What all these men had in common in the Americas was a passion for horses and bulls and a proclivity for horsemanship (González 1991, 4). As noted in the beginning of this chapter, rancheros are a phenomenon of the Western Hemisphere which developed after horses and cattle were imported from Europe in the mid-sixteenth century, that is, within decades of the Spanish conquest of Mexico. Vaqueros, the precursors to rancheros, were hired to control these animals; and a vaquero culture developed which blurred the distinction between work and play: "mounted labor included strong elements of play, and dangerous, vigorous equestrian contests employed 'real life' skills necessary to frontier survival and work" (Slatta 1990, 141).

This passion for horses and bulls continues to the present, and rancheros are associated with *jaripeos*,[1] which take place in both Mexico and Chicago. They are the folk version of the middle- and upper-class *charreada* of Mexico, but the games and contests of both traditions share an emphasis on skill and daring, as do rodeos in the United States. *Charreada* is not simply "a gathering of men on horses, nor fights on horseback, nor clusters of strings of horses; it is the organized spectacle, with well-defined, evaluated maneuvers, in which dexterity and agility reach the artistic and valor and daring are well appreciated" (Chávez 1993, 67). According to Octavio Chávez (1993), in some parts of Mexico women participate in *charreada*, although most exhibitions are performed by men. Some women in the region of the present study do participate, and more know how to ride and control horses. In the exercises performed on horseback for *la charreada* or in the bull riding in *el jaripeo,* boldness and daring, as well as agility and mastery of skill, are highly valued.

This valuing of daring and boldness is characteristically ranchero, not just in *charreada* or *jaripeo* but in the rest of life as well. Although rodeos, the U.S. equivalent to *charreada,* have been criticized for having "institutionalized many macho values and attitudes of the Old West" (Elizabeth Lawrence, in Slatta 1990, 211), among rancheros they affirm values important to both men and women, which would seem to apply to U.S. cowboys and cowgirls as well. Special dress for both men and women and other accoutrements for *charreada* as well as a variety of folklore genres, including legends, poetry, *corridos* (stories told in song), proverbs, and other sayings, all express the importance of this pastime to ranchero culture and identity. These days rancheros working, for example, for railroad construction companies in Chicago may never mount a horse or bull themselves. Nevertheless, they still go to *jaripeos;* symbolically, this sport/fiesta remains important, especially because it affirms the widely shared ranchero valuing of risk-taking, boldness, and physical skill.

These associations of horsemanship and valor with rancheros, as well as the ranchero life in general, were romanticized in some now classic Mexican films. The genre of the *comedia ranchera* (ranch comedy) began with *Allá en el Rancho Grande* (Out at Big Ranch), directed by Fernando de Fuentes, in 1936. As noted in Chapter 1, these films featured handsome ranchero heroes (often Jorge Negrete or Pedro Infante) who sang classic ranchero songs, won beautiful women, and, in general, represented men of honor. This enshrinement of rancheros led to a widely shared representation of them as "true" Mexicans from Mexico's "authentic" agrarian past, possibly in reaction to the social upheavals and changes that came in the wake of the Revolution (Montsiváis 1995). The idealization of rancheros rests upon a vision of a peaceful, and clearly hierarchical, rural Mexican society.[2] These cinematic representations persist even today in the collective imagination (both in Mexico and in the United States) as the somehow authentic and true Mexico of the past, even though they are juxtaposed quite paradoxically in the public mind with the disdainful attitude toward rancheros as uncultivated and uneducated peasants.

Francisco Scarano (1996) notes a similar use of the Puerto Rican *jíbaro* (native peasant) as a national icon following independence from Spain. Like the image of the Mexican ranchero, this image emphasized a creole heritage (Spanish descent, born in the Americas) along with an idealized rural identity. Equating this ethnicity with being "a native son" (or daughter) facilitated the dominance of creoles in the race/class hierarchy that continued beyond the colonial period. Also like the Mexican ranchero, the Puerto Rican *jíbaro* spoke a vernacular dialect and paradoxically shared a somewhat denigrated (uncultured) status despite being a national icon.

An anecdote from my time in the rancho illustrates the ongoing importance to contemporary rancheros of such public representations. One afternoon, while staying with a family I know well, we were all preparing for a *paseo* (outing) in the family pickup truck. Suddenly the father called out that *Allá en el Rancho Grande* was about to be shown on television (which came to them via their satellite dish, which, like virtually all the others on roofs of houses in the rancho, had been bought with money earned in Chicago). The members of the family, of all ages and both genders, became very excited, dropped whatever they were doing, and piled onto the double bed in one of the two bedrooms which was used for TV watching. We (myself included) attentively absorbed the images from this famous movie, with our eyes glued to the screen for hours, instead of going on our *paseo.*

This particular movie is notable in the history of Mexican film for inaugurating the golden age of Mexican cinema and for creating the first genuinely Mexican film genre (Medina de la Serna 1995): the *comedia ranchera,* a folkloric melodrama filled with song, set in the countryside. Its blockbuster success with the public even took its producer, Fernando de Fuentes, completely by surprise (García Riera 1995). What was (and is) its appeal? Produced in 1936, it appeared at a time of confusion arising from political, social, and economic upheaval in the wake of the Mexican Revolution (1910–1920) and the ensuing Cristero Rebellion (1926–1929) and exactly two years after President Lázaro Cárdenas began dismantling large plantations in a program of agrarian reform.

Yet *Allá en el Rancho Grande* does not include any of this; instead, it presents an old plot (a landowner threatens the honor of a young peasant woman loved by a young and honorable ranchero) set in an idealized countryside unaffected by such social changes. This movie and the genre it began may represent a backward-looking, nostalgic desire for the prerevolutionary Porfirian era (and dictatorship), when men were idealized as *machos* and women were idealized as pure and submissive. It appealed strongly to "a public that yearned for idyllic, utopian ranches" (García Riera 1995, 130) and that mythologized rural innocence in the face of increasing industrialization and urbanization (Montsiváis 1995, 118). Carlos Montsiváis (1995, 117–118) also points out that these films were educational, in that they served to socialize people who looked to their idols to learn ways of speaking, gesturing, and being—in short:

> . . . how to survive in a bewildering age of modernisation. At weekends, families went to the cinema to find and experience entertainment, family unity, honour, "permissible" sexuality, the beauty of the landscape and customs, and respect for institutions. Devotees of comedies and melodramas were not seeking to "dream," but to learn skills, to lose inhibitions, to suffer and be consoled in style, painlessly to envy the elites, happily to be resigned to poverty, to laugh at the stereotypes that ridiculed them, to understand how they belonged to the nation. In this school-in-the-dark the people were educated in suffering and relaxation.

The rancheros in the present study did not go to the movies on the weekends; nor did their parents, living as they did in a rural hamlet far from urban movie theaters. These films, however, are enduringly popular both in the rancho and on Chicago Spanish-language television; many Mexican ranchero families in Chicago own their own copies of the more famous ones, viewing them on VCRs both in Chicago and in Mexico. For these rancheros in Chicagoacán, the representations in the films affirm conservative ethnic and gender identities, the ideal and desired lifestyle of independent ranchers, and traditional values. Perhaps these films have special appeal now, in another era of confusion and upheaval, this time caused by massive migration to and labor in the United States, which have been essential for the economic survival of their families.

Migration and other processes are stimulating significant social and economic changes in the lives of these rancheros. Families now have sufficient money for food and other necessities, but only if they live and work in Chicago or have household members working there and sending money to the rancho. Both men and women, even married women, work in factories or construction in Chicago; and (mostly) unmarried women work in the recently established packing plants in the rancho, packing the avocados and other fruits grown commercially by these families and others since the mid-1960s (helped by migration dollars). Gender roles and relationships are changing, then, as are many other aspects of traditional agrarian life. In this context of change, traditional ranchero identities as represented in films and music may be particularly comforting, especially for men. These traditions of *mexicanidad* (Mexican identity) are particularly comforting and affirming in the context of being Mexicans in the United States. The Mexican neighborhoods of Chicago are full of signs of *mexicanidad* and of specifically ranchero identities: in churches, altars to the Virgin of Guadalupe; on the streets, pickup trucks driven by men with mustaches in cowboy boots, hats, and tooled leather (*pitiado*) belts, accompanied by women with large dark rebozos (shawls) wrapped around themselves and infants, with ranchera music pouring out of storefronts.

Music popularized in films and elsewhere as ranchero still sells briskly in Chicago as well as in Mexico, and classic songs (e.g., by Pedro Infante) are collected, treasured, and listened to by elite Mexicans of my acquaintance as well as by my (middle-aged) friends in the rancho today (and by me). These representations of ranchero identity, like those in the classic films, however nourishing (for various reasons) for different groups of people, contrast rather starkly with the realities of ranchero life and history, to which I now turn.

"Flesh and Blood" Rancheros in Western Mexico

Although missing until recently in much research literature on rural Mexico, rancheros as a specific type of rural Mexican appeared in published materials as early as the mid-nineteenth century (Brantz 1853; Hernández Galván 1926; Jacobs 1982; McBride 1923). Most recent studies have focused on western Mexico, although a few have described rancheros in other parts of Mexico and even in northern New Mexico (Shadow and Rodríguez-Shadow 1994). *El ranchero* is depicted in the early materials as presenting himself *sin formar curvas en la espina dorsal* (without forming curves in his spine, i.e., without bending forward in humility and deference) and as *ingenuo, cándido y sencilla a toda prueba* (ingenuous, candid, and completely down-to-earth) (Rivera 1855, 206–208). These characterizations match more recent studies of ranchero communities (Barragán 1990a; González 1991; Taylor 1987 [1932]) and the rancheros (and rancheras) of the present study.

González (1991, 4) describes the traditional location of ranchero homesteads, especially in western Mexico, as in "the hills, the high undulating plateaus and the hillsides in abrupt mountainous territory." These spaces, as Barragán (1990b) has pointed out, often are wild before rancheros clear parts of them for cultivation, but they are quite favorable for the extensive raising of cattle. Rancheros, in fact, are closely tied to cattle and related products (e.g., meat, cheese, sweets made from milk, and leather products). It is significant that these mountainous spaces are generally not the best for haciendas, because of their relative inaccessibility and undulating terrain. In the more level areas and larger valleys of western Mexico, haciendas were in fact an important chapter in the history of the region. Many traditionally ranchero spaces, in contrast, were not thoroughly dominated by haciendas, a historical fact that could contribute to the noted ranchero stance of independence, self-assertiveness, and pride.

Rancheros have pursued a range of economic activities: raising chickens and pigs; maintaining vegetable gardens, fruit orchards, and cornfields; hunting; raising and milking cattle; and making cheese. González (1991, 5) describes ranchero life as always having been "halfway poor, but very rarely extremely poor . . . for centuries they have lived in houses of little 'pomp and value,' with dirt floors, walls of adobe and roofs of straw . . . and in sum poor furniture but not miserable. Their clothing of habit has suffered many moves." As long as there has been an abundance of food, rancheros could not be considered extremely poor; but some rancheros have not always had such abundance. The members of the community under study here, in fact, began migrating to the United States because there was not sufficient food for their families. Some older (in their eighties) residents of the rancho, however, recall their youths as rich in land and food, though lacking in money.

As already noted, studies of rancheros in other regions of Mexico have shown them to be middle class, in fact a rural bourgeoisie (Schryer 1980). The rancheros in this study could be described as a community with such rural middle-class roots and with a potentially middle-class future; both of these aspects of their identity no doubt influence their behavior and self-presentation. Before dollars from migration and work in the United States began to flow into the rancho in recent decades, these rancheros were as poor as other campesinos of the region. Yet their status is clearly midway between the indigenous P'urhepecha (and "de-Indianized" campesino mestizos) and the urban, professional, and upper-class elite. Traditionally, rancheros in this region worked their fields (either as owners or as renters) as family units. In recent decades the region has become more integrated into the larger regional, national, and even international marketplace, so that many rancheros in western Mexico now sell almost all of their produce, from cheese (Barragán 1990b) to avocados (Damien de Surgy et al. 1988), sometimes employing one or two workers to help them.

Barragán (1997) argues that rancheros were the agents of the real conquest of Mexico, gradually over the centuries integrating ever more territory (usually remote from the Spanish center) into the nation-state, typically at the expense of indigenous communities. He traces ranchero society, and ranchero culture, to the lower orders of Spanish conquerors —soldiers, miners, sailors, farmers, and other working-class and peasant colonists. Hubert Cochet (1991), among others, corroborates Barragán's argument by documenting the late-eighteenth-century migration of rancheros from the Los Altos area in Jalisco to San José de Gracia and Cotija in northwestern Michoacán and the subsequent late-nineteenth-century migration of their descendants from there to Coalcomán in southern Michoacán. These migrations illustrate for this part of Mexico the "ordinary" conquest of land and its indigenous population by criollo (Spanish native to Mexico) and mestizo rancheros.

Cochet describes an agrarian system dominated by the great estate, the hacienda. In the Bajío (a large fertile agricultural plain slightly to the north of the region under study here) this system developed in the late sixteenth and early seventeenth centuries, when Spaniards passed through the area via the *camino real* (main road) from Mexico City west to the mines in Zacatecas and noted its agricultural potential. Both haciendas and cities developed across the Bajío to service the mining industry. Historical treatments of this agrarian system, however, have overemphasized the hacienda and its dependent peons, while, until recently, ignoring the presence of "an important sector of small and medium property owners" all over western Mexico, situated in the "large empty spaces between the haciendas" (Cochet 1991, 22–23). Cochet criticizes the traditional perceived dichotomy of hacienda owners and peons as the primary constituents of the countryside. Around the haciendas were small and medium-sized landowners whose properties lay in the interstices between haciendas, as well as the tenants and sharecroppers working hacienda-owned land. Frequently only a small inner circle of the best, irrigated land was actually worked by hacienda labor in the production of intense commercial crops. The unirrigated outskirts were often rented out to *arrendatarios* (tenant farmers) or worked *a partido* (sharing an agricultural yield with an owner) by *medieros* (sharecroppers) (Cochet 1991, 25). Rancheros, of course, constituted this missing population of small and medium property owners, tenant farmers, and sharecroppers.

In western Michoacán (including the region under study here) haciendas and ranchos predominated by the nineteenth century; the hacendados used rancheros as salaried labor, due to the relative scarcity of nearby indigenous populations that they could use for this purpose (Rouse 1988). Salaried labor, of course, can be quite different from debt peonage, resulting in different work relations as well as a heterogeneous class structure (as opposed to the more clear-cut dichotomy of dominant hacendado and submissive peon). A large middle sector of rancheros, businesspeople, muleteers, artisans, and various categories of tenant farmers blurred class boundaries, especially between the middle and lower classes; because the population was not clearly divided along class lines, a strong class consciousness did not develop. Moreover, an identifiable level of social mobility (often within one lifetime), kinship relations across classes, and frequently a single ethnic identity (predominantly criollo) also served to blur class distinctions. Thus much of the population shared a culture that integrated elite attitudes and so had a recognizably "liberal" character that valued independent businesses, ideally based in land, hard work, and a disposition to move in search of opportunity—all qualities believed to be characteristic of "whites" and not of Indians (Rouse 1988, 237).

So far in this chapter I have argued that ranchero culture and society developed in specific historical conditions, both material (the frontier) and structural (positioned midway between the elite and peons). Thus the specific history of this population, particularly within this region of Mexico, is essential to understanding their cultural identity as constructed in characteristic ways of speaking. Consequently I turn now to the history of rancheros in western Mexico, from the Spanish conquest to the present, the centuries during which ranchero society developed. This overview is intended to lay the groundwork for a better understanding of the aspects of ranchero identity and ways of speaking that I treat in Chapters 5 through 8.

Ranchero History in Western Mexico

The Colonial Period

In the first few decades following the Spanish conquest of what is now Mexico City in 1521, Spain was primarily interested in tribute from Indian subjects and in expropriating gold and silver, either through extant objects or through mining. Consequently a system of encomiendas (estates) divided up the territory, delegating the power of the Crown to conquerors and other Spaniards. Encomiendas created rights over the tribute and labor of the Indians but did not include rights to land. By the end of the sixteenth century, however, encomiendas had been abandoned, because the mines were exhausted and the Indian population that worked them had been dramatically reduced by disease. With the arrival of cattle, the conquerors' interest turned toward the land, and land was granted by the Crown in private property (Barragán 1997). The distribution of land began with *mercedes* (land grants), including *peonías* for foot soldiers (those *a pie* or on foot) and *caballerías* for cavalry (those *a caballo* or on horseback). The Spaniards receiving these modest properties (primarily *caballerías: peonías* were given mostly to the indigenous and were so small as to be undesirable to the Spanish) directly worked the land, along with hired Indian workers. They also resided on their land, unlike many large estate owners, who often lived in the cities as absentee landlords. Small nuclei of farmers and soldiers developed *caballerías* for farming and *estancias* (ranches) for cattle raising. These frontier people included "cowboys, adventurers, unattached men, those who roam in search of an opportunity to get themselves a piece of land which would permit them a more settled existence" and were the precursors to rancheros (Barragán 1997, 29).

Land tenure in western Mexico, then, consisted of either large haciendas or smaller ranchos, in contrast to the situation farther south in Mexico (e.g., Oaxaca), where the Indian village continued to own land communally "in the face of the expansion of the Spanish hacienda" (Brading 1978, 17). At the same time priests, encomenderos (owners of encomiendas), and governing officials began to congregate dispersed Indians into towns of European design near monasteries, ostensibly to convert them more effectively to Christianity but also to empty valuable agricultural land, which was then granted to new Spanish owners. The larger haciendas were often administered by members of the incipient ranchero society, who were thus stationed both physically and symbolically between the Spanish elite and the indigenous poor.

In the first half of the seventeenth century the conversion of land to private property was consolidated. Indians were progressively dislocated from their lands, largely through incessant pressure from mestizos and criollos, precisely the people who were forming incipient ranchero societies. Who were these rancheros? A large number originally were poor Spaniards, the lowest in the social hierarchy, those on the margin of society. They were only able to achieve land ownership on the margins of grand properties, on land which had been given to them by their Spanish bosses or in spaces left empty by dislocated Indians that were less desirable to large Spanish landowners. Those who did not own land at all, perhaps the majority, were relatively autonomous renters, either tenants or sharecroppers who shared the yield with the owner, often a neighbor or relative. These *estancieros* (people who lived on *estancias*), according to François Chevalier (1985 [1956]), were the lowest on the social scale among whites, when they were not mestizo, black, or mulatto.

The expansion of this population followed the expansion of the cattle population in the plains of the north and the hilly lands of the west (the site of the present study), and they were referred to as *hombres de a caballo* (men on horseback). In general they moved frequently, and they alternated between working for a fixed salary, working *a partido,* or getting half of the yield of animals sold for profit. They were *todistas:* they knew how to do everything, from breaking in a horse to roping cattle, making and fixing a saddle, building a house, cooking a meal, or making clothes (González 1974, 14). Whether free-floating travelers who moved around the country working here and there or more stable agriculturalists who worked land with their families, these people valued personal freedom, autonomy, and hard work.

According to David Brading (1978), who was writing about the Bajío, the large Mexican estate or hacienda was created during the first large cycle of agricultural exportation from 1570 to 1630, but yields sharply contracted after 1630. Many large haciendas went bankrupt; in an effort to bring in money without expenditure, the owners rented out much of their land to tenant farmers at very low, even nominal, rates. In some areas an extensive class of small property owners emerged. Eventually the hacienda system itself was threatened by the productiveness of such peasant farming, because these small holders and renters were supplying the markets with most of its products. Barragán (1997) describes these peasant farmers as rancheros, whose seminal characteristics—a love of liberty, great ambition, and a propensity for geographic and social mobility—led them to seize these opportunities. He adds that the decades from 1680 to 1740 "must have been like an epoch of gold for the *rancheros* of León, Guanajuato" (Barragán 1997, 43).

In the third century of Spanish occupation of Mexico ranchero societies consolidated and expanded along with the increase in Spanish-dominated territory. According to Brading (1978), the entire population in the diocese of Michoacán (which at that time included not only the region under study here but also the nearby Bajío of Brading's study) increased fivefold during the eighteenth century. A continuing policy of populating and colonizing peripheral zones throughout Mexico encouraged people to move from more settled and populated areas and from Spain. Eventually moving to the farther reaches of the frontier north and the southeast, rancheros integrated ever more territory into the nation-state (Barragán 1997). Often situated between large haciendas and indigenous lands, rancheros carved out their own spaces, perhaps on undulating terrain at the edge of hacienda properties or at the foot of mountains or on drier lands, but always in marginal spaces. In the far frontier north new colonies of people were supported by the government as a means of "pacifying" the region, using them as a wall of defense against the frequent incursions by "wild" Apache and Chichimeca Indians (Alonso 1995).

Thus criollo and mestizo ranchero communities were founded as "nuclei of permanent population in zones close to pre-hispanic indigenous settlements. These colonies had the double intention to serve as 'models of civilization' to the Indians and, at the same time, secure the *mestizo* and Spanish colonization of the area" (Lloyd 1988, 63). In an effort to populate these relatively inhospitable areas, colonial policy favored the founding of settlements that were ethnically mixed, assuring equal rights to all who would assume risks and move. In spite of this, most inhabitants of these communities were of Spanish descent, perhaps attracted by the possibility of maintaining, in a more isolated context, *pureza de sangre* (purity of blood), an attribute found to be important to rancheros in several different studies (Alonso 1995; Barragán 1990b; González 1974). Sephardic Jews may have populated some of these more isolated areas (possibly in an effort to avoid the Spanish Inquisition first in Spain and then in Mexico), because even today some Jewish practices can be found in some isolated ranchero societies (Chávez Torres 1998).[3]

The vastly expanding population during the eighteenth century, as well as the growing need for agricultural products, put pressure on available land. In addition Spanish laws of inheritance (specifying that all heirs inherit equally) worked to break up larger estates and ranches, which were only sometimes painstakingly pieced together again in subsequent generations (Brading 1978). Rancheros in particular were in a precarious position that often led to migration.

Cochet (1991) recounts a specific migratory flow over the generations in western Mexico at the end of the eighteenth century from the Los Altos region of Jalisco to the Cotija region of Michoacán, resulting in marked demographic growth in northwestern Michoacán, the site of the present study. González's history of San José de Gracia (1974) in northwest Michoacán also recounts the populating of abandoned hacienda land in 1791 by the settlement of families from nearby towns and other places as tenant farmers. The great majority of them were criollos, with a few mestizos and mulattos. These rancheros "were unruly people, who lived by the sling and the machete. The men, dressed in trousers of sheepskin or deerskin and coarse cotton shirts, rode as though they and their mounts were one" (González 1974, 16).

Although these colonists were largely criollo, they were enemies of the *gachupines* (Spaniards born in Spain), who were at the top of the status hierarchy in Mexico, followed by criollos and mestizos and then by Indians and mulattos (Brading 1978). Although they did not identify with local people of color (and in fact valued *pureza de sangre*), they were nevertheless closer to them than to recent arrivals from Spain (Spanish colonists were still arriving in significant numbers at the end of the eighteenth century). The war of independence from Spain in 1810 gave these criollo rancheros the opportunity to settle old scores with *gachupín* hacendados; in the century following the war, with the expulsion of the Spanish, rancheros as a group grew spectacularly. By the end of the third and last century of colonial rule, ranchero societies, with some variations, had sprouted up all over rural Mexico (González 1974).

Postindependence

After the war of independence from Spain (1810–1821), ranchero societies continued to expand, colonizing more isolated areas through generational migrations from the sierras of traditional ranchero occupation. According to Barragán (1997), the growth of ranchero societies followed two different dynamics: one was the result of the fragmentation of the old properties granted by the Crown, and the other the result of the accumulation of these lands. In the first case, when the time came for heirs to divide the lands of haciendas owned by absentee landlords, they were sometimes put up for sale and so fragmented into smaller pieces that they became ranchos. When haciendas did not fragment entirely, but still were subdivided by heirs, the smaller properties owned by some of the heirs also became ranchos. The owners of these smaller properties gradually came to be similar to other rancheros in the area. A second source of rancheros was the group that formed and strengthened in the orbit of the large properties. These rancheros did manual labor for the hacienda and also were tenant farmers and sharecroppers; they were producers without private property who, tied to the land, had to situate themselves in spaces ceded by the hacienda. In both cases, when local access to land was closed off or chances for accumulating any land were reduced, rancheros accelerated their movements toward less populated zones, where they might have a better future. In these frontier spaces, however, they were sandwiched between large landowners and the indigenous people, without reliable institutional support from the larger society. In this context they developed tenacity, flexibility, and a capacity for adaptation (Barragán 1997).

Ranchero migrations that occurred during this first century of nationhood were accelerated by liberal reform laws starting just after mid-century that promoted the subdivision of communal lands, including those owned by the church and those belonging to indigenous or mestizo communities, to encourage small property ownership. While this process was uneven and long-term, it took place in various regions of Mexico, principally in mountainous and poor areas, including Veracruz (Hoffmann 1994), Michoacán (González 1974), Hidalgo (Schryer 1980), and Jalisco (Chevalier 1982). Thus the population of rancheros continued to increase more or less rapidly (depending on their locations) throughout the nineteenth century, expanding principally from Los Altos of Jalisco and Cotija, Michoacán, toward poorer, more vacant lands in the south, the west, and possibly the north and northwest. Wherever they went, rancheros imprinted their presence on the land: agriculture based in private property and the complementary duality of raising cattle and growing corn, along with a wide range of other activities.

Only a few studies of rancheros exist for the twentieth century, but those that do shed light on ranchero participation in the four grand narratives of this century in Mexico: the Revolution (1910–1920), the Cristero Rebellion (1926–1929), the agrarian reform (1933–1943), and, throughout the century, migration, both to large cities within Mexico and to the United States to work. Migration to the United States, of course, has grown within the last three decades to the point that it has become institutionalized in the social and economic structure of western Mexico (Massey et al. 1987), where the vast majority of households have someone working in *el otro lado* (the other side).

The Mexican Revolution (1910–1920)

Several studies provide insight into ranchero experiences in the Mexican Revolution, albeit in contrasting ways. Both Frans Schryer (1980) and Ian Jacobs (1982) describe rancheros (in Hidalgo and Guerrero, respectively) who actively participated in, even instigated, revolutionary battles. In contrast, both Luis González (1974) and Paul Taylor (1987 [1932]) note the lack of involvement in the Revolution by rancheros in western Mexico (Jalisco and Michoacán, respectively). Thus although rancheros across Mexico may share cultural and linguistic identity, their political activities have differed according to local circumstances. The rancheros in the present study, like those described in other studies of western Mexico and in the early study by George McBride, generally were not involved in the Revolution, preferring "to be left alone, to cultivate [their] few acres in peace, unmolested by the march of troops or the raids of rebel bands" (McBride 1923, 102). González (1974) describes remote San José de Gracia, in northwestern Michoacán near the Jalisco border, as relatively uninvolved in the Revolution until its later stages, when it seriously and adversely affected life in this village. Revolutionaries began to appear, demanding food, horses, and money from rich families. Also, residents began consuming their own products, because roads were not safe for transporting agricultural produce to market, and trade declined.

Like many rancheros in this region, San José residents were disinclined to be patriotic, had not yet begun to identify with the larger Mexican nation, and had a strong distrust of government in general. Gradually and reluctantly, however, they became involved in the Revolution, as the town was increasingly besieged by bandits from various revolutionary factions. Some residents, usually small landowners, retained an enthusiasm for Francisco "Pancho" Villa, but no one supported any of the other factions. Whenever armed men were rumored to be in town, people ran to hide their daughters, horses, and anything else of value (González 1974, 127). Attacks by bandits worsened; some were clearly anticlerical, resulting in the plundering of churches and fleeing priests pursued by gunfire. The period between 1915 and 1917, when the Revolution was actually drawing to a close, was particularly devastating in terms of hunger, banditry, and chaos. One especially violent episode was the sacking, killing, and burning of the town by Inés Chávez García, a bandit still known in this region for the devastation he wrought (including the burning of archives in Tingüindín, the county seat for the rancho in the present study).

The new government promised both educational and agrarian reform, by bringing schools to rural areas and reallocating the land of large landowners to those who had none. In ranchero regions of western Mexico, however, resentment simmered, both over the agrarian reform and over the anticlerical attitude of the new government. Although the government meant to target the structure (and power) of the church in Mexico, the intensely Catholic people in this region of Mexico resented government interference in religious matters.

The Cristero Rebellion (1926–1929)

Soon after the Revolution a widespread rebellion against the new revolutionary government took place in western Mexico. Jean Meyer (1976) views this conflict as part of Mexico's long-term movement toward becoming a modern nation-state, with total control over its people and territories. The church had wielded considerable power throughout Mexico's history, and the new revolutionary government sought to curtail this power. In the Cristero Rebellion, however, the church as an institution did not confront the government; rather, the rural masses of western Mexico did. Meyer (1976) concludes that the impetus for this uprising was religious belief, based on a kind of sacramental Christianity that had been heavily evangelized in this region during the previous fifty years. *Cristeros* rose up against the government of President Plutarco Elías Calles when churches were closed following anticlerical government orders. Although the churches were later reopened, the eventual defeat of the *cristeros* led inevitably to more thorough state control over all regions of Mexico.

Meyer (1976) shows that 60 percent of the *cristeros* were manual laborers, including criollos, mestizos, and Indians. According to Meyer, when *cristeros* were faced with the withdrawal of the sacraments from their lives, which would mean spiritual death, they chose insurrection, even if it meant martyrdom and the bloody sacrifice of their lives. Thus *cristeros* of western Mexico rebelled against a government that was taking away their sacraments, but many of them also rebelled against a government that violated dominant local beliefs regarding land ownership. Some Indian *cristeros* hated both the government and its *agrarista* clientele, since some *agraristas* were attempting to take communal Indian lands. For example, Indians in Michoacán massacred *agraristas* (at Cherán) and expelled them from the mountains (at Charapán) during the Cristero Rebellion and, when not actively involved in the rebellion, sympathized with it. Many neighboring criollo and mestizo rancheros also hated the government and the *agraristas,* but for different reasons. On principle they hated the government as they hated any outside institution trying to impose control on them. This hatred was multiplied, however, against the *agraristas* and the government that sponsored their activities, because these actions went against ranchero ideology regarding hard work and private ownership of land. Thus some traditional Indians and criollo-mestizo rancheros had common foes: the government and those who profited from the government's interventions.

Although Meyer (1976) emphasizes more agency on the part of the rural masses than had earlier studies, both Marjorie Becker (1995) and Jennie Purnell (1999) argue that he overemphasized the homogeneity of "the people" rising up against an anticlerical revolutionary state. Purnell (1999, 7) shows instead that communities in this region, and factions within communities, were "deeply divided in their responses to revolutionary state formation." She traces these differences not to ethnicity or class, or even to religion (which was widely shared), but to varying historical experiences with land reform and local culture. In the case of ranchero communities, a history of a *lack* of agrarian conflict and a local ideology valuing private ownership of land led most people in these communities to resist the revolutionary government's efforts in this area. Indian communities, in contrast, had differing historical experiences of agrarian conflict. Those who had managed to retain communal lands could rise up as *cristeros* like the rancheros, with whom they had little else in common. In contrast, those who had histories of communal land loss pursued agrarian reform to regain traditional village lands and, as *agra-*

ristas, fought the *cristeros* for the government. This increased the polarization between *agraristas* and *cristeros,* in spite of the fact that many *agraristas* were as religious as the *cristeros* (Boyer 1998; Purnell 1999). Other *agraristas* expressed the polarization by burning Catholic icons (Becker 1995).

Meyer (1976, 97) notes that women often took an active part in the Cristero Rebellion, making explosives, teaching men the art of sabotage, secretly delivering arms and ammunition, and even participating in direct action. Many women regularly supplied food and other sustenance to *cristero* fighters, who would come down from the mountains into the ranchos when it was safe, to be fed and to restock their supplies. Meyer suggests that women were furious that the government was forcing the closing of their churches, thus taking away their sacraments; but closing the churches also took away the arena in which women held power, unlike the public domain of politics.

González (1974) provides a view of ranchero participation in the Cristero Rebellion in a particular village. In San José de Gracia, as in other ranchero areas in northwest Michoacán, people had a great deal of sympathy for the *cristeros.* Those who did not participate directly in military action provided food and supplies and served as spies for the rebels. According to González, virtually everyone in the mountains of this region supported the cause; 2 million people signed a petition for freedom to practice their religion. Battles were particularly fierce, and government forces regularly hanged *cristeros* from the trees (as they did in the rancho under study here) as reminders to sympathetic civilians. Although the government was ultimately victorious, Meyer (1976) notes that 100,000 people were killed during the Cristero Rebellion, two-thirds of this number being government troops.

Meyer (1976) details the remarkable organization and efficiency of the *cristero* army and government (in regions where they, and not the federal government, ruled), and their firm sense of morality and justice, including swift punishment for crimes such as rape. This grassroots movement's goals officially included agrarian reform (as well as votes for women), but only if previous owners were compensated for the property and only if the reform was carried out fairly (González 1974, 166). Much of their resentment of the government's plans for agrarian reform could be traced to their traditional distrust of the government and of any outside control. After all, priests in San José, as in other ranchero areas, for generations had been the primary source of information, entertainment, and authority and were local, not outsiders. Another source of the resentment against governmental agrarian reform was its undermining of the rancheros' own code of honor, which held that private property was sacrosanct and should only be earned through hard work. In spite of the best efforts of the *cristeros*, agrarian reform led by the federal government did come to northwestern Michoacán (although the churches were reopened).

Agrarian Reform

In spite of broad resistance to the new revolutionary government in this region and widespread support for the *cristeros*, small groups of *agraristas* continued to struggle for land reform, especially in indigenous communities attempting to regain lost village lands (e.g., Friedrich 1986). Even in ranchero communities, however, some applied for land via the agrarian reform policies of the government. Craig (1983) describes one such case in Los Altos of Jalisco, an intensely ranchero region. Here the agrarian reform movement was primarily an instrumental act, a means to obtain land, rather than a fight to reinstate historic rights. Moreover, those "who initiated local petitions for land reform . . . did so as the result of individual or, at most, family decisions. They were rarely chosen as leaders by community consensus" (Craig 1983, 9). Thus, like the agrarian reform in the microregion of the present study (see Chapter 3), these ranchero *agraristas* did not have widespread community support. Instead they pursued agrarian reform against a dominant local ideology that favored private ownership of land.

Although some efforts at agrarian reform in Michoacán had begun when Francisco Múgica became governor in 1920, his control over these efforts was tenuous; and forces opposed to his Socialist Party resulted in the fall of his government within two years (Boyer 1998). Agrarian reform primarily occurred in western Mexico during the presidency of Lázaro Cárdenas, a man from Jiquilpan in northwest Michoacán. Cárdenas had been governor of Michoacán from 1928 to 1932 and was president of Mexico from 1934 to 1940. The goals of agrarian reform, which he pursued both as governor and as president, were "to increase the number of landowners, encourage communal ownership of land [*ejidos*], and improve and expand agricultural production by opening new areas to cultivation, making use of irrigation, exploiting tropical crops, improving farm implements, and extending credit to farmers" (González 1974, 182). During his presidency, and partly through efforts at socialist education (Vaughan 1997), revolutionary beliefs and practice spread throughout Michoacán. This transformation was more difficult in ranchero areas, where the idea of agrarian reform was resisted by most. Ranchero commitment to private property did not square with the idea of the *ejido*, and "obtaining land as a gift meant losing face" (González 1974, 184). Sometimes, however, people put honor aside and petitioned for land under the agrarian reform, stimulated by the economic depression and hunger that followed the Cristero Rebellion.

Becker (1995) describes the Cardenista project in Michoacán as an attempt to transform the entire culture of the countryside, mobilizing a "cadre—teachers, agricultural agents, rural political bosses . . . [who] were to overhaul land tenure arrangements, to dispel illiteracy, to remake campesino habits" (Becker 1995, 9). Success was limited, partly because the Cardenistas misjudged the people they wanted to transform, assuming them to be ignorant and uncultured and in need of the modern "rational" practices they intended to impart. Nevertheless, at the end of "the triple revolution" (the Revolution, the Cristero Rebellion, and the agrarian reform), life in northwestern Michoacán had changed. Free secular schools provided by the government began to appear in small villages, and more people experienced formal schooling. Most importantly, however, "the triple revolution brought the end of isolation" (González 1974, 213): small towns became "Mexicanized," fused with the nation. Civil holidays were added to traditional religious ones, the radio arrived, and newspapers became popular. In spite of this, the traditional distrust of the government survived. According to González (1974), villagers hated every great figure of the revolution except Pancho Villa and Lázaro Cárdenas, who was revered not because of his agrarian successes but because he brought peace.

Migration

Rancheros, habituated to mobility over the generations, migrated during the twentieth century to other parts of Mexico and to the United States in search of better prospects. Significant Mexican migration to the United States had begun during the late nineteenth century, primarily in the post–Civil War industrial expansion and as part of the integration of the U.S. Southwest into the national economy (Massey et al. 1987). Mexicans worked in U.S. agriculture, mining, and railroading, especially after the 1882 Chinese Exclusion Act and the 1907 agreement with Japan curtailed these sources of labor. "As the railroads extended into western Mexico in the late nineteenth century, *enganchistas* (labor recruiters) sought Mexican workers to build and maintain the railroad lines, and then to work in U.S. mines and agriculture" (Cardoso 1980, as quoted in Hondagneu-Sotelo 1994, 20). The railroads were crucial in connecting "areas of labor surplus and shortage" (Massey et al. 1987, 41). This movement toward employment in the United States greatly increased during the Mexican Revolution of 1910–1920 and its aftermath, especially after World War I and the curtailing of European immigration to the United States in 1921 (Massey et al. 1987).

Although Mexican migrants at this time were concentrated in southwestern agriculture, they also worked in the Midwest, including Chicago, in various industries (Griswold del Castillo and De León 1996). Between World War I and the Great Depression, the first great wave of Mexican immigration placed Mexicans in the fields of the Southwest and the factories, packing houses, and restaurants in the Midwest and East. A more detailed history of the migration to the Midwest and Chicago is presented in Chapter 3. It can be noted here, however, that Taylor's (1987 [1932]) early study located five colonies of Mexican migrants in the Chicago area, three in Chicago (South Chicago and Irondale, Stockyards, and Hull House—where the University of Illinois at Chicago now stands) and two in Indiana (Gary and East Chicago). The overwhelming majority of these Mexicans, as surveyed in the 1920s, were from Michoacán, Guanajuato, and Jalisco (Rosales 1995). Not only are these states heavily ranchero, but the following description of Mexican workers from a steelworks superintendent reveals ranchero attitudes and values (as I demonstrate in Chapter 6): ". . . they are not so servile as some Europeans. If I go out in the mill, they may look at me and say good morning, but they don't cringe and curry as some of the Europeans do. I don't like men who do it, just because I am boss. I want men who can stand on their own feet" (Taylor 1987 [1932], 35).

After Mexican workers were deported during the Great Depression of the 1930s, a labor shortage brought about by World War II again led to the recruitment of Mexicans for (temporary) work in the United States as part of the Bracero Program (García 1996). When this program was initiated by the United States in 1942, rancheros (well used to mobility over the generations) signed up, probably in great numbers, to work in the United States as braceros (manual laborers). Although the program ended in 1964, it had already accelerated a migration process that had begun almost a century before. This process drew migrants, largely from the western Mexico states of Jalisco, Michoacán, Zacatecas, and Guanajuato (Massey et al. 1987), all heavily ranchero regions, to the United States to work, supposedly temporarily; it eventually resulted in "daughter" communities of various Mexican villages in the United States (Hondagneu-Sotelo 1994).

Roger Rouse's study (1988) of Michocacán migrants at both ends of their "transnational migrant circuit" includes one of these "daughter" communities, Redwood City, California, as well as the village of origin,

Aguililla, Michoacán. From the 1940s on, uneven economic development in Michoacán spurred migration to the United States. Mexican capital was diverted to urban industry, leaving local economies without sufficient investment in infrastructure and spurring people unable to make a living from their ranchos to migrate. Migration increased due to rising levels of health care and education in Mexico, "which put pressure on resources and equipped people with skills and ambitions that could not be realized locally" (Rouse 1989, 27). Finally, better transport and communications made it easier for people to leave the area. In short, a variety of "push" factors resulted in more migration.

Thus both "push" and "pull" factors promoted migration from western Mexico to the United States during this period (Massey et al. 1987). Conditions in the United States led again to the recruitment of Mexican workers. Conditions in Mexico unintentionally led to, and perhaps increased, the same migration process. Barragán (1990b) notes that for ranchos and villages around Cotija in northwestern Michoacán migration became all the more imperative because the highways built during this period of Mexican development bypassed them. Some of these small villages, in fact, effectively became ghost towns during the 1990s, in great contrast to a century earlier, when Cotija was a commercial center of much prosperity.

In the last several decades structural factors in both countries have continued to exert their "pushes" and "pulls" on migrants. Migration has not only continued but increased. These structural changes have notably included economic transformations in the United States in regard to globalization and the enduring economic crisis in Mexico. Ironically, whenever the "anti-immigrant" climate in the United States grows, each legislative act intended to curb this migration unintentionally increases it (Massey n.d.). With the maturation of migration as a social process, women and children have joined their husbands and fathers; and a shift from seasonal agricultural labor to year-round factory and service labor has encouraged settlement rather than "sojourning" in the United States. Moreover, hundreds of "daughter" communities sent about 14 billion dollars back to Mexico during 2003 (Malkin 2004; Thompson 2003), increasing to almost 8 billion in only the first half of 2004 (Dickerson 2004). The effects of these dollars are evidenced in western Mexico by housing construction, pickup trucks with U.S. plates, and new roads built to accommodate new vehicles bought with the money (Massey et al. 1987).

One important result of all this migration is the creation of what Rouse (1988, 26) calls a "transnational migrant circuit," or what Douglas

Massey et al. (1987) and others have called "binational" communities. These transnational communities are just that: communities of people living on both sides of the U.S.-Mexico border, both physically and metaphorically. Rouse (1988, 304) critiques the tendency for analysts to treat migration between places as a movement between two autonomous sites, arguing that the "continuous circulation of people, money, goods, and information" for many decades has woven together places in Mexico and the United States so tightly that "they can no longer be considered distinct," severing "the equation between community and place."

In the present study, a rancho reconstituted itself in Chicago, person by person and family by family; and within the social network of families in this study, someone is virtually always coming from or going to Mexico or Chicago. People keep up familial and other social relationships through telephone calls, e-mails, letters, visits, photographs, and videotapes of ritual celebrations such as weddings. In the next chapter I describe the two ends of this particular transnational circuit, the rancho as situated in its microregion in western Mexico and Chicago, particularly the Mexican neighborhoods in which these families live.

The brief history of rancheros in western Mexico presented in the second half of this chapter illuminates key characteristics of ranchero identity: a habituation to mobility, especially in search of economic opportunity; ingenuity and widely varying skills; a determined sense of autonomy, including profoundly antigovernment attitudes; deep religiosity; and, finally, entrepreneurial attitudes that take advantage of opportunity, even if that means enduring hardship, taking risks, and migrating long distances. In the next chapter I describe the geographic sites in which the people in this study live, on both sides of the U.S.-Mexico border. These places together form what can be called Chicagoacán. Chicago is omnipresent in the rancho, in terms of people, material goods, ideas, and of course language, both oral and printed. Likewise, ranchero culture from western Mexico, especially Michoacán, is omnipresent in Chicago, particularly in the densest Mexican neighborhoods in which these families live.

THREE

The Spatial Context

San Juanico, Illinois, and Chicago, Michoacán

Radio announcers on a Spanish-speaking station in the Chicago area frequently ask those who call in: "Where are you calling from?" After the caller responds with, for example, "Chicago," the announcer asks, "Where are you from in Mexico?" If the caller then says, for example, "Michoacán," the announcer gleefully shouts, *¡Bueno! Y en Chicago, Michoacán, ¿cuál manda?* (OK! And in Chicago, Michoacán, what [station] rules?), to which the caller responds, *¡La Ley manda!* (The Law rules!). La Ley, the most expressively ranchero FM station in the Chicago area, has named itself playfully, with tongue in cheek. "The Law" refers both to the top billing that the station claims for itself and to U.S. law enforcement, which is potentially troubling to migrants living in Chicago without legal papers. By appropriating this source of trouble as the very name of the station, the announcers, and by extension their listeners, enact a typically ranchero assertive stance by joking about such potential danger. This stance, though enacted by both men and women (see Chapter 6), usually indexes a dominant masculinity. Many well-worn phrases in Mexican Spanish personify "the law" and use *mandar* to invoke absolute authority, for example, of parents (particularly fathers) within the home: *¿Quién manda aquí?* (Who rules around here?). Such hierarchical authority is especially characteristic of ranchero-based societies that valorize order as *respeto* (see Chapter 7). The radio routine echoes the authority evoked by these phrases; and this is repeated many times each day, which delights and then becomes ingrained in the minds of thousands of listeners.

What is taken for granted in this routine is the cohesiveness of Chicago and Michoacán. The announcer seamlessly blends two distant places, each one far from the national border that separates Mexico and the United States (see Figure 3.1). This verbal blending of two locations accurately depicts the on-the-ground experiences of daily living in transnational social fields that characterize migrants' lives—of which radio announcers are well aware. For example, a recent Saint's Day fiesta in the rancho cost 30,000 pesos, one-quarter of which (about $850) was contributed by people in Chicago. Even more recently a committee in Chicago began to gather $100,000 (many individuals contributing $1,000 each) to construct a plaza in the rancho, complete with kiosk and water fountain. As noted in Chapter 1, the families in this study continuously maintain multiple links with people on both sides of the border and frequently move back and forth across the border themselves, either to visit or to live for varying periods over the course of their lives.[1] Such back-and-forth movement is easier and more frequent for those with legal papers; those without tend to remain either in the rancho or in Chicago for very long periods. Nevertheless, the multiple connections and cross-border mobility construct a transnational community in relatively constant communication; this is probably quite unlike migrant communities in past centuries that relied on letters rather than on the telephone for such transnational communication, as was the case during the massive German migrations to the United States in the nineteenth century (Kamphoefner et al. 1991).

Moreover, daily discourse, whether in Chicago or in the rancho, is peopled with those *en el otro lado* (on the other side); in fact, much talk is about talk that took place on the other side. Instances of *relajo* in Chicago in particular (see Chapter 8) often recount previous talk that took place in Mexico. Such talk reinforces the social bonds that include all those within the transnational community, whether they are in Chicago or in Mexico at the time. Many families in this social network want to own a home in Chicago and to construct one in the rancho, and many already have met this goal.

Chicago is evident everywhere in the rancho: English print, with references to specific institutions in Chicago (the Bulls basketball team, construction companies, television channels and radio stations, and restaurants), is omnipresent on clothing, ashtrays, dishes, and calendars.[2] Most houses have a pickup truck parked in front, usually with Illinois plates; one truck in particular exhibited a decal in the rear window depicting a Chicago winter complete with falling snow—in jarring contrast to the dry sunny climate in which the pickup sits.

If Chicago is endemic in the rancho, the rancho is also endemic in Chicago. People fill the streets of Mexican neighborhoods in Chicago dressed as they would be in western Mexico (see photos): men with cowboy hats, embroidered belts, tight jeans, and mustaches; women with rebozos tightly wrapped around themselves and the young children they carry, as protection from the early morning chill. Children skip home from elementary school clad in Mexican-style school uniforms (navy blue skirts or pants and light blue shirts). Mexican music spills out on sidewalks from nearby stores, and pedestrians cross themselves as they pass Catholic churches named for European saints that now have shrines to the Virgin of Guadalupe, Mexico's patron saint. Mexican street vendors sell *atole* (a corn-based drink) and *elote* (chile-sprinkled corn on the cob), just as they do in Mexico, as well as *paletas* (frozen popsicles), an industry built by ranchero settlements slightly to the west of the microregion in this study (Quinones 2001). Thus have transmigrants transformed both western Mexico and Chicago, imprinting themselves and their practices on the built environment. In the rest of this chapter I focus on these two sites, introducing first the rancho in Michoacán and then the Chicago setting in which network members live.

The Mexican Setting

Northwest Michoacán

The rancho is situated in northwestern Michoacán. The map in Figure 3.1 shows the drive between Chicago and the rancho and locates Michoacán in the west (*el occidente*) of Mexico, bordering Guanajuato and Jalisco—two other states, like Michoacán (and especially northwest Michoacán), with heavy migration to Chicago. Within northwestern Michoacán the rancho is part of the *municipio* (township) of Tingüindín; the city of Tingüindín, the township center, has about 5,000 inhabitants out of the total of 10,000 for the entire township. The rancho, located at the intersection of the highway and the railroad tracks, is about 4.5 kilometers northwest of Tingüindín—a distance that takes ten minutes to drive and forty-five minutes to walk (see Figure 3.2).

The microregion around the rancho, within which people from the rancho travel regularly, includes Zamora to the north (toward Guadalajara) and Los Reyes to the south. Because the rancho is located along a major highway, it is easy to travel by bus in either direction, and people do so frequently to purchase food, clothing, and agricultural products or (in some cases) to go to work or to school beyond the primary grades (*primaria*). The bus to Zamora takes about forty-five minutes, though driving a car there takes about thirty minutes;[3] the bus to Los Reyes takes only about twenty minutes, and driving takes only about fifteen. Another significant town on the highway from the rancho to Zamora, at which the bus stops, is Tarecuato, an Indian pueblo (village) with a large market where rancheras shop early on Sunday mornings. Tarecuato is a center of Indian life in this microregion and thus is used to index Indian identity in everyday conversation (e.g., remarking that someone came from

Figure 3.1. The route from Chicago, Illinois, to San Juanico, Michoacán

Tarecuato is equivalent to saying that he or she is an Indian). Another significant town on the map is Cotija (to the west of Tingüindín), known as an originally Spanish settlement (with many light-skinned people) and a center of ranchero society. Because of its history, Cotija is used in conversation to index non-Indian identity.

Michoacán is called the garden state of Mexico because of its high agricultural output: the rancho is part of Mexico's primary avocado-growing area, and Zamora is known for its strawberries. The highway south of Tingüindín (toward Los Reyes and even beyond), with its lower altitude and hotter climate, was long lined with sugarcane fields;[4] and an *ingenio* (sugar factory) near Santa Clara just south of Tingüindín still produces some sugar. Both Zamora and Los Reyes are hotter (because of lower altitudes) than the rancho, which (as can be seen in Figure 3.2) is nestled in a small hilly plain surrounded by mountains. The rancho, in fact, is situated on the slope (*la ladera*) at an altitude of 1,700 meters (a mile high). People refer to three different climates, based on varying altitudes, in this microregion: the higher up *tierra fría* (cold lands), the mid-range *tierra templada* (temperate lands), and the lower *tierra*

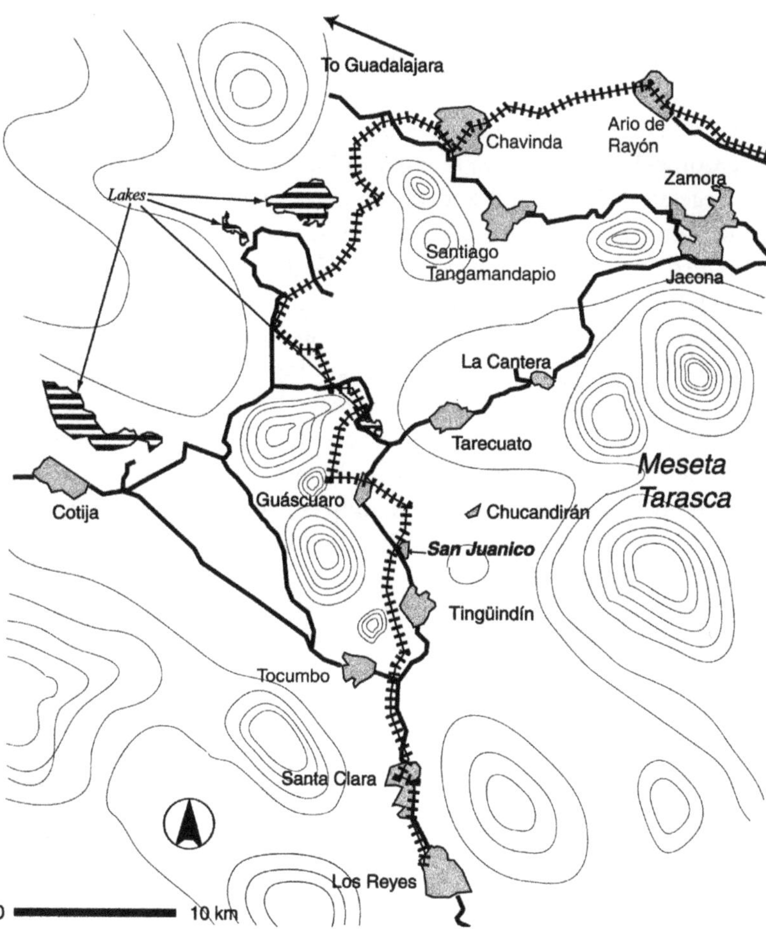

Figure 3.2. Map of microregion: Zamora to Los Reyes, Michoacán. Adapted from maps provided by the Mexican Instituto Nacional de Estadística, Geografía e Informática (INEGI).

caliente (hot lands). The rancho is temperate, with an annual average temperature of about 20 degrees C (about 68 degrees F). Thus there are both palm trees and pine trees here. Tingüindín, in fact, has a commons called El Pino that provides a cool, and sometimes beautifully misty, area for family picnics. The rancho can be quite cold in the evenings, especially during winter months, but it is rarely unbearably hot. In the *tierra caliente* of both Zamora (1,570 meters) and especially Los Reyes (1,300 meters), it is quite hot on occasion, particularly during spring before the annual rains come. In contrast, in the *tierra fría,* higher up in the Meseta Tarasca (Tarascan Tableland) with its many Indian villages, it even snows on occasion during the winter.[5] This Tarascan Sierra is a volcanic plateau with one active volcano, Paricutín, on its western end and the well-known Lake Pátzcuaro tourist site on its eastern end (West 1973). North and west of the Sierra are hills and plains, and the rancho is located on the western slope, long an area of ranchero settlement (see the Cotija-Tingüindín area in Figure 3.2).

Vegetation in the hill and plains areas surrounding the Sierra includes grasses and shrubs as well as pine and oak forests, now greatly denuded from past logging (West 1973). Soils around the rancho include *t'upurí* (fine sandy loam), productive for agriculture, and *charanda* (reddish brown clay soil), which can be planted only after the rains begin (West 1973, 10–11). These names for soil types are used in the rancho even though they are derived from *p'urhépecha,* the indigenous language of the Tarascans that the rancheros do not speak. Over time Spanish and mestizo settlements, interspersed among Indian villages, eroded the numbers of Tarascan speakers; only "small islets of purely Tarascan speech" (West 1973, 18) that continue to lose linguistic ground remain (Valdés and Menéndez 1987).

The Sierra was unattractive to large-scale Spanish exploitation (West 1973, 17), but Spanish settlers interested in stock raising established *estancias* and ranchos to the north and west of the Sierra, precisely where this study is located. Africans, mulattos, and Indians worked as cowherds in these settlements, and Africans and mulattos worked in the sugar mills (*trapiches*) and sugar factories (*ingenios*) in the warmer climate to the south of the rancho. Robert West (1973, 14) discusses the area to the west of the Sierra, the microregion of this study:

> At the beginning of the 17th century the large graben valley of Cotija was occupied by cattle estancias, and the settlement of Cotija was composed entirely of Spanish blood. As late as 1800 this valley . . . was an island of Spaniards and some mulattoes surrounded by Tarascans. A

few Spanish ranchers and traders settled also in Tingüindín, a large Indian village at the western edge of the Sierra. . . .

The rancho has two local sources of water: a narrow river over which a bridge (El Puente de San Juanico) has long been built and a natural spring (Pozo Verde) located across the highway, where there is now a dam (La Presa). The rancho utilized one for drinking and the other for bathing. Since 1958 the rancho has had piped water from a ravine near Chucandirán, next to the mountains (see Figure 3.2). In addition, this area counts on over 1 meter of rain annually, sufficient to grow a variety of crops (although many people now use irrigation from wells in their avocado orchards). The rainy season is from April through September, and the dry season is from October (a month of beautiful blooming flowers) through March. Avocados, the primary crop, are best harvested between December and March (*la cosecha* or *la fruta buena,* the "good harvest or fruit") but are also harvested during the rest of the year (*la fruta loca,* the "crazy fruit"), when the fruit sometimes drops to the ground. In addition to avocados, grown in vast orchards (*huertas*) farther up the mountains, people grow corn, beans, feed for their animals, mangos, oranges, and other fruit. Households often have citrus trees, chayote vines, chiles, and maguey cactuses for their own use. Typically, magueyes line avocado fields (sometimes marking property boundaries), and children are sent to suck the *aguamiel* (the sweet juice from the stem) through large tubes into buckets which they carry back home. This juice (for drinking) is said to have many healthful properties; it also can be fermented into pulque (an alcoholic drink).

The Rancho and Its Microregion

Traveling from Zamora southward to the rancho (see Figure 3.2), we see changes in the landscape, in people, and in vegetation. Leaving the urban twin cities of Zamora/Jacona, with their bustling traffic and multiple utility poles piercing the skies, we are suddenly in the countryside, first at the lower altitude shared by the cities. The mountains loom blue in the distance. For a while the *campo* (countryside) is sparse, in terms of both vegetation and people. We pass the rancho of Queréngaro then gradually gain altitude as we approach the Sierra. Here the vegetation changes: there are more trees, though they have sparse foliage. People begin to appear along the sides of the road; the women are usually wrapped in or carrying children or various items with the traditional Tarascan rebozo, with its black background and thin stripes of bright blue.

Two indigenous pueblos appear: first La Cantera and then the center of indigenous activity in this microregion, Tarecuato. Buildings by the sides of the road are one story tall, often painted in two colors: for example, reddish brown from the ground to about three feet and white up to the roof of red Spanish tiles. Even young girls wear the blue-striped rebozo, and many people look notably Indian. Children carry firewood to their mothers, who make tortillas over fires in small cooking huts. Graffiti on the side of a building with the words *los pochos*, a derogatory term for Mexicans in the United States who mix Spanish and English (Lara Ramos 1996), indicate that some people from here have been there. More graffiti say "*Vatos* Forever," *vatos* being another term for Mexicans, possibly gang members, in the United States.

By the time we approach Tarecuato, we are definitely in the higher-altitude Sierra, as is evidenced by the thicker stands of trees by the sides of the road and by the appearance of fir trees. As we leave Tarecuato, the road curves through a beautiful, spacious green landscape under clear blue skies, with yet more mountains in the distance. We pass the turnoff to San Angel on our right and finally reach Guáscuaro, the rancho nearest our destination, San Juanico. Guáscuaro, like San Juanico, is on a plain. There are bus stops, and people ride bicycles along the sides of the road. More electricity and telephone lines crowd the skies, and some nice-looking houses line the road, especially as we leave Guáscuaro.

Suddenly the road curves left and drops—and we see El Plano de San Juanico (the plain of San Juanico), edged by the Cerro de los Pulidos (the hill of the Pulidos, who historically owned it) on the west and the Sierra on the east. We immediately notice packing plants primarily for the avocados grown here, locally thought to be the best in Michoacán. Beyond the first packing plant on the right (west of the road, as we are traveling south) is Pozo Verde (green well, because it oozes water from natural springs), an area of planted fields so wet in places from the natural springs it contains that the ground squishes as we walk through it. On the left as we approach the rancho we see cows grazing in an open field. Thus we see the two foundations of this community's economy: livestock and agriculture (see photos). To the south of these areas on the right, we see El Campo (the soccer field) and La Presa (the dam), a small rectangle of water surrounded by cornfields. As we hear a rooster crow, we notice another packing plant on the left, as well as the entrance road lined with tall fir trees, up to the *huertas* where some families grow their avocados. We also see a field of old avocado tree stumps painted white; after twenty-five years, they are past their best yields and are cut down and replaced with new trees (or grafts onto the old trees).

San Juanico is located at the intersection of the highway and the rail-

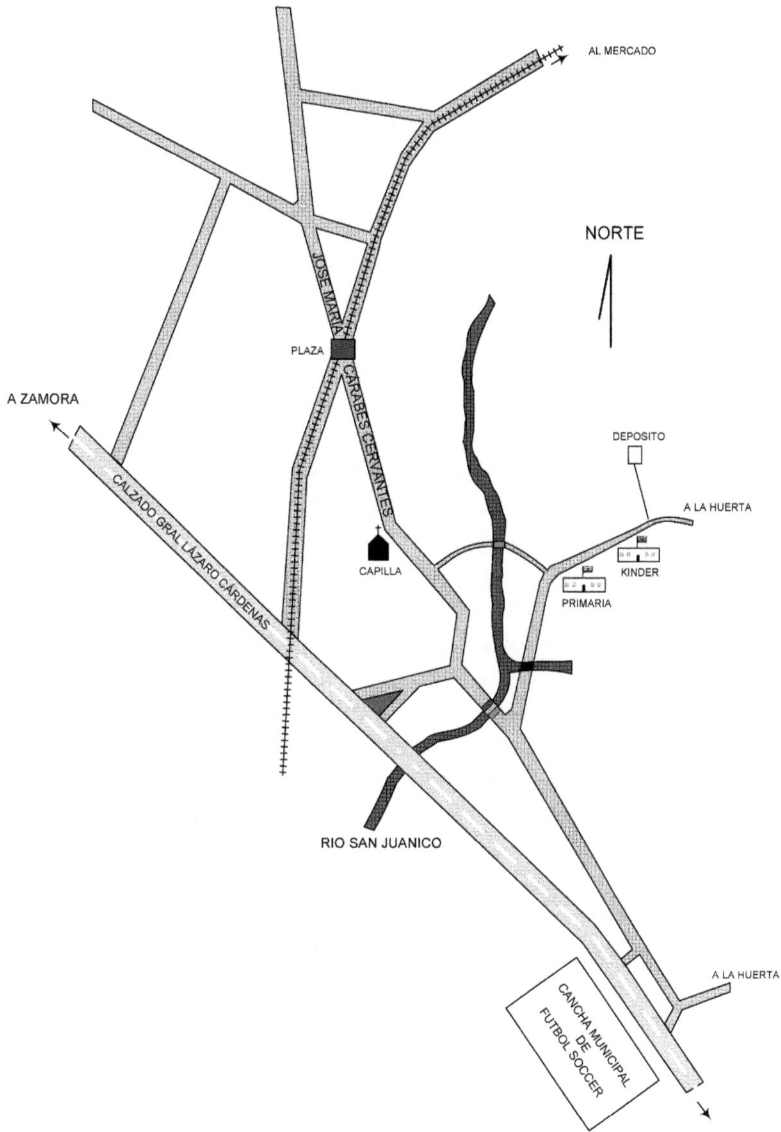

Figure 3.3. Map of San Juanico, Michoacán

road tracks. Although it now has an official entrance marked by flowers inside a triangular area bordered by a low white wrought-iron fence, three other dirt roads also lead into the rancho: two north of the official entrance (one following the railroad tracks) and one (directly across the highway from the soccer field) south of it. The hamlet itself has one main road (see Figure 3.3), which is partially covered with paving stones.

Although ranchos are not planned towns but haphazard settlements that grow up around fields, over time the residents here and in Chicago have collaborated on some urban planning. They built the official entrance; they paved more of the main road (and put in *topes* or speed bumps); and, like many other transnational Mexican communities during the 1990s, they constructed a plaza. Because there is no geographic center in a rancho, as there is in planned Mexican towns, this plaza could not be built in the center of town, flanked by the church and other official buildings. Instead the plaza was built where the tracks (no longer active) cross the main road of the rancho, down the road from the chapel, which in some ways has functioned as the center of town. Some residents, in fact, pride themselves in living near the church in what they refer to as *el centro*—a sign, like their urban planning efforts, of their aspirations to transform their rancho into a more modern town. The chapel itself was built only in 1962, when a family that had worked in Kansas and accumulated money donated the land to the rancho for its construction.

Houses lining the mostly unpaved roads of the rancho vary dramatically: some still small unpainted adobe huts with outhouses, but many others brightly painted, with indoor bathrooms, closed-in kitchens, and additional bedrooms added (see photos). Many houses are in various stages of construction, but many of those already renovated still have visible rafters where corn used to be stored. A few houses rival suburban U.S. houses in conveniences and surpass them in beauty, with brightly tiled kitchens and elegant hardwood cabinets, china closets, *artesanías* (Mexican crafts), and furniture. Many have *parabólicas* (satellite dishes) on the roof and pickup trucks parked out front or in carports.

Virtually all of this prosperity has come from U.S. dollars, and most houses can be clearly distinguished according to whether or not they have U.S. dollars coming in (either from workers in Chicago or from pensions or other investments) to support the household. Some houses follow the traditional Spanish architecture, with rooms around a center courtyard blooming with flowers and citrus trees; others resemble more closely the U.S. model: small front yards with wrought-iron gates and courtyards or patios, in the back. Even the best houses, however, retain the *pila* or outside concrete sink (see photos), for washing clothes and dishes (only rarely do houses have indoor plumbing in the kitchen). Many women, even when they have washing machines, continue to scrub some clothing on the concrete corrugated surface of the *pila,* claiming that the clothes become cleaner that way. And some people (even in Chicago) still prefer to drink their water out of a traditional brightly painted earthenware jug, with the cup functioning as the lid. Thus we see traditional ways of living juxtaposed with more modern ones.

The rancho is locally self-governed through nominations and elections. An *encargado del orden* (person responsible for order) serves for two years after having been elected. The elected *encargado* then chooses *el segundo* (the secondary deputy). When there is a change of *encargado,* a representative from the municipal *ayuntamiento* (council) comes from Tingüindín to the rancho; a committee is formed to propose projects, which are discussed at a *mesa de debates* (an open assembly). Committees organize various aspects of life in the rancho, including committees on potable water, social action, public works, and public school. The traditionally egalitarian character of ranchero societies (Barragán 1997) supports this system of committees. Although women vote and participate actively in committees (which have their own presidents, treasurers, and secretaries), only men are elected as *encargados* or chosen as *segundos.* On occasion these officials are called upon to enforce the peace with their own guns.

The father of the nine siblings who form the first generation of the social network in this study was elected *encargado* for twenty years, during which time modern services became available in the rancho. In 1954 a committee was formed in San Juanico to introduce piped water to individual houses, and José María Cárabes petitioned for this in 1962. San Juanico residents contributed most of the resources (15,000 pesos in cash and the equivalent of 10,000 pesos in labor) to this project, and the state and federal governments provided the rest. Insufficient water pressure in 1981 and again in the mid-1990s necessitated another water project, installing larger tubing. In the mid-1990s 50 percent of this effort was paid by San Juanico and 50 percent by various levels of government. In 1965 Esteban Navarro petitioned the governor to install electricity in the rancho, which was completed a few years later. Prior to the introduction of piped water and electricity, the highway was constructed to pass right by the rancho (around 1952) and was paved in 1964. Telephones were brought to the rancho in 1996. Dollars from Chicago have built bathrooms with plumbing in many houses in the last two decades.

Limited formal schooling began in 1940, and the rancho now has public schooling through the primary grades (preschool through grade 5).

Prior to such public schooling, people in many isolated ranchos in this region learned to read, write, and do elementary math, as well as read sacred texts, through church instruction (Barragán 1997). The current federal school, Melchor Ocampo, was authorized by the Secretaría de Educación Pública (SEP) in 1973. I discuss the history of schooling in this rancho, as well as current educational levels and attitudes, in more detail in Chapter 4. The next section provides a brief history of the rancho, developed from archival materials in Mexico and oral history interviews in the microregion.[6] This history focuses on the immediate area of the rancho and specifically on the social network of families in this study.

History of the Rancho

The first part of this brief history deals with the colonial period, roughly covering the sixteenth through eighteenth centuries, and the second deals with the nineteenth and twentieth centuries, following Mexico's independence from Spain after the Wars of Independence from 1810 to 1821.

COLONIAL PERIOD Before the Spanish conquest of Mexico, *tequecha* Indians lived in the area that is now known as Tingüindín (Pardo Pulido 1957; Romero Flores 1960). This group had been conquered by the Tarascans; by the time of the Spanish conquest they spoke the Tarascan language, *p'urhépecha,* and paid tribute to the Tarascan king. In 1519 Hernán Cortés and Cristóbal de Olid conquered what is now northwest Michoacán (Del Paso y Troncoso 1945); in 1522 Olid founded Tingüindín (based on an indigenous settlement called Chucandirán-Tingüindín) and orchestrated a ceremony in which the Tarascan king Calzontzín officially recognized the authority of the Spanish king Carlos I (González Méndez and Ortiz Ybarra 1980). Ongoing resistance from the Indians, however, delayed complete conquest until 1530, when another Spaniard, Nuño de Guzmán, definitively conquered Tingüindín (Del Paso y Troncoso 1945). After 1540 Franciscan priests arrived to evangelize the Indians (Romero Flores 1960). One such priest in particular is still remembered locally for his good deeds: Fray Jacobo Daciano, a Danish noble who had converted to Catholicism and become a Franciscan missionary (Pardo Pulido 1957).

The Europeans brought with the conquest unfamiliar germs, to which Indians had no resistance. This caused a drastic decline in the indigenous population during the sixteenth century: in 1530 Tingüindín had 3,000 persons; but by 1551 there were only 650, and in 1571 only 600 (Romero Flores 1960). With the rapid decrease in the Indian population, much land was distributed to Spaniards. Numerous *caballerías* (each one about twenty acres) were distributed to Spaniards who had served as soldiers on horseback (Florescano 1987), As noted in Chapter 2, these soldiers were an important source population for ranchero societies.

To compensate for the drastically reduced Indian population and to supply needed labor for a variety of endeavors, the Spanish brought African slaves to the region. The first to do so was Melchor Manzo Corona, who brought two slaves (a man and a woman) in 1564, giving them to his niece (González Méndez and Ortiz Ybarra 1980). After that, many peninsular-born Spaniards and Mexican-born criollos had African slaves working in their sugar mills. This "third root" of Mexico diversified the ethnic and cultural base in this region (and others).

Those Indians who did survive Spanish germs and subordination lived in scattered sites, making them difficult to control, so the Spaniards forcibly gathered them into *congregaciones* (congregations). Both Guáscuaro, a contemporary rancho close to the one in this study, and Tingüindín were such congregations. Tingüindín was moved in 1604 from its original site (now the rancho of Chucandirán) to its present location on the side of a hill (Esquivel Vega 1985), ostensibly for health reasons. After the conquest, indigenous people of various ethnic identities were homogenized into one category ("Indians"), forced to labor and pay tribute to their Spanish rulers, and Christianized (Morse 1987). Although Indians were relegated to their own "republic" apart from non-Indians, Spaniards dominated a colonial society composed of Spaniards, Indians, and a growing number of mestizos (Elliott 1987). Notably, Africans, who were allowed to earn their freedom as individuals, were not permitted to form ethnically based organizations (akin to the Indian Republics), so they eventually blended into the fast increasing mixed-race population (Lomnitz-Adler 1992).

After the conquest, some Spaniards were awarded *encomiendas* encompassing a particular geographic area. The Indians in that area were forced to pay tribute to the *encomendero* in the form of agricultural products, gold, and labor. The *encomienda* system, however, did not grant legal title/ownership to land (Gibson 1987; Mörner 1987). Antonio Caicedo received the *encomienda* of Tingüindín and Tarecuato in 1528, passing it to his heirs late in the century (González Méndez and Ortiz Ybarra 1980). At first such Spaniards were more interested in accumulating tribute than in owning land; but with the decline in the Indian population, the *encomienda* system waned.

In the middle of the sixteenth century the Spanish Crown began granting land to Spaniards in this region and allowed Indians to own (communally) certain types of land as well. Spaniards at this time were more interested in land for cattle raising than for agriculture, and many small ranches eventually grew into much larger ones (*estancias*), and even haciendas (Florescano 1987). By this time the Jesuits had arrived in the area, acquiring land in 1591 and eventually owning haciendas. Over the course of the seventeenth century, many ranches (often passed down in families) and three haciendas were well established in this area,[7] although it should be noted that the haciendas were at some distance from what is now the rancho in this study.

Throughout the colonial period, such landowners expanded their properties over time by taking communally owned land from Indian villages both legally and illegally. The historical record shows that various ethnic groups fought over claims to land: Spaniards (including the Jesuits), mestizos, *coyotes* (mestizo-*mulato* mixture), *mulatos* (Spanish-African mixture), and Indians. (See Chapter 5 for a detailed treatment of colonial racial categories.) Conflicts over land rights involving the church, various Indian communities (Tingüindín, Tarecuato, and Tacátzcuaro, all within the microregion of the rancho in this study), and the owners of land of various sizes, from ranchos to *estancias* to haciendas, continued throughout the eighteenth century. No doubt this century's heavy immigration from northern Spain (González 1995), including ancestors of the families in this study,[8] exacerbated the struggle over land. In addition to immigrants from northern Spain, this area received immigrants from Los Altos, Jalisco, the cradle of ranchero society in Mexico (Barragán 1997). Throughout western Mexico successive generations of rancheros moved from well-settled regions into more "virgin" areas in search of land for ranches; this probably includes other ancestors of the families in this study, whose family names can be traced to older ranchero settlements (Cochet 1991).

The conflicts over land reveal the stratified multiethnic mosaic into which Spanish immigrants and ranchero in-migrants arrived in this microregion. Although the Spanish Crown prohibited Spaniards, mestizos, and *mulatos* from living in Indian communities, Indian communal lands were rented or sold to non-Indians. Land ownership shows the colonial ethnic hierarchy: Spaniards (including the Jesuits) owned the haciendas, while ranchos and *estancias* were owned by lower-status Spaniards, mestizos, and *coyotes*. During the colonial period, Indians owned land communally, as *pueblos de indios* (Indian communities). By the eighteenth century Tingüindín had begun to transform itself from a community of Indians to a villa of Spaniards and various mixed-race *vecinos* (citizens), while Tarecuato and Tacátzcuaro retained their indigenous character.

Table 3.1. Chronology of Land Ownership in Area of Rancho

1528	Antonio Caicedo granted *encomienda;* Marina Montes de Oca (wife of Caicedo and later of Francisco Chávez) owned it upon his death
late 1500s	Isabel de Caicedo de Montes de Oca inherited *encomienda* land upon her marriage
1574	Francisco Torres de Saucedilla granted two *caballerías* of land in Guáscuaro
late 1500s–early 1600s	Manzo and Alcazar families own land in Guáscuaro; Jesuits own *estancia* of La Magdalena
1691	Luis de Govea owns mill in Guáscuaro
1698	Luis de Govea buys Guáscuaro land from Torres de Saucedilla family
1709	Don Joseph Valdés acquires title to La Magdalena hacienda
1709	Two haciendas, three *pueblos de indios,* six ranchos in area, including one owned by Doña Lucía de Cervantes near Cotija; Alcazar land bordered by "old community of San Juanico"
1758	Guáscuaro rancho owned (inherited) by Manuel Joseph and Antonio de Govea of Tingüindín; bordered by land of Joseph Pulido (formerly owned by Pedro de Alcazar); one *caballería* in "plain of San Juanico" owned by María Catalina and Bárbara Gertrudis López (inherited from Eufemia Ruiz)
1758	Juan Antonio Cárabes (Spaniard), administrator of La Magdalena hacienda; co-owner of Guáscuaro rancho with Francisco Zamudio, Miguel de la Torre (in various documents either mestizo or *coyote*), Joseph and Francisco Antonio Pulido (Spaniards)
1759	Mill owned by people of Guáscuaro, not by Indians of Tacátzcuaro; José Antonio Cárabes and Antonio Pulido witnesses to legal decree

The social network in this study can be traced to the eighteenth century in this area. As Spanish immigrants, they arrived in a region already populated by Indians, Spaniards, Africans, and various mixtures (*castas*) of these groups. Table 3.1 provides a brief chronology of the Spaniards and other non-Indians who owned the land in and around the present-day rancho.

The documents that provide the basis for the chronology in Table 3.1 reveal several important aspects of colonial society in this area. First, whereas Indian communities used Spaniards as witnesses to their land claims, rancheros used Spaniards, mestizos, and *mulatos.* That is, Indians preferred to buttress their legal claims with high-status persons, whereas rancheros presumably used their friends, neighbors, and possibly relatives. Second, some ranchos were co-owned by *parcioneros* (portion holders, possibly relatives); some of them were Spaniards, but others were of mixed race. This indicates that the nascent ranchero society in this area was multiethnic. Moreover, Juan Antonio Cárabes, who co-owned a rancho in Guáscuaro, was also the administrator of La Magdalena hacienda, a common pattern for rancheros, socioeconomically positioned in between elite Spaniards and Indians (as noted in Chapter 2). The early, and largest, landowners in this area were the Caicedo family and the Jesuits, although other Spaniards received smaller land grants. The early postconquest owners of small properties (the Manzo, Govea, and Alcazar families) were joined by other small property owners in the eighteenth century (the Cárabes, Pulido, and de la Torre families).

Those of Spanish origin were stratified into socioeconomic classes: higher-status Spaniards owned haciendas, whereas those of lower status ran the haciendas for the owners and owned smaller ranchos themselves. The hierarchy that placed Spaniards above criollos was also notable in terms of literacy abilities, which indicated access to education (or lack of it). Not all of those who were ethnically Spanish (e.g., the owners of Guáscuaro ranchos) could read and write, whereas hacienda owners signed documents and sometimes acted as local administrators. Finally, the slow but steady growth of ranchos, *estancias,* and haciendas in this area over time indicates how Spaniards and those of mixed race were gradually appropriating land from Indian communities, sometimes legally but also illegally.

NINETEENTH AND TWENTIETH CENTURIES The nineteenth century included several important wars (the War of Independence, 1810–1821; the War of Reform, 1857–1860;[9] and the French Intervention, 1862–1867), but it is unclear how much this microregion was involved in these wars. Interviews with older residents of the rancho indicate that in their own childhoods they overheard talk about Miguel Hidalgo (who led Independence) and the death of Benito Juárez (who led the Reform) and the presence of French troops in Patamburápio, an area contiguous to the rancho.[10] The rancho appears on a 1713 map, apparently becoming more populated in the early 1800s, and an 1823 document refers to a conflict over land between the Indian community of San Pedro in Tingüindín and the contiguous "*ranchería* [very small rancho] of San Juanico" (Pardo Pulido 1957, 81). The rancho, however, was not heavily populated until the end of the nineteenth century. The construction of the railroad in 1902 stimulated new in-migration, and conflicts over land increased. The 1900 census shows 400 persons in San Juanico, and many people still mention the inn for travelers that used to exist in the rancho.

During the nineteenth century the ownership of La Magdalena hacienda changed from the Valdés family to Eustaquio de Oruña,[11] who initiated a project to install a drainage system in 1877 with Doña María Concepción Martínez de Farias of Cotija (then a Spanish settlement) and Don Juan Heredia of Tingüindín. This costly project left Oruña with many debts,[12] and he passed the hacienda on to his niece, Carmen de Oruña.[13] Following this, the hacienda began to fragment into many smaller ranchos, a common pattern in this region at this time (González 1974). With the proliferation in ranches, new names began to appear in this microregion at the end of the century, notably Juan Heredia, who, in addition to being a partner in the costly drainage project, claimed to be the owner of land in Guáscuaro.[14]

During the reign of the dictator Porfirio Díaz from 1877 to 1911 the development of infrastructure increased, in large part with foreign investment encouraged by Díaz. The most significant development in this microregion was the railroad, which reached Tingüindín and some of its surrounding ranchos in 1902. The train enabled sugarcane growers in Los Reyes (a heavily Spanish settlement) to transport and commercialize the sugar and alcohol that they produced from cane (González Méndez and Ortiz Ybarra 1980). Building the railroad depended on exploiting wood from the forests and developing sawmills and a workforce to labor in them. Although the coming of the railroad brought an upsurge in the economy and richness to the region (Pardo Pulido 1957), it also furthered the invasion of "nonproductive" Indian lands.

Such rapid development augmented the already increasing number of both dependent and independent ranches (as well as smaller *rancherías*) in this microregion,[15] necessitating a new territorial division by the state of Michoacán in 1906. The town of Tingüindín was declared the head of the municipality of Tingüindín, which included one hacienda (La Joya) and numerous ranchos as well as several smaller administrative centers (*tenencias*) and congregations (Guáscuaro el Alto). Independent ranches included San Juanico, Guáscuaro el Bajo, Chucandirán, and Potrero de Herrera.[16] In 1910 various residents of San Juanico petitioned that it be moved (administratively) from the *tenencia* of San Angel to the township of Tingüindín, which was closer. The family names that appeared in this petition included Navarro, González, García, Huerta, Pulido, Francisco, Avila, and Ayala.

According to Vicente González Méndez and Héctor Ortiz Ybarra (1980), the socioeconomic structure of this microregion was as follows. The upper class owned haciendas and sugar mills. The upper middle class consisted of rancheros who either owned or sharecropped from 30 to 40 hectares (about 75–100 acres) of irrigated land; this class was small, with only eight owners of 150–200 animals and only twenty owners of 50 cows. The lower middle class included smaller-scale sharecroppers, cattle ranchers and farmers, small businesspeople, professionals, and teachers. The rest of the population lived in very precarious conditions.

One notable ranchero was José María Cárabes Navarro, who over time accumulated almost 800 hectares (about 1,975 acres) around Guáscuaro, including the areas called Pozo Verde, Guáscuaro Bajo, El Coyote, and La Españita or Jaral. In 1912 he gave legal rights to six lawyers to protect his properties, and many other rancheros signed the document, indicating that they were afraid of losing their lands because of the growing discontent of the landless. Moreover, the Revolution had begun (in 1910); General Zepeda in Tingüindín was known to favor agrarian reform (and was antagonistic to José María Cárabes).[17] Conflict over the 800 hectares that Cárabes owned persisted throughout the Revolution and many decades beyond it, through legal claims and counterclaims as well as illegal invasions.

The growing discontent among those who had no land or any possibility of obtaining any erupted in the Revolution and into the movement for agrarian reform, which lasted well beyond the Revolution itself. The economic boom of the Porfiriato had benefited primarily those who owned sugar mills and factories, and the region was controlled politically by the Pardo, López, Huerta, Rodríguez, and Pedraza families (González Méndez and Ortiz Ybarra 1980). With the arrival of the Revolution, dispossessed rancheros and landless peons joined either the Zapatistas or the Villistas, who predominated locally. Many others, primarily rancheros, firmly opposed the Revolution on ideological grounds, taking to the hills to hide when federal armies approached. Guáscuaro became an extremely conflicted place, with poorer rancheros and peons agitating for an *ejido* to be formed from both hacienda and ranchero-owned land. Since so many of the names on both sides are various combinations of the same family names, it would seem that this fight over land was not so much about ideology as about land. That is, although an individualist ideology of hard work and of earning one's properties is and was widely shared across the microregion, some families ended up with much less land than others or no land at all, perhaps through unequal inheritances, unrecognized progeny, or other means.

Meanwhile the agrarian reform ideology was promoted at different levels: by Cárdenas as governor of Michoacán and then president of

Mexico (during the 1930s when much agrarian reform was actualized) and by some locals, such as Francisco Múgica and General Zepeda of Tingüindín, providing an available discursive and legal resource for those agitating for land. Interestingly, the former president of the Ejidal Committee of Guáscuaro, whom we interviewed, referred to the *ejido* not as communal land but as small private properties,[18] indicating that agrarian reform in this area may have been primarily instrumental—a way to obtain land rather than a struggle over ideology. As with Craig's (1983) study of Los Altos, Jalisco, agrarian reform in this locality seems to have occurred within a climate that was dominated by antiagrarian ideology. Contemporary discourse in the rancho is markedly antireform, and the few *agraristas* generally are disdained.

A seminal event occurred in Guáscuaro in 1914 when José María Cárabes Navarro was assassinated at the door of his home by men sent by General Zepeda; they threatened to kill his kidnapped son, who yelled to his father not to open the door.[19] Upon his death, his land (almost 800 hectares) was distributed to his six children; he did not have a will, however, and they were unable to acquire written titles to the divided portions. Inheritors included Ignacia Pardo and María Dolores, Pedro, José María, Luis, and Emiliano Cárabes. At the beginning of the 1930s the *agraristas* in Tingüindín and around the microregion based a claim for an *ejido* in Guáscuaro on the supposed unity of this large property, as though José María Cárabes had still been living and a large landowner. His descendants argued that their lands were not one large property but had already been divided among them; each property was smaller than the 200-hectare limit for small properties and thus not eligible for agrarian reform. In spite of this argument and relevant documents, his heirs lost their lands. They later regained them but even later lost them again.

Such claims and counterclaims regarding either the *ejido* or various parts of the contested lands continued regularly throughout the 1930s, 1940s, 1950s, and even 1960s through 1980s. The *ejidatarios* argued that they should have the land because they had none and needed it to sustain their families, and the Cárabes descendants argued that they had been working the land all along and had bought it through hard family effort. The *ejido* was nevertheless created in 1933 and received its land—over 1,000 hectares—through a presidential decree in 1939. The original owners, however, continued to resist giving up their lands, arguing that as small properties they did not fall within the confines of agrarian reform laws. They were correct in this; but clearly the *ejido* was created anyway as a result of strong socioeconomic, political, and ideological forces. The final claim over lands in the *ejido* was settled in 1988, although a few later claims dealt with conflicts over borders.

A smaller agrarian reform movement was carried out in the rancho San Juanico by Felipe Estrada and Manuel González Pulido. In October 1970 an Ejidal Commission was created in San Juanico and granted 69 hectares by the governor of Michoacán. Two months later, in December 1970, Manuel Navarro and Manuel González, representing various people in the rancho, petitioned that the land not be distributed to the *ejido.* Although this same land was claimed to be part of the Indian community of Tarecuato in 1973, the *ejido* of San Juanico, consisting of eleven *ejidatarios,* received its land by presidential decree in 1979.

As already noted, people in San Juanico were also affected by the efforts to create the Guáscuaro *ejido.* In 1981 Noriberto Castillo Pulido, Esteban Navarro González, Salvador Andrade, José María Cárabes Cervantes, María Emilia Barajas, and Génaro Navarro González claimed to be dispossessed of their lands owing to an increase in the Guáscuaro *ejido.* José María Cárabes presented a bill of sale showing his purchase of 17 hectares of land referred to as "La Loma de San Juanico" from Emilia Cárabes in July 1973. Two subsequent legal efforts in 1985 and 1988 again asked that land be granted to the *ejido,* followed by a request for an investigation by the affected landowners in San Juanico in 1990. The investigation never occurred, however, because the municipal president of Tingüindín noted that the name of the agrarian community used in the document, "Puente de San Juanico" (possibly an ancient name for the rancho, which was built around a bridge over the San Juanico River), did not exist.

Ironically, although the Guáscuaro *ejido* ultimately was created, it stands idle while the owners are in the United States working as migrants. Some say that the owners are ashamed to cultivate it, because they know that they did not rightfully earn it, a central tenet of ranchero individualist ideology. Several small property owners in the rancho San Juanico lost their land in this mass of claims (including the late Esteban Navarro González and Noriberto Castillo Pulido) in 1976. Moreover, a similarity of names may have led to the invasion (repelled by force) of the land of José María Cárabes Cervantes in the mid-1960s. Now people are more mindful of written titles; and land is once again valuable, not for cattle raising and agriculture, but for avocado orchards and packing plants. In the next section I discuss recent changes in the rancho, focusing on the transformation wrought by migration to the United States since the 1960s. So fundamental is this transformation that even children immediately associate Chicago with earning money, as was indicated to me in the following exchange when a young girl of about nine asked me, during one of my extended periods in the rancho, where my husband was.

Marcia: *Se fue a Chicago.*	He went to Chicago.
Delia: *¿Porqué?*	Why?
Marcia: *A trabajar.*	To work.
Delia: *¡Ah! ¡Para diNERo!*	Ah! For money!

A Rancho Transformed

Whereas most *migradólares* (money earned by Mexican migrants in the United States and sent back to Mexico) are used for living expenses of families in Mexico, this rancho is unusual in that the money has been put to productive use, dramatically transforming the local economy in the process (Galetto 1999). This transformation illustrates aspects of ranchero identity explored here: independence, individuality, toughness, and, most importantly, an entrepreneurial spirit (see Chapter 6). According to the literature on economic development, several factors are necessary for such productive economic investment to succeed: first, sufficient opportunity (climate, money, innovators) that can be generalized across a population; and second, opportunity that is within the realm of the "thinkable" for the social agent. What is "thinkable" implicates "values, norms, capacities, experience, abilities, knowledge, customs, etc." (Galetto 1999, 152)—exactly the characteristics developed in ranchero societies across the centuries in Mexico's frontier regions (see Chapter 2).

These transmigrants, then, used Chicago dollars not only for subsistence needs (food, clothing, housing) but for productive use, at considerable personal sacrifice. Most of these families used money earned in Chicago to buy houses in Chicago and to buy land (and construct or improve houses) back in Mexico. If they decided to move back to Mexico, they rented the houses they own in Chicago, often to relatives. On the land bought in Mexico, they planted avocados to sell commercially. Two facts support the link between migrant dollars and the rancho's agriculture industry: first, "almost two thirds of the avocado producers worked in the United States"; second, "the establishment of almost 85 percent of the hectares of existing avocado orchards relied on capital of migrant origin" (Galetto 1999, 17). The intense growth in avocado production during the last two decades, in fact, resulted in the establishment of nine packing plants in the immediate vicinity of the rancho during the 1990s. Thus the rancho has undergone a fundamental transformation in the last several decades from an economy based on subsistence agriculture (corn and beans) and cattle raising to one based on commercial agriculture (growing, packing, and exporting avocados in the Mexican and international markets). This inclination toward the entrepreneurial is part of the ranchero ethos that I discuss more fully in Chapter 6.

These economic changes transformed the meaning of land: land traditionally was a marker of status and familial identity (Galetto 1999), but it now has material meaning. Specific areas of land have differential material value: *la sierra* (the hillside) is valuable for growing avocados, whereas *el plano* (the plain), where the rancho is located, is valuable for building houses and packing plants. Migration, as one woman told me, has changed everything. Before, everyone was

> *. . . muy pobre, no había trabajo, dormíen en petates. . . . El rancho tenía ni luz, ni carretera. No habían vegetales—comíen pura lechita y huevos.*
> . . . very poor, there was no work, they slept on woven mats. . . . The rancho had no electricity, no highway. There weren't any vegetables—they ate only milk and eggs.

With changed circumstances, however, this woman predicted that the migrant flow to the United States would slow down and that people there would return to the rancho. Although some (younger) people have remained in the rancho, many others have continued to find their way to Chicago; over time, some families have returned to live (either permanently or temporarily) in the rancho, but many more have continued to live, work, and go to school in Chicago.

The Chicago Setting

Original Settlements of Mexicans in the Midwest

A number of scholars have argued that the Mexican experience in the Midwest has differed from that in the Southwest (Gonzales 1999; Kerr 1976; Rosales and Simon 1987 [1981]; Valdés 1991, 2000). Five reasons are given for this. First, Mexicans followed several decades of eastern and southern European immigration. Second, they did not share the history of conquest, land loss, or mechanisms of subordination found in the Southwest. Third, urban settlement patterns more closely parallel those of European immigrants to the Midwest than those of Mexican immigrants to the Southwest. Fourth, whites in the Midwest show a higher degree of ethnic diversity that works against unity. And fifth, the larger presence of African Americans in the Midwest provides a buffer for Mexicans against racism on the part of whites (Valdés 2000).

Manuel Gonzales (1999, 147) adds: "The popular aversion to Mexicans in the racially charged atmosphere of the 1920s was not unique. All ethnic Americans were suspect. The lingering stereotype of the Italo-American as a Mafia gangster, for example, has its origin in the interwar period." Such prejudice against racialized southern and eastern Europeans led to the restriction of immigration from Europe; their labor was replaced by Mexican, African American, and Appalachian workers (the latter two groups were migrants from the South). Louse Año Nuevo Kerr (1976, 21) notes:

> Chicago . . . had been absorbing successive generations of uneducated and unskilled European peasants, most of them Catholics, for decades. By 1920 these immigrants had already established themselves in the city. They were part of the occupational structure, the parishes, the schools, the welfare system, and the social and political institutions. . . . To some extent the city received the Mexicans simply as the latest immigrants, obliged to suffer the traditional hardships of restricted and unstable employment at low wages, congested and dilapidated housing, and prejudice against alien newcomers. . . . Mexican immigration, however, came at a time when the need for unskilled labor was decreasing. It coincided, moreover, not only with the emergence of a more educated and skilled generation of white ethnics, but also with the large postwar migration of unskilled Blacks to Chicago. . . . Although this [racial and cultural] prejudice [against Mexicans] was less harsh and historically rooted than in the southwest . . . [it was still] a handicap.

The substantial presence of Mexicans in Chicago defies the traditional image of Mexicans as a regional minority group—by 1970 it was the fourth largest urban concentration of Mexicans in the United States (Kerr 1976). Chicago's distinctness also lies in the "city's ethnic and industrial diversity, its Roman Catholicism, its neighborhood-oriented political and social life, and [since the 1950s] . . . its unique combination of Latino populations" (Kerr 1976: 11). By the 2000 census these included people identifying as Mexican (530,462), Puerto Rican (113,055), Cuban (8,084), Dominican (1,651), Central American (23,339), and South American (20,828) (City of Chicago Department of Planning and Development 2001). These figures are for the city alone; presumably they would be much larger for the metropolitan area.

According to U.S. census figures, the Mexican population in Chicago increased rapidly in the final decades of the twentieth century, sometimes doubling from one decade to the next. Although this notable in-

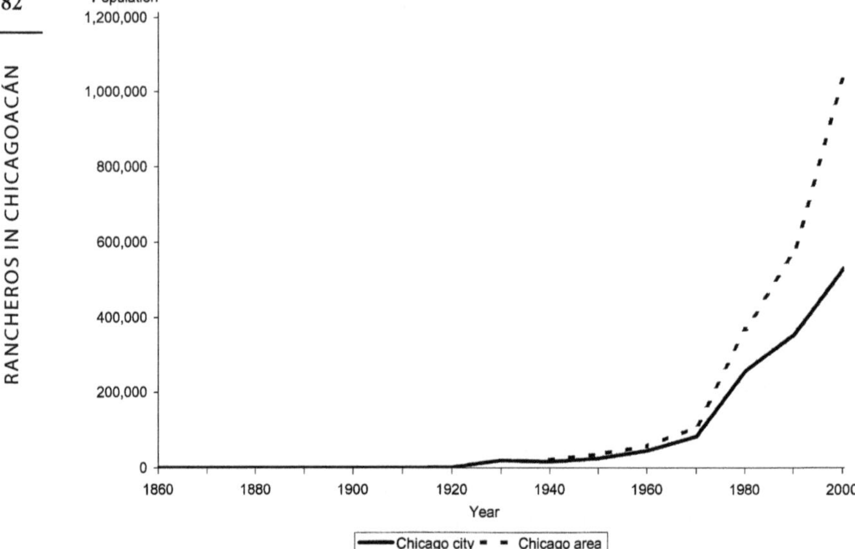

Figure 3.4. Mexican population in Chicago and surrounding area, 1860–2000

crease has occurred since 1960, Mexicans have had a recognizable presence in Chicago and in the Midwest more generally since early in the twentieth century. Both the recent growth and their historic presence can be seen in Figure 3.4, which is based on U.S. census figures.

Thus, although Mexicans started to appear in census counts in 1860, they first arrived in significant numbers from 1916 through the 1920s. Before summarizing the history of Mexicans in Chicago, I begin with a broader perspective, briefly encapsulating the early history of Mexicans in the Midwest more generally then focusing on the Chicago area to the present time.

Only recently have historians turned their attention to Mexicans in the Midwest (García 1996; Lane and Escobar 1987; Valdés 1991, 2000; Vargas 1993), with the exception of Kerr's 1976 dissertation on the history of Mexicans in Chicago. Many of these sources focus on specific decades; only Dennis Valdés (2000) and Kerr (1976) take the entire century as their scope. Both Valdés (2000) and Manuel García (1996) embed their narratives of Mexican migrations in discussions of broader social, economic, and political forces on both sides of the border.

In the late nineteenth and early twentieth centuries industrial expansion transformed the Midwest, leading to rapid urbanization. "Among the fastest growing cities in the nation and the world was Chicago, Illinois, which moved from the eighth largest city in the country in 1860 to the second largest in 1900" (García 1996, 4). Chicago developed as immigrants (first Germans and Irish then Scandinavians and eastern and southern Europeans) settled close to industrial jobs. Mexicans replaced earlier immigrants from eastern and southern Europe, moving into their neighborhoods and assuming their jobs as their descendants moved out of both. Throughout the Midwest, railroads were key to industrialization, urbanization, and migration, as they "stimulated international investment and commerce while making possible a rapid increase in labor migration between Mexico and the United States" (Valdés 2000, 24).

Midwestern settlements of Mexicans appeared in three distinct phases, according to Valdés (2000): first, from 1906 to 1910, the result of recruitment by railroad companies already employing Mexicans in the Southwest; second, from 1916 to 1919, in response to railroad and industrial labor shortages (in steel mills and auto plants) during World War I; and third, during the 1920s, with increasing employment (sometimes as unsuspecting strike breakers) in the steel industry and stockyards of Chicago. This last phase became the first large-scale movement of Mexicans into the Midwest generally (there were 58,000 Mexicans in the Midwest by 1930), although large-scale migration began in 1903 to Kansas (Valdés 2000, 29), where Mexicans worked on the railroad and in meat-packing plants in Kansas City (Vargas 1993).[20] All midwestern Mexican settlements arose directly as a response to labor needs in steel mills (in northwest Indiana and farther east in Ohio, Pennsylvania, and New York), automobile foundries (in Detroit), railroads, building and highway construction, and packing houses. During World War I the U.S. government instituted the first bracero (laborer) program (1917–1921) to assist these industries (García 1996). This program, like the later program begun during World War II (1943–1964), stimulated nonbracero migration as well, since migration processes, once established, build momentum (Massey n.d.).

Mexicans were recruited for these labor needs in Texas, in Kansas, or in the interior of Mexico partly because of the curtailment of Asian and then European immigration. The Mexicans who filled midwestern jobs were primarily from the western Mexican states of Michoacán, Jalisco, and Guanajuato as well as Mexico City, and most of them were single males who had worked in agriculture in Mexico (Valdés 2000). Mexican railroads, developed during the last two decades of the nineteenth century (passing by the rancho in 1902), provided a way for people who were unable to support their families because of economic and then political tensions (the Revolution of 1910–1920 was preceded by a depression) to reach employment. Moreover, from 1926 to 1929 "thousands of strictly devout Catholic immigrants flowed into the Midwest from west central Mexico, the site of the *Cristero* Revolution" (Vargas 1993, 143), a conflict described in Chapter 2. Often recruited in Mexico, many men "job-hopped" north, working on the tracks in Mexico and at the border and gradually moving farther into the United States, sometimes finding jobs in other industries wherever the tracks ended.

Some Mexicans recruited as field workers in the sugar-beet industry in the Midwest—by the late 1920s most beet workers in the Midwest were Mexican (García 1996, 15)—realized that better-paying jobs could be found in the cities and left agriculture for urban employment. For example, "[s]teel production helped transform Chicago into a Mecca for Mexicans migrating to the Midwest and into a staging area for those heading to other sections of the region" (Vargas 1993, 47). In addition, the railroads continued to be a heavily Mexican labor arena, with Mexicans constituting more than 91 percent of the workforce by 1927 (Garcia 1996, 6). Chicago, the hub of the U.S. railroad network, employed a similarly high percentage of Mexican workers by the mid-1920s (Vargas 1993). In fact the railroad, referred to by the families in this study as *el traque* (the track), still employs many Mexicans, including most first- and many second-generation males in this social network.

Researchers note the discriminatory behavior of European Americans and European immigrants toward Mexicans in obtaining housing and at work, even though this attitude was ameliorated somewhat by the preference for Mexicans over African Americans. Paul Taylor's early study (1987 [1932]) even quoted foremen in the steel industry who preferred Mexicans over European immigrants, saying that they were cleaner, harder workers and honest and trustworthy. Another early study, in the 1920s by the Reverend Robert McLean, also showed generally favorable attitudes on the part of foremen in a variety of industries toward Mexican workers, calling them "industrious and energetic, hard workers, steady and methodical, resourceful, and diligent" (quoted in García 1996, 61). In contrast to the prevailing stereotypes of Mexicans as docile and otherwise undesirable, many showed admirable strength and endurance in the difficult work in steel mills and other industries and would readily walk off the job if conditions were bad or supervisors harassed them. This sense of self-reliance also showed itself in the marked reluctance among Mexicans to ask for public assistance; instead they helped each other (Valdés 2000). In the housing industry the discrimination was about race; lighter-skinned Mexicans faced less negative attitudes than darker-skinned Mexicans (García 1996, 57), a situation that prevails today.

Various surveys documented "higher literacy rates and greater English-language proficiency among midwestern Mexicans" than among other immigrant laborers (García 1996, 74). Many Spanish-language publications circulated between 1914 and 1932 as well, indicating a literate readership. In addition to people from agricultural backgrounds in Mexico, there were many middle-class Mexicans in the urban Midwest (and especially in Chicago). Some of them came from the prerevolutionary middle class in Mexico, where they had been ranchers, businesspeople, and professionals (Griswold del Castillo and De León 1996). According to García (1996, 77),

> . . . many of these professionals earned better wages and enjoyed a higher standard of living than other Mexican workers. Emanating from the middle and upper classes in Mexico, they were well educated, fluent in English, and well schooled in the social graces. They also tended to be more noticeably White than other Mexicans, which served them well in employment.

The attribution of "social graces" in this description would seem to indicate an urban elite, rather than a rural ranchero, background for these particular migrants. Although there were many fewer women relative to men in these early Mexican settlements, women did work outside the home, albeit at lower wages than men. In Chicago a high proportion of women (47 percent) worked to supplement the family income (Kerr 1976, 26). Most men were still strongly opposed to the women in their families working, but economic necessity prevailed. Also bemoaned was the fact that by the 1930s young Mexicans had started to adopt American ways; and Spanish began to show borrowed English words, such as *baquería* for bakery instead of *panadería.* Public schools, of course, were a primary site for Americanization, although many Mexican children left school when they became old enough to work and contribute to the family economy. Another sign of acculturation was the increase in interethnic marriages (García 1996), often as a result of Mexicans' attending social events with other ethnic groups and becoming active in politics and labor unions. In addition, an unbalanced male/female ratio led many single Mexican men to marry European immigrant women (Valdés 2000).

History of Mexicans in Chicago

Kerr (1976) dates the beginning of significant Mexican immigration to Chicago to 1916, when 206 men were recruited to work on railroads. Although Mexicans had come to Chicago since the turn of the century (when the railroads were complete), the upheaval of the Mexican Revolution (1910–1920) accelerated this process, as did the Cristero Rebellion in western Mexico (1926–1929). Some of the immigrants were middle-class entrepreneurs and professionals whose lives were disrupted by the Revolution and strife, but most were peasants from rural western Mexico, especially the states of Jalisco, Michoacán, and Guanajuato. These three states accounted for two-thirds of Mexican immigrants to Chicago in the 1920s (Rosales 1995, 193) and still account for a majority of Mexicans in the Chicago area. Mexicans came to work on railroads and in the meat-packing and steel industries (wages were lowest for railroad work, somewhat higher for meat-packing, and highest in steel work). They settled close to these industries in three neighborhoods: the Near West Side (railroads), Back-of-the-Yards (meat-packing), and South Chicago (steel). Mexicans followed Italians, Poles, and Slovaks to these neighborhoods, which already had poor housing, serious economic disadvantages, and problems of discrimination and ethnic interaction, as well as gangs (Kerr 1976). Mexicans established communities that were firmly rooted by 1940; and the Near West Side "was the region's Mexican business, literary, and cultural capitol" (Valdés 2000, 36), with its proliferation of Mexican social clubs and societies, groceries, restaurants, bakeries, and other shops.

A fourth community emerged in the mid-1960s, after urban renewal (and the construction of the new University of Illinois at Chicago) forced Mexicans and Italians to move from the Near West Side. Mexicans moved a few blocks south to the Pilsen neighborhood at 18th Street (community 31 in Figure 3.5), a neighborhood that then became the port-of-entry for Mexicans until the 1990s. Pilsen, in fact, was the first neighborhood in Chicago to achieve a Mexican majority (in the 1960s). In addition to the three original neighborhoods, Mexicans also settled early in a number of industrial suburbs, including Waukegan (where one family in this social network lives), Joliet, Aurora (Cintron 1997), and Elgin (García 1996; Valdés 2000). Mexican communities were established during the 1920s in East Chicago and Gary, Indiana, located east of the southern part of Chicago along Lake Michigan (the Calumet region).

Kerr describes four periods of Mexican history in Chicago: 1916–1929, 1929–1943, 1943–1954, and 1954–1970. The first period was one of rapid growth; the second, of decline and repatriation during the Depression; the third, another period of recruitment to work in industries during and after World War II; and the fourth, of continuing growth. As already noted, from 1970 to 2000 the growth rate has been astonishing

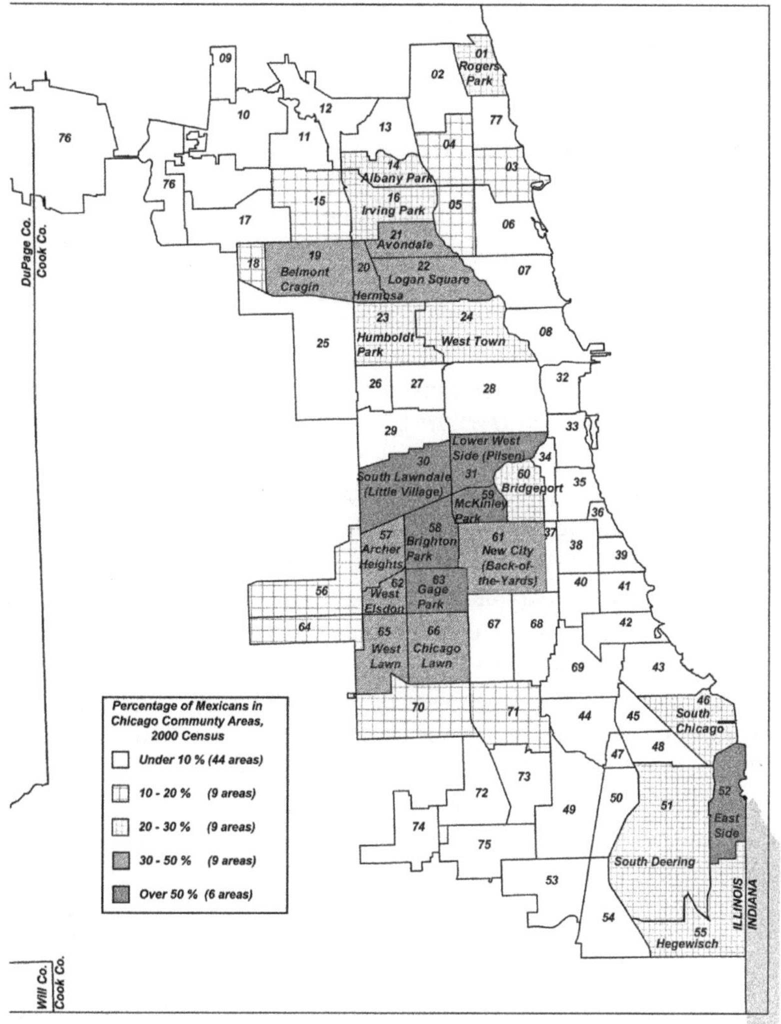

Figure 3.5. Chicago community areas, showing the percentage of Mexicans in each area

(see Figure 3.4). In the following sections I use Kerr's (1976) four periods, adding a fifth period to bring the history to 2000. In each section I integrate Kerr's findings with those of other researchers.

PHASE ONE: 1916–1929 Kerr's ground-breaking study is still valuable because of its emphasis on local phenomena in the three initial settlement areas, especially the varying experiences of Mexicans across the three neighborhoods. In this first phase of migration Mexicans were not a majority in their three original settlements, so they interacted (variously across the three neighborhoods and across religious and work domains) with the European immigrants already living there: Italians, Russians, Greeks, and Poles in the Near West Side; Poles, Slovaks, and Germans in South Chicago; and Poles and the Irish in Back-of-the-Yards. In Back-of-the-Yards, for example, Irish attitudes toward Mexicans were favorable compared to their attitudes toward Poles, who themselves were then less hostile to Mexicans.[21] In South Chicago, in contrast, which had the densest concentration of Mexicans, Poles were openly antagonistic. With cultural and linguistic similarities, Mexicans and Italians were friendlier, and some light-skinned Mexicans adopted Italian names when they took over Italian businesses (Kerr 1976).

Mexicans were known to help each other (more so than the Poles), rather than turn to public agencies when in need. They did, however, form mutual-aid societies; and they utilized local settlement houses: Hull House on the Near West Side (now a part of the University of Illinois at Chicago), the University of Chicago Settlement House in Back-of-the-Yards, and Bird Memorial Center in South Chicago. The Catholic Church in Chicago reached out to Mexicans as well (more swiftly than it had to Italians earlier), especially in view of potential threats from proselytizing Protestant sects. Cristero Rebellion refugee priests and nuns in the 1920s helped to create the first Mexican chapel, later a church, in Chicago, Our Lady of Guadalupe (the patron saint of Mexico), which was "built by the Illinois Steel Company for its Mexican workers, who had been excluded from the neighborhood's Polish and Slovakian parishes" (Kerr 1976, 56).

At the end of the 1920s, and the first phase of Mexican migration to Chicago, Kerr claims that there were "signs that the more than 20,000 Mexicans in Chicago had begun to benefit materially from the period of prosperity already beginning to pass" (Kerr 1976, 60), in terms of both housing and work. The next phase of Mexican history in Chicago, however, was not so propitious.

PHASE TWO: 1929–1943 With the onset of the Depression, Mexicans, most of whom were unskilled workers, faced high levels of unemployment and economic duress. Many returned to Mexico through repatriation programs in the early 1930s, promoted by both the United States and Mexico (the Chicago program also repatriated immigrants to Europe and Asia). "By the end of the 1930s, many of the early settlers and their families, including some American-born children, had already been removed, either voluntarily or forcibly, and new immigration had effectively been limited" (Kerr 1976, 74–75). Valdés (2000, 96) notes that Spanish-language newspapers, settlement houses, and political groups "organized opposition to abusive efforts to remove Mexicans" in Chicago more than elsewhere in the Midwest. The impact on the Mexican communities in Chicago nevertheless was drastic: the population was reduced by 30 percent from 20,000 in 1930 to 14,000 in 1933 and then by another 10 percent to 12,500 in 1934. In fact the Midwest had higher rates of repatriation than did the Southwest, especially in Chicago, East Chicago, and Gary, Indiana, partly as a result of determined efforts to reduce welfare costs (Valdés 2000). By 1940 the Mexican population in Chicago was 16,000; the small regain was due to new births and in-migration from Texas and other areas of the Midwest. Both unemployment and population loss, however, differed from neighborhood to neighborhood: the Near West Side (with the largest concentration of Mexicans) suffered the most, followed by South Chicago, and then by Back-of-the-Yards (Kerr 1976).

As minorities in all neighborhoods, those who remained developed interethnic solidarity as a response to the hardships everyone faced, especially in South Chicago and Back-of-the-Yards, where the Depression had a less severe effect on employment and where community formation solidified earlier. Moreover, as jobs increasingly were reserved for citizens, many immigrants became naturalized; and changes in policy instituted by the Roosevelt administration reduced some anti-Mexican hostility. Many single males had returned to Mexico, so the proportion of women and children rose, because much of the remaining population consisted of families (Kerr 1976). School attendance by Mexican children rose as well, leading to a language shift from Spanish to English. In response, Spanish language and Mexican culture classes were organized in settlement houses and other community organizations for children after school. Settlement houses also offered adult English classes, often in conjunction with naturalization classes, to increasingly interethnic groups. For recreation, neighborhood sports clubs focused on baseball (not soccer, as in Mexico). Kerr (1976, 83) thus shows a "gradual transition from the backward-glancing orientation toward Mexico of the 1920s toward the increasing insistence on Americanization which would prevail in the 1940s." Additional evidence of this Americanization process was the increased involvement in labor unions, especially the steel unions in the late 1930s, by Mexicans who participated not as Mexicans but as American industrial workers.

Participation in youth gangs increased too, but social workers at the time described this as "adaptation to the local community . . . learned by Mexican youth from the Italians and Poles who preceded them" (Kerr

1976, 95). Again, this varied by neighborhood: the Near West Side was more disorganized as a community, with more criminal and economic problems, whereas South Chicago was a more coherent and concentrated community and more traditionally Mexican. Back-of-the-Yards, with its lower proportion of Mexicans, evolved toward a multiethnic coalition, partly in response to the efforts of settlement houses there, including one led by Saul Alinsky and Ernest Burgess of the University of Chicago. Throughout the 1930s, then, Mexican communities in Chicago reduced but solidified: the remaining Mexicans gradually Americanized, as had the European immigrants who preceded them.

PHASE THREE: 1943–1954 U.S. entry into World War II marked the beginning of a long period of economic growth in the United States, led by midwestern cities, whose population peaked in the early 1950s (Valdés 2000). As a result of union struggles during the 1930s workers shared in this prosperity; many joined the middle class. Mexicans, however, fared worse in terms of job promotion or entry into the professions and public service than did others. Mexican Americans found the Americanization rhetoric promoted by schools and other institutions sharply at odds with their experiences of inequality (Valdés 2000). The Americanization programs, of course, had been established in the late nineteenth and early twentieth centuries for European immigrants, and Mexicans replaced Europeans in these programs as they had in housing and jobs. At the same time, wartime labor needs led to more agreements with Mexico for workers, and Bracero Programs were instituted in 1942 (for agriculture in the Southwest) and in 1943 (for industry in the Midwest and East). Chicago continued to be the fourth largest urban concentration of Mexicans in the United States.

After the beginning of the Bracero Program, attitudes toward Mexicans, and Mexican Americans, fluctuated. The first braceros brought to Chicago were railroad workers: more than 15,000 of them arrived between May and October of 1943. Many of these, as well as future braceros, used their stints in the United States as a way to familiarize themselves with the city for a future return, legally or illegally (Kerr 1976). In addition the labor shortage induced Mexican Americans from the Southwest (especially Texas) to come to Chicago, forming another important subgroup (Tejanos) within the larger Mexican community. Braceros were treated well during this period (and a social studies unit on Mexico was added to the public school curriculum); but, at the same time, hostility toward Mexican Americans, in contrast to Mexicans, was on the rise.

As the total Mexican-descent population increased, however, city officials became less tolerant of both groups. Kerr (1976, 117) notes: "In Chicago, Mexican Americans expecting to be assimilated were . . . outnumbered by new immigrants," and by the mid-1950s Puerto Ricans, Cubans, South and Central Americans, and people of Mexican descent from the U.S. Southwest added to the total Spanish-speaking population. In contrast to the earlier favoring of Mexican braceros over Mexican Americans, as the numbers of Spanish speakers increased, people began to lump them all together. Mexican Americans found their anticipated assimilation "aborted," in Kerr's term, fed by the stereotype of the Mexican as noncitizen. As Mexican inmigration continued and showed signs of becoming permanent, hostility increased against all those of Mexican descent, culminating in Operation Wetback in 1954—the rounding up and forced return of those who were undocumented.

In spite of their being perceived as one undifferentiated group by non-Mexican Chicagoans, in fact the total Mexican-descent population was quite varied in terms of class, skills, and nativity. Part of the upsurge in the number of Mexicans in the Chicago area (from 21,000 in 1940 to 35,000 in 1950) included "the more affluent and skilled from Mexico and Texas" who moved directly to the suburbs (Kerr 1976, 134), some to work in the new industries developed there after the war (Valdés 2000). The immigrants who continued to settle in the three traditional neighborhoods fared much better in terms of wages than the Mexican Americans there and in fact fared as well as (and had more schooling than) the foreign-born Poles and Italians who lived in these neighborhoods. Mexican Americans also had more schooling than their Polish and Italian neighbors but nevertheless earned the lowest wages. In spite of these inequities, wages were still higher for those of Mexican descent in Chicago than in Los Angeles.

The rise in anti-Mexican feeling led to community efforts to combat discrimination. Mexican Americans, many of whom had served in the war, formed ethnic organizations, although there were tensions between immigrants and Mexican Americans as the latter tried to represent the entire community (eventually including all Spanish-speaking groups). Ultimately outnumbered, Mexican Americans no longer dominated the ethnic scene (Kerr 1976). The term "Mexican American" dropped out of local rhetoric, and people identified simply as Mexican, in contrast to Polish, Irish, and so forth, and as an affirmation of the continuing connection with Mexico (Valdés 2000).

PHASE FOUR: 1954–1970 Numerous efforts to deport undocumented Mexicans in the early 1950s followed Operation Wetback in 1954. At the same time, however, bracero agreements were repeatedly renewed until 1965, although only for agricultural workers. Inmigration to Chicago nevertheless continued to increase, as workers left agriculture for better-paying jobs in the city, and as others were encouraged to migrate illegally. Chicago had gained a reputation in Mexico for having numerous well-paying jobs, and Mexicans in Chicago, though not without problems, were "relatively better off than Chicanos and other Latinos in large metropolitan areas elsewhere in the United States" (Kerr 1976, 204). Moreover, the 1952 Immigration and Nationality Act exempted Latin Americans from quota restrictions and contained provisions that favored Mexicans. In addition, the development of industry on the Mexican side of the border brought many Mexicans there, who soon realized they could earn higher wages by crossing the border. Finally, migration by social network, once established, tends to be self-perpetuating (Massey et al. 1987), as people join relatives and friends in the United States and as migration becomes a rite of passage for young people reaching working age.

Kerr (1976) documents the varying effects of this migration on the Mexican neighborhoods in Chicago until 1970. In both South Chicago and Back-of-the-Yards, inmigration slowed during the 1950s until the mid-1960s. Mexicans remained a minority during this period, having joined their Polish and other immigrant neighbors as workers, as Catholics, and (especially in Back-of-the-Yards) as relatives from interethnic marriages. Mexicans, like other neighborhood residents, were second- and third-generation Americans; especially in Back-of-the-Yards, where de-ethnification had taken place through labor organizing in the 1930s and 1940s, loyalty was to the community, not to ethnic subgroups. Some white ethnics, however, considered Mexicans a buffer against the perceived threat of African Americans (in South Chicago, preferring them to blacks).[22] Because of the steel industry, which expanded in the 1950s, Mexicans in South Chicago were better paid and had higher levels of schooling than Mexicans elsewhere in the city. When the stockyards closed in the early 1970s, established "Americans of Mexican descent," as they thought of themselves, began to disperse and leave the Back-of-the-Yards neighborhood for other parts of the city and suburbs, just as a new generation of single male Mexicans began to move in (Kerr 1976). A similar pattern occurred in South Chicago later, after the steel mills closed in the 1980s.

Meanwhile Pilsen, after the displacement of Mexicans from the Near West Side by urban renewal during the mid-1960s, grew to become a flourishing Mexican enclave. It rapidly expanded westward into Little Village, viewed then as a "Mexican suburb" by those living in Pilsen. This created a Mexican western corridor that extended to the edge of the city and in later decades into suburbs such as Cicero and Berwyn. By this time the corridor contained Mexicans, Tejanos, Chicago-born Mexican Americans, and a few Puerto Ricans and eastern Europeans (Kerr 1976), but the area increasingly became heavily immigrant.

Civil rights legislation in the 1960s stimulated a new round of community organizing by Brown Berets and others, some linked to the national Chicano movement. These ground-level organizations addressed problems in the schools (the need for programs for non-English-speaking students) and churches (the need to replace Polish and Slovak masses with masses in Spanish) and problems with harassment by police and immigration officials. They also worked for better health care, job training, and social services.

The Immigration Act of 1965, in the midst of the Civil Rights era, stimulated yet more migration, both legal and illegal. It replaced quotas for individual countries with quotas for hemispheres, and it lifted the ceiling for immediate relatives allowed to join family members in Chicago. As immigration from Mexico has dramatically increased since 1965, inmigration from Texas has trailed off, possibly as a result of civil rights legislation, which made Texas more acceptable to Mexicans living there.

RECENT DECADES: 1970–2000 The key characteristic of this most recent period in Mexican history in Chicago is the astonishing increase each decade in migration directly from Mexico (see Figure 3.4). In 2000 Latinos, two-thirds of whom are Mexican, constituted 26 percent of Chicago's population.[23] This migration occurred in the context of a numerically stable European American population and an only modestly increasing African American population. "While the majority of Mexican migration came from sending communities with long histories of links to the Midwest, it also extended farther into central and southern Mexico" (Valdés 2000, 215), increasing the regional diversity of Mexicans in Chicago. Higher proportions of immigrants have been undocumented, a trend that began in the 1950s, when the demand for bracero visas outpaced the supply (Massey et al. 1987).

During this period, economic restructuring eliminated previously abundant jobs in heavy industry, replacing them with jobs in smaller factories and in the service sector. Chicago became a global city in an increasingly globalized world. The transnational nature of Mexican immigrant life is part of the larger phenomenon of globalization, in which large numbers of people, capital, material goods, and cultural practices move across national borders regularly (Farr and Reynolds 2004).

The sheer presence of so many Mexicans in neighborhood after neighborhood in Chicago changes churches, schools, and other institutions in terms of language and other social practices. Churches in Mexican neighborhoods, for example, now have altars to the Virgin of Guadalupe, the patron saint of Mexico. Schools have Spanish-English bilingual programs. Voting instructions are mailed out in both English and Spanish (as well as Polish, Chinese, Russian, and other languages). Mexico, as noted earlier in this chapter, has changed as well because of the repeated influx of people, capital, goods, and practices from Chicago as part of migrants' return trips. The large number of Mexicans in Chicago also has affected other Spanish-speaking groups. Although a common Latino identity began to emerge in the 1970s and 1980s (Padilla 1985), the dramatic increase in (only) the Mexican population swamped this process (Valdés 2000). People in Chicago refer to themselves as Mexican, Puerto Rican, and so forth, rather than as Hispanic or Latino (Elías-Olivares and Farr 1991).

With such large numbers of Mexicans arriving in the Chicago area, settlement rapidly increased in the traditional areas of Pilsen/Little Village (communities 31 and 30 in Figure 3.5), New City/Back-of-the-Yards (61), and South Chicago (46). Southward from the Pilsen/Little Village area, large numbers of Mexicans settled in Brighton Park (58), McKinley Park (59), Gage Park (63), and other nearby community areas. In addition Mexicans began to settle in other Spanish-speaking areas of the city: for example, on the northwest side in and around the traditionally Puerto Rican neighborhoods of Logan Square (22), Humboldt Park (23), and West Town (24) and further north in Central and South American neighborhoods in Rogers Park (1). Furthermore, the city itself serves as a core that spreads out in several directions: toward western suburbs like Cicero, north toward Wisconsin (including Waukegan), and south (from South Chicago) and southeast toward northwestern Indiana (where Mexicans established a presence in the 1920s).

Most of the Mexican population in Chicago still is working class, although the number of professionals and entrepreneurs has increased in recent decades. Mexicans (and Puerto Ricans) are active in Chicago politics, especially since they were courted by Harold Washington, who, with their support, became the first African American mayor of Chicago in 1983. Richard M. Daley (the son of Richard J. Daley) also reached out to the Spanish-speaking population, especially Mexicans, when he successfully ran for mayor in 1989 and further developed such connections, especially in the business community, as mayor. Both Washington and Daley supported redistricting that resulted first in the election of three Latino (Mexican and Puerto Rican) aldermen to the City Council in

1987 and second in the election of Luis Gutiérrez, a Chicago-born Puerto Rican, to the U.S. House of Representatives in 1992. This electoral influence led to more political support for Latino causes in the city and state and increased the role of Mexicans in Chicago's school reform movement (Valdés 2000, 261). Clearly, numbers make a difference.

Mexican Neighborhoods

Pilsen, officially the Lower West Side (31 in Figure 3.5), is the best-known Mexican neighborhood in-Chicago and in the rancho as well, where it is known as *diez y ocho* (18) for its main commercial street. From the 1960s through the 1990s Pilsen was the primary port-of-entry for Mexicans; during the 1990s, however, Mexicans began settling directly in a variety of urban and suburban locations, rather than settling first in Pilsen and then moving out (and up) if and when their fortunes improved. This neighborhood is so Mexican in ambiance that a walk down 18th Street (see photos) could convince a person that he or she is in Guadalajara. Mexican music pours out onto the sidewalk from stores selling CDs and cassette tapes, Mexican bakeries and grocery stores advertise Mexican foods, dry cleaners announce themselves as *tintorerías,* and bars (*cantinas*) sport Mexican names or have bilingual signs (e.g., *Tenemos vía Satélite:* We have satellite TV). Pedestrians regularly make the sign of the cross as they pass by churches, with their altars to the Virgin of Guadalupe. *Tortillerías* (tortilla factories) pump out hundreds of thousands of tortillas for sale all over the city and region as well as tortilla chips and other products. Storefronts announce the availability of *carnitas* (a Michoacán pork specialty) or *birria* (goat stew). Mexican restaurants also line this street, drawing not only Mexican but also non-Mexican customers from all over the city.

The main commercial street in Little Village/La Villita (officially South Lawndale, 30 in Figure 3.5, contiguous to Pilsen, 31), 26th Street, has a similar abundance of Mexican stores, restaurants, tortilla factories, and other establishments. This street alone brings in more revenue to the City of Chicago than any area except upscale Michigan Avenue downtown. On weekends 26th Street is jammed with pickup trucks driven by men dressed in cowboy hats and boots and with non-Mexicans eating and shopping in a Mexican ambience. The street has been renamed Calle México, and an arch over the street holds a bilingual sign: "*Bienvenidos a* Little Village" (Welcome to Little Village).

In the 1990 census Pilsen and Little Village contained the greatest concentration of Mexicans in Chicago (Chicago Fact Book Consortium 1995), many of them immigrants. With new immigrants now settling more often outside the city than within it (Newbart 2003), these neighborhoods are no longer the main ports-of-entry. Yet even though these contiguous neighborhoods no longer contain the majority or the highest concentration of the Mexican population, they nevertheless continue to be focal points of Mexican culture and identity, functioning as centers of Mexican commercial and cultural activity (e.g., the Museo de Bellas Artes, the Mexican Fine Arts Museum in Pilsen). Thus Mexican Americans and Mexican immigrants living in the suburbs (or farther away), as well as many non-Mexicans, are drawn to Pilsen and Little Village precisely because they are so Mexican: to shop, eat, go to church, attend a cultural event, or otherwise spend time.

The families in this study primarily have lived in five heavily Mexican community areas on the south side of Chicago. The first generation of siblings to arrive in Chicago in the mid- to late 1960s lived crowded together in one small shared apartment in Pilsen (31). Eventually garnering enough money to purchase their own homes (through savings augmented by loans from each other), they settled in Pilsen. Later some of them bought better houses in Little Village (30), and more recently many have moved directly south into what they consider better neighborhoods: McKinley Park (59), Brighton Park (58), and especially Gage Park (63). In addition to a first-generation family, many in the second generation (now with families of their own) also live quite near each other in Gage Park, although a few live in Pilsen, Brighton Park, and McKinley Park. Because of their primary concentration in Pilsen, Little Village, and Gage Park, this description focuses on these three community areas.

Housing in these three community areas varies from small apartment buildings (with two to nine units), to two-flats (a type of housing with two units, one above the other, quite common in Chicago), to single-family homes. Pilsen, as the oldest neighborhood, has older and more dilapidated housing. But community-based organizations and individuals there have begun to renovate buildings, partly to avoid takeover by encroaching gentrification on the east side of Pilsen, encouraged by an expanding University of Illinois at Chicago slightly to the north. The primary housing stock in Pilsen consists of small apartment buildings and single-family homes; Little Village has these types of housing, but it also has many blocks of small brick bungalows. Gage Park's housing consists almost entirely of such single-family bungalows, a type of housing very characteristic of Chicago, especially on the south side.

All of these neighborhoods until 1960 were white ethnic enclaves of primarily eastern Europeans (Chicago Fact Book Consortium 1995). Pilsen, for example, was settled by native-born Americans, Germans, and Irish in the mid-nineteenth century. When the area began to develop around 1875, more Germans and Irish moved in, as well as Poles and Czechoslovakians (many of the latter from Bohemia). The neighborhood was fully developed by the end of the nineteenth century. Czechs predominated in Pilsen (giving the neighborhood its name) until 1930, when the predominant groups were Poles, followed by Czechs, Yugoslavians, Lithuanians, Germans, and Italians. Mexicans, and some Puerto Ricans, began moving in during the 1950s and by 1960 were only outnumbered by Poles. Since the 1960s Mexicans increasingly have predominated, reaching 83 percent by 1990. In the 2000 census Mexicans still were 82 percent of the population in Pilsen; Puerto Ricans were 2 percent, other Latinos 5 percent, and non-Latinos 11 percent.[24] Even though Latinos constituted 89 percent of the population in Pilsen, only 81 percent claimed to speak Spanish. Those who spoke only English (both Latinos and non-Latinos) were 17 percent, and those who spoke Polish or Italian (Chicago's Little Italy is located on one edge of Pilsen) together accounted for only 1 percent of the population.

Little Village, contiguous to the west of Pilsen, has a similar history even though it developed later, beginning in the last decades of the nineteenth century and reaching fruition in the first two decades of the twentieth. Little Village was originally populated by native-born Americans, Germans, and Dutch during the 1860s then by Czechs in the 1880s. After 1910 Poles were the majority population, and by 1950 Poles then Czechs and Germans predominated. These populations consisted of workers' families who followed the movement of industry west from the city. The 1950 census showed a few hundred Puerto Ricans, and since 1960 the area has become predominantly Latino. By 1970 one-third of the population was Latino; and by 1990 it surpassed 85 percent. According to the 2000 census, the population is 76 percent Mexican, 1 percent Puerto Rican, 6 percent other Latino, and 17 percent non-Latino, largely African Americans, who are concentrated in only two census tracts out of 20 (Bousfield 2001). Although Little Village is 83 percent Latino, only 78 percent of them claim to speak Spanish, while 22 percent claim to speak only English. Thus about 5 percent of Latinos here speak only English. Remaining speakers of Slavic languages constitute only 0.5 percent of the population.

Gage Park developed even later than Pilsen and Little Village, largely after the turn of the twentieth century. It is considered a middle-class residential homeowner neighborhood with neat brick bungalows and two-flats built between 1905 and 1919. German farmers settled the area in the 1840s and 1850s. In 1889, when it was annexed to Chicago, Germans and Irish settled there, replaced by Czechs and Poles following industry after the turn of the century. By the 1920s the neighborhood was fully developed, and it was more ethnically mixed, including Austrians, Italians, and some Lithuanians, Irish, and Swedes as well as more Czechs, Poles, and Germans. In 1966 it was still a white ethnic neighborhood and was "the scene of racial 'testing' and later of organized protest" (Chicago Fact Book Consortium 1995, 183). Two hundred African Americans lived on one corner of the community area by 1980, and during that decade Mexicans began moving in. By 1990 Mexicans, mostly young families, constituted 38 percent of the population. By 2000 Mexicans were 71 percent of the population; with other Latinos, this rises to 79 percent.

Mexicans are concentrated in a number of census tracts in Gage Park (ranging from 55 percent to 77 percent); and one census tract with a small population (417) contains most of the non-Latinos (it is 79 percent non-Latino). Presumably, given the lack of notable African American population in this community area (Bousfield 2001), these non-Latinos are white ethnics, even though the number of people speaking Polish and other non-English languages is quite low. In this one census tract 93 percent of the population was born in the United States, a figure which includes both Latinos and non-Latinos. The use of languages in Gage Park roughly parallels that in Little Village, with slightly more English-only speakers and slightly fewer Spanish speakers: 24 percent speak only English, and 73 percent speak Spanish. Another 3.5 percent speak Polish (largely concentrated in the one census tract) and other languages.

Mexicans in Chicago do not generally move into African American neighborhoods, located primarily west of the Loop in community areas 25–29 and on the south side of Chicago in community areas 36–38, 40, 42–43, 67–69 (see Figure 3.5) and farther south. Predominantly Mexican neighborhoods on the south side of Chicago, then, are situated between African American neighborhoods on the east toward the lake and white ethnic neighborhoods to the west, notably the heavily Polish neighborhoods in community areas 57, 62, 56, and 64 (Skertic and Lawrence 2002), where newly migrating Poles continue to arrive, especially in Archer Heights (57) (Herguth 2002). It is worth noting, however, that even Archer Heights has a 43.38 percent Hispanic (presumably heavily Mexican) population http://www.nipc.org/test/DP_1234_CA_2000.xls, accessed 12/15/05). Thus Mexicans have moved into eastern European-dominated neighborhoods and followed them west and south.[25]

Mobility is characteristic of ranchero societies, as noted in Chapter 2. This chapter has concentrated on this century's ranchero mobility as represented by the social network in this study. This detailed treatment of the spatial contexts in which these transnational families live their lives provides background for the next chapter, which describes the network itself and the social contexts in which the families live. These social contexts include the central domains of their lives: work, school, and church. Because language is so central to identity, the next chapter also briefly introduces their language (ranchero dialect) and its creative use in genre-rich conversation, a topic explored more fully in succeeding chapters.

FOUR

The Social Context of *La Familia*
Work, Education, Religion, and Language

In this chapter I describe the people in this social network of families and the primary social contexts in which they live their transnational lives, both in the rancho and in Chicago. This description includes some genealogical information, since the network is organized primarily around nine siblings who are now grandparents, although it also includes several other families with whom some of the sibling-families are closely connected (see Figure 4.1). Because these families interact regularly and intensely, they constitute a dense and multiplex social network (Milroy 1987); that is, members are linked to each other in multiple ways: through kinship, friendship, and work.

Figure 4.1 shows four generations. Two primary families are represented here as two sets of great-grandparents in the center of their offspring, whose birth order is shown with a number (1–9 and 1–7, respectively) and a solid arrow. Three other families, two of whom are not related by (recent) kinship, but all three of whom are very much a part of the network, are represented separately. The second generation of numbered siblings (in bold), with their spouses, are in turn surrounded by their children (and their spouses, when appropriate) in ovals, and their children's children in circles with initials. Additional kinship relations across the network are indicated with dotted lines.[1] Shaded shapes show those who live in Mexico; unshaded shapes show those who live in the United States (as of 2005).

This social network is based on interconnections among families for many generations over the past three centuries in the microregion in Michoacán in which the rancho is located. Marriage within the group has been and continues to be a frequent practice, as is evidenced by the overlapping of the same Spanish surnames in many families. This is so even in Chicago, continuing and reaffirming ties within the close-knit network. At the same time, as schooling and work experiences extend the range of acquaintances, both in the rancho and in Chicago, marriages outside the network are beginning to become more common.

Dense and Multiplex Interaction

Interaction within the network, not so long ago within the context of a face-to-face agrarian society, is frequent; and people within the network tend to turn to each other for information, knowledge, and advice bearing on specific problems and situations. For example, one woman in the rancho (a tortilla maker who taught me how to make them) once complained to me about her sister, who had bought a car with money sent by her son in Chicago without consulting those who know about cars—and who subsequently returned the car without getting her money back because it was a "gas guzzler." I recorded this conversation in my field notes:

> On the walk home she exclaimed to me, "Why didn't my sister go to someone who KNOWS about cars?! Like you asking me how to make tortillas!" Funds of knowledge are spread across the network, then, but shared. One should ask someone who knows for the appropriate knowledge and advice.

Other instances of sharing involve literacy skills (high school and college students in Chicago are called upon to deal with letters in English from U.S. institutions), financing (a number of people collaborate to lend home-buyers the money necessary for the purchase), and job-seeking (brothers from Mexico were sent for to fill jobs in railroad construction where original migrants worked). Such interconnections between individuals are based primarily on kinship, of both the genetic and ritual type (*compadrazgo*); people are aunts, uncles, nieces, nephews, and cousins, as well as *ahijado/as* (godsons/daughters) and *comadres* and *compadres* (literally co-mothers and co-fathers) to each other. *Comadres* and *compadres* are more important than godparents in non-Latino U.S. society, since *compadrazgo* emphasizes not only the relationship with the child for whom one has been chosen to be a godparent but also and especially the relationship with the child's parents, with whom one now has a special tie. Since these godparents are chosen for three to four ritual occasions over the life span—baptism, first communion, confirmation (sometimes now omitted), and marriage—there are multiple opportunities to celebrate and reinforce social ties within the network. The *compadres* of baptism are the most important, because they take over the raising of the child in the event of the death of the biological parents; next in importance seem to be the *compadre* or *comadre* for the first communion. Like choices for marriage partners, *compadrazgo* choices gen-

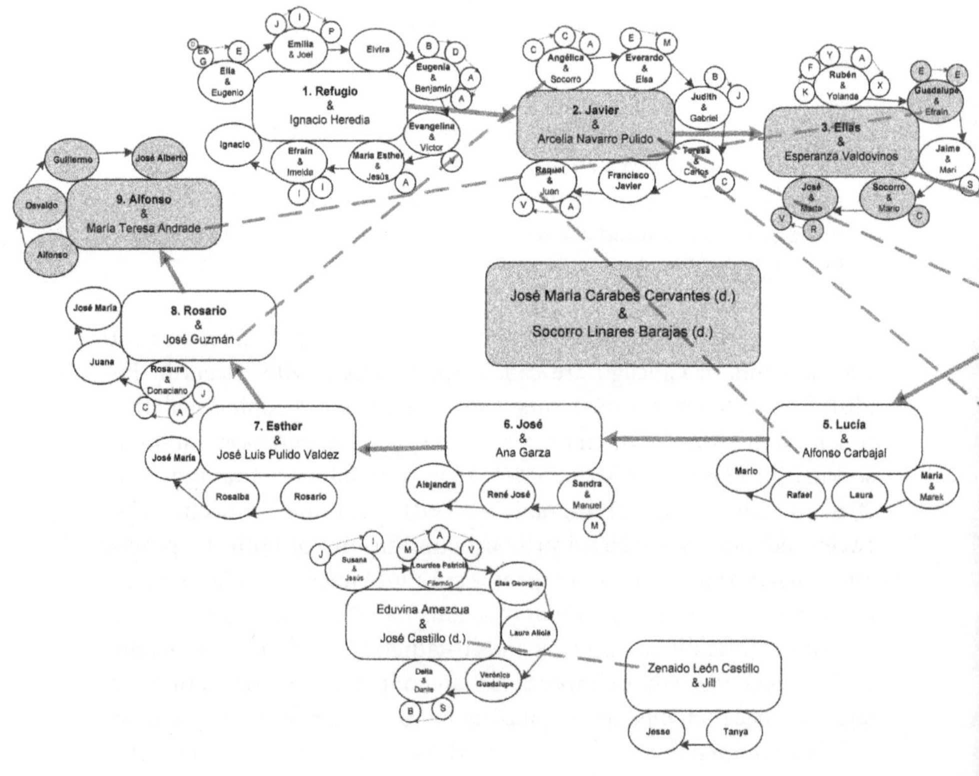

José María Cárabes Cervantes (d.)
&
Socorro Linares Barajas (d.)
1. Refugio
&
Ignacio Heredia
Ella
&
Eugenio
Emilia
& Joel
Elvira
Eugenia
&
Benjamín
Evangelina
&
Víctor
María Esther
&
Jesús
Efraín
&
Imelda
Ignacio
2. Javier
&
Arcelia Navarro Pulido
Angélica
&
Socorro
Everardo
&
Elsa
Judith
&
Gabriel
Teresa
&
Carlos
Francisco
Javier
Raquel
&
Juan
3. Elías
&
Esperanza Valdovinos
Rubén
&
Yolanda
Guadalupe
&
Efraín
Jaime
&
Mari
Socorro
&
Mario
José
&
Marta
5. Lucía
&
Alfonso Carbajal
Mario
Rafael
Laura
María
&
Marek
6. José
&
Ana Garza
Alejandra
René José
Sandra
&
Manuel
7. Esther
&
José Luis Pulido Valdez
José María
Rosalba
Rosario
8. Rosario
&
José Guzmán
José María
Juana
Rosaura
&
Donaciano
9. Alfonso
&
María Teresa Andrade
Guillermo
José Alberto
Osvaldo
Alfonso
Eduvina Amezcua
&
José Castillo (d.)
Susana
&
Jesús
Lourdes Patricia
&
Filemón
Elsa Georgina
Laura Alicia
Verónica
Guadalupe
Delia
&
Dante
Zenaido León Castillo
& Jill
Jesse
Tanya

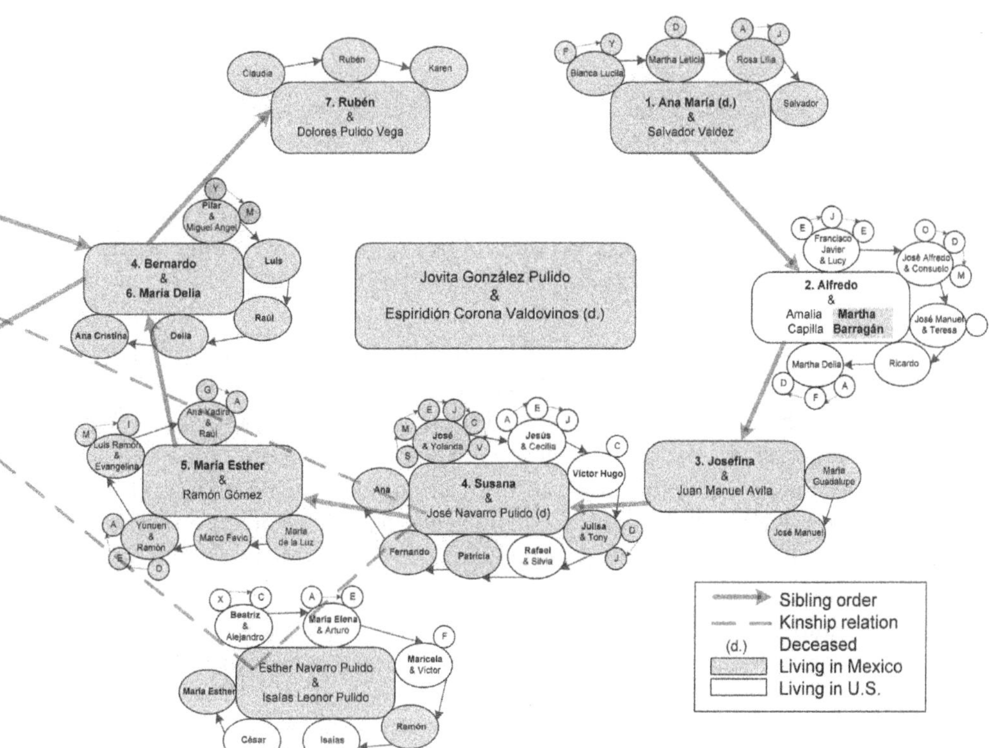

Figure 4.1. Social network of families

erally are kept within the group. They overwhelmingly fall within the extended family, then within the rancho; remaining choices are almost always from the microregion, and a very few *comadres* and *compadres* are friends from Chicago.

Beyond kinship and *compadrazgo* relations, network members relate as friends and as co-workers; the older generation especially works and socializes together, and age-equivalent cousins tend to be "best friends." It could be said, then, that network members largely form the fabric of each other's lives. I noted this *unión* (union, closeness) many times in my field notes both in Mexico and in Chicago; a typical example of this from Chicago follows:

> Belén [Judith's daughter] is taken care of during the day by Elsa [Judith's sister-in-law]. When Elsa works at the nearby supermarket in the evenings, she drives Lalo's [her husband's/Judith's brother's] car to take the children—sometimes—to Angelica's [Judith's and Lalo's sister]. Meanwhile, Lalo drives Chayo's [a cousin's] car to work. Judith watches Gordo [Lalo's son] at night for Elsa.

These multiple interconnections provide a real safety net for individuals and especially for young children, who attach emotionally to adults other than their parents and thus show little anxiety when parents leave them with others. People prefer to use this safety net rather than public welfare, a practice that also was noted among early Mexican migrants in Chicago (Kerr 1976) and which continues today. This practice is partly out of pride and partly the result of not having had any recourse to public assistance in Mexico, as noted by Carlos Heredia, director of a community center in the Little Village neighborhood of Chicago: "Mexicans come from a society with no welfare. You have to hustle, period. You don't come expecting to get anything . . ." (quoted in Casuso and Camacho 1995, 354). The advantages, both emotional and practical, of such a safety net are obvious.

The other side of this coin, however, is that there are few secrets and little privacy (especially in an Anglo-American sense) within such a social network, an aspect that is captured in a common Mexican *dicho* (saying): *Rancho chico, inferno grande* (Small rancho, huge fire). As a participant-observer in the rancho, I had to adapt (with some difficulty, but also with great pleasure) to this constant union and togetherness. I was consistently questioned about my comings and goings and greeted with puzzlement whenever I went to my room by myself to read or left the rancho for a few days to be (alone) in my apartment in nearby Zamora, where I was a Fulbright Scholar during 1995–1996 at El Colegio de Michoacán.[2] Even though members of the younger generations increasingly interact with others outside this network either at school or at work, it is nevertheless still the case that many members of the second and even third generation continue to participate actively in the network, including attending family events, which they sometimes organize themselves. Moreover, members of the second and third generations chat with each other by e-mail, whether in Mexico or in Chicago (those without computers in the rancho access their e-mail accounts in an Internet café in nearby Tingüindín). This underscores the continuing importance of the extended family (*la familia*) even within a context of increasing participation in U.S. social practices over the generations.

Work

Although work and school (discussed in the next section) are the most likely places for interacting with those outside of the social network and, in Chicago, with non-Mexicans, this is not frequently the case. As Guerra (1998) has argued, rather than deeply experiencing "contact zones" (Pratt 1991), members of this social network, especially the adults, are grounded in a "home front." This home front, largely due to the segregated nature of Chicago's ethnic neighborhoods as well as to the demographics that continually refresh Mexican cultural practices in Chicago (Kerr 1984), is overwhelmingly ranchero Mexican. In this dense, multiplex social network, much interaction is with each other, rather than with outgroup members such as African Americans or European Americans or even other Spanish-speaking populations such as Puerto Ricans. Many adult women in the network work with each other in Chicago at poultry-processing plants, printing companies, glass-painting and other factories, and catalog warehouses. Those young women with high school diplomas or GEDs (General Equivalency Diplomas) work as aides in schools and health clinics in the neighborhood or as clerks in nearby offices. Adult men work overwhelmingly (often with each other) on *el traque* (the track), either for railroad construction companies that build and repair tracks or for the city transit system; many others work for general construction (or demolition) companies; and a very few work in restaurants.

It is notable that the clear preference of both men and women is for factory or construction work, not for service positions such as cleaning offices or homes or busing tables in restaurants. Nor have they migrated to rural areas such as Carbondale, Illinois, for work in agricultural fields, as have large numbers of indigenous (Indian) *p'urhépecha* speakers from their region of Michoacán. As I discuss more fully in Chapter 5, rancheros define work itself as hard, physical labor, preferably for oneself, not for a boss (Barragán 1990a). For most of the first generation and some of the second, work in Chicago is a means to an end: supporting their families and accumulating enough money to live comfortably (and with self-sufficiency) in Mexico. They work hard at these jobs, but the characteristically independent spirit of rancheros often puts the jobs in second place after personal and familial desires and decisions—for example, to return to Mexico to live (without salaried labor). As Guadalupe Valdés (1996, 179) notes in her study of *mexicanos* near the Texas–New Mexico border, "the real dream . . . was becoming *comerciantes,* becoming part of the group that did not work for anyone else. Being one's own boss was, in fact, the real essence of the dream." Thus many families' ideal goal remains returning to Mexico and starting a business of their own. Barring a return to Mexico, they want to start their own businesses in Chicago, and some have done so.[3]

In the rancho most men and women are their own bosses in that they tend their own fields and animals. Those who have retired in the rancho after working for many years in Chicago have larger fields and more animals (cows and pigs), indicating their increased wealth. Even those men who have been quite successful in their jobs and have been promoted to well-paid positions frequently articulate a desire to retire to Mexico and grow avocados for commercial profit. One man in particular has been so successful in his job as a supervisor of railroad construction crews that his (middle-class) income was too high for his daughter to be eligible for financial aid at the university, and yet he too dreams of the day when he can retire to Mexico and grow avocados. (His Italian American wife, however, does not have the same feelings about the rancho as her husband.)

At both ends of the migrant circuit, all members of the family contribute to family economic projects and goals, as has traditionally been the case in their agricultural economy. With the transformation in the rancho's economy to commercial agriculture and the move to industrial jobs in Chicago, however, new work patterns have emerged; and gender figures significantly in these patterns, though differently in each place. Masculinity continues to be largely constructed through work, although a strong work ethic, especially regarding physical labor, pervades a sense of personhood for ranchero men, women, and even children.

In agrarian Mexico masculinity is closely associated with going to *el labor* (the fields) to work (Alonso 1995). With the move to industrial employment, manliness is linked to the dignity and respect that men are accorded for the wage-earning jobs that support their families, especially if these jobs require "strength, courage, and endurance" (Vargas 1993, 42). Men in this network are proud of doing demanding, even dangerous, jobs that can pose serious risks to their health and welfare. Part of a man's sense of self-worth has depended on the ability to provide total familial support, so that wives do not leave the home to work. With some difficulty, however, husbands have accepted their wives' working outside the home, at times out of necessity but at other times simply as part of the larger family goal of earning as much money as possible. Based on the traditional expectation of all family members contributing, in Chicago virtually everyone works for wages, even married women and teenaged (and older) sons and daughters, who manage jobs while attending school or university. This, of course, has accompanied significant changes in gender relations within families, as I discuss more fully in Chapter 7. At the same time, a new pattern is emerging within the second generation in Chicago: if finances allow it, some women are staying home to raise the children, reducing the tensions inherent in managing the family and household while working largely unsatisfying jobs outside the home.

In the rancho, almost all married women work only within their own households, which includes cooking, cleaning, and washing clothes as well as tending smaller animals and gardens and even helping out in the avocado fields when necessary. Young single women, widows, and occasionally married women, however, now work in the packing plants that were established during the 1990s. This work pays well in the Mexican economy, and teenaged girls are eager to enter this labor force in order to have their own money. Sometimes they keep half of what they earn, giving the rest to their parents. Other young women keep the money that they earn but spend much of it on groceries and other items for the household. Notably, in contrast to other places in Mexico, there is no wage differential based on gender in these packing plants: women earn the same as men do (Galetto 1999, 72). Although the hours are long and intense during peak packing seasons (and would be unacceptable to U.S. unions), many young women consider this work easier than helping out in the avocado *huertas* (orchards) that their families own.

Even young women with sufficient education for other jobs prefer to work in the packing plants, because they earn more money and are close to home and thus do not waste money on transportation or food. When I asked one young woman, María Elena, how things had changed with her working at the packing plant, she replied, "It's not a change. We've always worked! And this is easier than going to the fields!" The difference, of course, is that this work earns them their own money, which has inevitable implications for gender relations (see Mummert 1994), as women partially or fully fill the traditionally male role of providing economically for the family. When I began to ask another young woman about these changes, she finished my question for me:

Maricela: *¿Mas libertad? Depende en como te hagas. Si no tienes en su casa y puedes ayudar . . .*	More liberty? It depends on how you handle it. If there isn't enough in your house, and you can help out . . .
Marcia: *Pero los hombres—*	But the men—
Maricela: *Los hombres no piensan así. Piensan que estamos trabajando para ambición, para dinero y para su propia casa.*	Men don't think like that. They think that we are working for ambition, for money, and for your own home.

Thus, whereas women think that to help out in the household justifies their working outside the home, many men "don't think like that." They assume the women are working for their own personal betterment, not for the family. The individualist ethos of the rancho, however, concedes that even women have some right to money earned. As one man articulated it, "Cada quien su dinero" (To each his/her own money), when his wife bragged to me that he did not even know how much she earned. This married woman is exceptional in the rancho in working outside the home. With her comparatively advanced schooling (she received a *título de contador privado* [title of private accountant] from a *preparatoria técnica* [technical high school] in a nearby city, commuting by bus for three years), she works as the secretary in a public *secundaria* (middle school) in a nearby town, while an older daughter takes responsibility for younger siblings. Upon return from their avocado orchards (before the wife returns from work), the husband prepares the main daily meal. Although this is unusual in the rancho, other men also do some cooking (e.g., warming tortillas or grilling foods over fires). This is especially true for some (not all) men who have lived and worked in Chicago, where they learned to cook and do other household chores out of necessity when their wives and sisters were still in the rancho.

Education

Educación is not a direct equivalent of the English word "education." *Educación* carries broader meanings and is distinguished from the more focused term *enseñanza* (teaching). *Educación* includes raising children to behave well in terms of manners and morals (see Valdés 1996, 125), whereas *enseñanza* refers to direct teaching and usually to formal schooling. People from the rancho, then, can be *bien educado* (well brought up) even when they have little or no schooling. Parents, and other relatives, teach children proper behavior with *consejos,* "spontaneous homilies designed to influence behaviors and attitudes" (Valdés 1996, 125), proverbs, and traditional sayings. For example, one mother in Mexico supported her husband's restriction of their teenaged daughter's mobility at night with a proverb: "Más sabe el diablo por viejo que por diablo" (The devil knows more from being old than from being the devil), adding, "Tu papá tiene más años" (your father is older [and wiser]).

The rancho now has federal schools at the preschool (*pre-escolar*) and elementary (*primaria*) levels, the former for children over four years old and the latter for grades 1–6. A government *secundaria* (grades 7–9) is located on the outskirts of the nearby township center (Tingüindín), a short bus ride from the rancho. Those who continue their schooling into *preparatoria* (grades 10–12) must take longer bus rides (thirty minutes or more) to nearby towns, unless they want to attend the agricultural high school in Tingüindín. In addition to government schools, Tingüindín and other towns (e.g., Zamora) have private schools (*colegios*) which some children from the rancho, especially those with U.S. dollars, attend. Since schooling has only been available in the rancho since 1940, older members of the network have had limited exposure to it. According to interviews with members of the oldest generation still living there, people from the rancho began to petition the government for a teacher around 1937, and the first one arrived three years later. A succession of *maestros* and *maestras* (teachers) taught out of their houses for five centavos a week (virtually pennies, even in the undervalued pesos of that period). Yet even at this price, many could not afford to go to school, and others who had to help their families in the fields were unable to attend. Even when a public school was built in the 1950s (which at first had only one to two grade levels), some students only attended a few months a year, when they were not needed at home or in the fields. The current school, Melchor Ocampo, was authorized by the Secretariat of Public Education (SEP) in 1973.

In spite of the lack of educational opportunity, most people in the rancho know how to read and write, at least minimally. According to an educational census conducted in 1997,[4] only 19 of 362 persons living in the rancho reported themselves as unable to read and write, which matches the figure reported in the 1990 Mexican census for the rancho.

In the official school census conducted in 2002, 32 adults out of 407 reported no schooling. This figure, as well as the total population, may have grown through the attraction of nearby rural Mexicans from areas still without schools to jobs at the packing plants established during the 1990s.

Those who need to calculate numbers (*hacer cuentas;* e.g., to ascertain the amount of fertilizer to buy for their avocado orchards) know how to do so, whether they learned in school or *lírico* (see Farr 1994c). Learning to do arithmetic—or to read and write—*lírico* (lyrically) refers to a learning process carried out informally and orally, being taught by another person who knows how to do whatever it is that one is learning. This way of learning is extremely important among rancheros and is linked to the assumption that one should go to a person with the appropriate knowledge for guidance in particular areas. Whereas people in larger, more complexly literate contexts might turn to books for such guidance, people steeped in oral traditions in isolated, face-to-face agrarian contexts turn to each other. Thus even skills that appear decontextualized—using the alphabet to encode or decode written Spanish or manipulating numbers in arithmetic processes—are learned in a decidedly social way, as knowledge is transmitted from one person to another.

With the increase in schooling availability over the decades, years of attendance in school have increased over the generations in this social network, whether in Mexico, in Chicago, or at both ends of the migrant circuit over the course of individual lives. Educational opportunities in Chicago have, in fact, vastly increased the level of schooling for members of the second and third generations of this network. For the first generation who migrated to Chicago, formal schooling in Mexico generally did not exceed elementary school, ranging from two to six years in all. This level of schooling matches that of their generational counterparts who remained in the rancho rather than migrating to the United States, with the exception of those who were younger siblings in their families and thus able to continue their schooling at least through high school while their older siblings worked. Generations two and three, whether in the rancho or in Chicago, have almost invariably attained higher levels of schooling. Most members of the second generation in the rancho are more likely to have completed *primaria* and continued their schooling into *secundaria;* some have completed *secundaria;* and a few younger members of this generation have completed *preparatoria.* One young woman of the second generation even completed college in Mexico, commuting daily to nearby Zamora. A woman in the rancho commented on the increasing importance of education:

> *Sí, actualmente la educación es muy necesaria. Antes con la primaria bastaba, pero ahora la primaria no significa ni siquiera el nivel básico. Actualmente, en los trabajos piden como mínimo que tengan la prepa.*
> Yes, nowadays education is very necessary. Before primary school was sufficient, but now primary school doesn't even mean a basic level. Nowadays work[places] ask as a minimum that one have completed *preparatoria.*

Members of the second and third generations of the families that migrated to Chicago frequently have completed even more schooling than their generational counterparts in the rancho. For some, this has involved schooling in both Mexico and Chicago. A frequent pattern for second-generation members in several families is primary school in Chicago and secondary school in Mexico (then work, rather than high school, in Chicago). For two other families who lived during various periods in Chicago, Mexico, then Chicago again, the pattern of binational schooling is more mixed. Binational schooling experiences, of course, develop bilingualism and biliteracy. For example, those in the second generation who attended elementary school in Chicago learned English sufficiently to develop it further when they later returned to Chicago as young adults. These individuals easily speak a colloquial English that is difficult for others in the network, faced with learning English as adults, to attain. Yet there are some disadvantages to the pattern of dual schooling as well. The two school systems are quite different, as are the cultural contexts in which they are embedded. As Ramón Gómez, a teacher who lives in the rancho, notes,

> *Los [estudiantes] que vienen de allá son muy extrovertidos. Allá es otro el sistema de enseñar; los enseñan a participar más. Aquí uno está acostumbrado [a] que el maestro es él que enseña, él que habla, y los niños sólo escuchan.*
> Those [students] that come from over there are very extroverted. The system of teaching is different over there; they teach them to participate more. Here one is accustomed to the teacher being the one who teaches, the one who speaks, and the children only listen.

Thus children returning from the United States often are viewed critically for being "extroverted" in the way they behave in school. They also are criticized for their clothing styles (baggy, low-hanging pants and earrings for boys; short skirts and shorts for girls) and more "liberal" gender relations, both of which are seen as disrespectful and possibly gang-related. *Secundaria* administrators noted in an interview what was considered inappropriate for boys within the school: *vestirse como cholos, fumar, estar en bandas o tener novia* (dress like cholos [Mexican American delinquents], smoke, be in a gang, or have a girlfriend). Academically as well, some returning children are considered by both parents and teachers to be deficient in several respects. First, for their lack of (literate) Spanish:

> *Aún los niños que van en Estados Unidos en escuelas bilingües, no saben bien el español, ni tampoco leer ni escribir bien . . .*
> Even those children who go to bilingual school in the United States don't know Spanish well, nor to read or write [it] well . . .

Beyond a lack of Spanish, these children are perceived as having had inadequate academic preparation in other areas, as the teacher Ramón Gómez noted:

> *Varios papás de aquí me han dicho que ellos ven que la educación en México es mejor que la de Estados Unidos, y yo como maestro he notado que los niños que estudian allá vienen muy deficientes—bueno, en matemáticas llegan muy bien preparados, como que allá le dan mucha atención a esa materia; también en educación física y en actividades artísticas, porque allá hay un maestro para cada actividad y se tienen los recursos para apoyarlos . . . [pero] hay otras materias donde llegan muy mal, deficientes, como español, geografía, historia, ciencias naturales . . . hay veces que llegan niños de quinto o sexto grado y hay que bajarlos uno, porque no tienen el mismo nivel. Hay maestros que no los quieren recibir en sus grupos, porque dicen que implica mucho trabajo y no pueden retrasar a todo el grupo por un sólo niño.*
> Various parents from here have told me that they see that the education in Mexico is better than that in the United States, and I as a teacher have noted that the children who study over there come back very deficient—well, in mathematics they arrive very well prepared, since over there they give much attention to that subject; also in physical education and in artistic activities, because there they have one teacher for each activity and they have resources to support them . . . [but] there are other subjects in which they arrive very badly [prepared], deficient, such as Spanish, geography, history, natural sciences. . . . There are times when fifth or sixth grade children arrive and you have to put them back a year, because they don't have the same level [as children here]. There are teachers who don't want them in their classes, because

they say that they require a lot of work, and they can't hold back the entire class for one child.

Many people do note that U.S. schools have an advantage in that they provide computer instruction. Despite acknowledged advantages in specific subjects, however, many teachers and parents still believe that children study more subjects and are better schooled academically in Mexico, at least at the *secundaria* level and beyond, if not at the local elementary school in the rancho. Many parents see the elementary schools as inadequate, partially because the teachers are drastically underpaid and often hold down two jobs. Because of this, parents say, some teachers frequently arrive late or do not show up at all. Also, children only attend the *primaria* for the morning (9 A.M.–noon) or the afternoon (1–6 P.M.) session (the morning session is for those in the lower grades and the longer afternoon session for those in the upper grades).

Those members of the second and third generations who have been schooled entirely in Chicago generally go further in school and have fewer problems with language and literacy, especially writing English compositions. A few students with schooling both in Chicago and in Mexico have experienced difficulties in this regard, no doubt compounded by devalued dialect features in both their Spanish and English. Nevertheless, a number of second-generation individuals have completed college, and a few have entered graduate school. Most of these more advanced students are female, possibly because of social pressure pushing young men to work. For example, some young men are urged explicitly by older men to "get to work," because staying in school "too long" makes them vulnerable to the criticism that they are "lazy." Masculinity is tied to productive work, traditionally in the fields but increasingly in the United States. One older man now retired in the rancho urged his nephew as he came of working age: "¡Vete a la frontera!" (Get yourself to the border!), meaning get himself to Chicago to work. This same older man apprised me of his view of schooling on several different occasions: too much schooling can turn a person "crazy" or can "spoil" a person, taking away the drive to work. He pointed out several successful men in the rancho who had little or no schooling and contrasted them with those who had extensive schooling but considerably less success. What is truly important, he emphasized, is not formal schooling, but intelligence and drive.

Such views represent traditional ranchero attitudes toward work and school, but these attitudes are changing, especially among women. In fact, the man who adamantly espoused these attitudes on several occasions holds a quite different opinion than does his own wife, who once chastised her niece and another young girl for not liking school and for doing their homework at the last minute. She told them that if they did not go to school they'd be *burros trabajando en el campo* ([stupid] mules working in the fields) and then looked to me for affirmation: "¿Verdad, Marcia?" (Isn't that right, Marcia?). The girls objected, saying that she herself hadn't gone to school much, to which she quickly replied, "That's because we didn't have the opportunity! You do!" Nevertheless, many young women in the rancho now want to leave school at fifteen in order to work in the packing plants, to have "their own money." Others continue their education beyond that which their parents were able to attain.

In Chicago both males and females in the second and third generations take advantage of the increased opportunities for schooling and go further in school than their parents did; but proportionately more females do this, because many of their male cousins and brothers go to work. Thus there are both gender and age differences regarding attitudes toward education and years of education attained, both of which are tied to changes in the social and material contexts in which their lives are embedded, either in Chicago or in the rancho. Figure 4.2 shows actual levels of schooling (as of 2002) by date of birth for men and women. This figure includes only people born before 1981, since those born after that year are still of school age. Virtually all children in Chicago born in 1981 or after are fully schooled to their appropriate grade levels, as are many but not all of their age-mates in the rancho.

Figure 4.2 shows both age and gender patterns in the total years of schooling achieved (each square, circle, or triangle represents one individual). A clear pattern is the rise in years of schooling over time, reflecting increased opportunities in both locations. Even more striking, however, is the contrast between males and females. Over time, females achieve higher levels of schooling in both locations but especially in Chicago. Clearly, being female and being in Chicago leads to more schooling in this network. This is especially notable because there is little difference in schooling levels between males and females with dates of birth before 1950 (the first generation of migrants). For females born after 1950, however, levels of schooling skyrocket. Many females in Mexico born after 1950 achieve notably higher levels (note the white squares near the upper right corner of Figure 4.2: Women), but females in Chicago achieve even higher levels (note the cluster of black circles and triangles in the upper right corner of Figure 4.2: Women).

In contrast, many males born after 1950 do not avail themselves of the increased opportunities for schooling. Several male "outliers" with

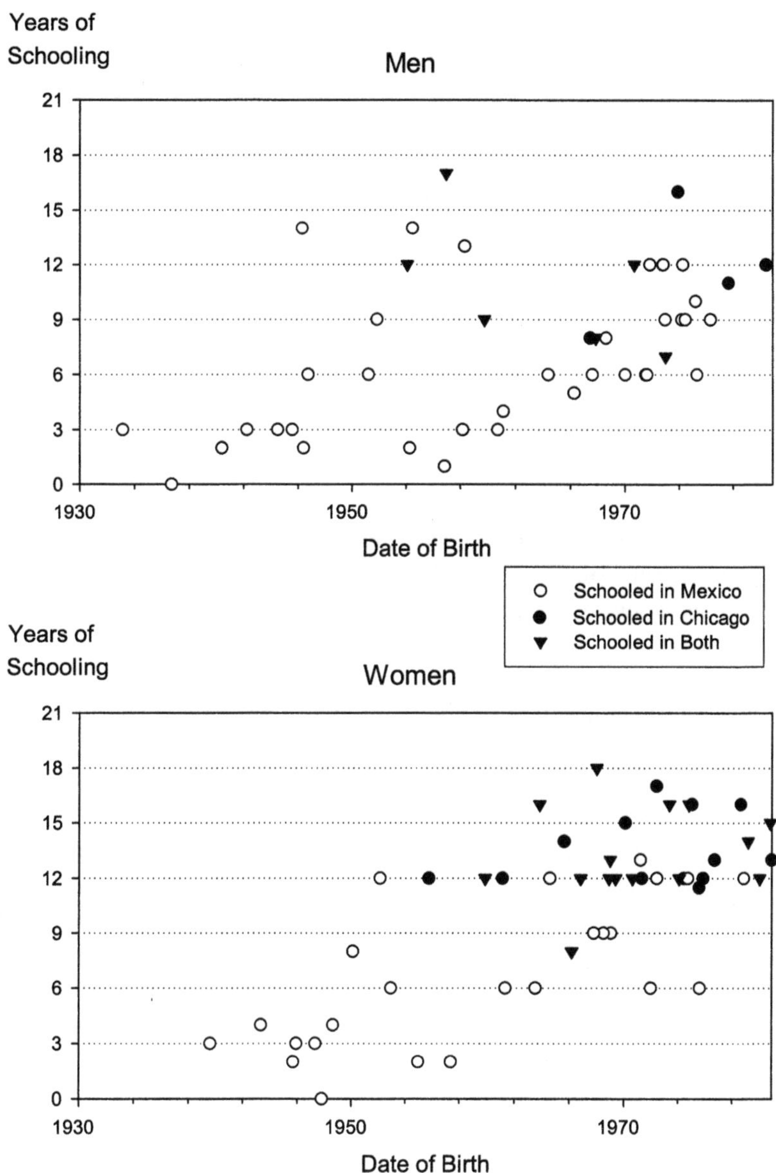

Figure 4.2. Years of schooling by date of birth and place of schooling

higher levels of schooling (near the top in Figure 4.2: Men) either married into the network (two teachers, one in the rancho and one in Chicago, and a computer programmer with a Chicago B.S. degree) or were younger siblings in the first generation who went to college while older siblings worked. Generally, however, unlike their male counterparts, women began to complete twelve years of schooling in Mexico late in the first generation and into the second. Overall, more second-generation women than men attended college or university, either in Mexico or in Chicago, but particularly in Chicago.

One explanation for the lower levels of schooling for males, even those with increased opportunities, is the cultural link between masculinity and work. A number of second-generation males, for example, migrated to Chicago to work and did not go to school. While some of their male cousins raised in Chicago continued in school, others dropped out because of gangs. In one case a young man dropped out of high school, moving to North Carolina to live with an older sister and work, to avoid the pressure to join a gang in Chicago. In another case a young man did join a gang and began to do poorly in school, so his entire family quit their jobs and school and moved back to Mexico to get him away from the gang.

Despite the lower levels of schooling achieved by males, overall there is a dramatic increase in high school and college degrees across time, a trend that is continuing into the third generation. In addition, many have pursued other kinds of schooling in Chicago, obtaining GED certificates (represented in Figure 4.2 as twelve years of schooling) and becoming certified electricians, chefs, photographers, and cosmetologists (none of which are included in Figure 4.2). Thus the ranchero ideology of hard work and progress (which I discuss in more detail in Chapter 6) encourages many in these families to take advantage of increasingly available opportunities to prepare themselves and their children for a better future.

Religion

Western Mexico is an intensely conservative Catholic region, and rancheros here are especially so (Barragán 1990a). González (1974, 50) contrasts the typical ranchero "refusal to submit to civil law and authority . . . with the obedience accorded to ecclesiastical government and to the commandments of religion." Being scrupulously Catholic is simply an assumed part of daily life. Women, especially, participate in masses, say the rosary, and even read the Bible. Sunday mass, both in the rancho and in Chicago, is *de rigueur,* although some in the second and third generations attend mass less often than weekly. One of these women even complained that priests in Chicago are irritating when they do not keep to religious topics but begin preaching about social issues. Other women, especially those in the rancho, attend mass more frequently than once a week, some carrying out promises made for the granting of prayed-for favors from the Virgin (e.g., to heal a sick child). Some first-generation women in Chicago also attend mass more frequently than once a week or attend other kinds of religious meetings, such as prayer circles that involve extensive reading and writing activities (Farr 2000; Guerra and Farr 2002).

Women in Chicago celebrate religious ceremonies in their homes, especially around Christmas. This includes *posadas* (in which small groups from the church visit homes in the parish enacting Joseph and Mary's search for an inn before the birth of Jesus) as well as the *levantamiento* and *acostamiento* (the "picking up" and "laying down" of a beautifully dressed baby Jesus doll while hymns are sung and prayers said, led by an adult woman in the network; see Farr 1994a for the literacy practices in this event). *Doctrina* (catechism) classes are sometimes held in families' homes on Saturday mornings, with teenaged women teaching young children. *Doctrina* in the rancho is also led by young unmarried women, although meetings are held elsewhere.

In the rancho various women, and men, are responsible for the religious ceremonies held in the chapel: some leading prayers, others reading the Word of God from the pulpit. The chapel itself (as noted in Chapter 3) was built in 1962 on land donated by a family that had accumulated some wealth working in Kansas. As a chapel in a rancho of about four hundred people, it has no resident priest. Instead, the priest from the township center visits on Sundays and religious holidays to celebrate masses. On special occasions, people from the rancho go to the cathedral in the township center for mass, as they used to before there were religious services in the rancho. Decades ago many people had to walk forty-five minutes to Tingüindín for this; today they can drive or take the bus. On the Day of the Virgin, December 12, many people choose to arise at 4:00 A.M. and walk to Tingüindín to enjoy the beautifully decorated shrine to the Virgin in the San Pedro neighborhood in the early dawn. This shrine, along one entire street, is meticulously built during the week prior to the Day of the Virgin. On the day itself, the priest begins mass at this constructed shrine around 6:00 A.M., then throngs of people follow him singing through Tingüindín's streets to the cathedral, named for La Virgen Santísima de la Asunción (The Most Holy Virgin of Ascension). They enter the cathedral on their knees, continuing on their knees all the way to their seats.

In addition to the Day of the Virgin, immensely important all over Mexico, a number of sacred days mark the annual calendar: Semana Santa (the Holy Week of Easter); the rancho's patron saint day, June 24; Tingüindín's patron saint day, August 15; and Christmas. The rancho fills with people from Chicago on these occasions, especially as they coincide with school holidays. San Juan, the patron saint of the rancho, occasions a week-long fiesta as well as many first communion ceremonies. On occasion people also organize day trips to special cathedrals in northwest Michoacán, getting up well before dawn to attend the early morning mass. I was included in one such trip early in my fieldwork. We arose at 4 A.M., piled into a van, picked up a few people at the other end of the rancho, and headed toward San Juan de Nuevo, the village rebuilt after the Paricutín volcano eruption in the late 1940s. We attended the 7:00 A.M. mass, visited the special shrine to the Virgin for special petitions, and breakfasted outside in the market. We spent the rest of the day touring Lake Pátzcuaro, an indigenous tourist site, and shopping for *artesanías* (crafts) then drove home, tired but content, in the evening.

Notably, people in the rancho do not celebrate the Day of the Dead at the end of October (All Saints' Day or Halloween), although this is celebrated widely in Mexico City and in the United States. Those who celebrate this day commune with ancestors in decorated graveyards, bringing them their favorite items, such as cigars and food. Rancheros, however, associate this holiday with its indigenous origins. Not being "Indian," they ignore it (see Chapter 5 on their decidedly nonindigenous identity). Ironically, however, a few members of the second and third generations in Chicago (those more acculturated to U.S. society) have learned to celebrate the Day of the Dead at the university, where it is viewed as quintessentially Mexican, and where an altar is erected.

Their Catholicism, then, is generally not a syncretic blend of Catholic and preconquest Indian traditions, as most descriptions of Mexican Catholicism have assumed (see, for example, Ingham 1986). Meyer (1976, 181), writing of the Cristero Rebellion from 1926 to 1929, which arose in this region, instead describes this Catholicism as part of a "popular culture whose lively traditions derived from the Middle Ages and the sixteenth century."[5] In addition to having rich oral traditions, many *cristeros,* 60 percent of whom were unschooled, had learned to read by themselves and "devoured" religious texts. Religion pervaded their daily lives at every level; the church was the center of "local life because it guaranteed entertainment, information, and education, and the priest was the head, the counselor, the 'natural' leader, at the crossroads of the scarce networks of co-operation existing in the rural world" (Meyer 1976, 187). Both Barragán (1997) and González (1974) note this characteristic of other ranchero societies, as does Meyer (1976), who describes honor, along with patriotism and religion, as central to the personality of the ranchero.

Oral history interviews with elders in the rancho identify relatives who fought as *cristeros* (one of whom was hanged by government forces at the railroad tracks and left for three days) and indicate that many people in the rancho hid from government troops in the mountains and secretly provided sustenance to the *cristeros.* Another interview with an elderly woman describes how a traveler once gave her some beautiful prayers (orally) in exchange for food. During the interview, she recited these prayers by heart.

Being Catholic, then, is an important part of identity for many in this transnational social network.[6] In spite of this, some young women unhesitatingly use birth control pills, even though they know this is against the church's teachings. The birthrate has been reduced by half (from six or more children to fewer than three) from the first to the second generation. Even divorce, traditionally unheard of, is beginning to occur in the microregion in which the rancho is located. A young woman in the network commented to me that divorce is becoming more acceptable in the microregion's larger towns, though it was not yet acceptable in the township center where she lived. Within this network, however, divorce is rare if not nonexistent. Moreover, young women within this network who become pregnant always marry the father rather than become single mothers, which is intensely disapproved of and greeted with shame by older adults (see Chapter 6 on *respeto*). But many young women now insist on only a *civil* marriage (a civil not religious ceremony), so that they can divorce their husbands if things do not turn out well. If they are satisfied after a few years of civil marriage, they are then willing to marry in the church, which is seen as a lifetime commitment.

Susana, a woman in her mid-fifties, explained this:

> *Como mi hija . . . ella sólo está casada al civil. Me dijo que no se casaba a la iglesia, porque si no se llevaba bien con su marido ¿para qué se iban a hacer la vida imposible? Se separaban y cada quien seguía su camino. Yo no veo bien eso; uno se casa para toda la vida—bueno, eso fue lo que a mí me enseñaran, pero mis hijas ya piensan de otra manera.*
> Like my daughter . . . she is only married by the state. She told me that she wouldn't marry in the church, because if she doesn't get along with

> her husband, why should they make life impossible? They would separate and each would go his or her own way. I don't see this as good; one marries for a lifetime—well, that's what they taught me, but my daughters think differently.

Susana's sister Esther, on a different occasion, echoed these sentiments but agreed with their daughters' point of view: "Más vale divorciada que viviendo con alguien que no la sabe sacar adelante o que la maltrate" (Better divorced than living with someone who doesn't know how to get ahead or who mistreats her). Although this is not a proverb or traditional saying (clearly!), she articulates it within a proverb-like structure, to increase its rhetorical effectiveness (see the next section of this chapter on language use). In spite of these and other changes, however, people in this extended network continue to interact most intensely with others within the network; most marriages, civil or religious, are to people within the network, the rancho, or the microregion. Even in Chicago, where there is more interaction and marriage outside these domains, many in the second generation marry others within the rancho and its microregion or marry rancheros from neighboring western Mexican states such as Jalisco and Guanajuato. Thus while the network expands to include these new relatives, many elements of ranchero tradition and culture, including religion, are maintained. Notably, members of the network who have "married out" in Chicago have done so with other Catholics (e.g., an Italian American, a Chicago-born *tejana* whose Mexican American parents came from Texas, and recently a Polish man).

Language: Rhetorical Competence, Poetic Genres, and Dialects

Families of this social network, like some other Mexican-origin populations, enjoy and esteem language competence (Briggs 1988; Limón, 1992, 1994). In particular, rhetorical abilities that include persuasiveness, expressiveness, grace, and wit are highly valued (Farr 1993). Although a primary framework for speech, in Erving Goffman's (1974) sense, involves being quite direct (see Chapter 6 on *franqueza*), playful uses of language also have an important place in their lives.

On the one hand, serious talk calls for directness, expressed both in direct questions and in frequent directives. For example, I was taken aback many times by direct questions put to me by men, women, and even children. Once in the rancho a young boy asked me in front of his family if I liked it better staying with them or where I had moved (I had to think quickly to answer tactfully); on another occasion a woman confronted me in front of her family, saying that she was *sentido* (sensitive) about my having been in the rancho for several days without visiting her, while her husband interrogated me with "¡¿Por qué tú no has venido?!" (Why haven't you come?!). This instance of directness, of course, is part of local politeness norms, showing that politeness does not always involve indirectness, as is often assumed (see Chapter 6).

On the other hand, the abundant direct speech is complemented by indirect playful speech. That is, in contrast to the primary framework of straightforward serious talk, much other talk is framed as "play." Being an *hablador* (skilled speaker) not only connotes being "boastful" but also invokes the entertainment value associated with good tellers of stories, jokes, and other genres. People routinely engage in wordplay, often through *doble sentido* (double meaning, one of which can be sexual). For example, Bernardo, a man in the rancho, used wordplay to tease someone coming into his home. Instead of saying the expected, "Pásale sin pena" (literally, Come in without embarrassment or Please do come in), he said, "Pásale sin vergüenza" (literally the same meaning, with *vergüenza* replacing *pena*). The humor here relies on ambiguity (in the stress pattern). His utterance, then, could be taken not for the two-word adverbial phrase *sin vergüenza* (without shame) but for the one-word noun *sinvergüenza* (a person who is shameless). Another example of such wordplay occurred in Chicago, when Santiago recounted a conversation that took place in his amnesty class at the local community center: "El maestro de nosotros nos dijo que los frijoles engordan" (Our teacher told us that beans fatten). He continued: "Pues una señora allí dijo, 'No maestro, los frijoles no engordan,' dice, 'los que engordamos somos nosotros' " (Then a woman there said, "No, teacher, beans don't fatten," she says, "those who fatten are us"). Much laughter followed this story.

Playing with language, in fact all kinds of talk, is so important that one woman complained to me about her niece's home in Chicago, where they "didn't even talk anymore, but just watched television." The older adults in this network, of course, grew up without television in the rancho, where genre-filled talk passed leisure time pleasurably. Such talk to them fulfills important social functions, entertaining, sanctioning, and knitting people together through the shared valuing of such linguistic abilities.

Throughout the tapes recorded for this study are many instances of the oral genres favored by this group: *dichos* (sayings), *refranes* (proverbs), *chistes* (jokes), *cuentos* (stories), *adivinanzas* (riddles), and especially *anécdotas* (personal anecdotes). These range from genres that are relatively independent of context, with established form and content (e.g., sayings, proverbs, riddles, and standardized jokes), to genres that are heavily tied to the context in which they are given voice (e.g., personal anecdotes). All of these genres, however, share an emphasis on poetics (Farr 1994b). That is, as these men and women generate these genres in their daily talk, they foreground the aesthetic potential of language. Roman Jakobson (1960) argues that the poetic function of language should be studied by linguists as much as other functions (phatic, conative, expressive, metalingual, and—the Anglo-American favorite—referential). Poetics is as characteristic of the oral mode of language as it is of the written (Bauman 1986; Hymes 1981; Sherzer 2002; Tannen 1989; Tedlock 1983). Jakobson (1960) noted that the fundamental principle underlying the poetic function in both modes of language is "equivalence," abundantly illustrated through the repetition and parallelism deployed in the oral genres that enliven daily speech within this network. Such patterns have been studied in a variety of languages and cultures, suggesting that the expression of poetics in oral language may have some universal properties (Hymes 2002).

An example of such poetic patterning (taken from Farr 1994b) is provided below, in a story told by a young woman in Chicago. In this story, she justifies herself to her peers for allowing her mother to take her newborn child back to Mexico with her. Her mother's concern was the welfare of the child while being taken care of by others when the young mother was at work. As she uses reported speech to quote her mother's persuasive words, the young woman structures them as a "constructed dialogue" (Tannen 1989) replete with parallelism in intonation and syntax, measured by the repetition of the connective *y* (and) between lines:

[*weepy, complaining tone*]	[*weepy, complaining tone*]
"¿QUIÉN se la va a cuidar?"	"WHO is going to take care of her?"
y "¡NO me le van a dar de comer!"	and "They are NOT going to feed her [for me]!"
y "¡ME la van a hacer llorar!"	and "They are going to make her cry!"
y "¿QUÉ, MIRA, qué si me le pegan ahora?"	and "LOOK, what if they hit her?"
[*laughter*]	[*laughter*]

In this short stretch of her story, the young woman repeats the same intonation pattern in each line (each line is followed by a slight pause), and she structures her mother's alleged words to her into the same repeated syntactic pattern. (Cleverly, the mother is represented as using

Spanish syntax to insert herself [*me* in the last three questions] in the repeated clauses, subtly laying claim to the baby as hers as well as the young mother's.) The young mother builds to a climax in her story by repeating and strengthening the rhythmic pattern of each line above: the words in capitals at the beginning of each line indicate their higher pitch and heavier stress relative to the rest of the words in each line (this cannot always be translated into English). The final line lengthens this initial emphasized stress and pitch into two words rather than the one of the previous three lines, possibly signaling the end of this mini-story to her hearers, who time their laughter perfectly with the end of her story.[7] Thus a story that could have been told quite prosaically is instead structured poetically, both to entertain and to garner sympathy and support from the immediate audience by detailing the considerable pressure on her that led to her decision. The tapes collected for this study are full of such poetic narratives, indicating that the poetic function of language is highly valued within this group and serves both to persuade others and to affirm high personal regard for those who can perform in this way. Such verbal abilities are examined in more detail in Chapters 6 and 8.

Other genres used in daily speech, the *adivinanza* (riddle), the *refrán* (proverb), and the *dicho* (saying), are traditional oral texts built around such poetic patterning. For example, on a Sunday afternoon at one young family's home in Chicago the young husband, Gabriel, hustled back and forth, going about the carpentry, tiling, and plumbing tasks that were part of his plan to improve their house and add on apartments for relatives to rent. The rest of us, including several visiting young families, sat in the living room chatting. Once as the young husband passed through, a visiting young mother teased him with a *dicho: A todo le hace y a nada le pega* (Jack of all trades, master of none). As everyone laughed, his wife's cousin Beatriz responded, "Sí, hizo una cosa muy buena! Nació Belén!" (Yes, he did one thing very well! Belen [his daughter] was born!). Even more, and more delighted, laughter followed this playful use of *doble sentido.*

Many other times, such as at breakfast in the rancho or during dinner preparations in Chicago, people initiated this speech play, often at the arrival of a third person (in addition to myself and one other woman). At these times it seemed to me that the very presence of a third person activated a reframing of the situation as a time for playful language, as someone immediately challenged the new person with a riddle to solve, or as the new person responded to being teased about something with a joke or riddle. On one occasion the new arrival was teased about a *novio* (boyfriend), and she responded with "¡Pasión de minga!" (minga passion [*minga* is a vulgar word for penis, here meaning sexual arousal]). When I asked what *minga* meant, the teaser and teased together chanted rhythmically, "¿Por qué minga? [pause] ¡Porque no mata pero sí chinga!" (Why minga? Because it won't kill you, but it certainly screws you). The wordplay relied on the sound parallels of *mata* and *chinga* with *minga:* the first sound of *mata* combined with the *-inga* of *minga* rhymes with *chinga.* The sexual connotations of both *minga* and *chinga* (from the well-known Mexican verb *chingar,* literally to have intercourse, but metaphorically to screw) create a message that a relationship leading only to sexual arousal won't kill you but will leave you messed up. The entire speech play not only commingled words but was structured poetically, utilizing rhyme and a measured rhythm.

Equally frequently people wove proverbs and other sayings into nonplayful conversation, performing a variety of functions. In Jakobson's terms, proverbs and other sayings always carry a poetic function, for they are structured according to poetic features, such as metrical rhythm, rhyme, and the "regular reiteration of equivalent units" (Jakobson 1960, 358). In addition to a poetic function, however, particular instances express at least one other function as well: emphasizing the relationship between the speaker and hearer, which Jakobson (1960), following Bronislaw Malinowski, refers to as the phatic function.

Domínguez Barajas (2002) explores four phatic uses of proverbs in the daily speech of Mexican transmigrants (censuring, teaching, uniting, and entertaining, all of which address the relationship between speaker and hearer). In the present study *refranes* and *dichos* also expressed these uses. For example, I was aroused from bed by a young woman late one morning in Mexico (and censured): "¡La vida es más bonita cuando se levanta temprano! ¡No sea floja!" (Life is more beautiful when one rises early! Don't be lazy!). Her brother later that day intoned, "La vida enseña más que la escuela" (Life teaches more than school does), as moral commentary on the importance of practical knowledge (a proverb uttered frequently by different people in the network). Others in the network supported me in Chicago at times of personal difficulty with "Uno debe tener valor y fe para seguir adelante" (One must have courage and faith to continue moving forward) and "Mientras que tengas esperanza puedes lograr todo" (When you have hope you can achieve anything) or "Querer es poder" (Where there's a will, there's a way). Once during conversation after a meal in Mexico, a woman and her elderly mother commented that I was *muy católica* (very Catholic), presumably because I went to church with them and took communion. I demurred, saying, well, not very Catholic but more or less, to which they nodded and responded:

"Ni mucho que queme al santo ni tanto que no le alumbre" (Not so much that you burn the saint but enough to illuminate him or her, using the metaphor of lighting a candle in church). In other words, I was not overly religious, but I was religious enough.

A final example of proverb use touches again on an incident already discussed: the ill-considered, and regretted, purchase of a car by a woman in the rancho. My field notes record her brother's use of a proverb to calm her down:

> . . . after buying the car and bringing it back to the rancho, she became very nervous (a nervous wreck by Sunday afternoon, I'd say), because men in the rancho told her the car was going to cost a lot for gas, and that she should have bought a smaller, more economical car. When [Sunday afternoon] she turned to her brother for advice, he said, well, the money's gone now. She protested that the man had said he'd refund it if she didn't like the car, but her brother was skeptical about this. He then tried to reassure her, to calm her nerves, with a *dicho: El dinero va y viene, la vida no* (Money comes and goes, life doesn't) and *Tenemos una vida* (We have one life, i.e., life is worth more than money).

This brief description of poetic genres in the daily speech of this network is intended to indicate the frequency with which they are used, the verbal creativity of those who weave these genres into their talk, and the high regard that network members have for those who excel in such verbal art. This propensity for, and valuing of, artistic and playful language is a key feature of the verbal portrait of these families provided in this chapter. That portrait would not be complete, however, without a brief description of the rural Mexican Spanish dialect characteristic of rancheros from this region and evident in the tapes made for this study. In the transcriptions of these tapes throughout this book, I have left these dialect features unchanged.

Research has begun to describe variation in Mexican Spanish (e.g., Moreno de Alba 1994), but many lacunae remain, especially for rural areas (Lipski 1994, 275). Otto Santa Ana and Claudia Parodi (1998) have described some regional variation, based on interviews in a city within the microregion in which the rancho is located, but no one has yet investigated social variation in this region, such as ranchero or indigenous (*p'urhépecha*) varieties of Spanish. As a step in that direction, features from the audiotapes for this study that diverge from standard Mexican Spanish and that occurred frequently in the speech of at least the older generation in this network are listed below. Although members of the younger generations do sometimes use such features in their speech, they also more frequently articulate the language ideology of purism that pervades modern schooling, a consequence of their increased exposure to formal schooling, either in Mexico or in the United States. People who have been formally schooled believe that there is a "correct" way to talk, and any deviations from this standard, especially those associated with rancheros (or Indians), are "incorrect."[8] This purist ideology applies to both Spanish and English (see Zentella 1997), although no systematic work has yet been done on describing how either variety in Chicago differs from its standard counterpart.

People on both ends of the transnational circuit experience this linguistic ideology, especially in regard to varieties of Spanish. A Spanish teacher (born in Argentina) at a heavily Mexican public high school in Chicago denigrated a young (second-generation) man's use of these linguistic features as *su español ranchereado* (your ranchero Spanish) and believed it his mission to "improve" his students' Spanish by insisting that they avoid these features in favor of their standard counterparts. An elderly woman in the rancho commented to me on the topic of ranchero Spanish: "¡Dice que somos mochos, pero nos comunicamos!" (They say that we are "mochos," but we communicate with each other!).[9] And yet her relatively highly schooled daughter and granddaughter regularly corrected their father and husband's use of *semos* for the standard *somos* (we are) and *venemos* for the standard *venimos* (we come).

Semos and *venemos* are part of a larger set of possibly archaic Spanish features (called *barbarismos* or barbarisms by purists) that have been maintained in ranchero dialect; many of these features (most of those in Table 4.1) can be heard on musical CDs by famous ranchero singers such as Jorge Negrete. These ranchero linguistic features are generally stigmatized as "uneducated speech" in elite Mexican society; but, paradoxically, they seem to be accepted nostalgically when they occur within classic ranchero songs. Thus they express both positive and negative connotations, a microlevel linguistic parallel to the ambivalence characteristic of all ranchero images and representations in the larger Mexican society (and in the United States), as discussed in Chapter 1.

In Table 4.1 ranchero dialect features are arranged according to apparent linguistic level, even though more analysis would determine whether a given feature is the result of lexical, syntactic, or phonological processes. According to extant research on varieties of Mexican Spanish, some of these features may be remnants of an archaic colonial Spanish, and others may have resulted from local indigenous influence (or are

Table 4.1. Ranchero Dialect Features

Standard Spanish	*Variants*	*Gloss*
	Lexical Items	
ahí	ái	over there
así	ansina, asina	in this way
donde (as in *donde está*)	on (as in *on tá*)	where is
mucho	muncho	much, very
nadie	nadien, naiden	no one
pues	pos, pue, pus	well, well then
sí (back channel cue for affirmation)	ehi	yes
	Verb Conjugations	
haya (subjunctive mood)	haiga	there is
quieren (present tense)	queren	they want
somos (present tense)	semos	we are
-ste (preterit past. 2nd sing. suffix)	-tes (dijiste > dijites)	you said
(dijiste; trajiste)	(trujiste > trujites)	you brought
traía (imperfect past)	traiba	I/he brought
trajo (preterit past)	trujo	he/she brought
venimos (present tense)	venemos	we come
veía (imperfect past)	vía	I/he saw
	Phonology	
-ado	-a'o (arado > ara'o)	plough (noun) or ploughed (past participle)
-e	-i (peor > pior; dale > dali; leche > lechi)	poor; give it to him/her; milk
-o	-u (sapo > sapu)	toad
fui/e-	jui/e- (fui/fue > jui/jue)	I was; he/she was
hui-/hi- (h not aspirated)	jui/ji- (huido > juido; hijo > jijo)	escaped (past participle); son

simply regional markers). Specifically, two phonological variables (*e* > *i* and *o* > *u*) parallel similar *p'urhépecha* variables. Paul Friedrich (1971, 171), investigating microregional (across villages) variants in *p'urhépecha*, notes "a general merger of both *e* and *o* with *i* and *u* in both suffixal and base root positions" for many Sierra villages. It is possible that this shift in *p'urhépecha* pronunciations influenced *p'urhépecha* speakers' use of Spanish, and, through interaction, the Spanish of rancheros; but the process seems to be more widespread, since this same feature occurs in many vernacular dialects of Spanish. Many of the other features in the list (perhaps all the remaining features except *ey* and *pues* > *pos, pue',* *pus*) seem to be traceable to "lexical, phonological, and morphological remnants of the old American Spanish koiné (see Cárdenas 1967, Parodi 1995, 39), which was formed in the New World during the sixteenth century" (Santa Ana and Parodi 1998, 35–36) out of the leveling of several peninsular dialects brought from Spain (Parodi 1995).

Interestingly, it is the archaic features that are generally stigmatized rather than those that are the result of other processes, even though the archaic features are not "peculiar to Michoacán" but are found in other parts of Mexico and Latin America (Santa Ana and Parodi 1998, 36). Santa Ana and Parodi claim that the potentially *p'urhépecha*-derived features are simply markers of this region (along with *ehi,* pronounced with a rising intonation, as an affirmative back channel cue); and José Moreno de Alba (1994, 43) provides support for this claim. In contrast, archaic usages such *fui/fue* > *jui/jue, naiden, asina/ansina,* and *haiga,* as well as archaic verb forms such as *ser* > *semos, traer* > *truje, trujiste, trujo, trujimos, trujeron,* and *ver* > *vía* (Cárdenas 1967), are viewed pejoratively as rustic and uneducated, at least when they occur in ordinary speech, if not in commercial ranchero songs.

In this chapter I have provided descriptive background information about the people in this study within the important social contexts of their lives, both in the rancho and in Chicago: their work experiences and attitudes; their educational levels and attitudes, as well as the perceived advantages and disadvantages of binational schooling experiences; the important domain of religion; and, finally, their language use, including a valuing of rhetorical competence and poetic speech and a description of their ranchero dialect. These dimensions of their lives form a basis for better understanding of the remaining chapters of this book, which focus more specifically on particular aspects of identity and language use. In the next chapter I explore the racial aspects of their ranchero/ranchera identity as expressed and constructed in their daily discourse. This provides the background for understanding how this racial ideology underlies their primary framework for speaking, *franqueza* (frank language), the topic of Chapter 6.

First house built in rancho

The plain of San Juanico: agriculture and livestock

Traditional house in rancho

Newer house in rancho

Gathering *aguamiel* from maguey plant in rancho

Back road in rancho

Washing clothes at *pila* in rancho

Chicago Cubs fan with his children in rancho

Author with tortilla *maestra* in rancho

Cooking for family celebration, Chicago

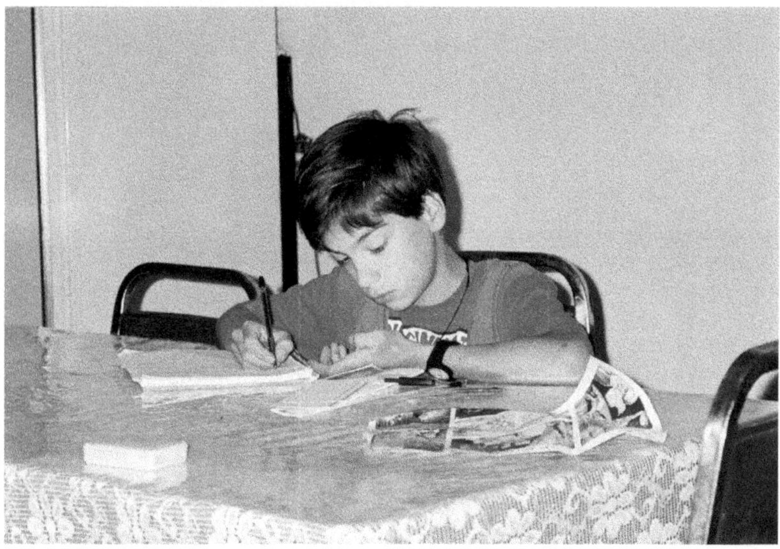

Doing homework in rancho

Learning to be ranchero, Chicago

First communion in rancho

Grandparents and *quinceañera* from Chicago at her celebration in rancho

First communion in Chicago

Family celebration in Chicago park

Receiving blessing before marriage in rancho

Baptism in Chicago

At church in Chicago

After church, 18th Street, Chicago

Father and daughter, 18th Street, Chicago

Dancing at family party, Chicago

Fifth birthday party, Chicago

Women joking at birthday party, Chicago

Classroom in rancho

Children at home with book in rancho

FIVE

Rethinking *Mestizaje*

Racial Discourse among Rancheros

Los Cárabes vinieron de España, los primeros como detectives. . . . *El rey de España los mandó a buscar los restos de un sacerdote o un . . . fraile que había muerto aquí. Le dijeron a dos personas Cárabes, "Tú vas . . . a esa parte, aquí está el mapa, consigues dónde enterraron esos el cuerpo de aquella persona y me traes los huesos."*

Tenían que investigar 'ónde había sido, 'ónde lo . . . posiblemente lo haigan matado o se murió, pero allí lo enterraron. Y el rey . . . o la reina quería los huesos de ese fraile allá. Duraron parece que nueve u once años. Pero lo llevaron, uno, y otro se quedó. Y el que lo llevó allá duró, cuando pudo . . . regresó, pero regresó a Michoacán. Le gustó aquí la tierra, la . . . las güares. [*laughs*]

Y los mandaron a ellos porque eran hombres muy vivos. Ya tenían misiones cumplidas en ese ramo . . . Salieron de España, llegaron a México . . . se quedaron en Michoacán . . . y tuvieron familia con la Malinche si tú quieres [*laughs*] *y, y así se fue el apelativo . . . siguiendo. Y de esa manera se extendieron los Cárabes.* [*chuckles*] *D'ese es la . . . descendencia de los Cárabes.*

The Cárabes came from Spain, the first ones as detectives. The king of Spain ordered them to look for the remains of a priest or a . . . friar who had died here. They told two Cárabes men, "You go . . . to that part, here is the map, find out where they buried the body of that person and bring me the bones."

They had to investigate where it had been, where it . . . possibly they had killed him or he died, but there they buried him. And the king . . . or the queen wanted the bones of that friar there. It seems they lasted nine or eleven years. But they took [the body back], one [of them], and the other stayed. And the one who took it back stayed there, [and] when he could . . . he returned, but he returned to Michoacán. He liked the land here, the . . . the *güares* [indigenous women].[1] [*laughs*]

And they sent them because they were very quick-witted men. They

> already had completed missions in that line [of work]. . . . They left Spain, they arrived in Mexico . . . they stayed in Michoacán . . . and had family with Malinche,[2] if you want [*laughs*], and, and so the surname . . . continued. And in that way the Cárabes spread out [*chuckles*]. That is the . . . lineage of the Cárabes.

These words were spoken to me by a man at the kitchen table in his house in the rancho. He was the first from the rancho to travel to Chicago to work, coming as a contract worker in 1964 during the last year of the U.S. Bracero Program. He is now retired and living back in the rancho where (as noted in Chapter 3) his forebears have lived for centuries. He, like many other adults in this social network of families, carries on his life both in the rancho, where he now spends most of his time, and in Chicago, where five of his six children live, most of them raising families themselves. (One daughter lives with her husband and son in California; another daughter, with her husband and two children, recently returned to Chicago after several years in the rancho, before which they had been in Chicago for twelve years.)

This man and/or his wife frequently visit Chicago, sometimes staying for months at a time (e.g., around the birth of a child), and their children's families in the United States regularly return to the rancho for several weeks' vacation or even for several months to work on special projects (constructing their own houses, helping in the family avocado orchards at crucial times of the year, attending weddings and other fiestas). These visits, of course, are constrained by work and school schedules in Chicago. Construction workers, for example, who sometimes are laid off in Chicago's harsh winter weather, have the flexibility (which comes with no paycheck) to extend their stays in Mexico. Those women and men who work in factories usually do not have such flexibility unless they too are laid off or they quit their jobs, intending to find new ones when they return to Chicago. Sometimes, however, relatives work temporarily in the place of those who go to Mexico for an extended visit, especially when employers want to retain valued employees. Children enrolled in Chicago public (or sometimes Catholic parochial) schools generally are restricted to Christmas, Easter, and summer vacations for their returns to the rancho. Preschool children, however, unconstrained as yet by school schedules, are sometimes sent to be with their grandparents for extended periods. Moreover, many children even into the third generation still are socialized partly in the rancho. This pattern of course varies, as some children go to school entirely in Chicago and grow up and begin to work there, making acquaintances and friends outside the social network in the process. Nevertheless, there is a tie to the rancho that extends into the third generation for most families in the network.

The story related above is the oral tradition that traces the family's origins to Spain, which was told to this man, the eldest brother in his natal family, by his father, who presumably learned it from his own father. Some other families in the rancho trace their ancestry back to Spain. One especially prosperous family, with professional members in Guadalajara, has a Spanish coat of arms on the wall of its architect-designed house. Most people nevertheless readily acknowledge that their ancestors (and those only a few generations back, after the Revolution of 1910–1920) "mixed their blood" with indigenous Mexicans. In a conversation among several women on the morning after we had all spent the night in the "female" bedroom of her home,[3] a young woman whom I know well remarked that *mestizaje* in the rancho is reputed to be relatively recent, having occurred primarily since the Revolution. Others outside of the rancho also have indicated that this rancho was known for being populated by whites.[4]

Although most people in the rancho acknowledge a partially indigenous heritage and thus would be categorized as mestizo (racially mixed), many individuals and even entire families in this rancho are perceived as "white" in the United States until they speak Spanish or Spanish-accented English. That is, many people have blue or green eyes, blond or light brown hair, and light skin (with freckles) that turns red, not brown, in the sun.[5] Others look more evidently mestizo, with tan skin and some indigenous features.

Photos of a number of family forebears show light eyes, skin, and hair. *Mestizaje* in this family is traced to a grandmother and a great-grandfather of the man who told the story quoted above; one of these forebears had both Spanish and Indian ancestry and the other had Spanish, Indian, and African ancestry.[6] This "origins" story, however, illustrates an intensely felt non-Indian (and non-African) identity. Several family members have told this story on different occasions, noting first their Moorish then Spanish then Mexican origins (other families in the rancho omit the Moorish origin but talk of Spain then Mexico and *mestizaje*). One woman even noted that in Chicago people of Middle Eastern origins expected her to speak their language.

During my long-term fieldwork both in Chicago and in the rancho, this sense of ethnic identity emerged in countless conversations. Thus while easily acknowledging their mestizo heritage, the families from this rancho identify nonequivocally as nonindigenous, a claim that is supported by the physical appearance of many individuals and families.

People here sometimes refer to themselves as *blancos* (whites); for example, one man said to me, in reference to distant relatives from another rancho, "Son blancos como nosotros" (They are whites like us). Many of these rancheros are light-skinned and light-eyed, even blond (*güero/a*), which attests to the presence of Spanish, French, and possibly other Europeans in these parts in the past. French troops, for example, were stationed contiguous to the rancho for several years during the French Intervention in Mexico (1862–1867); among other French influences, bakeries in Tingüindín produce *pan blanco* (white bread), also called *pan de vapor* (steamed bread), that closely resembles what is called French bread in the United States.

While the Spanish of this network is lightly sprinkled with *p'urhépecha* words, particularly words for various types of soil and place names, such borrowing of vocabulary is not unusual in language-contact situations. Beyond vocabulary items, some individuals can sing particular songs in *p'urhépecha,* especially the well-known "Flor de canela" (Cinnamon Flower; note the Spanish title), but this knowledge is framed as Other and kept separate, which only confirms a primarily nonindigenous identity.

Thus these rancheros, like others in pockets all over western Mexico, construct themselves as nonindigenous, even while acknowledging their *mestizaje.* Alan Knight (1990, 99) argues that such claims are particularly vocal in contexts (especially "Indian zones" like northwest Michoacán) in which "lower-class *mestizos*... cleave... to their eroding ethnic privilege" as Indians begin to compete with them economically and socially. Though Knight offers a plausible explanation from a research perspective, when this racial ideology is explored at the local level, it is revealed as more than a simple claim to higher social status. It calls into question the category *mestizo* itself. Although this term is widely used in the research literature on Mexico, it is not a category that is emically derived, at least not for all so-called mestizo communities. Rather, it is a term created from outside such communities that is closely tied to colonial racial ideology and, as such, evokes that ideology when used.

Although "race" has been shown to be a social construct rather than a genetically determined category (American Anthropological Association 1998; AAPA 1996), conventional thinking continues late-nineteenth-century notions of "races" (e.g., in U.S. census forms);[7] and the terms *mestizaje* (race mixture) and *mestizos* (those who are "mixed" racially) invoke this ideology. In this sense, it is difficult to "think outside the language"—that is, as long as we use these terms, we perpetuate the assumption that separate races exist and that they have "mixed."

Research literature on Mexico often specifies whether the site of a particular study is an "Indian" or a "mestizo" community, for example. I have rarely, however, heard the word *mestizo* used by the rancheros of this study to refer to themselves. When asked about mestizo communities, many refer to formerly indigenous communities that have gradually become hispanicized over time, through the "crossing" of Spaniards and Indians. Such distancing from *mestizaje,* even while acknowledging some indigenous heritage themselves, clearly reveals ambiguities and locally perceived differences in racial identity among what are lumped together and generically referred to as mestizo communities. After all, communities can become mestizo from a primarily Spanish as well as Indian base, and these two types of mestizo communities can differ sharply on a variety of linguistic and cultural dimensions. As Guillermo de la Peña (1984) has noted, Mexican villages that are physically quite close to one another often contain populations that contrast sharply as social groups and categories within the larger society, and this is especially true in this part of western Mexico. These complexities of identity can be understood better by briefly reviewing *mestizaje* in Mexican history, to which I turn in the next section.

Mestizaje in Mexican History

Race and ethnicity have a complex history in the New World in the confrontation of Europeans, and Africans, with Indians. After the Spanish conquest of Mexico, a hierarchical society based on caste or "race" was established, with Spaniards at the top, followed by *castas* (mixed bloods of various types), then Indians, and then Africans. Although this caste hierarchy evolved toward a more class-based system, especially during the nineteenth century, colonial racial ideology endured and continues to underlie Mexican society even today (Lomnitz-Adler 1992). Most studies of Mexico and Mexicans have assumed that *mestizaje* has been so thorough that the two resulting social categories, the (remaining) indigenous Indians and mestizos, are generally indistinguishable from one another (e.g., Foster 1988 [1967]). That is, it is widely assumed that there has been so much genetic and cultural mixing in both groups that one cannot tell who is Indian and who is mestizo by physical characteristics alone.

For example, Claudio Esteva-Fabregat (1995) shows that *mestizaje* in Mexico, as in all of Ibero-America, was rapid and thorough for several reasons. First, the conquistadors mated freely and frequently with Indian women. In the early stages of the conquest, Spanish women were rare;

and when they were present, they usually lived in urban centers, so *mestizaje* was more intense in the countryside. According to Benedict Warren (1985), the P'urhepecha royalty offered their daughters to the high-status Spaniards in order to establish kinship ties with them. The gathering of recalcitrant Indians into settlements called *congregaciones* furthered contact, and thus mixing, between Indians and nonelite Spaniards who lived in the towns. The municipal township center in this study, in fact, was created as just such a *congregación* in 1601 (Del Paso y Troncoso 1945), so we can assume that rapid mixing took place in this microregion as well, at least early in the conquest.

Another reason that Esteva-Fabregat (1995) gives for the rapid mixing was that many of the Spanish who migrated to Mexico for conquest and colonization were already "Euro-*mestizos*" (like the family in the origins story at the beginning of this chapter), who had a more flexible and positive attitude toward *mestizaje* because they had "mixed" in Spain with those of north African origin. Ramón Gutiérrez (1991, 198) notes that many people (in New Mexico) described as mestizos racially were identical in skin color to those listed as *españoles* (i.e., their skin was "dark"). Whatever the reasons, racial mixing seems to have been so extensive that mestizos relatively quickly overtook Spaniards in number. According to Woodrow Borah (1954), Mexico had few people of unmixed blood by the late eighteenth century. These official numbers may even be an undercount of mestizos, since illegitimate offspring of Spanish fathers who were not recognized by them were raised in indigenous communities by their mothers and thus were counted as Indians. Such early, rapid, and widespread *mestizaje,* however, does not account for the diversity of racial/ethnic identities in contemporary northwestern Michoacán. Not only are communities locally distinguished as either "indigenous" or "nonindigenous," but the "nonindigenous" are further distinguished as either Spanish in origin or indigenous in origin.

Thus another common assumption in many studies of Mexico that is problematic in this region is that mestizo (i.e., nonindigenous) communities have been, in Guillermo Bonfil Batalla's (1996) term, "de-Indianized" historically. That is, they were originally indigenous communities which, through mixture with Spaniards and/or acculturation to "Spanish" culture, gradually lost their indigenous identities, as in the community studied by David Frye (1996). Jane Hill and Kenneth Hill (1986, 49), in another such study, explore a syncretic language (*mexicano*) in central Mexico that shows historical traces of the indigenous language mixed with Spanish, even though Indian identity there is "covert and ambivalent."

On a national level, state ideology since the Revolution of 1910 has promoted Mexico as a mestizo nation, valorizing, at least officially, Mexico's indigenous past but promoting the acculturation of Indians to the mestizo state (Knight 1990; Lomnitz-Adler 1992). In contrast to the widely accepted representation of Mexico as a mestizo nation, Bonfil Batalla (1996, xvi) argues that *mestizaje* in Mexico has not been complete, at least in cultural terms. He critiques the official representation of Mexico (calling it "the imaginary Mexico") as the synthesis of two different cultures, that of Spain and that of indigenous, preconquest Mexico. He argues instead that two world views and civilizational bases simply co-exist (though they interpenetrate) in modern Mexico. What has occurred is not a true transformation in culture, he claims, but only a transformation in ideology. The official government ideology promotes images of racial and cultural mixture and integration. But in reality Spanish (or more generally Western) culture has only been superimposed upon a Mesoamerican indigenous base which still underlies most of Mexico, what he calls "México profundo" (deep Mexico).

From colonial times to the present (and even Bonfil Batalla does not question this) a dichotomy has dominated perceptions of Mexico: urban/Spanish/elite vs. rural/Indian/peasant. Since much of Mexico's population is rural, Bonfil Batalla claims the predominance of a Mesoamerican (rural) base in Mexican society. Although the urban elite disdain what is rural/Indian/peasant, even they have appropriated some Mesoamerican cultural practices over time, such as celebrating the Day of the Dead (see Chapter 4). Bonfil Batalla further argues that mestizos who claim to be non-Indian, especially those who are rural peasants, actually have only been "de-Indianized" superficially, by having had a Western ideology imposed on a basically Mesoamerican civilization. The process of "de-Indianization" is "the loss of these groups' original collective identity as a result of the process of colonial domination" (Bonfil Batalla 1996, xviii).

Although Bonfil Batalla in some respects accurately describes two coexisting Mexicos (a "first world" country on top of a "third world" country), he unfortunately generalizes rural Mexicans as fundamentally "Indian." In stark contrast to both the imaginary Mexico and "México profundo," the rancheros in this study represent yet another alternative. Like other ranchero communities in western Mexico, they emphasize, and often physically reflect, their Spanish and/or other European heritage. Yet most anthropological research on this region to date has focused either on the indigenous P'urhepecha (e.g., Friedrich 1977, 1986) or on mestizo groups that are presumed to be "de-Indianized" campesinos (e.g., Foster 1988 [1967]; Dinerman 1982). This may reflect a preoccupation with what is presumed to be more "authentic" or a desire to study, and identify with, the most politically and economically oppressed groups (i.e., the indigenous). Les Field (1998), for example, argues that mestizos have been understudied and not well understood because they are seen as lacking in cultural authenticity. Mestizos, then, either are considered uninteresting because they are not Indians or are interesting only because they have an indigenous past. Either one, of course, involves an Othering of Indianness, even when it is positively valorized (and romanticized), that generally ignores communities that are not indigenous or at least evidently "de-Indianized."

In spite of this public representation of Mexico as a mestizo nation, a more complex variety of identities has endured at the local level, especially in rural western Mexico. Several studies of isolated rancheros in western Mexico who identify strongly with the Spanish side of their heritage (Taylor 1933; González 1974; Barragán 1990b) have revealed this complexity. Spanish predominance in such ranchos might be the result of the increased immigration from Spain, especially from northern provinces (González 1995) at the beginning of the eighteenth century. Such origins might have been maintained through the ranchero tradition of endogamy (Barragán 1997) in order to maintain *pureza de sangre.* In Spain this concept had distinguished Christians from Moors and Jews as well as *conversos* (Jews who had converted to Catholicism under pressure); many of them escaped persecution, at least temporarily, by migrating to the New World as Spaniards (Sanders 1978).[8] Purity of blood formed part of the Spanish code of honor that was brought by the conquistadors to the New World, resulting in a racially based status hierarchy (Gutiérrez 1991).

During an interview about the history of the rancho, a man from a family of non-Moorish Spanish origins volunteered to me in a confidential tone that a particular family was not really Spanish (*No son españoles*) because they were *moros* (Moors from Spain). Although this term is sometimes used elsewhere in Latin America simply to mean "dark-skinned," here it only refers to those who were "mixed" during the seven hundred years of Moorish dominance in Spain before coming to Mexico as colonists. Thus a doctrine of racial purity that was brought from Spain more than five hundred years ago was alive and well in 1996 (the date of the interview) and the families who have lived side by side in this microregion for centuries are still distinguishing among themselves according to their (original) ethnic identity in Spain.

Although the racial hierarchy has evolved into one based more on class, colonial racial ideology has persisted in Mexico; race still inflects class distinctions (Lomnitz-Adler 1992), and, as already noted, rural mestizos are "Indianized" by urban elite Mexicans. This point has not been lost on the rancheros of this study; while quite aware of their lower, Indian-like status in the eyes of the elite, they consistently distinguish themselves from the Indians.

As noted in Chapter 3, oral tradition traces the family under study here to Asturias, a northern province of Spain; and other family names in the rancho are traceable to other northern provinces (e.g., Galicia and Basque Country). Many marriages in this community are endogamous (i.e., with others from the rancho or the microregion or with rancheros from neighboring states in western Mexico such as Jalisco or Guanajuato), whether the courtship developed in Mexico or in Chicago. As already noted, oral tradition in this region also indicates that *mestizaje* primarily has occurred in recent generations, since the Mexican Revolution of 1910–1920. Some families in the rancho are experiencing *mestizaje* now, through the marriage of *güeros* (people with light skin, often blond and blue-eyed) with *prietos* (people with darker skin, sometimes described as swarthy) or *morenos* (people with tan or brown skin). Whatever the historical trajectory of individual ranchos and ranchero families, however, studies of ranchero groups in this region reveal significant differences from studies of so-called mestizo societies, especially in terms of self-perceived identities and individualist ideologies.

Taylor's (1933) early study, for example, describes the "Spanish Mexican" peasant community of Arandas, Jalisco, located in Los Altos of Jalisco, a region directly northwest of northwestern Michoacán and (as noted in Chapter 2) the cradle of ranchero society. Western Los Altos (including Arandas) was colonized by Spaniards at the end of the sixteenth century, and ranchos were created there primarily for pasturing sheep, cattle, and horses. The people of Arandas experienced some *mestizaje* with Indians and Africans (who were brought to the region as slaves), but the non-Spanish contribution to the mixture was slight. Taylor, tracing archival records from the eighteenth and nineteenth centuries, shows a rapid absorption of mestizos and mulattos by dominant whites, both through marriage and through "irregular liaisons" (Taylor 1933, 17).

The works of González (1974, 1991), Barragán (1990b, 1997; Barragán et al. 1994), Cochet (1991), and others similarly describe rural communities that are neither indigenous nor de-Indianized, illustrating the Mexican saying *la güera del rancho* (the white/blond of the rancho). The present study continues in this tradition, providing a contemporary ethnography of rancheros similar in identity to those studied by Taylor,

González, and Barragán; but it departs from this earlier work by focusing on rancheros who are less isolated from regional indigenous communities and who live within a transnational context.

The Local Setting, Michoacán: *Nosotros y los Otros* (Ourselves and the Others)

As explained in Chapter 3, the rancho is nestled amid rolling hills on the western edge of the highland plateau called the Meseta Tarasca in northwest Michoacán. The Tarascans or, in their own language, the P'urhepecha in the *meseta* primarily live in villages or towns recognized as indigenous. Many adult women wear distinctive skirts, belts, embroidered blouses, and, most significantly, a particular type of rebozo or large woven shawl, black with thin, bright blue lengthwise stripes and complexly knotted ends. This distinctive clothing and their distinct language, *p'urhépecha,* mark an indigenous identity in this part of Mexico, and ethnic boundaries between the P'urhepecha (referred to in Spanish as *tarascos*) and rancheros are scrupulously maintained here.

The status hierarchy of this region of northwest Michoacán places the indigenous P'urhepecha at the bottom, rancheros in the middle, and the urban elite at the top. Rancheros mostly live in rural hamlets and make occasional excursions to nearby cities, although increasingly they live in small towns and cities as well. While people who index a noticeably ranchero identity with their clothing, their dialect of Spanish (as detailed in Chapter 4), or other behavior sometimes suffer disdain in the cities, they themselves show disdain for *catrines* ("citified" people) (see Chapter 6). As Barragán notes, rancheros approaching cities are aware that *Desde lejos nos conocen* (They recognize us from afar) (Barragán 1990a, 87). Yet except when doing business (e.g., receiving medical services) in cities that have an urban elite population, these rancheros can avoid most contacts with those above them in the regional status hierarchy, interacting primarily with other rancheros or with *indígenas.* In interactions with other rancheros, their demeanor and language are relatively egalitarian. In interactions with the indigenous people, in contrast, these rancheros expect and often receive deference, at least publicly. Friedrich (1977) notes the extreme hostility toward these "outsiders" on the part of the indigenous P'urhepecha of this region, which suggests that such public deference may be a form of resistance, a "weapon of the weak" (Scott 1990).

Identities are clearest in their contrast with others; in fact, identities are constructed in opposition to these others: "we" are not "them."

Within northwest Michoacán rancheros and P'urhepecha distinguish themselves from each other, sometimes fiercely. As Barth (1969, 15) noted, it is "the ethnic boundary that defines the group, not the cultural stuff that it encloses." Otherwise, ethnic groups in interaction, as rancheros and *indígenas* have been for centuries in Mexico (Barragán 1997), would tend to exchange "cultural stuff" over time. In fact, such exchange has occurred here in both directions, including the movement of individual people, and yet the boundary between these two groups has remained distinct.

The rancheros in this study maintain racial boundaries between themselves and the indigenous people in both linguistic and nonlinguistic ways, as I detail in this chapter. Many instances recorded in my field notes illustrate the racial ideology that values lighter skin, with which these rancheros construct their identity. Talk that indexes a primarily nonindigenous racial identity is frequent within these families, in both Mexico and Chicago, especially among the older generation. Such talk (at least on some occasions) entails ambivalence and acknowledgment of their own (partial) indigenous heritage among the younger, more schooled generation, because in federally supported Mexican schools they are taught the nationalist ideology that proclaims pride in Mexico's indigenous heritage. In school they are taught *Todos somos indios* (We are all Indians) and *Todos somos iguales* (We are all equal) (Levinson 2001). Yet their families' comments about the indigenous people, whether positive or negative, always make it clear that they are different (and usually of lower status). This ambivalence and ambiguity about racial identity is revealed in the analysis of tape-recorded discourse in the last section of this chapter. In the next section I discuss the variety of ways, both linguistic and nonlinguistic, in which racial boundaries are maintained between rancheros and *indígenas.*

Maintaining Differences

Barth (1969) explores the persistence of ethnic groups as discrete categories despite the flow of people across groups. He notes that the traditional, and simplistic, view that it is geographical isolation and social isolation that sustain cultural difference is inadequate to explain the "social processes of exclusion and incorporation" that result in the persistence of these categories (Barth 1969, 9–10). Rather than each cultural group developing its values and characteristics over time in interaction with its environment exclusive of other groups—what Michael Omi and Howard Winant (1994) call the primordial view of ethnicity—ethnic groups and identities are created and maintained precisely because of interaction with those perceived as Others. In-group members share understandings of criteria that distinguish themselves from outsiders; and social relations cover all domains for in-group members but are restricted, often to a commercial domain, with those outside the group. This "structuring of interaction . . . allows the persistence of cultural differences" (Barth 1969, 16).

Rancheros and their neighboring indigenous Others in this region are a classic example of Barth's theory. They clearly signal their own identity through various signs, and their individualist ideology supports criteria that distinguish them from the indigenous people (see Chapter 6). Boundaries are sharply maintained by these rancheros through racial discourse, styles of clothing, and other social practices. They are not isolated from interaction with the indigenous, yet this interaction generally is restricted to the commercial domain of their lives. Not extending these contacts to other domains (e.g., kinship or friendship), in fact, is one way of structuring and thus maintaining the ethnic boundary between these two groups.

COMMERCIAL INTERACTION Ranchero men and women interact with indigenous persons for commercial purposes. Early most Sunday mornings many of the women in the rancho travel (by bus unless a man drives them) to the nearby Indian market, where they purchase most of their fresh food for the week, returning in time to go to mass at 10:30 A.M. At the market—a visual splendor—they buy vegetables, meat, and other household items such as wooden spoons and earthenware cooking pots (they raise their own chickens and birds, and some have fruit orchards, so they do not generally buy these items). On a daily basis families buy bread and other food that is made and marketed by the indigenous woman known as "Margarita" who walks door to door late every afternoon in the rancho. The *cena* (evening supper) is often made up of this bread and food: various kinds of *atole,* tamales, and whole-wheat *gorditas* (shaped like English muffins).

Sometimes ranchera women buy *güanengas* (heavily embroidered handmade blouses) from indigenous women in nearby villages, which form part of the traditional P'urhepecha female attire. Young ranchera girls are dressed in these blouses and sometimes in an entirely indigenous outfit (with skirt, apron, special belt, and rebozo), to celebrate the Day of the Virgin on December 12 or on other occasions, including ethnic heritage days celebrated at school in Chicago. Although these rancheras sometimes dress their children and grandchildren in this indigenous clothing, however, it is important to note that they only do so on special occasions, when the clothing symbolizes the traditional dress of their state, Michoacán, and not indigenous personal identity. Such occasions frame the wearing of this clothing as "special," not as a part of their regular, daily expression of identity.

Ranchero men who can afford it hire indigenous men or younger ranchero relatives as their *trabajadores* (workers) to help them in their avocado orchards and with other tasks on their property. Sometimes indigenous bands are hired to provide the music at a birthday party, but at more important fiestas like the annual Patron Saint's Day, *quinceañera* celebrations, or weddings, much more money is spent on ranchero-style mariachi bands. Thus the interactions that ranchero men and women have with the nearby P'urhepecha are almost entirely restricted to commercial exchanges in which they buy services and products of indigenous labor.

SIGNS OF DIFFERENCE Clothing is a visible means for expressing ranchero identity. For men, this includes cowboy hats and boots, fancy leatherwork (*pitiado*) on their belts, and fitted shirts and jeans (see photos). In contrast to the upper-class elite of Mexico City (seen, for example, on television) and to many indigenous men, rancheros usually have mustaches. For married rancheras, daily clothing includes crisply ironed blouses, knee-length skirts with gingham aprons over them, and a solid-color rebozo in the evening or during winter. On dressier occasions special fitted suits or dresses, bought in Chicago or nearby Zamora, and *tacones* (high heels) show their respectability. For young, unmarried women, T-shirts (*playeras*) with jeans and hair either worn long or pulled back in a ponytail, with large curving "bangs," are their daily badges of identity. On dressier occasions these young women expertly apply makeup and wear spotlessly clean, freshly ironed blouses with either skirts or pants. Young girls are clothed in fancy dresses with abundant lace and ruffles for Sunday mass or other special occasions. For all women, special gold earrings with semiprecious stones made in nearby Cotija, long known as a traditionally white ranchero settlement, are treasured items worn on special occasions. (Indigenous women, in contrast, wear large thick gold hoops that index their own identity.)

Other social practices that index ranchero identity include food consumption and visiting to socialize, both within the rancho and when traveling to other villages or towns in the region. All socializing is with other rancheros in other ranchos and towns. Although they eat many indigenous foods made from corn (tortillas, tamales, etc.), they also frequently eat breads and other foods made with wheat, a grain introduced by the Spanish; and a preference for foods made from wheat, such as *pan de vapor* (French bread) and *tamales de harina* ("white bread" tamales), still carries some prestige.

These rancheros continually express their difference from the indigenous people, especially since, with increasing *mestizaje,* they are less and less distinguishable from them physically. They reaffirm values, primarily a liberal individualist ideology (see Chapter 6), that they perceive as uncharacteristic of the indigenous, and they dress and speak in ways that express a clearly non-Indian identity.

LANGUAGE DIFFERENCES Language, of course, is a prime medium for indexing ethnic identity. The clearest distinction here is the use of *p'urhépecha* rather than Spanish. Those rancheros who know some *p'urhépecha* frame it as "special," not as part of their regular Spanish language identity. Others make a display of not knowing this language at all, claiming that its sounds are too difficult for them to pronounce. Many people in the rancho remark on the similarity between *p'urhépecha* and English sounds, claiming that such similarities enable *p'urhépecha* speakers to learn English more quickly than they themselves do. The implicit assumption that *p'urhépecha* is "strange," even though its speakers supposedly learn English easily, effectively distances monolingual Spanish speakers (the rancheros) from the indigenous people just as surely as do their clothing styles.

A second way in which rancheros here distinguish themselves from the indigenous people through language involves the use of Spanish. People note that the indigenous people speak with *un cierto tono* (a certain tone) or that "they don't speak Spanish very well." Conversations with them accomplish business but are not characterized by *confianza*—in fact, quite the opposite. While a lack of such trust is the norm between strangers, people begin to build *confianza* (through talk that establishes network connections) when these strangers are determined to have similar ranchero backgrounds, rather than maintaining distance as they do with people perceived to be Indian. Thus these rancheros use language, both *p'urhépecha* and dialectal Spanish, as a sign that identifies indigenous Others.

They also use language in a more global way to distinguish themselves from indigenous (and other) Mexicans. A characteristically ranchero verbal style, *franqueza* (frankness), enacts a self-assertive, proud stance that indexes the individualist ideology deeply ingrained in ranchero identity (see Chapter 6). Because this verbal style marks people as ranchero, it is a particularly clear way for them to distinguish themselves from indigenous Mexicans, whom they perceive as shamefully humble. In the following section I explore another way in which language is used to maintain boundaries between these two groups: discourse in which racial differences are explicitly remarked upon. Although my presence, especially early in my fieldwork, was no doubt a catalyst for some of this discourse,[9] it has been constant enough across contexts, topics, and time (and recorded on audiotapes in my absence) to indicate an ongoing and acute concern with racial identity.

RACIAL DISCOURSE Not all examples of discursive boundary maintenance involve negative evaluations of the indigenous, although many do. Some people note that they are particularly healthy because they have some "Indian blood," but the reverse comment is never made, indicating that a non-Indian or primarily Spanish identity is the unmarked norm. Others note, "Sí, hay morenos aquí, pero no son indígenas" (Yes, there are darker-skinned people here [in the rancho], but they aren't indigenous).[10]

Finally, some attribute positive characteristics to the indigenous but in doing so describe them as different from themselves. One woman explained: "Somos de la misma raza, pero ellos son indígenas. Todos somos mexicanos; somos iguales. Nos llamen 'señora' y 'señorita,' pero es 'María' a las indígenas" (We are of the same race, but they are indigenous. All of us are Mexicans; we are equal. We are called "señora" and "señorita," but it's "María" to the indigenous women). She continued: "El indígena es muy trabajador, sabe mucho de agricultura, sabe hacer textil, sabe trabajo de barro, madera, muebles, cucharas, bueno, todas. Es una persona muy inteligente" (The indigenous are hard-working, they know a lot about agriculture, they know how to make textiles, they know [how to make] pottery, woodwork, furniture, spoons, well, everything. They are very intelligent). This way of talking about the indigenous people is contradictory about differences in status. On the one hand, "we are all equal"; but on the other, different terms of address are used. Indigenous women are addressed with a generic "María," indexing their lower status, while rancheras are addressed with a respectful "señora" or "señorita."

DIFFERENT PERSPECTIVES ON DIFFERENCE An interview with "Margarita" (the young indigenous woman from Tarecuato who walks door to door daily in the rancho selling fresh breads and other food and drinks made from corn and wheat, as did her aunt before her) provides an indigenous perspective on these naming practices.[11] At the very beginning of the interview, smiling knowingly, she somewhat defiantly announced that the name by which we knew her was not her real name. When we asked, she revealed her real name to us, explaining that she came to be known as "Margarita" when people in the rancho simply assumed that her name was the same as her aunt's, whom she replaced selling bread in the rancho. Thus she claimed the false naming herself, remaining "closed" to the rancheros, who in turn describe such a "closed" demeanor as linked to a lack of *confianza.* One man noted in this regard: "Los indígenas, no [nos] tienen confianza" (The indigenous don't trust us). He continued, "Primero dicen una cosa y luego otra cosa" (First they say one thing, then another), flipping his hand over to emphasize their changeability: "Son muy cerrados" (They are very closed).

When asked to describe the differences between people in her indigenous pueblo and the people in the rancho, "Margarita" claimed that the only difference was in the way the indigenous people were treated (those in the rancho looked down on them) but that in other respects, including the way in which people in both communities lived, they were the same: "Vivimos igual" (We live in the same manner). She may have been referring here to the traditionally shared level of poverty, but in this she is now mistaken. Largely because of dollars earned in Chicago, people in the rancho enjoy a substantially raised standard of living that includes indoor plumbing, electricity, renovated houses, and pickup trucks. Certainly some indigenous families also benefit from migrant dollars, but the indigenous homes I visited in this microregion, including this one, do not share the comforts of almost all houses in the rancho. These homes, for example, had dirt floors, outhouses, and sometimes bed frames but no mattresses. The ongoing improvement of ranchero homes, both in the rancho and in Chicago, is emblematic of their commitment toward *el progreso* (progress), a value which they believe the indigenous P'urhepecha do not share with them. Thus the indigenous "don't progress" (unspoken: as we do, in going to Chicago, making money, buying land in the rancho and homes in Chicago, and planting avocados as an entrepreneurial enterprise).

As already noted, such an unequivocal claim to a nonindigenous identity is most often and most clearly expressed by the older generation, people in their forties and up who belong to the first generation to migrate to Chicago. Members of the second generation express this identity variably: some express it flatly;[12] others do not express it at all; and still others express it, but with an ironic detachment. Members of this second generation have experienced more formal schooling than their parents, although there are mixed patterns in this schooling (see Chapter 4). Some have received formal schooling only in Mexico and are working in the United States. Others have received virtually all their formal schooling in the United States, and still others have experienced schooling in both places. Wherever they have been schooled, however, they learn that Mexico is a mestizo nation; pride in Mexico's indigenous heritage, taught explicitly in Mexico, is also promoted by community organizations and a few schools in Mexican neighborhoods in Chicago. Many in this generation also have noted that non-Mexicans in Chicago, especially whites, assume that Mexicans are "mixed-race," although these same white people also sometimes claim that white-looking Mexicans must really be "white."

Many members of the second generation who live in Chicago thus express ambivalence and ambiguity regarding ethnic/racial identity, as explored later in this chapter in an analysis of an excerpt of discourse tape-recorded for me (I was not present) in a van that was traveling to Mexico for the Christmas holidays. The talk on this tape shows that a nonindigenous identity is still a basic assumption, but here it is joked about (as is ranchero "progress"), perhaps due partially to the mixed messages that they have learned at home and at school and partially to the transnational perspective that they acquire in moving back and forth between Mexico and the United States. Before turning to the analysis of this discourse, however, I first consider racial categories in the United States and the place—or lack of it—of Mexicans within them.

Chicago: Racial Categories

Mexican ethnicity in the United States historically has been structured into a disadvantaged minority position; that is, Mexicans as a group have had a disproportionate share of low-level jobs. Yet this historical legacy is changing: U.S. Mexicans are now principally located in urban areas, which have a wider range of employment opportunities (Nelson and Tienda 1997). Massey (1981) cites the declining isolation of the barrio and a degree of assimilation into Anglo society, with less residential segregation for Mexicans than for Puerto Ricans and others (Massey and Denton 1989, 1993). Candace Nelson and Marta Tienda (1997, 13) predict that "class divisions could become more salient than ethnicity as Chicanos become more integrated into the non-subordinate part of the labor force," though this depends on the process of immigration and the vitality of the economy. Fernando Peñalosa (1995) also claims that caste is moving to class, as the Mexican-origin population in the United States becomes more and more class-stratified.

Omi and Winant (1994, 66) argue that the United States is moving from a "racial dictatorship" to a "racial democracy," albeit slowly, painfully, and unevenly. They distinguish between race, a social and historical construct that fluctuates in meaning, and racism, the use of "essentialist categories of race" (Omi and Winant 1994, 71) to structure domination. Although racism persists, it is, like all hegemonic projects, incompletely dominant—there are "cracks" in it that allow for challenge and thus change (Ortner 1996). From an imagined community of whiteness (Basch et al. 1994, 40) that was used to unite various European groups in a new nation against Others, then, the United States is moving toward an imagined community of cultural pluralism (Basch et al. 1994) and no doubt toward newer forms of *mestizaje,* mixtures of what are now considered different ethnic and/or racial groups.

Historically, however, racial categories in the United States developed according to a dichotomy between white and nonwhite, with race perceived as being biologically or genetically based (Denton and Massey 1989; Omi and Winant 1994; Rodríguez and Cordero-Guzmán 1992). The white category itself, of course, emerged in response to the presence of nonwhites, initially Africans and Native Americans and then Asians and Hispanics/Latinos (Omi and Winant 1994); and "black" or "African American" was defined, both socioculturally and legally, by the presence of any African descent (Denton and Massey 1989; Omi and Winant 1994). As Víctor Rodríguez (1997) has pointed out, only whites were included in the imagined community of the United States; and recent research by Nilda Flores-González (1999) has shown that this imagined community ("real Americans") is still perceived as white by Mexican and Puerto Rican college students in Chicago. Moreover, a categorical perception of race is still evident in the U.S. census item on race, which proceeds from white to black then to the rest of the nonwhite categories (Elías-Olivares and Farr 1991); and it is evident as well in the coding procedures that have been used by the U.S. census (Denton and Massey 1989). Although the 2000 census allowed Americans to indicate more than one race and put the item regarding Hispanic background before rather than after the race item, racial categories still remain, at least partly in order to count population groups for entitlement programs.

When Mexicans or other Hispanics/Latinos migrate to the United States, they confront a racial scheme that differs from the one they are familiar with in their countries of origin. In contrast to the categorical view of race in the United States, in Latin American countries, including Mexico, racial descriptors constitute a continuum, from white to black and/or Indian, depending on the predominant lower-status population. For example, Puerto Rico had a negligible presence of Indians and a substantial presence of Africans as well as white Spaniards, whereas in Mexico Indians outnumber Africans historically (Denton and Massey 1989). In the U.S. scheme, with a persisting white/nonwhite dichotomy, Mexicans have had an ambiguous place: at times categorized as white and at other times categorized as a nonwhite minority, although regional differences have been significant in this regard. Texas, for example, "where Mexican Americans have come closest to being treated like a racial caste" (Skerry 1993, 20), is quite different from other parts of the Southwest; and the entire Southwest is strikingly different from the Midwest. In Chicago, for instance, Mexicans are sometimes treated as yet another "white ethnic" population (especially politically); and Mexican as well as Puerto Rican politicians have ties to the Democratic organization in the city.

Peter Skerry (1993) claims Mexicans are an ambivalent minority, sometimes identifying as white and other times as a racial minority akin to African Americans. He cites census data from 1980 and 1990 to illustrate this split: 53.2 percent of Mexican Americans self-identified in 1980 as "White," 1.8 percent as "Black," and 45.0 percent as "Other Race"; 50.6 percent self-identified in 1990 as "White," 1.2 percent as "Black," and 48.2 percent as "Other Race" (Skerry 1993, 17). Identity categories are not always chosen, however, but are imposed by dominant groups and ideologies. Recent research indicates that some second-generation Mexicans and other Hispanics/Latinos in Chicago are beginning to view Latino/Hispanic as a racial category in itself, to which they belong (Flores-González 1999). Nicholas DeGenova (1998) indicates a similar kind of racializing of the Latino category among adult Mexicans in Chicago. All research indicates that few Hispanics/Latinos, even those with a partial African heritage, identity themselves as black (Denton and Massey 1989), possibly because of the benefits of being white and the disadvantages of being black in the United States and perhaps also because they are not African American culturally. Since the more limited African presence in Mexico was forced to blend into the general mestizo population (Lomnitz-Adler 1992), even fewer Mexicans than other Hispanics/Latinos in the United States would identify themselves as black. Consequently, the "Black" category is irrelevant for most Mexicans in the United States; only the "White" and "Other Race" categories are potentially relevant.

In a Chicago study that explored reasons for the undercount of Mexicans during census taking, Elías-Olivares and Farr (1991) found the race item the most problematic of all on the 1988 census form used in the study. Virtually all residents who participated in the study objected to the racial categories listed as choices, claiming that an option should have been included for their race. As in other studies (see Rodríguez 2000), most participants in this study did not view themselves as either "White" or "Black"; rather, they self-identified as Mexican, Puerto Rican, and so forth, and even (a few) as Hispanic or Latino, after using the "Other Race" category. Statements such as "We're not here—we don't count!" were common responses to this item. One resident said, code-switching from Spanish to English, "*Pos blanco, quiere decir un americano, no? Completamente* a white person" (Then white, that means an American, no? Completely a white person).

Both in Mexico and in Chicago, the rancheros in this study use U.S. racial categories in their discourse, due both to the heavily intertwined history of the United States and Mexico and to the extensive transnational flows of people, goods, and ideas during the last century. In Chicago people make categorical references to groups in conversations: for example to *gente mexicana* (Mexican people), *gente güera* (white people), or *los güeros* (the whites). Similarly, the terms used for African Americans, *negro* (black) or the more polite *moreno* (brown), are used both in Mexico and in Chicago, always in a way that distinguished them as different. A woman who has long lived in Chicago once noted in a conversation about education that there had been much racism between Mexicans and blacks at a particular high school in Chicago but that things were better (in 1995), because they had new directors at the school. During a conversation in the rancho, a man who had worked in Chicago for a few years before being deported compared the Indians in Mexico with lower-class blacks in the United States in terms of social problems such as a high birth rate (an ironic comparison, as this man has five children). In spite of such stereotypic generalizations, however, it is invariably the case that when members of these families meet individual African Americans or U.S. Native Americans they treat them as individuals and even develop friendships with them, sometimes commenting explicitly on how important it is not to judge people on first appearances.

Sometimes generalizations about groups link them to specific characteristics, often in a way in which ranchero values and identities are affirmed by contrast with others. In two typical conversations in a kitchen in Chicago, people noted the differences among whites, blacks, and Mexicans in terms of the ability to do hard work. As she cooked in her kitchen, Rosario talked about the number of white and black women who "leave the line" (quitting the factory job of painting mottos and other material onto plastic drinking glasses) after only a few hours or days, implying that only Mexican women can endure the very hard work. Similarly, her husband, José, on another occasion in their kitchen claimed that only Mexican men could endure the hard work on *el traque* (the railroad track): "Todos son mexicanos, es que los güeros no—pa' el traque no. . . . No pueden con el trabajo, es muy pesado" (All are Mexican, it's that the whites, no—on the track no. . . . They can't endure the work, it's very hard).

These rancheros, then, use U.S. racial categories in their discourse, especially since they are not entirely different (in the racial order) from the colonial racial ideology that still persists in Mexico. What is different in the two systems is the race/class continuum (Mexico) vs. discrete racial categories (United States). Peñalosa (1995, 411) argues that, given the diversity among people of Mexican descent, researchers should stop "trying to find the 'typical' or 'true,' and seek rather to establish the range of variation" among Mexicans in the United States. He suggests first differentiating among the Mexican American regional subcultures of the Spanish-descent Hispanos of New Mexico/Colorado, the Tejanos of Texas, and the Chicanos of southern California. The Midwest, especially urban areas like Chicago, is yet another regional subculture, one where the Mexican presence has been built entirely by immigration (Kerr 1977) in the context of a predominantly immigrant milieu (Holli and Jones 1995 [1977]; Farr 2004, 2005). In addition to such diversity within the United States, there is diversity among Mexicans in Mexico, including their various identities as rancheros, different groups of indigenous Mexicans, and urban Mexicans of all socioeconomic classes.

Given such diversity (including phenotypic diversity), how are Mexicans placed in the discrete racial categories of the United States? Manuel Gamio's work in the 1920s showed that white Mexicans were not segregated, especially if they spoke English. In contrast, darker Mexicans were not allowed into segregated facilities (Peñalosa 1995). More recently, Edward Telles and Edward Murguia (1990) showed that income differences among Mexican Americans could be traced to discrimination based on phenotype; that is, light and medium-complexioned Mexican Americans had significantly higher incomes than dark-skinned Mexicans.

Some members of the social network in this study have had experiences similar to those reported by Gamio in the 1920s; that is, the lighter-complexioned among them have been taken to be white, at least initially, in a variety of contexts. Several different people have joked, for example, about how easy it is for Mexican *güeros* to cross the border without papers. On one occasion when three members of one extended family were crossing into the United States, the father, Javier, handed the border officials some papers for himself and his daughter-in-law (who did not in fact yet have her own papers), but his son Lalo was not even asked for papers: "Because," he said with a broad smile, "I'm *güero!*" Another story recounts the crossing of a young blonde woman from the rancho who was told to speak a few words of English in front of the officials (the only words she in fact knew at that point); as they had hoped, she successfully crossed into the United State without papers. On a less successful occasion Ramón, another *güero,* was caught by the Immigration and Naturalization Service (INS) right after he had crossed the border, but only after they discovered he did not speak English. His brother Isaías, similarly *güero,* had already successfully made it to Chicago without papers. When the brother who made it to Chicago found a construction job with the Chicago Transit Authority (CTA—another version of the predominant male employment on *el traque*), as part of job orientation he was sent into a room with English-speaking whites and blacks, while other Mexicans were sent into a room to see a video.

Resisting Categories

Although Mexicans in the United States are often assumed (on various institutional forms) to be Hispanic or Latino, an ethnic category (within "Other Race"), the term "Hispanic" has never been used to my knowledge by the members of the social network in this study. The term "Latino," in contrast, is used, but only rarely and only by those who live or have lived in the United States. As a category it is contested by these Mexicans both implicitly and explicitly. As Suzanne Oboler (1995) points out, the terms "Hispanic"/"Latino" function as a two-edged sword. On one hand, they are a forced category imposed externally by the U.S. government starting in the 1980s; in the 1970 census, for example, Mexicans were coded as white, according to Nancy Denton and Douglas Massey (1989). On the other hand, however, even though there is resistance to these labels, their use has provided a platform on which various Latino subgroups have been able to organize to combat discrimination (Padilla 1985). Ground-level resistance to the labels has been shown in several studies, which indicate that most immigrants of Latin American descent prefer to identify according to their nationality (i.e., as Mexicans, Cubans, Puerto Ricans, etc.) (Elías-Olivares and Farr 1991; Oboler 1995), although this varies for second- and third- (or more) generation Latinos (Flores-González 1999; Oboler 1995). An exception to this may be (some) Mexicans, who find it especially easy, when speaking Spanish, to use the term *mexicano* regardless of generation.

Resistance to the terms "Hispanic"/"Latino" is, first of all, due to the way in which they homogenize a population that is extremely diverse in racial, socioeconomic, national, cultural, and historical terms (Oboler 1995). Resistance to these terms is strengthened by the awareness among those with U.S. experience of the stereotypic and denigrating connotations of the terms in U.S. media discourse, conjuring up images of crime, gangs, drugs, high welfare use, and illiteracy. In short, the terms "Hispanic"/"Latino" not only homogenize a very diverse group of people who may not feel any natural allegiance to each other but place individuals in a racial hierarchy, with whites at the top, that defines them as nonwhite. That this category includes Europeans of Spanish descent illuminates the ideology upon which the racial hierarchy is based, which assumes the superiority of northern over southern and eastern Europeans. Although explicit statements of this assumed superiority that attribute it to genetic grounds are rarer now than they were a century ago, the ideology that underlies this categorizing persists in government forms and in the general populace, even among those who do not benefit from it.

Members of the social network in the present study contest the U.S. racial hierarchy in various ways. First, they implicitly question the discreteness of the categories with jokes about some of them being taken as white; their very phenotypic diversity essentially undermines the white/nonwhite dichotomy that is conventionally assumed in the United States (and the terms *güero* and *güera* are used to refer both to U.S. "whites" and to "white Mexicans"). Similarly, they deconstruct the white category by explicitly referring to Italian Americans as Latinos (most marriages within the social network that have been exogenous—not to other Mexicans, let alone to others from the rancho or its microregion—have been to Italian Americans). Esteban, an older man who was born in Kansas but retired in the rancho, one of whose daughters married an Italian American she met in Chicago, said to me, "¡Italianos, pues, son latinos!" (Italians, well, they're Latinos!). He argued that Italians and Mexicans shared customs such as spicy food, a focus on the family, and Catholicism. Another man in the rancho, who has never been to the United States, told me that the Italian American wife of Zenaido, who lives and works near Chicago, is not *pura güera* (pure white) because she is Italian. Such comments echo a belief articulated historically in the United States to justify preferential treatment first of Anglo-Saxons and then, more generally, of northern (but non-Irish) Europeans (Oboler 1995). Both of these men, perhaps imposing the more finely graded Mexican racial hierarchy on the U.S. black-white dichotomy, undermine the white category by separating out Italians.

A second way in which members of this social network challenge U.S. racial categories also involves the use of the term "Latino." Several people have contested this homogenizing label (even though on occasion others have used it positively) by distinguishing themselves from other Latinos. Refugio, for example, was critical of Puerto Ricans, saying that they did not have family values like Mexicans, since their children leave home at eighteen like *los anglosajones* (the Anglo-Saxons). Dionisio criticized Latinos who do not speak Spanish, calling into question the lumping together of non-Spanish-speaking Chicanos with Spanish-speaking *mexicanos;* he complained of people who "have a nopal [an edible Mexican cactus] engraved on their forehead" (i.e., look very Mexican, perhaps with indigenous features) but do not speak Spanish! José was critical of upwardly mobile Cubans: "Esos cubanos, aquí entró uno de . . . quién sabe qué de barredor en la pinche CTA, ¡y 'orita es el mero jefe ya!" (Those Cubans, one entered here as the . . . the, the who knows what—the sweeper in the damn CTA, and now he's the boss!)

Neither Here Nor There: Playing with Race in Transnational Space

The contesting of U.S. racial and ethnic categories of white and Latino by these rancheros is paralleled by their resistance to being racialized as Indians, or as de-Indianized mestizos, in Mexico. Given their ambiguous place in each racial hierarchy, they sometimes play with the categories, enjoying the ambiguity and perhaps their own dexterity in sliding from category to category, depending on the context. All such play, of course, deeply questions the validity of the categories themselves, as is illustrated in the following tape-recorded excerpt of joking among women in a van traveling from Chicago to Mexico for the Christmas holidays one year.

This excerpt occurred during a longer joking session among women of various ages in the van. Partly to pass the time, and partly for the sheer pleasure of *echando relajo* (a joking activity that is the topic of Chapter 8), these women moved from topic to topic in their talk, led by various individual contributions. According to José Reyna, quoted in Briggs (1988, 231), an "immense desire to be verbally adequate" is often realized through humor in *mexicano* culture. Often people take the floor during *relajo* to tell narratives that pleasurably entertain and simultaneously function to draw the group together. As a Mexican language and cultural practice, *relajo* affirms group identity and solidarity, and it socializes younger listeners into Mexican, and ranchero, ways of speaking and being.

In this particular instance, the floor is predominantly shared; at other times, women take turns telling humorous narratives. Here laughter is most notable, and highly significant, in two places: first, when Lupe uses Polish and then comments on the progress that it signifies (lines 9–15); and second, after Beatriz and Dalia play with the ambivalence of Indian identity in lines 29–34. Following Lupe's suggestion that, being Mexican, they should know the indigenous language of their region of Mexico (*tarasco* or *p'urhépecha*) in line 28, both Dalia and Beatriz utter comments that are "double-voiced": their speech incorporates different voices or ideologies from their social world (Bakhtin 1981; Tedlock and Mannheim 1995). On one hand, "Oh *sí*," they should know Tarascan (lines 29–30); but on the other, the Indians are (to use a phrase common in the rancho) *pinche indios* (damn Indians), as Dalia says ironically while giggling in line 31. They end by acknowledging their partial Indian heritage: first Beatriz playfully insists that she herself is Indian, so don't talk that way about them in front of her; and then Dalia agrees, noting that all of them are Indian, really, for you can see the nopal coming out of their foreheads.[13] In the unstated background of this conversation are two racial orders embedded in two different nations. Their ambivalent positions in these two hierarchies, and the fact that they are traveling from one to the other, intensify the ambiguity with which they joke. In this excerpt three women (Beatriz, Dalia, and Lupe) are *echando relajo* in the presence of a larger (all-female) audience.

1. Dalia: *Yo no te veo delgada.*	I don't see you as slender.
2. Beatriz: *Pues no pero—*	Well, no, but—
3. Lupe: *Pero ella quiere más—*	But she wants more—
4. Beatriz: *Estoy como la calidad del tordo al revés.*	I am like a bird, but in reverse.
5. Dalia: [*laughs*]	[*laughs*]
6. Lupe: *Ella quiere tener más—*	She wants to have more—
7. Beatriz: *Más piernas. Más—*	More legs. More—
8. Woman: *No, un poquito más pompis.*	No, a little more rear end.
9. Lupe: *¿Tú sabes qué es dupa?*	Do you know what *dupa* is?
10. Beatriz: *¿Es qué?*	It's what?
11. Lupe: *¿En qué idioma te estoy hablando?*	In what language am I speaking to you?
12. Beatriz: *No, no sé.*	No, I don't know.
13. Lupe: *Polaco.* [*laughs*]	Polish. [*laughs*]
14. Beatriz: *Ay, en polaco es todo—*	Oh, in Polish it's all—
15. Lupe: *Fíjate nomás el progreso.* [*ironic tone*]	Just look at the progress. [*ironic tone*]

16. Women: [*laughter*]	[*laughter*]
17. Beatriz: *Ya de lo que—¿ya pasastes al qué?*	Now from that—now you've passed on to what?
18. Lupe: *No, no todo.*	No, not really.
19. Woman: *¿A cómo—?*	How—?
20. Beatriz: *¿Cómo se dice en inglés pompi?*	How do you say *pompi* in English?
21. Dalia: Butt.	Butt.
22. Beatriz: *Ya de eso ya pasastes a polaco y todo. Para el próximo año ya vas a hablar chino y* [*laughter*] *chan chan chan.*	Now from that you've passed on to Polish and everything. Next year you're going to speak Chinese and [*laughter*] chan chan chan.
23. Dalia: *Como el novio de Vero dice, "Yo sí se francés, yo sí sé francés" y le hace Vero bien callada, "Sí, pero cuando se le acaba el francés le entra el italiano."* [*laughter*]	Like Vero's boyfriend says, "I can speak French, I can speak French," and Vero says real quiet, "Yes, but when the French stops, the Italian enters." [*laughter*]
24. Beatriz: *¿Por qué? ¿De dónde es él?*	Why? Where is he from?
25. Young Women: *¡Es mexicano!*	He's Mexican!
26. Dalia: *Pero es puras mentiras, no sabe.*	But it's just lies, he doesn't know.
27. Beatriz: *¡Mexicano, hasta las cachas!*	Mexican, to the hilt!
28. Lupe: *No, el mexicano va a saber pero tarasco.*	No, the Mexican is going to know Tarascan.
29. Dalia: *Oh sí.*	Oh yes.
30. Beatriz: *Oh sí.* [*pause*]	Oh yes. [*pause*]
31. Dalia: *¡Pinche indios!* [*giggling*]	Damn Indians! [*giggling*]
32. Beatriz: *Ehi, calmada con los indios. Yo soy india.*	Hey, take it easy on the Indians. I am Indian.
33. Dalia: *Todos nosotros, todos. No me ves el pinche nopal, que me sale una tuna ahí.* [*laughs*]	All of us, all. Don't you see the damned nopal, that the fruit comes out here. [*laughs*]
34. Beatriz: *El nopal.* [*laughing*]	The nopal. [*laughing*]
35. Lupe: *Ay ay ay.*	Ay ay ay.
36. Beatriz: *¡Ay, como son tremendas!*	Oh, you all are really audacious!

Synopsis and Interpretation

Immediately preceding this excerpt, the women were joking about comparing their own bodies to the idealized ones found in magazines and other public media. Beatriz then states, at the beginning of this excerpt, how she would like to change her own body, with more legs and rear end. This reminds another woman of the word for rear end in Polish, something she may have learned through contact with Polish immigrants, the next largest non-English-speaking group in Chicago after Mexicans. (Such contacts sometimes happen in neighborhoods, in English classes, or at work, and one young woman married a Polish man.) After using the Polish word *dupa* (rear end), she asks if anyone knows what this means and then, when no one does, tells them its meaning. She ironically links her learning of some Polish with progress, in line 15, by saying, *Fíjate nomás el progreso* (Just look at the progress). Progress, as noted earlier in this chapter and explained in more detail in the next, is an explicitly articulated value which these rancheros use to contrast themselves with indigenous Mexicans, who are seen as communal and not progressing. Moreover, progress is an expected benefit of going to Chicago to work. Cognizant of the fact that they are returning to Mexico from working in Chicago, Lupe makes explicit what is perhaps in the back of everyone's mind and jokes about it, since the move to Chicago, while certainly resulting in substantial material progress for virtually all of these rancheros, has not been without pain or loss. This disjuncture is a ripe topic for joking, and the women reward her comment with hilarious laughter.

The topic of speaking other languages then brings to Dalia's mind the insistent claim of her sister Vero's boyfriend that he can speak French (line 23), which she says her sister quietly and sarcastically called into question by noting, *Sí, pero cuando se le acaba el francés le entra el italiano* (Yes, but when the French stops, the Italian enters). This too is rewarded with much laughter, at someone who is trying to be more than he is. Beatriz, not knowing this young man, asks where he is from. When the others delightedly and loudly chorus, "He's Mexican!" (and Mexican *hasta las cachas* or to the hilt), Lupe comments that, really, a Mexican (from their region) who knows another language should know Tarascan (*tarasco* or *p'urhépecha*). Dalia affirms this right away (*Oh sí* in line 29), since the official public discourse in Mexico, promoted by the government and federal schools, valorizes the indigenous languages and heritage of Mexico. Beatriz repeats and affirms Dalia's *Oh sí.*

Following a slight pause pregnant with meaning, Dalia then playfully utters a phrase common in the rancho: "[Those] damn Indians!" This phrase calls into question the nationalistic racial ideology that they had just affirmed with *Oh sí.* Moreover, it invokes their shared reality of ranchero attitudes toward Indians and their shared assumption of nonindigenous identity. Here the disjuncture is between a national official discourse that valorizes an Indian heritage and the local-level reality of what it actually means to be Indian in Mexico. As rural campesinas who are often Indianized by the elite in Mexico, these rancheras are well aware of the disadvantages that this implies and of their own family histories, which disrupt the widespread imaginary dichotomy between Spanish/urban/elite and Indian/rural/poor.

Dalia and Beatriz's use of the English "Oh" rather than the Spanish *Ay* in their *Oh sí* responses, while no doubt unconscious, may not be accidental. This code switch, though minor, indexes the transnational context in which they live and within which, at that very moment, they are traveling. Moving regularly between two nation-states, and two racial schemes, highlights the differences between them and leads to a deepened sense of relativity. The "place" of these women and their ranchero families in a racial hierarchy depends entirely on context; and even then, their knowledge of who they actually are (and what some of them look like) disrupts the logic underlying the racial order in both the United States and Mexico.

Although Beatriz appears quite "white," with brown wavy hair, light skin, and blue eyes, her own racial identity is multifaceted, depending on context. On this tape from the traveling van, Beatriz seems to affirm Mexican nationalistic racial ideology (we are all Indians), but playing with this topic suggests her ambivalence about it. Dalia, in revoicing a common ranchero denigration of Indians, clearly questions their automatic affirmation of the government ideology. Yet perhaps she also is critiquing the ranchero claim to a nonindigenous identity, making fun of the fact that, in spite of this claim, in this conversation they seem to be playing the Mexican government's game (we should value our indigenous heritage and perhaps know Tarascan). Beatriz noted (on another tape) that co-workers question her claim that she is indigenous. Because she is so white, they tell her, she can't really be Indian. Her claim to those at work that she in fact is Indian can be interpreted as a response to the U.S. racial dichotomy of white/nonwhite. If she has any Indian blood, then she is not completely white, according to this logic, so she makes this claim herself rather than having this category imposed on her by others. She has told me that she has been taken for white until she speaks (either Spanish or English with a Spanish accent) and then has suffered job discrimination. Here, however, within the social network, she and Dalia joke about these categories and invoke the shared knowledge that they are not truly indigenous according to the local logic of their microregion within Mexico. There the truly indigenous do speak *p'urhépecha* and live in indigenous communities, excluding and being hostile to these "outsider" rancheras, who consider themselves to be of higher status.

When (immediately after Dalia's counterdiscursive *¡Pinche indios!*) Beatriz playfully says, in line 32, *Ehi, calmada con los indios. Yo soy india*

(Hey, take it easy on the Indians. I am Indian), she ambiguously invokes both positions: in the United States she might as well be Indian since she is nonwhite (conveyed by the literal meaning of her words), yet in Mexico she knows that she is not Indian, in spite of the government's official position (conveyed by the playful tone in which she expresses the words).

The joking on this topic begins to come to a close in line 33 when Dalia points out that they are all (ambiguously) Indian, like Beatriz, and then invokes the common metaphor for looking (very) Mexican: having a nopal on one's forehead (with a *tuna* or cactus fruit coming out of her forehead). They laugh, and Beatriz ends the episode with an evaluative comment on those who would joke about such things in line 36, *¡Ay, como son tremendas!* (Oh, you all are really audacious!). The word *tremenda* is often used positively, not pejoratively, by these women to refer to those who do not keep to "traditional" demure female behavior and are not afraid to speak out against such norms. Beatriz uses it here in that sense, showing her, and their, pleasure in this counterlanguage, so characteristic of *relajo.*

Verbal Play as Racial Critique

An extensive literature on joking reveals its capacity for social inversion (Bauman 1986, 70–77; Briggs 1988, 171–232), and Mexican *relajo* functions as a microfiesta in this regard, since the fiesta, or carnival, is similarly an antistructural process (Farr 1998). In both verbal and nonverbal play such as *relajo* and fiesta, the usual norms and structures of society can be turned upside down, at least for the moment. José Limón (1982), Richard Bauman (1986), and Charles Briggs (1988), among others, stress the creative and performative power of such play, especially verbal play, arguing for the transformative power of language and that change is indeed facilitated by the critical perspectives engendered by joking. In the above excerpt, Beatriz and Delia express a Bakhtinian "double-voicedness." One voice expresses the official Mexican ideology of pride in their Indian heritage, while the other voice is critical of this ideology, given the local categories of Indian and ranchero in the countryside. Their own movement back and forth across the Mexican-U.S. border and their familiarity with two different national ideologies that implicate race in different ways (in Mexico the imagined national community is officially mestizo, and in the United States it is white) provide them with a perspective from which to critique these ideologies. This critique is implicit in their joking.

The ambiguity of their position in both national racial orders provides fertile resources for such humor. They consider themselves non-indigenous in Mexico, even as they are Indianized by elite Mexicans because they are rural peasants; and in the United States they are not easily placed in a single racial category. Although many of them are initially perceived to be white in the United States, they know they are not *güera güera* (really white) because of their mixed heritage. Neither are they black, Asian, or Native American. In this excerpt of joking, however, these women play with the ambiguity inherent in their not fitting neatly into either country's racial categories. Such critical verbal play can lead to an eventual realignment of traditional racial identities and attitudes, leading those who engage in this verbal play to question and undermine existing racial hierarchies.

Conclusion: Race, Rancheros, and Nations

I have described the traditional racial ideology of this group of rancheros in relation to colonial and postcolonial Mexican racial categories as well as U.S. racial categories and the place (or lack of it) of Mexicans within the traditional white/nonwhite dichotomy. Nation building in both Mexico and the United States has utilized the idea of shared descent and thus race in constructing imagined communities—Mexico with a new "mixed" race (*la raza cósmica*) and the United States with whiteness—ignoring differences in class, gender, and ethnicity in the attempt to homogenize national communities. According to Linda Basch et al. (1994), transnational migrants have the potential to disrupt these homogenizing forces of nationalism. By resisting inclusion in either nation's racial categories, as well as by resisting the impositions of both governments, these rancheras affirm their difference from both nation's dominant identities. This in itself provides a space for counterhegemonic effects, as Basch et al. (1994, 46) have pointed out:

> However, the issue of resistance is a complex one that must be contextualized within the always partial and unfinished construction of identities shaped by the pressures of national hegemonies. Subordinated populations may internalize many of the meanings and representations that pervade their daily surroundings, but that internalization remains partial and incomplete. Meanings are often subverted and there is always, at the level of daily practice, some opening for innovation.

These rancheros, and thousands of others, "vote[d] with their feet" (Dinerman 1982, 10) in migrating to the United States, where their increasing presence alone disturbs the traditional racial order. In their daily practices, which include *echando relajo* (as in the excerpt above), they resist both Mexican and U.S. hegemonic constructions of identity, playing with their ambiguous places in the racial orders of both countries. In daily verbal practices such as *relajo* they perform identities somewhere between the two racial poles in both countries (in Mexico: urban/Spanish/elite vs. rural/Indian/poor; in the United States: white vs. black). Through these daily verbal practices, they illuminate ground-level nuances in identities that do not fit easily within the categories of a racial hierarchy.

Rancheros traditionally have existed far from the centralized powers of government and its ideologies of race, on the moving frontiers of the nation state. They have lived, at least in the remembered past, without government and historically are quite antigovernment (González 1974; Barragán 1997). Antigovernment comments are quite common in the rancho: "Son chuecos" (They're crooks), one man succinctly said to me, whatever the country. In two oral history interviews in the rancho in 1998, similar attitudes were expressed. One elderly man said, in explaining events that occurred during his childhood, "No había ley" (There was no law or government). Another older man recalled seeing armed men on horseback on the horizon and running to tell his father, "¡Viene el gobierno!" (The government's coming!). It is significant that he did not say that armed men were arriving but that the government was coming.

This no doubt reflects the opposition of many rancheros in western Mexico to the post–Mexican Revolution national government, which was anti-Catholic. The ancestors of these rancheros, like many others in this region, opposed this government during the Cristero Rebellion in the late 1920s (see Chapter 2), and they are no fonder today of either the Mexican or the U.S. government. With their deeply ingrained individualist ideology of progress through hard work, they prefer to avoid both governments and make their own way within their own ranchero society. They have always managed to survive and, they hope, prosper, but this has always been through their own considerable efforts, without the help of government. One man, now retired with a U.S. pension in the rancho, commented to his daughter's family during a visit in Chicago that the U.S. government provided so many benefits that it was practically Communist! Although he earned this pension, he nevertheless seemed to assume that such benefits were not to be expected. In the next chapter, I explore further this ranchero ideology of liberal individualism and how these rancheros construct in their speech on a daily basis the self-assertive, autonomous identity that accompanies this ideology.

SIX

Franqueza and the Individualist Ideology of Progress

As discussed in earlier chapters, rancheros often have not been distinguished from other Mexican campesinos. Most research literature in both the United States and Mexico has long ignored the differences among campesinos, either assuming "peasant" to be the significant category (and "Indianizing" all peasants) or distinguishing only between *indígena* (Indian) and mestizo peasants. As illustrated in the previous chapter, however, all mestizo peasants are not alike. The rancheros in this study own (or wish to own) their own land individually, even relatively small parcels; and the valuing of such private property, and the hard work that gained it, is central to their identity. They do not own land communally, as do Indian communities and *ejidatarios.* Dominant ranchero ideology, in fact, holds all *comuneros* (people who communally own land) in disdain, including Indians and *ejidatarios* as well as the *agraristas* who worked to create the *ejidos.* According to the honor code prevalent in ranchero societies (see Chapter 7), private property is highly valued, but it must be earned through one's own efforts.

Lomnitz-Adler (1992) traces ranchero discourse which constructs this ideology to liberal individualism from late-nineteenth-century Mexico, but it is also likely that such discourse evolved in the material historical conditions of Mexico's changing frontier, where rancheros have been socially, economically, and geographically mobile for centuries (Barragán 1997). Whatever the origins, however, it is clear that upward mobility and a belief in progress through individual effort are fundamentally important to the rancheros in this study. This ideology is the central underpinning of their identity, because it is the basis upon which they distinguish themselves from other subgroups of the larger Mexican society. The ideology is generally shared by both men and women, although age and gender affect the cultural practices in which it is embedded.

Rancheros traditionally are "ranch" people, able to control horses, shoot guns, butcher livestock, and, in their view, create their own destinies through hard work. Even those who no longer ride horses or live in ranchos nevertheless construct themselves as tough, "no-nonsense" persons—that is, according to definitions of personhood that are tied to "New World" frontiers. In defining themselves this way, these rancheros distinguish themselves from those who identify as *indígenas* on the one hand (whom they view as communally oriented) and from *catrines* (city people whom they see as effete dandies) on the other. In this view, Indians work hard but do not "progress"; similarly, many (elite) city people do not really work, since "real" work involves manual labor. In contrast to these other identities, rancheros espouse an individualist, upwardly mobile ideology that is constructed in a verbal style or "way of speaking" (Hymes 1974b), characterized by *franqueza.*

The history of the origins and development of rancheros in western Mexico after the Spanish conquest (as detailed in Chapter 2) involves the socioeconomic conditions in which the ranchero way of life, and its ways of thinking and speaking, developed. Briefly, within the material conditions of Mexico's ever-moving frontier, rancheros emerged in the Americas as the cowboys who handled cattle and horses and domesticated land wrested from the Indians, for small-scale agriculture and cattle raising. When not fighting Indians, they were struggling with them over land or otherwise dealing with them on behalf of the elite Spaniards who owned the haciendas but often lived in urban settings, at a distance from them. That is, rancheros frequently found themselves positioned, both literally and figuratively, between the lower-status rural Indians and the higher-status urban Spaniards.

Ranchero societies thus emerged in western Mexico from lower-status Spaniards who mixed with some Indians and Africans and who handled the cattle, imported from Spain, on large haciendas. They were the original cowboys of the Western Hemisphere, who were always on the frontier of the colony, domesticating land (smaller ranchos based on less desirable land not part of large haciendas) and dominating indigenous populations. They are known as *hombres de a caballo* (men on horseback), because the land on which they lived (and on which some still live) could only be traversed on horses (González 1991). This history of isolation and geographical movement made their housing perennially provisional and led to a culture in which mobility (both geographic and socioeconomic) was valued and achieved through hard work, autonomy, and toughness, particularly for men but also for women. In light of this tradition of mobility, migration to the United States can be seen as only the latest chapter in their history, part of their continuing strategy to progress or improve their circumstances in the world.

A history of frontier isolation and mobility also facilitated the development of strong ties of reciprocity for mutual support in hostile conditions and common ways of living, dressing, and speaking. Although self-reliance was and is of utmost importance, so were and are ties of kinship, both real and fictive (*compadrazgo*). This valuing of both autonomy and affiliation undermines the often-invoked dichotomy between Mexicans and Anglo-Americans as being communal or group-oriented and individualistic or self-oriented, respectively. Rather than being only one or the other, these rancheros evidence both orientations (as discussed more fully below).

In traditional ranchero society, an antigovernment attitude coexisted along with a social system based on honor which depended on one's word (*la palabra*) and the legitimation of violence to settle conflicts. *Franqueza* as a way of speaking is particularly emblematic of the ranchero identity that developed under these material conditions. *Franqueza* is direct, straightforward, candid language that goes directly to a point: *Rancheros no se andan con rodeos* (Rancheros don't beat around the bush); their language can be blunt and rude (according to more "cultured" people), sometimes peppered with obscenities. It is a direct, "no bull" approach to communication. As Eduvina remarked in a comment critical of people who are not candid about who they are (referring to Mexican-origin young men in Chicago who introduce girlfriends as "friends" rather than being straightforward about their presumed intimacy),[1] "¿Para que andan ahí con medias copas, podiendo ir directamente?" (Why go around beating around the bush, when you can go directly?).

This style, of course, is not the only style in which these rancheros, including this woman, speak (nor are they always communicatively "direct"). But it is a predominant style, and in use it evokes a deeply held ideology that is tied historically to the ecology of ranchos, traditionally isolated from large urban centers of sophistication and schooling. As exemplified in the history of the rancho in Chapter 3, men and women have coped for centuries in isolated ranchos, creating their own housing, growing their own food, raising their own livestock, and making their own cheese, clothing, and many other items out of necessity. Now, of course, many rancheros, like those in this study, are producing food for commercial purposes (and/or working for wage labor both in the United States and in Mexico) and buying food at nearby markets. Nevertheless, the deeply ingrained *habitus* (Bourdieu 1977) of the independent rancher persists, and this includes a propensity to use direct, frank language. This *franco* (frank) style of language constructs an identity for rancheros that contrasts sharply with other identities in Mexico.

Lomnitz-Adler (1992, 199–200), who studied rancheros in another Mexican state (although there they dominated the region politically and economically), describes this rough talk as "bold, frank, and open," full of "regional sayings and down-to-earth obscenities." Its very frankness, he argues, created a populist and egalitarian stance for these rancheros, who used this verbal style and stance quite effectively in gaining political dominance in their region. In this study, unlike Lomnitz-Adler's, the rancheros are not regionally dominant; nor are they rich. Yet they nevertheless evidence the same ideology and verbal style as the more powerful rancheros of Lomnitz-Adler's study and of other studies (see Chapter 2). González (1991, 7) traces this stance of authority and pride on the part of rancheros to their Spanish heritage:

> They inherited from their Spanish parentage a practice of arrogance. They never owe anything to anyone, and they are very sensitive to humiliation. Being haughty they are individualists and disrespectful of authority. They regard honor highly and look down on the humility of the indigenous, as well as on the shame of the *ejidatarios.*

Primarily, then, ranchero *franqueza* contrasts sharply with the stereotyped image of the *humilde peón* (humble peon), standing with head bowed and hat in hand before a powerful landowner or boss, in many popular representations of Mexican peasants. In contrast to this humble image, which is found in both popular fiction and research literature, rancheros enact a proud stance, with heads held high and gazes direct, even when interacting with those who are more powerful than they are. The rancho in this study is situated in a microregion in which there never have been large landowners with haciendas, unlike other regions in the state and nation. In regions in which haciendas long existed, relations of domination and subordination presumably would be more deeply established, such that ruling families could expect and probably received verbal and bodily deference from their workers and other landless peasants dependent on them for material resources.

The land in this particular microregion of northwest Michoacán (see Chapter 3), consisting of rolling hills on a high plateau, is not as conducive to large-scale agriculture as the flatter, more easily exploitable, expanses of land on which the closest nearby haciendas were located. The shape of the land in this microregion may have contributed, along with other factors, to the predominance of ranchos here. It has always been ranchero territory (i.e., the province of small landowners rather than plantation owners). Thus the microregion does not have an entrenched tradition of a *patrón* (boss), usually from a dominant family, to whom workers owe deference, so these rancheros do not habitually assume a humble, deferential stance toward more powerful others (even bosses in Chicago). In contrast, an interview with an older man living a half-hour's drive away (over the hills to the west) in the flat expanse of land that had been part of an hacienda contains the frequent deferential use of *el patrón* and *la patrona* (the boss, male and female respectively) to refer to members of the family that owned the hacienda until the Mexican Revolution.[2]

The directness of this verbal style also serves to contrast rancheros with more educated and "cultured" urbanites, who consider people rude whose language does not conform to *cortesía,* an elaborate and often indirect verbal politeness style (Chodorowska-Pilch 1998; Haverkate 1994). *Cortesía* in polite Mexican society requires verbally elaborate greetings and leave-takings, for example, whereas the *franqueza* of rancheros is usually much more concise, allowing people to leave (appropriately) with a simple *Ya me voy* (I'm leaving now), unless the situation specifically calls for more formality.

In this chapter I explore the construction of this aspect of ranchero identity in informal verbal performances within homes both in Chicago and in Michoacán. Performances "stand out" in the flow of ordinary conversation because the audience orients attentively to the performer, who is often telling a story or joke (Bauman 1984 [1977]; Hymes 1975, 1981). Such verbal performances are especially important sites for constructions and interpretations of identity, because they are instances of heightened aesthetic experience for both performers and listeners-as-audience and are intended for display. Instances of ranchero direct verbal style (*franqueza*) in such performative talk illustrate how language and ideology are intertwined in the construction of individualist ranchero identity. As a linguistic style or way of speaking, *franqueza* relies on devices that are quintessentially "bald-on-record" according to politeness theory (Brown and Levinson 1987). It is not that rancheros are not polite; rather, they have a different definition of politeness than more "cultured" Mexican society, in which particular linguistic devices are required to mitigate or soften the effect of potentially threatening speech acts on hearers. In contrast, rancheros speaking frankly use language notable for the virtually total absence of such devices as well as the use of other devices (e.g., direct questions and directives) that can impose strongly on the hearer.

Studies of Mexicans within the United States have characterized them as being "collectivist" (Delgado-Gaitán 1993) or "deeply familistic" (Valdés 1996) and thus more committed to family and other reciprocal relationships than are many members of the dominant U.S. Anglo "individualist" culture that, according to Robert LeVine and Merry White (1986), has been inculcated by mass schooling. While encapsulating some truth, these contrasting characterizations of "collectivist/familistic" vs. "individualist" too often are perceived as a dichotomy. In my ethnographic experience with ranchero Mexicans, such a dichotomy dissolves into a "both" rather than an "either/or." These ranchero Mexicans evidence an individualist orientation, even though they do so within the context of familism and networks based on reciprocity. That is, although the family and human relationships are of central importance in social life, individuality is also highly valued, both within and beyond the family. It is possible, then, to be both "individualistic" and "collectivist/familistic," autonomous without being isolated. What is significant may be the differences between U.S. Anglo and Mexican ranchero individualism (which coexists with an emphasis on familism). The rancheros in this study see themselves as differing from other Mexicans in terms of such individualism, especially from those who identify as Indian Mexicans, who are seen as communal.

Studies of Mexicans within Mexico also have avoided, sometimes explicitly, characterizing particular groups of Mexicans as individualistic. As noted previously, many studies of Mexican and Latin American peasants have characterized them as community-oriented and even anti-individualistic, especially if this individualism is linked to the development of capitalism. For example, Hill's (1995) study of *mexicano* discourse by an elderly peasant man in the state of Puebla illuminates the ways in which this discourse represents a resistance to capitalist penetration of traditional indigenous communities. This man (one of the last surviving speakers of this indigenous language in his town of 800 people) clearly links the Spanish language and culture, and the death of his son, with capitalist "business for profit," as his occasional use of Spanish for a "business" lexicon "falls out" of his otherwise fluent narrative about his son's death. Citing a number of studies (Dow 1981; Taussig 1979; Warman 1982) for making similar claims, Hill notes that "a [Latin American] peasant consciousness is at least partially constituted as a domain of ongoing ideological resistance to a capitalistic ideology" (Hill 1995, 138). This anticapitalist stance cannot be generalized to all peasants, however, since the rancheros in this and other studies explicitly and implicitly construct themselves in opposition to such a communal, noncapitalist (and indigenous) orientation.

Some studies of nonindigenous (i.e., mestizo) communities in Mexico interpret the high value placed on autonomy by members of these communities either as resistance to capitalism, specifically the wage labor associated with it (Rouse 1992), or simply as a desire for autonomy that is not linked to capitalist individualism (Nugent and Alonso 1994). The rancheros in this study, however, do identify with an ideology of individualism linked with business-for-profit, and other studies of rancheros in western Mexico also have noted such an orientation (Barragán 1990b, 1997; González 1974).

We cannot assume, of course, that all those who identify as rancheros are entirely similar in their orientations to capitalism. Even in the present study there is variation in this, and people are often critical of the materialism and consumerism of U.S. society, contrasting it with the emphasis on family and human relationships in Mexico. Many express ambivalence about the material comforts that they enjoy as a result of work in Chicago, since achieving those material comforts requires living *a prisa* (in a rush, on a schedule) and working virtually all the time.

Moreover, although an individualist ideology is dominant among these rancheros, it is not above criticism. Rubén, a man with considerable education (one year of medicine in Mexico City) and professional employment with the Mexican federal education agency, had attempted to organize people to work a community-owned plot of land together in order to generate money for public work projects in the rancho. His effort was unsuccessful, which he attributed to an attitude characteristic of small property owners:

> *Aquí casi todos son pequeños propietarios, así que la gente nada más ve por lo suyo y no piensa en el bien de la comunidad, o si se trabaja en común sólo quieren recibir los beneficios. La gente hablan de mí, pero me doy cuenta que los que hablan son los que no cooperan.*
> Here almost everyone is a small property owner, and because of this they only look out for themselves and don't think about the good of the community, or if they work together they only want to receive the benefits. People talk about me, but I notice that the ones who talk are those who don't cooperate.

Rubén gives voice here to an unusual perspective in the rancho (which is consonant with his advanced education and federal employment), even though he himself also owns a small property and generally speaks with *franqueza,* as befits his ranchero background. Although he is critical here of what he sees as too much individualism, his comments indicate that such an ideology is in fact characteristic of the rancho.

As already noted, even though rancheros across Mexico vary in some respects, they apparently share certain cultural practices, beliefs, and the frequent use of a frank verbal style (*franqueza*). They can be rich or poor, dominant or "middle class," that is, sandwiched between an elite dominant class and those on the bottom of the status hierarchy (Jacobs 1982; Lomnitz-Adler 1992). Yet no matter what the size of their land holdings, and thus their relative wealth and influence, they share certain cultural values (Brading 1994), including the overriding importance of hard work and autonomy, ideally living off their own land on livestock and other food products and being their own bosses (Barragán et al. 1994). In addition to valuing hard work and autonomy, however, the rancheros in this study and others also value individual efforts at entrepreneurship, although never at the expense of family. Both men and women practice such entrepreneurship: in Chicago men and women fix up and rent apartments within the houses they own, men buy items (e.g., car batteries, guns) in Chicago and sell them in Mexico, women buy jewelry in Mexico and sell it in Chicago, and women sell Tupperware and other commodities, apart from their regular factory or construction jobs. One teenager airbrushed and sold T-shirts while still in high school in Chicago; this was proudly announced by aunts and other family members, who reported that he was "doing really well" at this endeavor.

These rancheros espouse a liberal individualist ideology (Cosío Villegas et al. 1995, 114–115) in which people are believed to be equally free and able to work their way up in the world through their own hard labor and enterprise, rather than having their social status determined at birth. As a political philosophy, nineteenth-century liberalism in Mexico argued for "freedom of work, trade, education . . . [and] small property owners" (Cosío Villegas et al. 1995, 95). This was based on the belief that, rather than relying on established traditions, new paths must be forged for the future greatness of Mexico. Private property was seen as inviolable; and in the "liberal scheme of things, the force which drove society forward was the self-interest of the individual proprietor, operating in a market free from state intervention" (Brading 1991, 652). Progress was central to this philosophy and was seen to emerge from the individual interests of a large class of proprietary farmers.

Thus land reform by liberal governments made land formerly owned by the Catholic Church and Indian communities available for small property owners, who also created ranchos out of pieces of former haciendas as these were sold off (Arias 1996; González 1974). Although many liberals were opposed to the power of the Catholic Church, others maintained that "true Christianity, as distinct from the practices and dogmas of the contemporary Church, was very close to the ideals of liberalism" (Brading 1991, 673). This understanding resolves an apparent paradox of this study, as these rancheros are both liberal individualists and intense Catholics (whereas rancheros elsewhere can be anticlerical).

Work, Autonomy, and Progress

Productive labor, especially working with one's hands, is highly valued, especially for men but also for women. One of the worst criticisms that can be leveled at a ranchero or ranchera is to be *flojo/a* (lazy). Although it is considered an extremely negative evaluation of both women and men, a man's very masculinity is impugned by this charge, whereas a woman can still be feminine yet lazy. This echoes the observation by Marit Melhuus (1996) that men in Mexico are evaluated according to degrees of masculinity, whereas women are evaluated dichotomously according to their moral character: either as good/decent women or as bad/immoral women. Yet good or bad, decent or immoral, they are still women and thus feminine. Because a man's very masculinity is questioned if he does not work hard, this value standard has a particularly harsh effect on men. Men boast of their abilities to work twenty-four hours at times on *el traque* in Chicago, even though this might endanger them. One conversation in a kitchen in Chicago described a man (forty-eight) who continued to work even with damage to his cranium. This man worked even though he walked bent over (*Que caminaba pandito*), claiming that it no longer pained him.

The emphasis on work, especially for males, is so great that those who continue their schooling beyond the age at which they can begin full-time work (usually in their mid-teens) are considered *flojos* by traditional rancheros (see Figure 4.2). Nowadays a young man in the rancho can also be labeled *flojo* if he doesn't "get himself to the border" (*¡Vete a la frontera!*), so that he can "get to work" in the United States.

Other qualities related to the high value placed on work include the ability to be practical and efficient, captured in the common saying *el ingenioso ranchero* (the ingenious ranchero), which is applied to both men and women. The frontier past, in isolated settlements lacking in modern conveniences, gave rise to the importance placed on clever, spontaneous solutions to emergent practical problems. Men and women are expected to come up with their own solutions to everyday problems in the household or in the fields. Susana, an expert tortilla-maker (and my teacher) in the rancho, for example, discovered one day that animals had broken her *comal,* the large earthenware platter lodged over an outdoor wood fireplace upon which tortillas are cooked after having been formed from the raw *nixtamal* (milled corn dough). Although she accepted my offer to buy her a new one since she had taught me how to make tortillas, several trips to a nearby Indian market where they are sold ended up being fruitless searches for the right size. Needing to make tortillas, she came up with her own solution: she used a large old casserole, lodging it into place with wet mud, and she was back in the tortilla business (literally, as people in the rancho paid her for her tortillas made by hand rather than by machine).

Another man, José, recounted a long story at a kitchen table in Chicago of his practical expertise at work. Working for the Chicago Transit Authority constructing the switches (where the trains change tracks) below O'Hare Airport, this man realized that the engineer's designs were faulty. When he objected to them, he was not believed at first, and they laughed at him: "Se rieron, han de haber dicho 'Este pinche mexicano 'sta loco' " (They laughed, they must have said, "That damned Mexican is crazy"). So he said, OK, I'll do the work exactly according to the engineer's designs, with the stakes in the wrong places (derailing trains). Validated by the resultant surprise and chagrin on the faces of those who had not believed him, he says that he then explained the problem to men who flew in on a private plane to discuss the matter. Finally, he was told by the engineer, no less, "Sabes que, tira las estacas y haz lo que quieras" (You know what, throw out the stakes and make what you want). He was vindicated, especially since it cost the company another three days' work to rectify the problem. This anecdote illustrates not only the valuing of practical, hands-on knowledge and expertise (as opposed to the "book learning" of the engineer) but also ranchero self-assertiveness in the face of authority (a subject discussed below, in two tape-recorded narratives).

Certain men in the network are respected because they are *todistas* (jacks-of-all-trades). Gabriel, for example, has skills needed for everything from fixing cars to renovating houses. Such abilities are linked to knowledge and intelligence, as in the saying *De todo le sabe, a todo le hace* (From knowing everything, one can do anything). This kind of knowledge, however, is not learned in school, but *lírico* or *liricamente* (literally "lyrically," but meaning practically, orally, informally). Elsewhere I have described how even literacy has been learned *lírico* by many adult rancheros with very limited formal schooling (Farr 1994c). This kind of learning is fundamentally a social process, with one person showing another how to read or write, how to work with numbers, how to play the guitar, how to fix a car, how to do electrical wiring, plumbing, tiling, and so forth. Reading, writing, and arithmetic are treated like other useful skills: learned, and then used, in the context of daily life.

Thus we see that work, especially manual labor, and practical, efficient knowledge are seen as the basis upon which people can progress in this world. It is key that individual enterprise, not organizing to demand rights, is the recognized path to upward mobility. *Agraristas* who organized beginning in the 1930s in this region to gain land for communal *ejidos* commonly are called *ratones* (rats) or *ladrones* (thieves), because they are viewed as not having earned the right to land legitimately. Yet as important as work is, simply working hard, as a slave might, is not enough. Anyone who cannot *defenderse* (defend himself or herself; i.e., stand up for oneself) or is overly deferential is disdained. One must have a sense of autonomy, a "take this job and shove it" attitude if one is not respected (both men and women have quit jobs in Chicago over such issues). The attitude of pride (rancheros are said to be *orgulloso* or proud), or even arrogance, that González (1991) traced to their Spanish heritage is expressed in a ranchero *dicho: ¡A mí no me manda nadie!* (No one orders me around!).

An example of this surfaced when one woman in the rancho, Esperanza, commented to me that she was quite happy to be back there after years working in Chicago. Even though she had been "good with her hands" at the tool-making factory where she had worked, and had taken pride in being good at her job, now no one told her what to do, which was much better. Her attitude illustrates how independence and autonomy are valued by both men and women; as such, this part of ranchero identity provides a platform upon which women can assert themselves against restrictive gender norms (as illustrated later in this chapter). It is a "crack" in male hegemony, as Sherry Ortner (1996) would term it, that rancheras can and do exploit.

Constructing Rancheros against the Indigenous

While their historical legacy as frontier people is a primary source of ranchero identity, it is also important to consider other factors that support the persistence and continual reproduction of this category over the centuries. As Fredrik Barth (1969) notes, ethnic boundaries persist, signaled by language, clothing, food, and value standards, in spite of the fact that individual people often radically change their ethnic identity through intermarriage and other factors. Chapter 5 describes such boundary maintenance via language, clothing, and food; this chapter illustrates the differentiating power of ideology and its implicated cultural values, as constructed in language practices.

For the lower-status Spaniards among the first rancheros, intermarriage with (often female) Indians and Africans, or perhaps more frequently mestizos with partial Indian and African backgrounds, brought those with non-Spanish ethnic identities into ranchero society. Most research literature on Mexico emphasizes the syncretism that resulted from the blending of Spanish and Indian cultures (and until recently generally ignored the African contribution). Yet such syncretism was probably not distributed evenly across Mexico. The primarily Spanish identity of rancheros seems to have predominated in these "mixed" unions, for example, in certain regions (see, for example, Barragán 1990b; Taylor 1933) because of proportionately larger numbers of Spaniards than of Indians or Africans. As *mestizaje* has increased in the microregion under study here, the traditional ranchero identity has been reaffirmed by defining itself primarily against Indian but also against other identities, including that of *catrines* (urban dandies, a subject to be taken up later in this chapter).

Usually Indians are described by rancheros as having fixed and, significantly, very nonranchero characteristics. As noted in Chapter 5, they are seen as "closed" (and they undoubtedly are to outsiders like rancheros) and as not willing to develop *confianza* (trust) with non-Indians. Indians are viewed as rigid: as one man said to another in my presence once, "El indio va con una idea" (The Indian goes with one idea—i.e., persists in one kind of thinking rather than flexibly choosing among alternatives). Thus Indians are not *gente de razón* (people of reason), using rationality in a "civilized" manner. They are said to lack "culture" (*que todavía no tienen cultura*). Indians live in isolated villages, where (in Michoacán) they weave sweaters and make furniture and other objects crafted of wood that are sent to cities to be sold, so they are unfamiliar with the ("civilized") city and its ways (*que no conocen el pueblo*). Even when positive comments are made about the intricacy of these artisanal crafts and "pretty" houses in Indian villages constructed entirely of wood ("Y se miraban unas casas nuevecitas, bonitas, muy blancas, bien bonitas"; And you could see some brand new houses, pretty, very white, very pretty), Indians are constructed as exotic and different. Finally, and perhaps most importantly, it is said that Indians do not "progress"—that is, while they do work, they do not work toward upward social and economic mobility. Instead they are said to do everything "together": to work together, have fiestas together, and, crucially, own property (i.e., land) together. This last distinction refers to the communal land tenure of Indian villages, traced to pre-Hispanic tradition in Mexico as well as to policies of colonial Spaniards that affirmed Indian identity as tied up with rural land-holding communities (Taylor 1979).

These rancheros (in contrast to their view of the indigenous people) centrally value progress, which they hope to achieve by amassing private property, traditionally land and cattle. As Alonso (1995, 61) points out in her study of the Namiquipans who colonized northern Mexico and fought the Apache Indians with government support, "Property rights in land, including *derechos de posesión* [rights of occupancy], were a sign of work, of the activity that transformed nature, and as such were indexes of civilization." Historically,

> In the confrontation of "civilization" with "barbarism," a "work ethic" emerged on the frontier. As an activity that transformed nature, work became a sign of ethnic honor that distinguished the gente de razón from the bárbaros. In contrast to the Center, where to work with one's hands was a sign of infamy, on the frontier even forms of manual labor, such as agricultural work and livestock herding, became signs of ethnic honor (Jones 1979, passim). (Alonso 1995, 107–108)[3]

Thus the elite Spaniards of the center disdained labor, especially physical labor, while on the frontier it became a "badge of honor" and ethnic (i.e., non-Indian) status. In the next section I explore how this distinction is used to construct ranchero identity.

Constructing Rancheros against the Urban Elite

If a belief in progress and individual rather than communal effort distinguishes rancheros from their Indian neighbors, work (particularly hard, physical labor) distinguishes them from those that they consider "effete" city dwellers. Rancheros are quite distinct from the urban elite in Mexico City (where rural Mexicans are called *nacos*) or Guadalajara, or even in mid-sized cities like Zamora in northwest Michoacán. The rancheros in this study quickly acknowledge the higher education of people in the cities, yet they do not hesitate to ridicule "citified" people (*catrines*), especially men who, if they do not work with their hands, are thought not to work at all. Clearly, then, these two identities are sharply differentiated by both the urban elite and rancheros. As discussed in Chapter 1, from the viewpoint of those in the city, rancheros are backward and uncultured; this contrast is discussed more fully below, especially in terms of its linguistic ramifications. The candid and even blunt predominant linguistic style of rancheros (*franqueza*) contrasts sharply with a favored verbal style of the urban elite: *cortesía* (courtesy), which is verbally elaborate and polite by indirection. Whereas *cortesía* is language of polite society that is often indirect, sensitive to the feelings of others, and verbally elaborate, *franqueza* is direct, straightforward, candid language (sometimes peppered with obscenities) that does not mince words. Such bluntness constructs a ranchero identity that emphasizes independence and self-assertion. As a verbal style it is direct, powerful, and blunt and as such invokes an individualist, egalitarian, and even entrepreneurial ideology.

Thus many rancheros disdain those who are not autonomous "self-made" men (and women), whether they be communal Indians or effete city dwellers. Office workers in particular, part of a hierarchy in large organizations (and thus not at all independent), are sometimes made fun of: such *asalariados* (salaried workers) become, in a ranchero pun, *al sal diario* (for the daily salt) (Barragán 1990a). This pun relies on the belief that salaried work is only valuable for the "daily salt" it can buy; in itself, such work (for others) is disdained. From these distinctions rancheros construct their own identity, based on an ideology that values work as a way toward progress—even wage labor if necessary, but only as a means to an end. As explained in Chapter 3, such labor on their part, enabled by migration to Chicago, has transformed their lives as well as their Mexican village. They have indeed progressed socially and materially, though not without great personal cost.

Franqueza as a Verbal Style

The authoritative, self-assertive stance of rancheros easily lends itself to a frank verbal style that is termed "bald-on-record" in politeness theory (Brown and Levinson 1987), which relies on the notion of face, or "the public self-image that every member [of a group] wants to claim for himself" (Goffman 1967, 61). Depending on context (such as power relationships, distance or closeness, and cultural values), certain linguistic acts on the part of a speaker can be "face threats" to a hearer:

> Doing an act **baldly, without redress**, involves doing it in the most direct, clear, unambiguous and concise way possible (for example, for a request, saying "Do X!"). . . . By going *on record* [baldly], a speaker

can . . . enlist public pressure against the addressee or in support of himself; . . . get credit for honesty, for indicating that he trusts the addressee . . . [and] for outspokenness. . . . (Brown and Levinson 1987, 69–71)

A speaker who wishes instead to avoid threatening a hearer's face either speaks "off record" (very indirectly) or "on record" uses "redressive action" which "gives face" to the addressee. Spanish address terms such as *tú* and *usted* (informal and formal "you"), for example, can be used strategically to emphasize either positive (solidarity-oriented) or negative (deference-oriented) politeness. Bald-on-record, in contrast, is communication that is stripped of conventional linguistic politeness devices that serve to reduce the face threat to the hearer by humbling the speaker. For example, a directive formed as a syntactic imperative—*¡Venga, apague esa luz!* (Come, turn out that light!)—is bald-on-record communication. In contrast, the same directive formed as a question—*Apaga esa luz, ¿quieres?* (Turn out that light, would you?)—includes redressive action in order to be polite, that is, to reduce the face threat to or be more respectful of the hearer (Haverkate 1994, 167).

The rancheros in this study frequently use direct, bald-on-record directives that do not humble the speaker. Such directives support a stance of autonomy and self-assertion, indexing their individualist ideology. Men, women, and children all use such directives frequently, often but not always (e.g., daughters on certain occasions use such directives to mothers) to someone lower in the family hierarchy. In one instance of this general pattern (mentioned in Chapter 1), an eight-year-old girl in the rancho who was attending to a cut on her ten-year-old brother's arm said to him as he grimaced from the pain, "¡Aguantase, si es hombre!" (Handle it, if you're a man!).

Linguistically, the devices that construct *franqueza* cohere in a "grammar of self-assertion," which is virtually a mirror image of the "grammar of helplessness" described by Lisa Capps and Elinor Ochs (1995). A grammar of helplessness emphasizes nonagentive roles, that is, semantic roles other than that of agent or actor, in which the speaker is sometimes completely omitted from the sentence. Various linguistic devices are used for diminished agentive roles, including verbs of necessity (e.g., "got," as in "I've got to get out of here. I'm not—I'm not *feeling* good"), hypothetical past constructions (e.g., "If I wanted to leave"), "try" constructions (actions are "tried" but unsuccessful), negation (actor fails to complete a given action), and intensifiers ("really" as in "really afraid") and de-intensifiers (e.g., "sort of," "like," "kind of," "maybe") to construct a portrait of helplessness.

In stark contrast to this grammar of helplessness, the rancheros in this study employ a grammar of self-assertion that emphasizes agentive roles in which speakers cast themselves as actors controlling situations (such as the man who described how he repaired the engineer's mistakes on the railroad track), directives in the form of verbal imperatives (*¡Vete a la frontera, muchacho!;* Get yourself to the border, young man!), direct questions (*¿Cuanto te costó esos zapatos?;* How much did those shoes cost you?), and other statements that can impose upon the hearer. Notably absent in this grammar of self-assertion are the linguistic devices used in *cortesía verbal* (verbal politeness) common in elite Spanish-speaking society, such as indirect requests (*Quisiera que me platiques de tu paseo;* I would like you to tell me about your trip) or other mitigating devices that reduce the imposition of a speech act (Chodorowska 1997; Chodorowska-Pilch 1998; Fraser 1980; Haverkate 1994).

According to Penelope Brown and Stephen Levinson (1987), such bald-on-record communication is used primarily in two situations: first, when there is little distance (much intimacy) between speakers; and second, when there is a hierarchical relationship between the interlocutors in which the speaker has more power than the hearer. In other words, it is used between intimates (where there is by definition little distance between speakers) or is used by a higher-status speaker to a lower-status speaker. In the first case, the use of bald-on-record communication assumes a relationship of trust (*confianza*) between speaker and hearer(s), and it also indexes honesty, lack of manipulation, and candor among equals in ranchero society. When the interlocutors are not equals in terms of age or gender (i.e., male/female or older/younger), such communication indexes the power differentials between them. Of course, bald-on-record language not only expresses status and power differentials; it also attempts to create them on the spot. An incident from my field notes provides an example.

Early in my fieldwork in the rancho I was introduced to a man outside of the chapel following the weekly Sunday morning mass. I reproduce this dialogue below:

Esteban: *¿Qué eres?*	What are you?
Marcia: *Soy Marcia Farr.*	I am Marcia Farr.
Esteban: *No, ¿QUÉ eres? ¿Inglés, alemán, qué?*	No, WHAT are you? English, German, what?

Marcia: *Bueno, pues, inglés, alemán, y un poquito de francés e irlandés.*	Well, English, German, and a little French and Irish.
Esteban: [*nodding and smiling*] *Bueno, ¿cual religión eres?*	[*nodding and smiling*] OK, what religion are you?
Marcia: *Fui bautizada católica.*	I was baptized Catholic.
Esteban: [*nodding and smiling*] Well then, you are very welcome here in the rancho.	[*nodding and smiling*] Well then, you are very welcome here in the rancho.

As shown in the first line, the very first thing this man said to me was "What are you?" Thinking that I had misheard him asking me who I was, not what I was, I replied with my name. "No," he said firmly, "WHAT are you? English, German, what?" Somewhat taken aback, I replied honestly with my ethnic background as I understand it. Nodding approval, he continued to interrogate me: "OK, what religion are you?" I replied that I was baptized Catholic (true, but in saying this I avoided claiming that I was a practicing Catholic). He smiled, slowly nodded, and then said, switching to English, "Well then, you are very welcome here in the rancho." The code switch itself was an added layer of welcoming, since the use of my native language indexed this welcome in addition to stating it explicitly.

This incident not only illustrates the *franco* (frank) verbal style that is bald-on-record (especially its use of direct questions); it also shows how such a verbal style constructs a powerful stance on the part of the speaker toward the hearer. Not knowing anything about me except that I was from the United States, instead of acknowledging distance (and possibly higher status) through various verbal politeness devices, he used direct questioning and a bald-on-record verbal style. Moreover, he used *tú* (second person singular, familiar pronoun) rather than *usted* (second person singular, formal pronoun), as indicated in verb endings (*Qué eres* [*tú*], not *Qué es* [*usted*]). The use of *tú*, of course, like *franqueza,* indexes either intimacy or higher status on the part of the speaker vis-à-vis the hearer. Since we were virtual strangers, his use of *tú* did not index intimacy; it indexed a claim of equal or perhaps higher status on his part.

His verbal choices here must be understood against the widespread awareness in the rancho of the power of the United States over Mexico, both historically and currently. Virtually all of the families in this rancho have members who are working in the United States and sending money for daily necessities like food and clothing or who have worked there in the past and now live off those earnings. Moreover, Javier, the man within whose household I often stay when in the rancho, has pointed out to me explicitly that the United States has exerted much control over affairs in Mexico. His younger son even told me once that the United States was planning to annex some northern Mexican states. Although this struck me as a wild rumor, it nevertheless vividly evoked the Mexican-American War of 1848, in which the United States took over half of what was then Mexico and incorporated it. In the interaction in front of the church, then, all of these background understandings inevitably came into play. Although I was in some respects of a higher status (more educated, with more money, and from a powerful nation), this man chose to use *franqueza* with me, to assert himself and possibly to claim his own high status, at least equal to if not higher than my own.

It is interesting to consider whether my interrogation, evaluation, and then (fortunately for me) welcome in front of the church would have happened in this way had I been male, a gringo rather than a gringa. Certainly the fact that I am female facilitated a man's use of a bald-on-record verbal style in this traditionally patriarchal ranchero society. Looked at this way, I was being incorporated into the local status order: the use of *franqueza* with me communicated that, although I might be of arguably higher status than he was in some respects, I was after all a female and so could more easily be confronted with such direct questioning than could a male of my class and national status. This is not to say that *franqueza* is not used between men (it most certainly is): *franqueza*'s bald-on-record style indexes either an egalitarian ideology among equals (e.g., male to male or female to female, when both are of roughly equal age) or a patriarchal ideology of hierarchy (e.g., older to younger or male to female). Depending on the context, *franqueza* constructs somewhat varying meanings. In this context, however, the fact that it was a male-female interaction unavoidably invoked gender relations, especially in a society in which gender is such a fundamental principle for social ordering (see Chapter 7).

It is also interesting, however, to consider this interaction in the light of critiques of politeness theory. Nieves Hernández-Flores (1999) views Brown and Levinson's positive and negative politeness as grounded in the characteristically Anglo-Saxon cultural value of individualism, inasmuch as face wants (mutual consideration for public self-image in an interaction) "focus on the individuality of people, on their right to privacy . . . [a] value [that] is not shared by other communities" (Hernández-Flores 1999, 38). Following Diana Bravo (1996), Hernández-Flores argues for autonomy and affiliation to replace the concepts of negative and positive face, respectively. Autonomy and affiliation, seen as universal categories, are "filled" with the cultural content of each case.

In Spanish society (the locus of Hernández-Flores's study), autonomy and affiliation are not opposed to each other but are linked in a common emphasis on group belonging: autonomy is the wish to be seen as an original individual standing out from his/her group (and therefore worthy of group acceptance); and affiliation is the wish to achieve closeness within a group. Autonomy is expressed as self-affirmation, so that one is seen as having qualities attractive to the group. Affiliation is expressed through the search for *confianza,* such that open, candid communication can occur. In order to fulfill the face requirement of autonomy, "the individual is expected to display her/his self-confidence by means of assertive behavior" (Hernández-Flores 1999, 40). In order to fulfill the face requirement of affiliation, developing *confianza* (which presumably follows from self-affirmation) allows speakers to speak openly and intimately, as though they were in a family context, which is highly valued in Spanish, and ranchero, society. Distance, then, and a corresponding lack of *confianza,* is negatively valued.

In the interaction above in front of the church, I was taken aback by the *franqueza* expressed in direct, blunt interrogation, which I initially interpreted as a face-threatening act (FTA). My interrogator, however, may not have perceived this as an FTA. Rather, his *franqueza* may have been intended as an appropriate expression of self-assertiveness, putting "one's best foot forward," so to speak. Possibly, then, he was incorporating me into his group on local terms, laying the groundwork for *confianza,* wherein such candid language is appropriate. At the same time, of course, he was impressing me with his own positively valued ranchero qualities of assertiveness and self-affirmation.

In similar interactions between men, *franqueza* either can index an egalitarian or trusting relationship or can index a relationship of unequal status. The latter often occurs in interactions between rancheros and the occasional *indígena* who comes to the rancho to work for or do business with them, especially if the person is unknown. The former often occurs within ranchero society, where a direct unadorned verbal style sets up expectations of a basically egalitarian social order based on *respeto* (respect) between independent, authoritative men (and between women or children equal in age). For both men and women, at least when they are communicating within their own gender or with those with whom they have *confianza,* the ethic invoked is that of a frontier society in which the individual must be strong and independent in order to survive.

Rancheras, although sometimes publicly deferential to men, are physically and emotionally tough and resilient. Given the ranchero emphasis on individuality and self-affirmation, they would lose esteem as persons if they were exceptionally deferential. Moreover, women work not only in the kitchen but also in the fields when necessary, and they take care of smaller animals, killing, gutting, and plucking chickens to prepare meals. Some know how to use guns and ride horses. They learn at an early age, like everyone else on the rancho, to take care of themselves in the natural and social world in which they live, defending themselves both verbally and physically when necessary. Thus when women use *franqueza* it directly indexes strength and self-assertion, as it does for men; but when men use *franqueza* it indirectly indexes masculinity as well (Ochs 1992). Notably, the most *franca* women are widows, who are perhaps permitted more self-assertion because their behavior will not affect a husband's public esteem.

Franqueza Constructed in Narrative Performance

As is shown in the interaction in front of the church described above, *franqueza* is an emergent quality of discourse constructed by interlocutors as they speak. Thus the self-assertion of *franqueza* is an emergent quality of performance (Bauman 1984 [1977]; Hymes 1975) initiated by a speaker and either accepted or challenged by others. As self-assertion, the emergence of *franqueza* indexes either social equality (e.g., between age-equivalent males or females) or social hierarchy (e.g., older to younger or male to female).

In the following excerpt from a tape made early in the research, when we were relative strangers to each other, *franqueza* is constructed in a narrative recounted by the senior male (the eldest brother) of the extended family. At the time, the man was visiting from the rancho, where he had retired after many years working in Chicago and where he managed the family avocado business. The interaction took place in the kitchen of a home in Chicago. The kitchen was filled with people, since this house and family served as a center for the entire social network in the early years of the study. We had finished eating and were about to teach a class that would help family members prepare for examinations and interviews in the amnesty process that would make them legal residents. Don Javier, unlike many other family members, already had a green card that granted him residency in the United States, although in this excerpt he tells about his interactions with the immigration authorities when he was still working without legal papers.

Juan Guerra begins the conversation by saying, "Bueno Don Javier, me dicen que usted, cuando primero vino a los Estados Unidos, fue a Harlingen" (Well, sir, they tell me that you, when you first came to the

United States, went to Harlingen).[4] After some discussion of where Harlingen is located near the Texas-Mexican border, Juan tells Don Javier that he was born there. Although he is familiar with the town, Javier says, he does not like it, because he was incarcerated twice there by the immigration authorities before he was legally sanctioned to work in the United States. Then he notes that he was the first to come here illegally from his rancho and that eventually about a hundred people followed him to Chicago. He continues to explain that, with money earned in Chicago, many of them bought land back in the rancho and planted avocado orchards; so today the rancho is vastly different from the pre-Chicago days, when only a few people had money and most of the rancho was very poor (see Chapter 3). After two interruptions by others in the kitchen (and in the midst of multiple conversations being carried on by others), Juan and Javier continue their conversation, and Javier launches into his story:

1. Javier: *Este, a mí la ley americana NUNCA me dobló la vista. O sea nunca le tuve su puro miedo. Me decía mira que esto y que l'otro. [Decía yo] "Está bien, tú estás en tu derecho. Yo voy a hacer el mío. Cometí un error, lo voy a pagar, nomás que allá en México."*	Well, to me, the American law NEVER made me look down in fear. That is, they never made me really scared. He would tell me, look, this and that. [I would say] "OK, you're within your rights. I am going to assert mine. I made a mistake, I'm going to pay, only over there in Mexico."
2. Juan: *Sí, sí.*	Yes, uh huh.
3. Javier: *Dice—ya después me encontré con un emigrante de, en, Detroit, Michigan. Y me agarró allá . . . entonces había un muchacho qu'empezó a decirle, "Que mira," le digo, "Mira, dile, dile nada más que eres de México, y, este, no tienes que decirle cómo llegaron."*	He says—then after that I encountered an immigration officer of, in, Detroit, Michigan. And he grabbed me over there . . . so there was a young boy who began to tell him, "Hey look," I told him, "Look, tell him, tell him nothing more than that you are from Mexico, and, well, you don't have to tell him how you got here."
4. Juan: *Sí.*	Yeah.
5. Javier: *'Tonces m'empezó a hablar el, el emigrante, "Sabes qué [le dije], me da pena con él. Apenas es un muchacho y siento feo que lo, este, que lo estés investigando así." Dice, "Oye, me gustas como pa' emigrante," y me rogó tanto que*	So the immigration official began to speak with me, "You know what, [I told him], I feel sorry for him. He is just a boy and I feel bad that, well, that you are investigating him this way." He says, "Listen, I'd like you as an immigration official," and he

me quedara en, en Michigan para donde la frontera de, de Canadá pero, "Pero yo [dije], ¿qué voy a hacer aquí? Todo está afuera y yo no sé hablar inglés." Dice "No, tienes un sentido . . ."	begged me so much to stay in, in Michigan for, at the Canadian border, but [I said], "What am I going to do here? Everything is foreign and I don't know how to speak English." He says, "No, you have a feel for it . . ."
6. Juan: *Sí.*	Yeah.
7. Javier: *"Vete a la frontera* [*slight pause*] *y vas a—" "¿Y voy a denunciar a la gente?" le digo. Dice, "Sí." "¡Pos no-o-o!"* [*marked fall rise intonation*]	"Get yourself to the border [*slight pause*] and you're going to—" "And I'm going to denounce my people?" I say to him. He says, "Yes." "Oh-h-h no!" [*marked fall rise intonation*]
8. *Al poquito ya me volví a venir aquí, fui a traer a mi esposa, nacieron dos niños.* [*pause*] *La—nos admitieron aquí en este país por medio de esos dos niños, ya 'tán grandecitos, aquella es m' hija, ella es mi hermana y, y así.*	After a little while I returned here, I went to bring my wife, two children were born. [*pause*] The—they admitted us here in this country because of those two children, now they are grown, that one is my daughter, she is my sister and, and, that's how it is.
9. Juan: *Sí.*	Yes.
10. Javier: *De veras fue reduro.*	Really, it was very hard.
11. Juan: *Es muy difícil al principio, ¿verdá'?*	It's very hard at the beginning, right?
12. Javier: *Sí.* [*pause*] *Muy difícil.*	Yes. [*pause*] Very hard.

In this excerpt Javier tells a story within a story: while telling Juan the story of their migration to the United States, he recounts the story of his capture (along with a younger male migrant) by the immigration authorities in Michigan. This capture occurred during the period when he was a migrant without legal papers, after he had been a legal bracero and before he became legalized through the birth of his two youngest children in Chicago. In this story, he stands up to the immigration officer (referred to colloquially as *el emigrante*), saying that American lawmen *never* made him look down in fear (*NUNCA me dobló la vista;* literally, "look down at the ground," meaning in fear). Since, as I have argued, rancheros generally enact pride with erect posture and direct eye gaze, for them this colloquial phrase is particularly apt. To be strong (*not* afraid) is to maintain direct eye gaze, literally to stand up to another person.

In this story Javier not only stands up for himself in front of *el emigrante;* he also stands up for the younger male who is captured with him and who, possibly out of fear, begins to tell *el emigrante* more than he needs to. Javier stops him, saying, all you need to say is that you are from Mexico, not how you got here. Javier is aware of his rights under U.S. law and points this out to the representative of this law who is arresting him: You are within your rights to arrest me; now I am going to assert my rights. By assuming this stance, Javier constructs himself as an appropriately masculine ranchero, that is, he assumes the role of patriarch, dealing with the immigration official on behalf of both himself and the younger male with whom he is traveling. His use of *franqueza* (as explained below) indexes qualities associated with masculinity: active control of a situation, the use of reason and seasoned judgment to deal with a crisis, and the assumption of hierarchical authority.

This storytelling exemplifies the performing of ranchero masculinity in the face of authority. Yet this particular performance is not unusually highlighted as a verbal performance. Though fleeting, it is a performance in the sense that Javier is aware of his attentive audience (Juan) and crafts his language in aesthetically pleasing and persuasive ways (Bauman 1984 [1977]; Hymes 1975; Tannen 1989), even though it is not as highly performative as Javier's storytelling language is on other occasions. Such performances by males within this network (especially in male-only contexts) usually involve humor and some "coarse" or taboo language. Here Javier is quite matter-of-fact in recounting how he stood up to the immigration official.

How is this performance, then? In other words, how does it differ from Javier's ordinary conversational language? The primary device which he utilizes to make this story performative is reported speech or what Deborah Tannen (1989) more accurately calls "constructed dialogue." Javier quickly shifts back and forth between his own voice and that of *el emigrante* in the recounted episode and by doing so embellishes a simple narrative with artfulness, constructing a dramatic dialogue between himself and the immigration officer in which he is placed in a position to decide whether or not he would denounce his people by becoming an immigration official himself.

As Javier shifts between these two voices, he sometimes includes and sometimes omits *digo* (I say) and *dice* (he says), but the speakers are clear to Juan, the listener, through marked changes in pitch level, pronominal reference (through verb endings in Spanish), and semantic context. Displaying these various voices within his story allows Javier to construct his own identity in contrast to the others. First, he contrasts himself with the boy, who is frightened and talking too much; in his recounting of this episode, Javier calmly stops the boy in mid-sentence and then speaks on his behalf to the INS officer. Second, he contrasts himself with the INS officer, whom Javier represents as trying to get him to switch allegiances. Here Javier constructs himself as a self-assertive individual who is sophisticated enough to know his rights and insist on them in the face of authority and as someone who is responsible and loyal to his people. Note here the construction of an identity that evidences both individuality and group solidarity (i.e., both autonomy and affiliation). Since identity construction relies on the creation of salient contrasts with other identities, the constructed dialogue here is crucial to Javier's representation of himself through *franqueza.*

Below I extract the constructed dialogue from the story within the story told to Juan Guerra in Chicago to clarify this artfulness and identity construction (I include here only the English translation; the original Spanish is provided in the full story above, lines 1–7).

Constructed Dialogue within Story

Javier (to official): OK, you're within your rights. I am going to assert mine. I made a mistake, I'm going to pay, only over there in Mexico.

Javier (to boy): Look, tell him, tell him nothing more than that you are from Mexico, and, well, you don't have to tell him how you got here.

Javier (to official): You know what, I feel sorry for him. He is just a boy and I feel bad that, well, that you are investigating him this way.

Official: Listen, I'd like you as an immigration official . . .

Javier: But what am I going to do here? Everything is foreign and I don't know how to speak English.

Official: No, you have a feel for it. Get yourself to the border [*slight pause*] and you're going to—

Javier: And I'm going to denounce my people?

Official: Yes.

Javier: Oh-h-h no! [*marked fall rise intonation*]

Javier enunciates *¡Pos no-o-o!* (Oh-h-h no!) with a marked fall rise intonation pattern, marking this particular speech as especially performative. These words also serve as the resolution to the climax of the story-within-a-story: when urged by the immigration official to become an *emigrante* himself because he has "a feel" for the work, Javier refuses so that he will not have to denounce his own people.

Javier's own voice in the story clearly shows the self-assertive verbal style of *franqueza,* which constructs him as independent, strong, and in control in the face of authority. His first words to the official in line 1 are direct and unadorned: they are all in the active voice, and he casts himself in an agentive role (i.e., he is an active agent, not an object of action or omitted from the sentence): "I made a mistake, I'm going to pay, only over there in Mexico." He assumes authority in the interaction, granting the officer his rights and then asserting his own, explicitly and directly stating that he is doing so. His constructed dialogue is notable for its lack of de-intensifiers—that is, he did not mitigate the force of his statements with qualifiers. Instead of saying, for example, that "perhaps" he made a mistake (*Quizás cometí un error*), he unequivocally announces, "I made a mistake."

Está bien, tú estás en tu derecho. Yo voy a hacer el mío. Cometí un error, lo voy a pagar, nomás que allá en México.	OK, you're within your rights. I am going to assert mine. I made a mistake, I'm going to pay, only over there in Mexico.

With their uniformly pronominal *tú* (you) and *yo* (I) subjects, both a syntactic and a semantic parallelism develops that aligns the equally short independent clauses into a staccato-like rhythmic pattern, which signals performance. The first two clauses parallel each other, one focusing on "your rights" (the rights of the officer to arrest him) and the other focusing on "my rights" under your law. The staccato-like rhythm is especially notable in the last two clauses and final phrase which begin with *Cometí un error* (I made a mistake):

Cometí un error,	I made a mistake,
lo voy a pagar,	I'm going to pay,
nomás que allá en México.	only over there in Mexico.

These poetic qualities affirm Javier's authoritative stance. Moreover, he uses *tú* with the official, rather than the more self-humbling and respectful *usted;* and in his account the official accepts Javier's claim of equality (and possibly friendliness) between them with his own use of *tú* (here in second person singular Spanish verb endings). Thus their words immediately construct an egalitarian relationship between the two men, even though one is an immigration official arresting the other, a migrant without legal papers. In Javier's account, his self-assertive claim to rights is not contested; in fact, it is admired so that the official begs him to consider becoming an INS official himself. These men are the two equals; the younger man, whom Javier also addresses with *tú* (line 3), here indexing that the hearer is of lower status due to his age, is under the protection of Javier.

What is important in this story is not its truth value, although it may well be factual. Of more interest here is the frank verbal style used in the story and its construction of ranchero identity. Javier recounts that the official *never* made him look down in fear (*NUNCA me dobló la vista*); instead Javier addressed him directly, with a bald-on-record verbal style, using linguistic devices that cohere in a grammar of self-assertion. This is the rhetoric of the self-made man, an independent individualist that nobody orders around. He is, after all, in a foreign country to work and thus to improve the social and economic well-being of himself and his family and, in his view, deserves respect for doing this.

Gender and *Franqueza*

As noted, women as well as men construct themselves as self-assertive and independent through *franqueza,* even though ranchero society is traditionally patriarchal and ranchero men frequently use *franqueza* to construct relations of power so as to dominate others. *Franqueza* is a verbal style that is emblematically ranchero and, as such, indexes qualities (e.g., self-assertion, autonomy) that are valued widely in ranchero society. Men and women, children and adults, all frequently construct themselves as strong and independent, even dominating, through *franqueza.* Yet these qualities are publicly associated with "superior" masculinity (Stern 1995) in the larger Mexican society, in contrast to "ideal" femininity expressed through self-abnegation, docility, and subservience to men (Melhuus 1996).

Rancheras, however, often do not enact such "ideal" femininity. Instead, they frequently use *franqueza* to assert their own strength, autonomy, and even dominance. Often this occurs within the verbal play frame of *echando relajo* (joking around) (Farr 1994b, 1998), which I explore in Chapter 8. When this happens, the two styles (*franqueza* and *relajo*) overlap, but *franqueza* also occurs in serious, "nonplay" talk. In both ways of speaking, however, talk is often constructed for aesthetic pleasure, and performances of such verbal art are frequent. The transcript below, like the one analyzed above, exemplifies both *franqueza* and verbal art which occurs conversationally, as a mother recounts in an extended narrative to her daughters how she stood up to her late husband when they were young.

1. Mother: *Yo ya la había halla'o como dos tres veces, adentro . . . de la casa. Primero andaba jugando arriba de la cama con Ramundo, y después con Juan.*	I already had discovered her two, three times, inside . . . of the house. First she was playing around upstairs on the bed with Ramundo, and later with Juan.
2. Daughter 1: *¿Con mi Pa?*	With my Pa?
3. Daughter 2: [*mutters*]	[*mutters*]
4. Mother: *¡Cállate, no andes diciendo así! Tienes que tener respeto.*	Shut up, don't go around talking like that! You have to have respect.
5. Daughter 2: *¿Y qué dijiste tú?*	And what did you say?
6. Daughter 1: *Am—¿QUIEN?*	M-ma—WHO?
7. Mother: *Yo, nada.*	Me, nothing.
8. Daughters: *!¿Porque?¡*	Why?!
9. Mother: *Porque yo tengo—yo tengo dentro de mí, toda la vida, una decisión. Que el que quiera hacer de su vida—que haga lo que sea, y a mí no me va enojar eso, porque hay que respetar las decisiones de otra persona.*	Because I have—I have inside of me, all my life, a decision. That whatever a person wants to make of his life—that he make what he want of it, and I'm not going to get myself angry about it, because one has to respect the decisions of other people.
10. Daughter 2: *A mí que me hiciera eso yo la mandaba a la chingada, que chingara su pinche madre a otra parte.* [*laughter*]	If someone did that to me, I would send her to the devil, the bitch—have her do her damn screwing around somewhere else. [*laughter*]
11. Mother: *Porque entonces—*	Because then—
12. Daughter 1: *¿Quién? ¿Quién, Ma?*	Who? Who, Ma?
13. Female Friend: *Tu padre.*	Your father.
14. Mother: *Cuando—*	When—
15. Daughter 1: *No, babosa.* [*side comment to sister*]	No, dopey. [*side comment to sister*]
16. Mother: *Cuando su hermana—cuando ella era chiquita, yo le—acá vivíamos en San Juan. Acá en San Juan, y ellos ya vivían ahí, y yo me fui, a llevarle a Juan el café. Como—serían como las seis o cinco y media . . .*	When your sister—when she was little, I—we were living over here in San Juan. Over here in San Juan, and they were then living over there and I went to take Juan his coffee. About—it was about six or five-thirty . . .
17. *Porque él 'taba tisando la campaña, o el horno que le dicen ustedes, estaba quemando. Y la vide cuando*	Because he was stoking the fire, or the oven as you say, it was burning. And I saw her when she crossed

se atravesó y se metió . . . pa' su casa, porque no había cerca.	and entered . . . her house, because there wasn't a fence.
18. *Entonces, yo no he de 'ber ido de mucho humor, y le dije a Juan, "Te traje ya el cafecito." Y me dijo, "Yo no quiero café 'orita, ya tomé."*	So, I wasn't in a very good mood, and I said to Juan, "I brought you your coffee." And he said to me, "I don't want coffee now, I already drank some."
19. *"Eso me 'bieras dicho," le dije, "pa' no venirme con la niña abrazada desde allá, y tenerla hasta que levantar." Y le dejé la olla. Dijo, "Llévatela." Le dije, "No, no la voy a llevar porque yo voy al molino. ¿Cómo crees que yo voy a ir con la muchacha y la cubeta del, del nixtamal?"*	"That you should have told me," I said, "so that I didn't come all this way with the little girl in my arms, and having to wake her up." And I left the pot. He said, "Take it." I said, "No, I'm not going to take it, because I'm going to the mill. How do you think I'm going to go with the little girl in my arms and the bucket of, of *nixtamal* [milled corn dough for tortillas]?"
20. *"Llévatela."* [*insistent command*]	"Take it." [*insistent command*]
21. *Que me regreso y que le doy una pi:nche patada a l'olla y que—cayó echa mil pedazos. Se la aventé a tu padre en las patas. "¡Trágate el café!" le dije, "o levanta los telpalcates y te los comes."*	I went back and kicked the da:mn pot, and it broke into a thousand pieces. I threw it at your father's feet. "Drink your coffee," I said to him, "or pick up the shards and eat them!"
22. Daughter: [*slight giggle*]	[*slight giggle*]
23. Mother: *Umm, y me fui. Y él se fue a almorzar p' allá. Y le dije, "Otro día, que yo vea, que Mariana está ahí, a putisa les voy a meter a los dos—a ti y a ella, cabrón!" Le dije, "Pa' que se le—a ti pa' que se te quite lo inrespetuoso porque estoy—yo estoy supuesta, a que tú me respetes a mí. Si no a bien—si no por bien, a güevo. Y ya sabes."* [*daughters giggle*] *Pero entonces era yo delgadita. A pus, ya me vi'tes en el retrato. Entonces—*	Umm, and I left. And he went to eat over there. And I said to him, "Another day, if I see, if Mariana is there, I'm going to give you both a blow—you and her, you son of a bitch." I told him, "So that—for you, so that you quit being disrespectful because I am—I am supposed to, you are supposed to respect me. If not nicely—if not nicely, then, with balls, by force. And now you know." [*daughters giggle*] But then I was slim. Ah, well, you've seen me in the photo. Then—
24. Daughter: [*giggle*]	[*giggle*]

25. Mother: —*Enton's era yo delgadita. Y entonces ella, entonces él me dijo, "¿Qué qu'eres que le haga?" dijo, "Pu's, yo no sé desde a qué horas se fue y ahí e'taba."*	—Then I was slim. And then she, then he said to me, "What do you want me to do?" he said, "I don't know when she went and there she was."
26. *Le dije, "Estaba porque tú querías."*	I told him, "She was there because you wanted it."
27. Daughter 2: *La saco a chingar su madre si yo no la quiera ahí.*	I'd take her out and mess with her if I didn't want her there.
28. Mother: *Entonces que voy—que voy y que le digo a esta mujer Ramona. Porque esa mujer Ramona también es mi prima, por parte de mi padre. Y el finado Ignacio, padre de la muchacha, también era pariente de nosotros por mi Pa, también. Enton's fui y le dije a Ramona, "Yo vuelvo a ver, Ramona, a ella, junta con Juan, y no le voy a pegar a ella, a ti te voy a mandar chingar tu madre. Y acuérdate que soy [apellido], cabrona. No se te olvide que soy [apellido] y no se te olvide de 'onde dependes, hija de tu chingada madre."*	Then I go—I go and I say to this woman Ramona. Because that woman Ramona is also my cousin, on my father's side. And the late Ignacio, father of the girl, also was our relative on my father's side. Well, I went and said to Ramona, "If I come back, Ramona, and see her together with Juan, I'm not going to hit her, I'm going after you to mess you up. And remember that I'm a [family name], you bitch. Don't you forget that I'm a [family name], and don't you forget who you depend on, bitch."
29. Daughter: [*giggle*]	[*giggle*]
30. Mother: *Y sale la vieja muy arrebatada,* [*high pitch*] *"¿Y yo qué culpa tengo, si Juan la invita?" Le dije, "Ya le dije, hija de su puta madre. Y acuérdese quiénes son los [apellido]." Umm. Le dije—*	And the old woman, very furious, spat out, [*high pitch*] "And me, what fault is it of mine, if Juan invites her?" I said to her, "I already told you, bitch. And remember who the [family name] are." Umm, I told her—
31. Daughter 1: Yeah, Ma, ROUGH HER UP! [gruffly and rhythmically]	Yeah, Ma, ROUGH HER UP! [gruffly and rhythmically]
32. Mother: —*"Pa' que sepa." Porque—*	"—Just so you know." Because—
33. Daughter 2: *Cállate pinche linguini* [*to sister*].	Shut up you damn linguini [*to sister*].
34. Daughters: [*giggle*]	[*giggle*]
35. Mother: *Yo nunca supe que fuera otra vez.*	I never knew her to go again.

This excerpt illustrates rough, candid, extremely frank language. As this mother recounts events from long ago in Mexico to her teenaged daughters in Chicago, she is facilitating the transformation of traditionally restrictive gender norms. As a socialization experience for the daughters, it illustrates that the changes in gender being made across the generations in such transnational communities are not simply the achievements of the younger generation. The older women are integrally involved with the younger generation in changing these norms, negotiating them verbally in conversations such as this one. Inasmuch as such language practices construct social reality for the participants, gender relations themselves are transformed during the storytelling. At the very least, these verbal sessions "push the envelope" of gender and allow both mothers and daughters to experience and even practice the changes that many of them are making in their daily lives. Although the transcript here seems to include only women (a man is within hearing distance but is silent), these changes also involve men, as young married women talk to and convince their husbands of the advantages of such changes for both of them.

Research on gender among contemporary Mexicans, either in the United States or in Mexico, has investigated the changing roles of women (Hondagneu-Sotelo 1994; Mummert 1994) as well as men (Gutmann 1996). Some studies have focused on the changing construction of gender among migrants in the United States: for example, on women's relative empowerment through their involvement in community building (Hondagneu-Sotelo 1994) or working outside the home (Espinosa 1998). Other studies have focused on changes in Mexico, pointing out that ongoing gender role changes are not restricted only to those who migrate and that such changes can be traced to several factors, such as the employment of women in recently commercialized agriculture in Mexico as well as the migration of men, leaving women in charge of households in Mexico (Mummert 1994). Because of the nature of transnational communities, of course, it is difficult if not impossible completely to disentangle the relative effects of factors such as U.S. or Mexican ideologies of gender and family, migration processes, and labor force participation on both sides of the border on changes in the social construction of gender in both Mexico and the United States. Nevertheless, many studies have made it clear that gender is changing among Mexican transmigrants, both in the United States and in Mexico.

Although such change is often described as occurring mostly in generation two (or one and a half) (Hirsch 1999), such changes inevitably involve several generations. Not all of the older generation remains stuck in a traditional gender frame, and not all of the second and third generations have changed this frame; moreover, many women of all generations talk of such ongoing changes. Several factors are a part of this process within the network under study here. First, the emphasis on individuality and autonomy within traditional ranchero culture provides a platform upon which women can initiate such changes. Second, young couples are collaborating in working out some of these changes and their effects on family life by talking through differences.[5] Finally, as is evident in the tape-recorded discourse here, mothers and daughters collaborate in the transformation of familial gender relations, as women support each other in such conversations.

The mother begins her narrative in line 16 with *Cuando su hermana—cuando ella era chiquita* (When your sister—when she was little). She then sets the stage for the story, telling her daughters where they were living and that on one occasion she gathered up her sleeping daughter and carried a pot of coffee to her husband, to the house of relatives near where he was working and where he went for meals. And she notes the time: about 6:00 or 5:30 P.M. On the way she saw a young woman, whom she had discovered fooling around with her husband previously, crossing the street and entering her own house, which put her in a bad mood. Upon seeing her husband, she said, "I brought you your coffee," to which he responded, "I don't want coffee now, I already drank some" (line 18). Here coffee may have metaphorical meaning (as sexual intimacy): she, as his wife, is properly offering some to him, yet he refuses it because he already drank it elsewhere. With increasing though restrained anger, the mother tells her husband that he should have told her that he had already had his "coffee" so that she did not have to come all this way with the baby in her arms, having had to wake her up to do so, and sets down the pot of coffee. This response on her part focuses the confrontation and leads to the climax of the story, which the mother artfully presents as constructed dialogue (Tannen 1989). The dialogue consists of her voice and his, both constructed by her on this occasion many years later in her Chicago backyard. Here I provide only the English translation.

Husband: Take it [the coffee pot].

Wife: No, I'm not going to take it, because I'm going to the mill. How do you think I'm going to go with the little girl in my arms and the bucket of *nixtamal?*

Husband: Take it [insistent command].

Wife: [returning and kicking the pot so that it breaks into many pieces] Drink your coffee, or pick up the shards and eat them!

At this point a daughter giggles in support and pleasure at her mother's self-assertion. The story continues: the father leaves to go eat, but the conversation continues, and the mother recounts the ultimatum that she gave her husband:

Wife: Another day, if I see, if Mariana is there, I'm going to give you both a blow—you and her, you son of a bitch. So that—for you, so that you quit being disrespectful because I am—I am supposed to, you are supposed to respect me. If not nicely—if not nicely, then, with balls, by force. And now you know.

Here the mother appeals to ranchero norms of *respeto.* First, a married man should not commit adultery; but if he does, he should never do so publicly, because this shows lack of respect for his wife's reputation. She tells him that if he does not respect her in this way *por bien* (being reminded of this obligation nicely) then it will happen *a güevo* (with balls, by force). The mother continues the dialogue between herself and her husband, who, perhaps caught by the logic of her appeal to traditional norms, begins to back down:

Husband: What do you want me to do? I don't know when she went and there she was.
Wife: She was there because you wanted it.

Here the husband weakly defends himself by saying that the young woman showed up without his knowledge, presumably seducing him. His wife, however, does not let him off the hook, saying that the young woman showed up because she knew he wanted her to. After a daughter (again) comments that she would go after the young woman involved, the mother extends her story by recounting how she then went and confronted an older female relative whom she believed was involved in the young woman's actions and who had been hostile to the mother.

Wife: If I come back, Ramona, and see her together with Juan, I'm not going to hit her, I'm going after you to mess you up. And remember that I'm a [family name], you bitch. Don't you forget that I'm a [family name], and don't you forget who you depend on, bitch.
Relative: [furiously] And me, what fault is it of mine, if Juan invites her?
Wife: I already told you, bitch. And remember who the [family name] are.

Again the wife/mother constructs herself as a not-to-be-messed-with ranchera. She relies on two warrants for her argument here: first, on her traditional right not to be disrespected by her husband; and, second, as she says both to her husband and to the older woman, if that does not work, on the reputation of her family name, one that is known locally for a willingness to fight. She may be a woman, but she still carries the name of that family and so has the wherewithal to apply "might to make right."

Throughout her recounted narrative, the mother constructs herself as having qualities usually associated with men in Mexico: bravado, self-assertion, forcefulness, and even dominance. At least in her account, she makes both her husband and the older woman back down and do what she wants. At the end of her story she says, quite satisfied, "I never knew her [the young woman] to go again." Linguistically, the bald-on-record style is most evident in her use of imperatives (e.g., line 21, when she orders her husband "Drink your coffee or pick up the shards and eat them!"). Her frequent use of *groserías* (swear words) reinforces her powerful stance.[6] Also, it is notable that she uses *tú* rather than the more respectful *usted* throughout the talk addressed to her husband and to the older woman. Moreover, as in the use of *franqueza* by Javier in the previous transcript, there is a notable absence of mitigating devices in the mother's direct confrontational style. She does not soften the effects of her face-threatening speech acts with such linguistic devices as *pues* (well), which her husband does use when he begins to back down. Finally, like Javier, she casts herself in agentive roles, finally threatening violence if her husband and then the female relative do not comply with her demand for respect.

A feminist reading of this narrative would note the power asserted by the mother/wife in effectively confronting a situation that offended her sense of personal dignity. Yet such a reading would also note the fact that the mother's final comment, that she never knew this offensive behavior to happen again, as a potentially ambiguous victory inasmuch as it might only have reaffirmed traditional gender norms: married men can fool around with other women, but they must not do so publicly. Also, it must be noted that daughter 2's angry comments (in line 10 and again in line 27) are directed at the young woman in question, not her father, possibly in response to her mother's earlier scolding (line 4), in which she insists that her daughter show respect for her late father. Taken in context, however, the mother's verbal moves were quite assertive and did achieve the goal of retaining, or regaining, public respect for her. Moreover, the narrative provides her daughters with a model of verbal confrontation with one's husband as well as a female stance of self-respect, self-assertion, and strength.

Noteworthy in this transcript is the co-construction of the narrative by both performer (the mother) and audience (the daughters). Although at first glance it may appear that the mother relates the story on her own, closer inspection reveals how her daughters contribute to the shape her story takes. Notice, for example, lines 8 (in which the daughters exclaim) and 10 (in which daughter 2 says, "If someone did that to me I would send her to the devil, the bitch"): both are daughters' responses to finding out that their father had fooled around with another woman early in his marriage to their mother. At first (in line 4) the mother commands them to show respect for their father, not to talk badly about him: "Shut up, don't go around talking like that! You have to have respect." When a daughter asks what her mother said when she first discovered the infidelity, and the mother responds that she said nothing, the daughters quickly protest, "Why?!" The mother explains (in line 9) that she said nothing because all her life she had felt that one had to respect the decisions that other people make in their own lives, rather than getting angry about them. This explanation, however, does not satisfy the daughters, one of whom says (in line 10) that she would go after any woman who did that to her!

After the daughters' disapproving responses to discovering infidelity and saying nothing about it, the mother tells how she eventually directly confronted her husband, using quite frank language to do so. As the daughters listen intently, giggling in appreciation and support, the story gets better and better. When the mother tells of her confrontation of her husband, daughter 2 again interjects a comment (in line 27: "I'd take her out and mess with her if I didn't want her there"). This comment may spur the mother on to extend her story, this time about how she confronted an older woman that she believed was involved in the infidelity. Again the mother uses self-assertive, rough language to threaten the older woman, as she did her husband. And again the language of the story is *franco,* replete with imperatives (in the constructed dialogue) and obscenities, which emphasize her personal and even physical strength. Clearly, like Javier in the previous story, this woman casts herself in agentive roles: she is a person who makes things happen, not someone who is passively the object of others' actions. She uses no de-intensifiers (e.g., "kind of," "maybe") but confronts people who are causing her trouble with direct, unmitigated language that is anything but self-effacing. Several of the daughters' comments are equally *franco,* with their strategic use of *groserías,* agentive roles, and the notable lack of mitigating devices such as de-intensifiers.

The analysis of this transcribed discourse illustrates that these women are co-(re)constructing gender, with their use of *franqueza,* on the spot, as it were. That is, through the self-assertion enacted by *franqueza,* both the individualist ranchero and ranchera identity and a reconstruction of gender relations are emergent in the verbal performance. This supports two main aspects of my understanding of gender within this transnational community. First, even within a patriarchal structure, the rancheras of the older generation in this transnational community have not been and are not now passive, self-abnegating women. Women who can survive in the conditions of relatively isolated ranchos, of course, are not likely to be either self-abnegating or passive.

Second, their daughters, nieces, and granddaughters (and some of their male progeny as well) are transforming gender, often with their guidance, in the form of co-constructed verbal performances. Keeping in mind the inevitable variation across the network (such changes are not always supported or welcomed—certainly not by men, but also not by all of the women), instances of discourse like the one explicated here are nevertheless frequent; they are more typical than not of the largely female conversations within these families. This family in particular, with its lack of a patriarchal father, has more such conversations; and the daughters have used the support from these conversations to achieve much in the world (e.g., college and even graduate education for several of the daughters). But such collaborative verbal practices are also found throughout the network of families. A careful look at these practices shows the important role of language in the social construction of (new) realities.

Conclusion

The analyses of discourse presented in this chapter show how *franqueza* works to construct ranchero identity. The bald-on-record verbal style of *franqueza* indexes a self-assertive, individualist ideology, and it is a predominant verbal style among the rancheros I have known for over fifteen years now. It is perhaps the most salient characteristic of this group, creating a sense of personhood that is straightforward, candid, and honest, on the one hand, and self-assertive, tough, independent, and proud, on the other. Qualities of sincerity and honesty are believed to support an egalitarian and stable social order, while self-assertiveness protects that order and assures one's (family's) own progress.

While evoking all these qualities of personhood, this verbal style often indirectly indexes masculinity, since these are characteristics usually associated with men in the larger Mexican society. Women, though, also use *franqueza* and thus also frequently construct themselves as tough and independent individuals in specific contexts. Even children use this style of speaking. Thus it is an ideology that is generally shared throughout the community and so underlies cultural, not just individual, practices, although some individuals are known to be *más franco/a* (franker) than others. Yet virtually all rancheros participate in and generate cultural and linguistic practices that evidence self-assertion and a belief in their own abilities to progress through hard work and effort.

Such examples of a belief in and commitment to upward mobility through hard work, independence, and interdependence abound in these families. Their discourse uses such constructs implicitly or even explicitly to distinguish themselves from other groups of Mexicans, notably indigenous Indians, who are perceived as hard-working but as not valuing private property or upward mobility. In verbal style rancheros also distinguish themselves from "citified" people, who, it is said, do not really work because they do not work with their hands for their own benefit. That is, they do not create things, and their own (and their family's) material well-being, with their own hands and effort. These rancheros, in contrast, are proud of doing and making things themselves, including their own houses and, for some, businesses; with their own labor they convert raw land and other resources into something that benefits themselves and their families. Migrating to Chicago, then, can be seen as one important manifestation of an ideology that is fundamental to their identities and permeates their discourse. As Javier once said to me, referring to Chicago, "Es una herencia" (It's an inheritance) for his children, giving them a base from which they can *mejorarse* (improve themselves) and, in another common phrase, *salir adelante* (move forward).

These beliefs constitute the liberal individualist ideology central to ranchero identity. This chapter has focused on *franqueza,* the primary framework for speaking among rancheros that verbally constructs this identity. The next chapter expands this verbal portrait of rancheros to include another way of speaking: *respeto,* a marked verbal style that constructs a different aspect of social order within ranchero society. In contrast to *franqueza,* which primarily indexes egalitarian social relations between families, *respeto* builds age and gender hierarchies that together form the basis of traditional family relations and of traditional ranchero society.

SEVEN

Social Order among Rancheros
Equality and Reciprocity, Hierarchy and *Respeto*

As noted in Chapter 6, rancheros are both intensely individualistic and family-oriented. Although families are the basic unit of their social order, individuals within these units are expected to be able to defend themselves (*defenderse*) both verbally and otherwise. Men, women, and even children are notably self-assertive in many contexts. As detailed in the previous chapter, they construct this aspect of their identity in their speech through *franqueza,* a way of speaking that is direct, self-assertive, and notably lacking in *cortesía.*

This chapter further explores social order in this social network of rancheros, discussing the principles and ideologies that traditionally underlie it as well as the norms for interaction that are expected to maintain orderliness in roles and relationships and relating social order to verbally framed disorder or *relajo* (the subject of Chapter 8). Here we focus on the ways in which individuals cement the social order through practices of reciprocity and the verbal code of *respeto.* Whereas *franqueza* is the primary framework (Goffman 1974) for speaking, *respeto* and *relajo* are marked ways of speaking that are framed as special.

Before exploring reciprocity and *respeto* in detail, I first consider more closely the age and gender-based social hierarchy that coheres ranchero society, relying on Steve Stern's (1995) definition of patriarchy and focusing on dichotomous notions of ideal masculinity and femininity and how these interact with the color-class hierarchy of the larger Mexican society. Whereas Stern focuses on the larger Mexican society, placing rancheros within its vertical hierarchy, the ranchero community itself is pervaded by an egalitarian ethos. Within ranchero families, however, an age and gender hierarchy orders relations. Relations in the community and within families are organized by norms for interaction: reciprocity (primarily family to family within the community) and *respeto* (primarily individual to individual according to family, or family-like, roles). Reciprocity is enacted in mostly nonverbal ways, whereas *respeto* heavily emphasizes norms for language use.

In this chapter I delve into reciprocity as a core value of these rancheros, contrasting this deep expectation of reciprocity with the perceived communal orientation of Indian Mexicans. I also describe linguistic norms for *respeto,* exemplified by language use within these families. Linguistically, *respeto* (and a hierarchical social order) is often contrasted with *relajo* (the democratic leveling of that order), which I take up in Chapter 8. Because of the oppositional relationship between these two ways of speaking, an understanding of *respeto* is clarified by some consideration of *relajo.* In this chapter I describe the orderly social background within which *relajo,* as verbally framed disorder, is made meaningful.

Social Order: Overview

Traditional ranchero society is undergirded by a liberal individualist ideology (see Chapter 6). This ideology, promoted during the late-nineteenth- and early-twentieth-century Porfirian dictatorship, was no doubt reinforced because many rancheros in northwestern Michoacán did very well during this period, accumulating land from fragmenting haciendas or from indigenous communities (see Chapter 2). Mexican society at that time was a pyramid, with a few wealthy large landowners on top, smaller property ranchers and farmers (rancheros) in the middle, and the large mass of workers and (relatively) landless peasants, especially Indians, at the bottom. Becker (1995, 11–13) describes this hierarchy in the early twentieth century as it was spatially arranged in northwest Michoacán:

> . . . the Spaniards and their descendants . . . constructed lucrative haciendas [in the northern plains] out of what once had been Tarascan land. This was particularly true of the northwestern corner of the state, dominated by the town of Zamora. Yet they refrained from building haciendas on a nearby plateau, the *meseta tarasca.* Located across the mountains, the plateau was studded with old volcanic cones running into basins or long depressions. By the early twentieth century, Tarascan Indians had taken refuge in this remnant of their former lands. . . . Owners of the large estates that dominated the state economy . . . lived in the best houses, fronting on the plazas. Their homes were spacious, frequently sporting two kitchens, always staffed by a number of servants and supplied with bountiful foodstuffs—chicken, eggs, chocolate, tamales. But the further one went from the plaza, the sparer lives became. Behind the most conspicuous houses were the dour homes of

> the middling mestizos, men who were muleteers, hacienda administrators, merchants, and the wives and servants who performed domestic chores . . . they may have owned a few chairs, a table or so, but little else. These were people who ate reasonably well but whose children, the daughters in particular, regularly lacked shoes.
>
> Past this tentative middle class lived the mestizo men and women who had been cast adrift . . . [and] lacked the barest security that their children would be nourished. . . . Crowded in the alleys or adrift toward the estates were the homes of the peons. Their sons wore the minimal white pajamalike outfits and the huaraches so prevalent in the period. In even worse straits . . . were the Tarascans, wandering into town, then returning to their sparse homes across the mountains.

Becker's "middling mestizos" (whom she calls a "tentative middle class"), although located in towns, have much in common with ranchero families from whom the network in this book descended. Rancheros, however, lived in relatively isolated rural areas which, until recent decades, variably experienced integration into regional and national life (see Chapter 2). Although Becker does not acknowledge ranchero society in the northwest Michoacán she describes, rancheros were the muleteers and hacienda administrators in her middling stratum: they sometimes had land but no money or food and only a few possessions (including female children who had no shoes).

Becker (1995) describes in detail how the Catholic sermons in this area during the first several decades of the twentieth century affirmed a hierarchical social structure. Clearly the church hierarchy was implicated in this socioeconomic structure, even while individual priests and other reformers urged a more egalitarian order, and small landowners were the favored model for agrarian reform (Cosío Villegas et al. 1995). Yet families, rich or poor, continued to be patriarchal, with the male head of household responsible for order within their stratum of the larger societal pyramid. Becker (1995, 22) notes the compensation that men lower in the social order received in the widely accepted dominance (in both Spanish and Tarascan cultures) of men over women and in the possibility of becoming overseers over other peons.

Ranchero society, then, is patriarchal (de la Peña 1984), although this is nested within an egalitarian ethic among heads of families. Ranchero families, like the rural Spanish villagers described by Julian Pitt-Rivers (1966), consider themselves equals. Slight differences in status among families (based on land ownership) are not marked linguistically in displays of deference. Moreover, such status is highly fluid over time, due both to the dividing of land through inheritance and to dollars earned through migration and used to purchase land. Thus (heads of) families relate to one another within an egalitarian ambiance. Within families, however, and publicly between individuals (based on family-like roles), gender and age organize interaction and power relations. That is, females ideally defer to males and younger people ideally defer to older people. Marked deference is proffered toward the eldest male in an (extended) family, even by other male heads of households. Within the family, age-based authority underpins strict discipline (from the father, to the mother, to the eldest child, to the second eldest, etc.).[1]

Even today among families from the rancho, whether in Mexico or Chicago, reciprocity and *respeto* still generally predominate as social organizing principles, although migration and other changes have begun to transform this traditional social order. Thus whereas gender and age still heavily influence rules for interaction (under a code of *respeto,* as described below), this is now more fluid than it is described as having been in the past. Several men in a number of different contexts have decried these changes in family gatherings or to me personally, saying that *antes* (before) was much better, when everyone was poorer but more "united" (more on this below). One older woman, Jovita, once talked to me nostalgically about how people used to work their fields together, singing songs to make it more pleasurable. There were no fences, she said, although everyone knew where the boundaries were between different families' lands.

On another occasion in the rancho, Bernardo (a man who had worked in Chicago for a few years) emphatically described the Mexican neighborhood of Pilsen as *desorden, un desastre* (disorder, a disaster), with gangs, drugs, and crime. He blamed much of this on U.S. laws which give children and women the right to call the police, who would then (unthinkable in Mexico) intervene inside the family. Acknowledging that sometimes true abuse merited calling the police, he still attributed what he saw as rampant disorder to the breakdown of family, and patriarchal, authority, the basis of traditional social order. Even in the past, of course, the social order was undoubtedly more varying, more fluid, and less static than is its usual representation in the present, but the pace of such flux may have increased with migration and transnational life. What follows should be read as a general description that is neither monolithic nor unchanging.

Gender Ideologies and Patriarchy

Gender is a central means for organizing social relations and linguistic interactions among rancheros. By "gender" I mean culturally constructed, relational notions or ideologies that represent femininity and masculinity. Gendered meanings are relational in the sense that they are constructed in contrast to one another: to be masculine is not to be feminine (Poovey 1988). They are also relational in the sense that they structure power relations within a group; that is, these ideologies position men and women hierarchically within the social order. These notions are culturally constructed (in that they are not determined by biological sex but differ from culture to culture and also differ from group to group within complex societies such as Mexico). As indicated in previous chapters (see especially Chapters 5 and 6), these rancheros as women and men construct themselves as different from other kinds of Mexicans, particularly Indians and urban elites. Both men and women are notably self-assertive, independent, and individualistic, as expressed in their primary way of speaking, *franqueza;* moreover, ranchero men (in appropriate contexts) are expected to embody a daring, confrontational, and authoritative *machismo* in their relations with other men and with women and children. Rancheras, while also constructed as independent and self-assertive, are nonetheless constrained in their confrontational behavior toward men, at least in public (although they do not hesitate to confront other women and children, including visiting ethnographers, when the occasion arises). While they do not display much public deference toward men, neither do they often confront them publicly.

Matthew Gutmann's (1996) study of masculinity in a working-class barrio of Mexico City emphasizes such variation in gender identities even for Mexican men, who are commonly stereotyped as domineering *machos.* Embedded in this view of gender, like that of culture, are several notions: first, that gender is socially and culturally constructed around biology; and, second, that it is not an unvarying set of meanings and relations in any group or across groups. This is particularly salient regarding rancheras, as I note above. They are distinguished from elite Mexican women, especially in their stance of toughness, independence, and willingness to fight, both verbally and physically. Just as Gutmann (1996) and particularly Stern (1995) describe multiple masculinities, so are there multiple femininities within Mexico, beyond the duality of the "good" woman symbolized by the Virgin of Guadalupe and the "bad" woman symbolized by Malinche.[2] Actual men and women work creatively within such constraints to construct their own particular identities. Gender identity is an ongoing process, constructed and reconstructed in daily life. *Respeto* in language use reaffirms these identities, whereas *relajo* provides a space within which people can challenge gender and other identities (as illustrated in the next chapter). *Relajo,* then, is a key place to look for what Raymond Williams (1977) called emergent cultural practices, whereas *respeto* is a site for traditional cultural practices.

The third notion embedded within this perspective on gender is ideological. Gender is ideological in the sense that the cultural constructs of which femininity and masculinity consist position men and women within the social order and thus involve power relations. Stern (1995) analyzes the interplay between masculinity and power in colonial Mexico in terms of three planes or dimensions: the vertical, the horizontal, and the familial. The vertical dimension involves color-class distinctions among men; the horizontal dimension involves relations among men within generally the same color-class grouping (in this study ranchero men); and the familial dimension involves relations within the family between men and women. Patriarchy, broadly defined, explains the dynamics of social relations within these three dimensions:

> . . . patriarchy refers to a system of social relations and cultural values whereby (1) males exert superior power over female sexuality, reproductive roles, and labor power; (2) such dominance confers both specific services and superior status upon males in their relationships with females; (3) authority in family networks is commonly vested in elders and fathers, thereby imparting a generational as well as a sex-based dynamic to social relations; and (4) authority in familial cells serves as a fundamental metaphorical model for social authority more generally. (Stern 1995, 21)

This understanding of patriarchy as a broad system of social relations and cultural values explains not only male power over women but also rankings among men and among women based on color-class (in the larger Mexican society) and the intricate interweaving of age and gender privilege that sometimes allows older women to exert power over younger men. Most importantly, however, it relates "gender culture" to "political culture" (Stern 1995, 19), illustrating the connection that feminists have noted between the oppression of women and other kinds of oppression in society (Ortner and Whitehead 1981). Specifically, it shows how an honor code (see Chapter 5) based on the control of women's sexuality buttresses a color-class hierarchical social order.

The honor code functions most effectively for elite men, whose masculinity relies upon the deference of others. The honor code itself, in fact, "tended to equate masculine honor with color-class privilege" (Stern 1995, 161). Such superior masculinity has more room for decorum and politeness (indexing high rank and Spanish descent) than does subaltern masculinity, which can only stand up courageously, refusing to show either fear or anger in the face of degradation by elite men; such degradation makes them metaphorically feminine or at least puts them into a female (dominated) position. Ranchero men, sandwiched as they are between elite Mexican men and truly subaltern Indian men, are positioned ambiguously in regard to this honor code. On one hand, they potentially face the "verbal taunting and humiliation" (Stern 1995, 163) of elite men (although I have never observed this or heard of it in conversation). On the other hand, they themselves sometimes verbally degrade and humiliate lower-status Indians, with whom they are in more frequent contact. Moreover, in their horizontal relations with each other they experience not only solidarity but also competition, in which they joust for superior status and the dominant male position of power. Thus *valentía* (courage, daring) and *hombría* (manliness) are highly valued ranchero character traits on two fronts. If faced with putdowns, they ideally evidence such courage and manliness as well as a quick willingness to fight to defend one's honor. One also evinces such traits, as well as superior masculinity, when displaying dominance over Indians, based on their deference.

Among themselves, at least in the colonial period, Indians relied more on a "communal ratification of their manliness" (Stern 1995, 182) than on the attempted imposition of superior masculinity employed by both elite men and men from the middling ranchero stratum. Moreover, the masculinity of Indian men, like that of other men, is supported by a gender contrast that emphasizes competence and empowerment for men and incompetence and weakness for women. As for women themselves, for all strata (elite, ranchera, and Indian), "the ideal code of female comportment" requires "submissive obedience to family superiors, sexual purity and fidelity, and discreet self-enclosure" (Stern 1995, 17). This code, however, like the code of honor for men, may constrain elite Mexican women more than others (although no doubt with spaces for challenge). Like rancheros, rancheras do not have the luxury of elaborate decorum and politeness but have emerged from a material history of frontier life and ambiguous in-between status with space for maneuvering the constraints of a patriarchal system. Whereas Indian men and women no doubt creatively challenge these constraints, ranchera women have the comparative advantage of an equivocal place in society. In the Indian/rural/poor vs. Spanish/urban/elite duality that pervades perceptions of Mexico, they (like rancheros) are "out of place" and can use this creatively to construct varying identities for themselves (see Chapter 5).

Within the horizontal dimension of ranchero society (in both Chicago and their Mexican rancho) men have ultimate authority, although women also wield considerable authority, especially within domestic and religious contexts. In fact, houses are often talked about as having been bought for the women by their husbands, and women effectively control all activities within the home and family, especially when the men are not there. Thus although patriarchy organizes the life of the network, the women are far from powerless; in this regard they are similar to the French peasant women described by Susan Carol Rogers (1975), who publicly submit to male dominance while in reality controlling virtually everything within the peasant household, the significant unit in that economy. I have witnessed many within-the-home interactions in which women (and some women more than others) exert control over household resources and even over the men by whom they are presumably controlled. Such control is increased by the fact that mothers are expected to be the spiritual center of the family, itself the center of network life. Women's authority, then, is partly built upon their expected superiority in spiritual matters; and within the domains of family and church their authority is rarely challenged. In public and political arenas, however, men usually dominate, although, notably, the township center near the rancho recently had a female mayor.

In a culture in which the family is a centrally valued unit managed by women, women do exert considerable power. A particularly patriarchal man, retired in the rancho, neatly articulated this for me: *un hombre solo es nada* (a man alone [without a family] is nothing); and a young woman in Chicago once commented caustically, "They all come crawling back!" (implying that even after much indiscretion a man will return to his family, since family is so important within his world). Nevertheless, the public performance of masculinity relies substantially on the ideology of patriarchy. Some men, for example, publicly display dominance over their wives and daughters (which is sometimes responded to with a "rolling of the eyes" or casually ignored and at other times taken seriously and resented). In short, although rancheros are dominant, rancheras are not weak or submissive, in contrast to the ideology of ideal femininity. While some aspects of *marianismo* (a suffering, self-sacrificing femininity; see Alonso 1995) sometimes characterize these women, more regularly they display a tough, independent, and self-sufficient demeanor. Rancheras, like rancheros, have led lives that require these qualities, and children of both sexes are still socialized according to these values. Girls are restricted in their mobility, and boys are not, but girls nevertheless learn to be strong and *defenderse* (defend oneself), especially verbally.

The apparent contradiction between the Catholic gender ideology (see Becker 1995) dominant in Mexico and the reality of tough rancheras can be resolved with the treatment of gender imagery in what Melhuus (1996) refers to as mestizo Mexico. Melhuus argues that there is an inherent ambiguity in the gender system: the society is male dominant, yet places its highest value on the feminine (the Virgin of Guadalupe), leading to a split between power and value. Ortner (1996) might call this contradiction a gender hegemony that is nontotalistic. In other words, patriarchal ideology is hegemonic in ranchero society, but it is not uniformly so. As I have noted, other ideologies (notably *franqueza* in the construction of self-assertive personhood) conflict with it, and rancheras can and do exploit this "crack in the hegemony" to construct personal authority and assert power. Thus rancheros dominate, but not always or everywhere, and rancheras are frequently as tough and authoritative as the men, in some contexts more so. In the next section I explore the more egalitarian aspects of ranchero society, at the level of the community rather than the level of the family. From this perspective, an egalitarian ideology (interfamily) coexists with a patriarchal ideology (intrafamily and interindividual across families).

Norms for Interaction: Reciprocity

According to Barragán (1997), being ranchero means being part of a ranchero society, although having this identity does not necessarily mean (now) that one was born and raised in a traditionally isolated rancho. Many people who self-identify as rancheros now live in cities in Mexico and the United States, yet they retain many fundamental values and customs tied to the traditional ecology of ranchos (see Chapter 6). It is commonplace in the Mexican neighborhoods of Chicago, for example, to see men dressed in ranchero style, with cowboy hats, boots, jeans, and tooled leather belts, often driving pickup trucks with miniature lassos hanging from the rearview mirrors. Many ranchero communities (sets of interrelated social networks) have reconstituted themselves in cities (González de la Vara 1994; Rouse 1989) and have continued the frequent interaction that characterized their lives back in the rancho, even when it means travel across neighborhoods in large cities or from city to nearby city (e.g., Waukegan, Illinois, to Chicago), as well as transnational movement. This interaction relies on a deeply ingrained base of reciprocity, or cooperation in many endeavors, that forms the basis of multifamily community. In traditional ranchero society, activities involving cattle complemented activities involving agriculture, and the two together constituted the work of the rancho.

Most importantly, organizing this work called on different kinds of cooperation or reciprocity out of necessity. Barragán (1990b, 72) lists three typical forms of such work organization:

1. When the owner (of land and cattle) carries out the activity;
2. When an administrator carries out the activities by means of an (unwritten) contract called *a partido* (sharecropping), in which the administrator usually keeps one-half of what is produced as compensation for the labor expended;
3. When the owner pays for someone to take care of work (e.g., agricultural) during some part of the year, usually while the owner is carrying out other activities (e.g., milking and cheese-making).

Usually administrators were sons or other relatives, and half of what was produced referred either to agricultural products or to newborn calves and cheese. With the increasing absence of landowners due to outmigration, the third form of work organization, paying someone to do the work, has become more frequent, according to Barragán.

The well-established tradition of working *a medias* (an agreement to share halves), out of necessity, was grounded in an egalitarian ethos. Because parties to these agreements were often relatives or close friends, contractual arrangements did not lead to a marked sense of social stratification. Even though some people owned more land than others, the values and customs were shared by everyone; and those without land aspired to having land, either through inheritance or through hard work and savings. This sense of cooperation extended beyond the (male) work domain to include other aspects of life, and even today in Chicago there is a profound sense of such give and take among those who share *confianza.* People frequently borrow and repay money to help each other buy houses or to respond to emergent economic needs. Women exchange food and other household items, bring clothes from Chicago to people in the rancho, send local cheese and breads up to Chicago, and so forth. I have received cheese and jam, embroidered doilies, and (many) handworked cloths to keep tortillas warm, and given U.S.-made bed sheets (highly valued), various food and drink items, books, children's games, clothing, tutoring (for the GED in Chicago and with English in the rancho), and help with college tuition (in Mexico). Once when returning to Chicago from the rancho I arrived at the Dallas/Fort Worth airport so laden with boiled chayotes (a vine-grown squash), home-made *chongos* (sweetened boiled milk curd), and *gorditas* (whole wheat buns) that my arms ached from moving from gate to gate to change planes.

Early in my fieldwork in Chicago, I fell into the habit of bringing, among other things, twenty-pound bags of rice when I arrived at people's houses, for they frequently fed me delicious Mexican meals. Such gifts are never remarked on (something I found puzzling at first, as I was expecting to be thanked) but are simply accepted as part of the understood reciprocity and, more importantly, as commitment to the relationship. During a conversation in the rancho one woman complained that a man from another family who hunts birds used in cooking has never given her even one—and, worse, his wife, who is her *cuñada* (sister-in-law by virtue of being the sister of her late husband), has not done so either:

Susana: *A mí nunca me ha regalado una güilota.*	He has never given me one bird.
Jovita: *¿Y Flora a escondidas?*	And Flora hasn't given you any secretly?
Susana: *Menos. Tampoco ni Flora ni Carmen.*	No, even worse. Neither Flora nor Carmen.
Jovita: *No te quieren.*	They don't like you.
Delia: *No te quiere Flora.*	Flora doesn't like you.

Breaches in the expectations of reciprocity only serve to reaffirm the significance of the exchanges: because the brother- and sister-in-law never share the results of his hunt, they are not committed to the friendship, so there are no *alianzas* (ties) between them.

Those who do share such ties can rely on a substantial safety net in times of need. When someone is sick, others visit to check on the sick person and bring food. In the rancho this happens on a daily basis; in Chicago it is more often done by phone, unless people are living in close proximity (e.g., renting an apartment in the house owned by someone else in the network). As I lamented one time about the lack of such closeness in my own life in Chicago and searched for a word to describe it, Arcelia (a woman with whom I often stay in the rancho) quickly finished my sentence for me with the word *unión.* She immediately understood this contrast between life in the rancho and in Chicago. Such *unión* might be expected in a small, face-to-face agricultural community in which everyone is related by either biological or fictive kinship; but even though the pressures of working and living scattered across a large urban area may have begun to dilute it in Chicago, many people in the network work hard to maintain it.

Of primary importance in this system of reciprocity is the understanding that you must respond if you are asked for help by someone who has helped you. Not to do so is interpreted as not holding up your end of the implicit contract. At the same time the high value placed on independence means that people who receive help, if they do not reciprocate equally, suffer in terms of status. As Jovita said once regarding those who bring her gifts from Chicago, "Yo no quiero regalos pos pa' qué, no tengo nada para ti. Nomás quiero ver tu persona nomás yo a ti" (I don't want gifts, well, because, for what, I don't have anything for you. I only want to see you in person, just you and me). The status accorded to those who help others furthers the reciprocal nature of interaction and builds solidarity; in fact, for rancheros, as in many other societies, such reciprocal gifting closely parallels social bonds and status (Mauss 1990 [1950]).

Another institution that reinforces reciprocity is the system of *compadrazgo,* in which women and men are asked and become co-(god)parents (*comadres* and *compadres*) with biological parents, for the purpose of looking out for the welfare of individual children (and forming bonds between adults and children but also between the adults involved). *Compadres* and *comadres* (in this network almost always relatives) are selected for each child for baptism, first communion, and marriage (at one time they were also selected for confirmation, but this practice has fallen into disuse). *Comadres* and *compadres* often call each other by this title rather than by their first names, which signals intimacy and trust (*confianza*), and involve themselves in guiding and providing *consejos* (verbal advice) to their godchildren (see Valdés 1996, 125–128, for a detailed explanation of the verbal genre of *consejos*). The overlapping and multiple relationships of *compadrazgo,* then, fortify the reciprocal basis of ranchero community, and they also distinguish between parts of social networks who may have fallen into discord with each other and thus may no longer share *confianza.* When social networks come apart, which happens very infrequently, it is usually because of a breach in the expectations of reciprocity and *confianza.*

Significantly, a reliance on *alianzas* (alliances) and reciprocity is not the same as being communal, because reciprocity in fact requires the independence of both parties. Although there is certainly a commitment and orientation to the importance of the group (usually the extended family), this coexists with a sense of independence, individualism, and autonomy (as explained in the previous chapter).

Norms for Interaction: *Respeto*

In contrast to the egalitarian ideology underlying norms of reciprocity, the norms of *respeto* construct a hierarchy of social roles. *Respeto* guides both verbal and nonverbal interaction between network members:

> *Respeto* in its broadest sense is a set of attitudes toward individuals and/or the roles that they occupy. It is believed that certain roles demand or require particular types of behavior. *Respeto,* while important among strangers, is especially significant among members of the family. Having *respeto* for one's family involves functioning according to specific views about the nature of the roles filled by the various members of the family (e.g., husband, wife, son, brother). It also involves demonstrating personal regard for the individual who happens to occupy that role. (Valdés 1996, 130)

Thus respect is owed to people not simply out of a sense of personal dignity but also because of the roles that those persons play. Fathers and mothers are always to be respected, even when they do not live up to the obligations of their positions. Even adult children, if they are still living at home (e.g., unmarried daughters), are expected to obey their parents and do what they are told to do. The roles in the family (father, mother, brother, sister, grandmother, etc.) include rights, obligations, and privileges. Fathers, for example, are expected to work hard and provide for the family, and they have the right to have their commands followed. Mothers are expected to manage the entire household, be the spiritual center of the family, and socialize the children so that they are *bien educado* (well brought up), disciplined, and responsible. As noted in Chapter 4, *educación* has broader connotations than does the English term "education" (Valdés 1996). In Mexico it includes both home socialization regarding manners and sociability and more explicitly formal teachings (*enseñanza*), often but not always at school. Sisters and brothers also have parts to play within the family system of roles. Brothers assume responsibility for and control over sisters, especially if the father is no longer living; and sisters are expected to take care of brothers, including protecting their honor, especially by restricting their own sexuality and mobility. Since both age and gender organize these social relations, older siblings often have more control over and responsibility for younger siblings, regardless of gender.

Anthony Lauria (1964) defines *respeto* (among Puerto Rican men) as a quality or image of the self which ensures the *dignidad* (dignity) of both oneself and one's interlocutor. He ties *respeto* not only to dignity but also to *honor* and to the "ceremonial courtesy" of adult males, depicted as "haughty Hispanic individualist[s]" who conserve within themselves an "inviolable residue of pride" (Lauria 1964, 55). Such an understanding of selfhood has much in common with (self-)representations of ranchero individualism and their notions of *respeto:*

> Respeto . . . signifies proper attention to the requisites of the ceremonial order of behavior, and to the moral aspects of human activities. This quality is an obligatory self-presentation; no Puerto Rican is considered properly socialized unless he can comport himself with respeto. (Lauria 1964, 55)

Both Valdés's and Lauria's definitions of *respeto* invoke honor. The honor code of Spain, brought to Mexico by conquistadors, priests, and colonists (see Chapter 5), has two interrelated aspects: honor-precedence and honor-virtue (Alonso 1995; Gutiérrez 1991; Pitt-Rivers 1966). Honor-precedence refers to one's status or position within a hierarchical social order: those with more honor are higher in the social order than those with less, or no, honor. Honor-virtue refers to one's public reputation, ideally based on behavior but sometimes based on talk about alleged behavior, and involves clearly demarcated gender roles and practices that attribute physical courage to men and modesty (especially sexual) to women. In Spain, prior to the conquest of the New World, honor as status was linked to purity of blood, that is, blood without Jewish or Moorish descent (Sanders 1978). According to Julio Caro Baroja (1966, 123), "in the north of Spain an idea existed . . . in which the people of the south are in general the product of mixtures and bastardies, which affect their morals . . . it is with reference to the dubious Moorish ancestry, not to the Jewish, that the Andalusians, and southerners in general, are considered a 'bad breed.' " Spaniards continued the *reconquista* (the reconquest of Spain from seven centuries of Moorish domination) in Mexico by establishing a social, economic, and political hierarchy based on honor as ethnicity. As noted in Chapter 5, some families in the rancho are still, almost five centuries after the conquest, referred to as "not really Spanish, but Moors." Ironically, the ancestors of the family referred to were from the province of Asturias in the north of Spain, not the south, where mixture among Christians, Muslims, and Jews was more common. Nonetheless, their family name (and some facial features, according to some) indexes their Moorish descent.

Thus although the old Spanish code of honor has undergone some changes in ranchero western Mexico, many of its basic tenets still hold. The word "honor" itself rarely is used, but a sense of honor is still evident in sanctioning misbehavior, often but not always sexual. Shame or modesty (*vergüenza*), however, is frequently heard and remarked upon, and within this network it is used in reference to both women and men. The term *sinvergüenza* (a shameless person) is considered to be the worst epithet. When a woman is a *sinvergüenza,* it is usually the result of her sexual (mis)behavior or excessive drinking. When a man is called this, he has been terribly lax in maintaining his responsibilities to his family. Men or women who are simply *flojo/a* (lazy) are severely criticized, but they do not quite merit being called *sinvergüenzas,* a term which is reserved for more serious moral lapses. A man who abandoned his wife and many children in the rancho after he went to Chicago to work (a rare occurrence in this community), for example, and who eventually married a relative there is considered a *sinvergüenza.* His former wife, who clearly labels him so, said to me, "Like an animal, he has no shame."

Honor/shame distinctions within this social network, then, evaluate people on moral grounds—honor-virtue, rather than honor-precedence, given the egalitarian ambiance of ranchero society. This restriction of honor/shame (here *vergüenza* and *respeto*) to virtue is strikingly similar to that of the rural Spanish villagers in the classic studies by Pitt-Rivers (1971 [1954], 1966). In both cases honor/shame judgments are restricted to moral considerations (especially regarding sexuality), because status considerations are generally irrelevant, given the egalitarian relations among farmers/rancheros. Both men and women are expected not to commit adultery, although women are more severely judged for this moral failing than men. A man's masculine reputation (among other men) is even reinforced by such behavior, especially if the dalliance does not interfere with his family responsibilities. For the urban middle class, in contrast, honor/shame constraints include not only honor-virtue but also honor-precedence, because considerations of status are relevant for them, unlike their poorer rural counterparts. Finally, members of the upper-class elite, secure in their honor-precedence, are freer to disregard the constraints of honor-virtue. In Spain this includes upper-class women as well as upper-class men (Pitt-Rivers 1966, 63–64).

Among these rancheros, a person, usually a man, who is honorable holds true to his word (*la palabra*), is honest in financial dealings, and is candid and frank (*franco*). Moreover, he and others generally adhere to the moral code that underlies the social order: *respeto.* One man's words to me, "Respeto es vivir en paz" (respect is to live in peace), emphasize the function of this code to ensure social order. As noted in Chapter 1, this use of *respeto* alludes to a well-known quotation by a nineteenth-century president of Mexico Benito Juárez: "El respeto al derecho ajeno es la paz" (Respecting the rights of others is peace). This understanding of *respeto* as social order is universally shared in the rancho: "Respeto es casi igual con vergüenza" (Respect is almost the same as shame or modesty). Responses from all the people I talked with were practically, and remarkably, identical. Dionicio's words sum up this agreement:

Respeto es vivir en paz, no ofender a una persona, respeto al derecho ajeno, amistad. Si quieres vivir bien, no peleando, tienes que tener respeto. . . . Si tienes vergüenza, no haces nada para ofender. . . . Es lo mismo para hombres y mujeres porque son partes iguales.	Respect is living in peace, not offending other people, respecting the rights of others, friendship. If you want to live well, not fighting, you have to have respect. . . . If you aren't shameless, you don't do anything to offend. . . . It's the same for men and women because they are equal parts.
Hay mas respeto aquí en México—más en el rancho que en una ciudad—que en los Estados Unidos, donde cada quien, cuando hay chanza. Pues, depende en la persona.	There is more respect here in Mexico—more in the rancho than in a city—than in the United States, where it's every person, whenever there's a chance. Well, of course, that depends on the person.

Two proscribed activities cause someone to lose *vergüenza* (become shameless) and thus undermine *respeto: andando con otro/a* (running around with someone else's wife or husband) and *agarrando cosas* (stealing the property of others). I have spent enough time with the women in this transnational community to know that they do not, with rare exceptions, *andar con otros* (run around). Given my gender, my direct observations of the men are limited except when they are in large family gatherings. What I have learned through conversations, however, suggests that those men who have extramarital encounters do so at a distance from family life or, while in Mexico, have fleeting encounters with Indian women. Yet if such encounters are not publicly acknowledged as *andando con otras,* it does not humiliate the man's wife, publicly at least. If and when such behavior becomes public knowledge, however, it is considered humiliating and even shameful by many, certainly by women. Yet, in general, many in the older generation still assume that "men will be men" and judge them by a different standard than they do women. Yet many women of the younger generations in both Mexico and Chicago are very critical of such behavior and are exceedingly careful in choosing mates. Early in the study, my efforts not to be judgmental led Dalia (a young woman in Chicago) to exclaim to me in exasperation (in English): "Haven't you noticed, Marcia?! There's a double standard!" This young woman and others are initiating significant changes in gender roles and expectations.

Language and *Respeto*

A mother and her teenaged daughter in the rancho, Delia and Pilar, added a linguistic aspect to *respeto:* a person should not use taboo language (*no habla maldiciones*). They criticized both a man and his wife in the rancho for having a *boca suelta* (loose mouth) or a *lengua floja* (lazy tongue), saying that the wife in particular was *siempre hablando en doble sentido* (always talking with double [sexual] meaning), even about her own daughter. This daughter recently had begun flirting (*coqueteando*); and the mother, complaining, told people (ironically) that she would send her to Tijuana to a *lugar para todos* (house of ill repute). Delia and Pilar strongly disapproved of such public talk; both the daughter's behavior and the mother's public talk about it undermined the family's *respeto* as well as community norms. Their opinion was that, even if a daughter flirts (although she should not do so), it should not be publicly acknowledged, least of all by her own mother.

Thus the public knowledge of behavior is more important than a private reality; and a person's (or family's) public face (Goffman 1967) is the basis for *respeto.* Consequently, *respeto* involves "both the presentation of self before others as well as a recognition and acceptance of the needs of those persons with whom interactions [take] place" (Valdés 1996, 132). In the above scenario, the mother's presentation of self was lacking in *respeto* in two senses: she herself was using inappropriate language (with sexual *doble sentido*), and she was publicly acknowledging behavior that lessened her family's respect in the community. In doing so, she was not acting with respect toward her interlocutors either, who were offended by her (linguistic) behavior.

Language, then, while not the only kind of behavior important in maintaining *respeto,* plays a crucial part in doing so; in this sense, *respeto* involves language ideology or beliefs about language that implicate social standing (Woolard 1998). *Respeto* in interaction is basic to the social contract and thus is essential to the life of the community. In this particular community *respeto* is colored by values, attitudes, and beliefs that stress independence and self-assertion and a certain amount of direct, frank talk (*franqueza*) that enacts such individualism. Yet a preponderant style of *franqueza* does not preclude a complementary emphasis on politeness, locally defined. That is, urban elite Mexican society defines politeness differently than do these rancheros. Because elite politeness has been dominant in the larger society, popular representations of contemporary rancheros stress their coarseness and lack of social (notably verbal) skills.

Henk Haverkate (1994, 11–12) traces this dominant Spanish language ideology to the life of the court at the end of the Middle Ages, where "courtesans began to distinguish themselves from the common people, creating a system of manners that served as a standard of social distinction." People then became preoccupied with socializing children into "current norms of politeness" and viewed the lack of good manners as "characteristic of the style of life of people of humble extraction." A consequence of this is the stereotype of rancheros as uncultured hillbillies. As explained in Chapter 6, *cortesía* in elite Mexican society entails some indirectness and much verbal elaboration, whereas the *franqueza* of rancheros is stripped of all nonessential verbal elaboration. Yet rancheros have their own notions of politeness, notably a code of *respeto* that is enacted verbally. As with most cultural differences, these distinctions are matters of degree and appropriateness across contexts rather than sharp qualitative differences between the two groups.

Ranchero politeness involves brief verbal formulas that are used regularly: *¡Que milagro!* (What a miracle!), uttered when greeting someone not seen in a while; *¿Porque te vas tan pronto?* (Why are you leaving so soon?), used as the first response to a guest who has indicated an intention to leave; and *¡Que le vaya bien!* (May things go well with you!: i.e., Have a safe trip home!), uttered when a guest leaves. Another verbal aspect of politeness involves a general interdiction against swearing in mixed (gender) company or in front of children, although this is a norm held more at the level of ideology than in practice. In mixed company, however, swearing is rare. Women especially are judged negatively if they use swear words (*maldiciones*); and yet, when they do swear, especially during *relajo* (see Chapter 8), laughter rather than criticism can result. Of course, given the prohibition against women swearing, it is especially funny when they, not men, do it.

Tú and *Usted*

In spite of the local construction of *respeto* as egalitarian (living in peace, respecting the rights of others, male and female roles being complementary and equal), ranchero politeness and *respeto,* like *cortesía,* involve systematic use of *tú* and *usted* (informal/intimate and formal/distant "you") in ways that build hierarchy. A number of studies have concluded that *tú* is gaining ground over *usted* in many Spanish-speaking communities in Spain, Latin America, and the United States (Blas Arroyo 1994–1995; Carricaburo 1997; Correa-Uribe 1995; Sigüenza-Ortiz 1996). This is more true of younger than older generations and sometimes is correlated with urbanization and other social changes, such as a move toward more egalitarian politics. Among Spanish-English bilinguals in the United States, the influence of English, which has only one second person singular pronoun, is another factor in the simplification of this pronominal address system.

Most studies of *tú* and *usted* utilize the politeness theory of Brown and Levinson (1987), linking *tú* with informality and/or solidarity and *usted* with formality and/or distance. Such studies view pronoun choice as reflective of social relations that are preexistent in the context in which the language is used: that is, these pronouns are referential indexicals (Silverstein 1976), linguistic signs that point to aspects of the context. These pronouns not only refer to specific persons (e.g., the addressee), but they also point (more abstractly) to the relationship between the two people. In other words, the choice of *tú* or *usted* signifies the speaker's affective disposition (Ochs 1990) or attitude toward the addressee—either equal status due to intimacy and/or solidarity or unequal status, whether from an inferior toward a superior or the reverse. From this perspective the use of *tú* or *usted* not only reflects such attitudes and power differences but constructs them on the spot. In other words, a person who uses *tú* is communicating an attitude of either intimacy/solidarity or higher status/power, depending on the context (and the perceived status of the addressee). For example, reciprocal *tú* is normally expected (i.e., it is unmarked) either between speakers of relatively equal power or status or between intimates. Reciprocal *usted,* in contrast, is expected between those who do not know each other well and/or to convey formality. In nonreciprocal use of these pronouns, *tú* is expected from those with more power or higher status in addressing those with less power or lower status. Conversely, *usted* is expected from those with less power or lower status in addressing those with more power or higher status.

Role relationships (especially familial ones) as well as the domain of interaction (e.g., home, church, work), generational group, and speech event are important influences in the choice of *tú* or *usted* (Sigüenza-Ortiz 1996). As a rural, culturally conservative population, rancheros tend to preserve such verbal distinctions even in an urban setting like Chicago, although this is more true of older than younger generations, especially those who are bilingual and thus possibly influenced by English.

Within the families in this study, traditional norms for *tú/usted* usage are generally followed, with some exceptions. First, as has been noted in one other study (Sigüenza-Ortiz 1996), although parents usually use *tú* when speaking to their children, they sometimes use *usted,* notably with commands and directives. This use of *usted* clearly does not index deference but rather authority and distance as well as some formality. Second, in addition to this use of *usted,* wives and husbands of the older generation frequently address each other with *usted* in front of others, a conservative usage that emphasizes their family roles, as in the following excerpt from an audiotape made in a kitchen in Chicago:

Wife: *Ay viejito, no hay tortillas. Encargue si por favor.*	Oh, dear, there aren't any tortillas. [you formal] Get someone to get them, please.
Husband: *Ahh?*	Huh?
Wife: *Encargue tortillas.*	[you formal] Order tortillas.
Husband: *Ay vieja, pero usted no se fija nunca en nada . . . ¿no ya está usted grandota?*	Oh [wife], but you [formal] never ever notice anything. . . . Aren't you [formal] grown up already?

Third, there are regularly occurring instances of apparently "meaningless" variation on the tapes in which *tú* and *usted* alternate within the same utterance without seeming to carry any attitudinal meaning. According to Carmen Silva-Corvalán (1994), such "meaningless" variation can be expected when a linguistic change is in progress, as may be the case with some uses of *tú* and *usted.*

Apart from this kind of fluctuation, traditional norms generally are maintained on the tapes for this study, although the solidarity of gender plays a larger role than has been acknowledged in previous studies. As *maestros* (teachers), my then doctoral student and co-ethnographer Juan Guerra and I were accorded *respeto* and addressed with *usted,* at least initially. Within a month or so, however, a shift occurred. As my friendships with the women grew, most of them began to address me either by my first name or with *tú,* although they persisted, even against his expressed wishes, in addressing Juan with *usted* and as *maestro.* He argued with several women that they certainly should address him with *tú* because we all had known each other for four months; when they did not, he jokingly called them either *alumna* (student) or *señora* with their last name. They chuckled at his humor but nevertheless continued to use *usted* with Juan and *tú* with me, as in the following example (although *tú* and *usted* are not explicitly used here, the -*s* suffix on *quieres* is the equivalent of *tú* and its absence in *quiere* is the equivalent of *usted*):

Rosario (to Marcia): *¿Quieres una tostada? ¿Quieres una tostada?*	Do you want a tostada? Do you want a tostada?
Marcia: *No, gracias.*	No, thank you.
Rosario (to Juan): *¿Uste', maestro, no quiere una tostada de jamón?*	You, teacher, don't you want a ham tostada?
Juan: *Una.*	One.

The women's discomfort with using *tú* with Juan most likely is due to its potential interpretation as indexing (potentially sexual) intimacy, at least according to traditional ranchero norms. In contrast, after getting to know him, men often address Juan with *tú* (unless foregrounding his status as a teacher) but vary in addressing me either with *usted* or with *tú*, depending on context. When calling attention to my status as a teacher or as someone with whom they are not close, they often address me with *usted*. When men address me with *tú*, it may index my lower status as a female, rather than indexing intimacy, as in the instance below from an audiotape made quite early in the study. In this example, my senior male interlocutor, Don Javier, shifts from formal "you" (*habla*) as he addresses me for the first time to informal "you" (*hablas*) as he evaluates my use of Spanish. Switching to the *tú* form with me may subtly invoke his status as the male head of the extended family, with the right to evaluate my use of his native language. Also, given this status, he generally uses *tú* with everyone on the tapes.

Javier: *¿No habla español muy bien?*	You [formal] don't speak Spanish very well?
Marcia: *No, un poquito.*	No, a little.
Javier: *Lo bueno es lo hablas correcto.*	What is good is that you [informal] speak it correctly.
Marcia: ¿Hmm?	Hmm?
Javier: *Lo hablas correcto, lo poquito que hablas lo hablas correcto.*	You [informal] speak it correctly, the little that you [informal] speak, you [informal] speak it correctly.

In sum, a number of factors affect the choice of *tú* or *usted* in this network. Status (based on age, gender, and profession) is important, but gender alone can override the influence of status on pronoun choice. The solidarity of gender, as well as relatively equal status among adults of the same gender, most often generates reciprocal *tú* between women and between men, at least after they have become familiar with each other. Men and women do not use *tú* across genders, however, except occasionally to close relatives. This avoidance of *tú* may be due to its potential interpretation as indicating inappropriate intimacy. When men do sometimes use *tú* with women in some contexts, it may be indexing the status differential between genders. Thus although other studies have concluded that sex/gender is not influential in the choice of *tú* or *usted* (Carricaburo 1997), it clearly is the most influential aspect of pronoun choice in this social network.

Both linguistic and nonlinguistic aspects of *respeto* serve as glue to bind the family, and the community, together. The norms of both *respeto* and reciprocity cement connections between otherwise independent individuals; and, as Valdés (1996) claims, *respeto* helps to avoid drawing energy away from common family goals. Because the family is the basic unit for maintaining order in ranchero society, families are the center of social life. Of course, in order for families to form, people must marry. Tradition holds that men who do not marry cannot go to heaven when they die, and (as explored in the next chapter in an instance of *echando relajo*) women sometimes joke about "saving" men from such an unpleasant fate. Not only do single men forego the respect of their (potential) wives and children, but neither do they have wives and children to respect in return. In a society in which family is so focal, men without their own families have a less important place in the social order. Given the key role of mothers in families, these assumptions allow women a substantial degree of control and power within the private domain. Men who have extramarital liaisons are expected always to return to their family, especially after they have sown their wild oats while younger, although this is less tolerated by women of the younger generations. One young woman even urged her mother to divorce her own father, who was drinking and seeing another woman for many years. Ultimately, however, her mother did not divorce him; he totally reformed (after being on the verge of death from alcoholism) and returned to the family; and the children hosted a 25-year marriage celebration for the entire social network.

Families are the building blocks of ranchero society: if families are orderly, then the larger community will be. *Respeto* as a moral code entails *lo que es bien y lo que no es bien* (what is good and what is not good: i.e., right and wrong). Respecting the rights of others, within the family and in the larger group, ensures peace and friendship. Such rights include the linguistic encoding of deference or solidarity, and they include, as Bernardo put it, not invading land belonging to other people: "Respeto al derecho ajeno es vivir en paz, dijo Benito Juárez. Quiere decir, ¡no invadir!" (Respecting the right of others is to live in peace, Benito Juárez said. That means, no invading [of land]!). This comment ties *respeto* as a moral code to live by in order to maintain social order with the liberal individualist ideology (discussed in Chapter 6) so characteristic of ranchero societies. Private property is sacrosanct; those who invade another's land, as has happened to this extended family, are called *ratones* (rats) and *ladrones* (thieves) by members of this social network. These terms especially are directed at agrarian reformers, who—in occupying or otherwise claiming land owned by others—are intent on undermining the current social order.

Thus these rancheros insist on a particular kind of social order and emphasize orderliness and discipline in social life. Women are evaluated on the basis of how clean their homes are; and children are socialized with unambiguous authority by parents, grandparents, aunts and uncles, and older siblings or cousins. Children are taught *lo que es bien y lo que no es bien* unambiguously as well. Actions considered wrong are immediately responded to with criticism and sometimes punishment. Children are coddled and allowed much leeway as babies and young toddlers; but at about the age of four they begin to be held responsible for chores and taking care of themselves (e.g., bathing, dressing, and, in the dusty and sometimes muddy rancho, cleaning their shoes). The alacrity with which many children and youth in this network take up such chores and other responsibilities may be directly related to the clarity of roles and discipline which they learn to expect. As noted earlier, physical discipline is an expected part of child socialization.

This focus on discipline and order was illustrated in a comical performance of *enanitos* (dwarfs) at the rancho's elementary school in 1996. Most of the humor across a variety of skits contrasted *desorden* (disorder) with *disciplina* (discipline); for example, in a skit about soldiers the largest laughs from the audience came when the leader repeatedly (and literally) failed to keep his foot soldiers in line. The social function of such skits, as for circus sideshows, is "to clarify for patrons what the ordering and limits of their basic frameworks are" (Goffman 1974, 31). Moreover, since humor is enhanced with the forbidden, those aspects of the skits which the audience considered to be most humorous were precisely those that disrupted normal order: lack of discipline and scatological subjects (i.e., bathroom humor). Such an inversion of normal order is characteristic of carnival (Da Matta 1991; Limón 1992) or fiesta (Pérez 1998; Vaughan 1994) as well as verbal joking.

Inversions would not be humorous without the stability of what is inverted, as is evident in *relajo* as framed, and thus permitted, disorder (see Chapter 8). Thus *respeto,* associated with discipline and order, is countered by *relajo,* associated with disorder. Framed as verbal play, behavior that would normally be considered out of bounds is permitted during *relajo,* a verbal activity in which people purposely invert the ordinary social order. Because ordinary social relations are organized according to a gender- and age-based hierarchy (i.e., as a patriarchal system), it is this system that is frequently inverted in *relajo.* Before moving to the next chapter and an exploration of gender during *relajo,* the next two sections explore how gender and place are mutually articulated, how *respeto* and *relajo* are associated with both gender and place, and, finally, how language ideologies underlie the *respeto-relajo* contrast.

Gender and Place

Most activities among rancheros are divided by gender, men with men and women with women. Knowledge is perceived as similarly divided between the two sexes: for example, men know how to drive, and women know how to make tortillas. (Bernardo was quite disconcerted to discover that I not only could drive but knew how to drive a stick shift, saying, "¡Bueno, pues, sabe todo!" (Well, then, you know everything!). When a sufficient number of people gather in homes, women congregate in the kitchen, and men congregate in the living room. If (as in some homes in the rancho) the house has no separate living room, men gather on porches or around the television.

These gatherings are full of talk, which can engender the space as female or male. If men happen to enter the kitchen where women have gathered (perhaps to get a glass of water or juice), they leave quickly, sometimes after a comment or two that is picked up by the tape recorder. On some of the tapes you can hear the door creaking as people enter and leave the kitchen, and sometimes the storyteller pauses temporarily in response to the creaking (and the presence of a man). If women are gathered in the kitchen but are only chatting (*echando plática*), the men sometimes stay, joining in the talk. When women engage in *echando relajo,* men generally do not join the discussion but may make a humorous comment about the activity and leave quickly (see Chapter 8). This suggests that certain kinds of talk engender spaces more readily than others; and the taboo topics treated during *relajo* intensify the gendering of the space. As one man, reluctant to join the women, put it, "¡No, son puras mujeres!" (No, it's all women!).[3]

Much of the separation between men and women is symbolically organized around the places with which they are predominantly associated. This results in a perceived binary opposition between the male street and the female house, with their associated characteristics of unpredictability vs. control and disorder vs. order (Da Matta 1991). Women, in fact, spend much of their time within their homes; and, while men can roam freely, women generally use the streets only in groups on their way somewhere (e.g., to church or to a sister's house or, in Chicago, to work or school). A woman alone on the street risks her reputation, and what goes on in public (the street) has more impact on reputation than what might go on in private (within homes and thus not generally known).

The opposition between house and street is paralleled by the opposition between *respeto* and *relajo* as ways of speaking. The hierarchical organization within the house is signaled, even constructed, by the regulated use of *tú* and *usted* according to the code of *respeto.* Similarly, the unpredictability and the potential for social inversion characteristic of the street are mirrored in the democratic leveling and verbal misbehavior that takes place during *relajo.* Although these symbolic oppositions are used to produce and understand behavior as meaningful, in actual practice the boundaries of these binary terms are regularly transgressed. *Relajo,* after all, emerges frequently within the house (as people *desahogan* or "let their hair down"), providing a kind of mediation between these two categories in both single and mixed gender settings, frequently around meals.

Carnival, or in Mexico fiesta, is also a "special space where street and house might meet," and carnival in Brazil transforms "public social space [the street] into one big house," with naked and seductive women on parade (Da Matta 1991, 103, 108). As I argue in the next chapter, *relajo* functions as a microfiesta in the midst of the house; so whereas carnival brings the house into the street, *relajo* brings the street into the house. Either way, these polar opposites are mediated by a special space: "We thus create a special space where the routines of the everyday world are broken, and where the real world, viewed upside down, can be observed, analyzed, criticized, and presented to us as *relative*" (Da Matta 1991, 104). *Relajo,* like carnival or fiesta, emphasizes "open exhibition, as opposed to modesty and constraint," exaggeration in which the "powerless . . . represent the powerful" (e.g., the poor act as the rich, women act as men), and the treatment of sin as normal: "What in the everyday world is considered a 'sin'—i.e., the intense provocation of the public and men by women—comes to be regarded as something completely normal, as part of the style of the festivity" (Da Matta 1991, 105–106). Likewise during *relajo* what would normally be considered sinful behavior is permitted and even approved as appropriate for this verbal activity.

Gender and Language Ideologies: *Respeto* and *Relajo*

Much of the ideology that constructs gender is language ideology (Hirsch 1998; Ochs 1992). That is, beliefs about and attitudes toward language are embedded in understandings of gender. For example, the interplay between masculinity and power on Stern's (1995) vertical dimension revolves around the display, primarily verbal, of deference and dominance encoded as *respeto. Respeto* implies a hierarchical social order in which dominance and deference are expressed, in fact constructed, with specific linguistic devices, prototypically the informal and formal "you" pronouns *tú* and *usted.* Thus men of higher status use verbal humiliation to force deference from men of lower status, which in itself constructs their dominance and thus superior masculinity. On the horizontal dimension of male interaction as well, male camaraderie and play can lapse into conflict and sometimes violence, often over perceived verbal insults.

Within this ranchero social network, men ratify their masculinity in a number of arenas: community political meetings in which men's voices dominate; "metaphorical spectacles of masculine valor" such as cockfights; and a "culture of male play . . . tinged by jousting and risk, a solidarity achieved in part through competition" (Stern 1995, 176). As part of the culture of male play, verbal games such as *albures* (joking competitions with sexual innuendos) result in winners and losers who are considered more or less masculine, respectively (Cintron 1997), which can but need not end in conflict and violence, especially in the context of drinking. Such contests and drinking usually occur in cantinas and elsewhere, rather than at home.

Swearing is another use of language that is heavily implicated in *respeto* or the lack of it (*una falta de respeto*). That is, it is not clear who can swear at whom in what context without an understanding of who is above whom in the *respeto* hierarchy. Stern (1995, 166) recounts colonial incidents in which Indians were cited for the indecency of swearing in front of their social superiors. In this network, moral femininity precludes the use of *maldiciones.* Dominant gender ideologies from the larger Mexican society reinforce this local proscription: elite, cultured women definitely do not use *maldiciones* publicly. For elite women, such proscriptions may not conflict with other ideologies. Rancheras, however, often must choose from conflicting language/gender ideologies in any given interaction: on the one hand, the use of *franqueza* to assert themselves as self-sufficient and strong individuals, in accord with local ideals of personhood; yet on the other hand, the use of *respeto* in interactions with men and the avoidance of *maldiciones* to construct themselves as moral rather than immoral women. Because the latter two constraints (part of the language ideology of *respeto*) conflict with the first one (the ideology of *franqueza*) rancheras face conflicts that rancheros do not. This conflict provides fertile resources for the inversion that is called for during *relajo* (as illustrated in the next chapter).

Language ideologies, then, are reciprocally fused with the gender ideologies that support a patriarchal system. At the core of these ideologies is the code of *respeto,* which organizes social interaction. Order, of course, breeds disorder; and *respeto* is challenged by *relajo.* Sabean's (1984) definition of culture as argument is relevant here (see Chapter 1), for no social orders or cultures are uniformly organized; nor is their social order entirely consented to. Instead there is cultural argument between groups (based on gender, generation, class, ethnicity, or race) and individuals (based on different life experiences and personalities). The patriarchal system organizing ranchero society contains tensions and disagreements over the allocation of power; for example, men compete with each other to establish their masculinity, younger men dispute their elders' authority, and women dispute the authority of men, most frequently in the mediated activity of *echando relajo,* where they can play with and practice new ways of being and talking within a supportive and thus relatively safe space. Virtually all this contestation takes place through language, by using language in culturally established ways that undermine regular social order or *respeto.* Much of the language use during *relajo* would be proscribed outside of this verbal play frame, and most of the stories told during *relajo* involve conflict, as illustrated in the two instances of *relajo* analyzed in Chapter 8.

Stern's (1995) study of gender and power in late colonial Mexico significantly reveals conflicts over *respeto* to be at the core of (gendered) contestations of power relations in both familial and political contexts. To affronted superiors *una falta de respeto* defied the

> . . . inherent prerogative and status of the superior. One owed respectful deference to a family elder, a patriarch, or a community official or *viejo* [community elder] even if the inner self questioned the rightness of specific acts, demands, or excesses of the superior. To lose the fear of disorder or punishment, to dare to question bluntly or to lift the hand, to lose the restraint that kept the sense of quarrel more or less inside the self and weakened its outer expression—this was to lose respect . . . [and] turned subordinates into "shameless" people. . . . (Stern 1995, 212)

Thus *respeto* as a gendered language ideology connects the familial with the political, resting on "a core idea of restraint, a deference to order, place, and legitimacy" (Stern 1995, 213) and providing the community with a shared language for argument. *Relajo* is a key site (Philips 2000) for this argument, which is basically about *respeto* or organized (and hierarchical) social relations. In the next chapter I provide examples of this in analyses of two instances of *relajo,* one all-male and one all-female.

EIGHT

Relajo as (Framed) Disorder
The Carnivalesque in Talk

Although people in this social network describe *relajo* (joking or fooling around) as purely for diversion and fun, a close examination of actual instances of *relajo* shows it to be more significant, particularly as it challenges (within a verbal play frame) the existing social order. María Moliner's *Diccionario del uso de español* (1998) defines *relajo* as (1) the act of permitting oneself an extravagance or unusual recreation, (2) tranquillity and rest (as opposed to work), (3) laxity in the performance of something, (4) disorder and lack of discipline, (5) immorality of customs, and finally (6) a dirty joke (*broma pesada;* this definition pertains in Argentina, Cuba, Mexico, Puerto Rico, and Uruguay). As is evident in the progression of these dictionary meanings from 1 to 6, *relajo* encompasses fun and relaxation but also carnival-like inversion of normal discipline and order.

Relajo is treated here in two primary aspects: first as poetics, the aesthetically pleasing rhetorical skills in the story and joke telling that goes on in this speech activity; and second as politics, jointly constructed meanings regarding how language framed as *relajo* indexes and critiques social life. The critical evaluation of social life can threaten the usual social order in two ways during *relajo.* First, the verbal frame itself allows, in fact requires, laxity in the usual discipline that organizes life (e.g., respectable women swearing). Second, the sometimes relentless teasing that frequently goes on during *relajo* goads people to (learn to) defend themselves as unique individuals within a tightly knit group. Individuals learn during *relajo* to control and assert themselves within the group. Teased individuals must maintain their self-composure (not showing vulnerability by showing hurt or anger) and then, by retorting, take the offensive by turning the teasing around.

All of this requires a balancing act: when everyone stays within the play frame, social order is maintained even as individuals assert themselves, sometimes against the prevailing order (in which case the other participants join the initiator in such counterdiscourse). In *relajo* that occurs in schools, for example, students join an initiator in humorously undermining teacher-led activities and formality (Levinson 2001; Saucedo Ramos 1998), but such *relajo* does not necessarily undermine all teaching and learning. Too much self-assertion can threaten social cohesion, either within a *relajo* play frame or outside of it, in serious talk (*franqueza*). When either *relajo* or *franqueza* goes too far, group cohesion is threatened. During *relajo* this can happen when people tease too much or too sensitively, or the target does not manage to defend himself or herself and expresses hurt and/or anger (and thus loses face): the frame is broken and so, possibly, are interpersonal relations. In contrast, when all participants stay within the frame, *relajo* affirms group solidarity, and the participating individuals maintain their dignity and respect. After all, participants must share *confianza* in the first place, even to initiate *relajo.* Just enough self-assertion, then, on the part of both teaser and teased during *relajo,* or outside of it during *franqueza,* affirms ranchero values that emphasize individuality and autonomy. Too much of either runs the risk of causing dangerous friction between people in a group that is valued because of its close familial (or family-like) relations.

An example of self-assertion that challenges the existing social order but affirms the group creating the *relajo* is illustrated below in the transcript of a remembered anecdote from Mexico. This anecdote was recalled during *relajo* among men in the living room of a house in Chicago in 1989. The participants are all men, although women are nearby in the kitchen. At one point, the host's daughter approaches the men, asking if they want to eat, but she is ignored. In recalling the story from Mexico, the men marvel at the nerve of a young boy who, in a threat to familial patriarchy, challenges his own father in public. Yet the story ends (after some tension) with a humorous punch line by the father, who saves both his own and his son's face by noting that the rebellious son is at least of strong character, like his father!

The incident took place at a sugar-processing plant (*ingenio*) south of the rancho, where it was customary for children to bring lunch to their fathers during the workday. This particular son is late with the lunch, to which his father responds angrily by throwing the lunch sack. Rather than being afraid of his father and perhaps apologizing for being late, the son angrily kicks the lunch sack back toward his father, in full view of the father's co-workers. Tense moments ensue, and the father finally breaks the tension by saying, "That's it, son of a bitch, he has to turn out just like his father!" The father thus turns a tense moment of interpersonal conflict, and a threat to the patriarchal order, into a moment of face-saving humor. He locates the interaction within an acceptable "play" frame rather than allowing it to result in explicitly and publicly expressed anger by a lower-status male (young boy) to a higher-status one (the boy's father), which would imply a loss of (masculine) reputation, or dominance, for the father. The transcript of the story as told in Chicago follows:

José: *Una vez a, una vez traían—platican estos de Santa Clara también estos viejones que—*	One time, one time they had—those of Santa Clara say, also these old guys that—
Zenaido: *¿Los Tamboras?* [*nickname for family*]	The Tamboras? [*nickname for family*]
José: *Tamboras.* [*pause*] *Que:* [*pause*], *no ve que le llevan de comer a los que andan allí en el ingenio, y que, una vez—*	Tamboras. [*pause*] Tha:t [*pause*], don't you know that they take the food to those that are over there in the sugar mill and that, one time—
Zenaido: *Voceros, voceros, le dicen vocero.*	Criers, criers is what they call them, crier.
José: *El chiquillo le llevó de comer a su papá, un chiquillo—* [*pause*]	The kid took his father food, a kid— [*pause*]
[*female voices in background*]	[*female voices in background*]
Rosaura: *¿No quiere alguien comer?*	Doesn't anyone want to eat?
José: *Un chiquillo* [*pause*] *llegó tarde, compadre se enojó y—el papá—y agarró el, el, como le dicen el costal de la, costalito de la comida del lonche y lo avienta, entonces, todo, verda', toda la gente allí viendo y—Ehi. Pos pensaron que el chiquillo se iba a espantar o algo. ¡No! Que llega el chiquillo y que le da un patadón al—* [*laughter*]	A kid [*pause*] came late, the compadre got mad and—the father—and grabbed the, the, what do they call the sack, the lunch sack, and throws it, then, everyone, right, everyone there watching and—Yeah. Well, they thought that the kid was going to get scared or something. No! The kid came and gave a good kick to the—[*laughter*]
Zenaido: *Al costal.*	The sack.
José: *Al costal.* [*laughter*] *¿Se imagina? Pinche muchachillo como quiera de ley, ¿eh?*	The sack. [*laughter*] Can you imagine? Fucking kid, at least of strong character, huh?
Zenaido: *No pos sí.*	Oh yes.
José: *De ley porque en vez de que se había espantado—pos el papá era de esos hombres recios y—lo aventó el costal y el chiquillo fue, pensaron que lo iba a levantar, n'hombre que,*	Of strong character because instead of getting scared—well, the father was one of those rough men and—he threw the sack and the kid went, they thought he was going to pick

que le da un patadón, [laughter] que le dijo, "¡Eso, hijo de su chingada madre, tiene que salir igual que su padre!" [laughter] ¡Se imagina!	it up, no, man, he, he gave it a good kick, [*laughter*] and he told him, "That's it, son of a bitch, he has to turn out just like his father!" [*laughter*] Can you imagine!

This retelling of a favorite story illustrates tension over power and dominance and, moreover, inherently conflicting mores in ranchero society. On the one hand, the son, who has been raised to respect his elders, explicitly—and publicly—challenges his father's authority by not being deferential to him in front of the father's co-workers and friends. Thus the boy has shown *una falta de respeto* (a lack of respect). On the other hand, the young boy must learn to assert himself in accord with male-inflected ranchero values of self-assertion and autonomy in order to become a respected masculine adult. Here he takes a risk and asserts himself against his father. The crowd watches, waiting for the father's response. One way for the father to save face would be to punish (dominate) the son. The father, however, rather than punishing the boy, reframes the interaction as humorous and in so doing saves face—both his own and his son's: he accepts his son's self-assertion by noting that the "son of a bitch has to turn out just like his father!" Thus he compliments both his emerging-male son and himself as strong individuals, granting respect for autonomy even under a threat to his own masculinity and, ultimately, the social order.

Had this been a daughter kicking his lunch, rather than a son, however, his response might have been different. Rancheras, though, like the son in this excerpt, also frequently rely on the shared valuing of autonomy and self-assertion in enacting themselves as challenging rather than submissive to patriarchal dominance (as illustrated later in this chapter in a transcript of all-female *relajo*). But they rarely do so directly and in public.

Relajo, then, is a way of speaking which is framed as play. The psychological notion of frame is based on "the physical analogy of the picture frame" (Bateson 1972, 186); it refers to the "bracketing" of a stretch of behavior (here discourse) to be understood by participants in a particular way. As Gregory Bateson (1972) notes about animals and extends to humans, the message "this is play" is a metacommunicative one that distinguishes "primary frameworks"—ordinary, serious behavior central to a social group (Goffman 1974, 27, 46)—from the kind of behavior or discourse to be taken nonseriously.

Relajo is framed as play rather than as the serious language of *franqueza* or *respeto*. Play frames are signaled by keying, which transforms a strip of activity from unkeyed, ordinary behavior to playful, joking behavior (Goffman 1974, 40–50). Without such keying, the very same behavior would be taken entirely differently (i.e., seriously and with consequences). Within verbal play frames, however, many normal boundaries are transgressed without such consequences. Within the verbal play frame of *relajo*, individuals excel as performers of verbal art, telling personal anecdotes (*anecdotas*), stories (*cuentos*), and jokes (*chistes*). In Bakhtinian terms, these secondary genres occur within the primary genre of *relajo* (Bakhtin 1986). In this sense, *relajo* can be understood as a communicative activity which frames traditional oral genres as playful and nonserious. When these oral genres are performed by skilled individuals, participants experience aesthetic pleasure and are often persuaded to adopt the performer's perspective on the topic at hand. Thus *relajo* simultaneously affirms both the individual performer and the social bonds of the group. Jorge Portilla (1966) claims that, in its emphasis on disorder, *relajo* is antisocial and undermines community; but among rancheras and rancheros it conversely affirms social bonds and group identity, even while allowing space for individuation through rhetorical performance. In what follows, I explore the aesthetic dimension, or poetics, of *relajo* and consider how the poetics of *relajo* necessarily includes the politics of *relajo*.

The Poetics of *Relajo*: Rhetorical Competence and Aesthetic Pleasure

People in this social network highly value rhetorical competence (Farr 1993), and this value is captured in two expressions that they use: *tener gracia* (to have grace or wit in talk), and *hablar sabroso* (to speak deliciously or with flavor) for pleasure and entertainment. These rhetorical qualities are abundantly illustrated during *relajo*. Framing speech play as *relajo* allows individuals who excel at telling jokes and funny stories to perform their verbal competence in front of others, and the making of *relajo* by a group of people affirms relations among them. *Relajo* often occurs within homes, when work and household chores are finished and when three or more persons are spending time together or preparing food for a celebration; the intent is to pass the time pleasurably with playful and clever talk. As one older woman remembers it back in Mexico during her own childhood:

Eduvina: *Como no había en todas las casas—o más bien no había radio, estoy hablando de México, televisión, ¿verdad?, luz eléctrica.*

Since there wasn't in any of the houses—or rather there wasn't radio, I am talking of Mexico, television, right?—electricity.

Marcia: *Uh-hum, sí.*

Uh-huh, yes.

Eduvina: Okay, *se juntaban en una esquina. Yo me acuerdo. Todos los señores grandes—*

Okay, they would gather together on a corner. I remember. All the older men—

Marcia: *Uh-hum.*

Uh-huh.

Eduvina: *En lo oscuro se sentaban en unas piedras a fumar su cigarrito y a echar chistes, a platicar de las novias que ellos tuvieron en su juventud, a cantar, a reír y eso es lo que se—lo que se llama echar relajo.*

In the dark they would sit on some stones to smoke their cigarettes and to tell jokes, to talk about the girlfriends that they had in their youth, to sing, to laugh, and that is what—what is called doing *relajo.*

Marcia: *Sí.*

Yes.

Eduvina: *Porque no era nada serio sino que tú sabes, platicando, reírse y eso—de eso se trata, de echar relajo.*

Because there wasn't anything serious but, you know, talking, laughing, and that—that's what *echar relajo* means.

Marcia: *Uh-hum.*

Uh-huh.

Eduvina: *Y eso era bonito, fíjate, porque todo el mundo se divierte a su manera en cada parte, ¿no? En qué se podían esas personas divertir ¿con el radio? No, porque no había ni siquiera luz contimás radio.*

And that was really nice, listen, because everyone enjoys himself or herself in his or her own way, no? How could those people enjoy themselves, with the radio? No, because there wasn't even light [electricity] much less radio.

Marcia: *Sí.*

Yes.

A younger woman articulated what many others also stressed: the use of *relajo* as temporary relief from the worry and pain of daily problems:

Beatriz: *Relajo es cuando tú estás—o sea las cosas no las estás tomando en serio. O sea que, es como para el—ahm, levantar el humor. Por ejemplo, si tú tienes un problema, ¿verdá'? Un ejemplo, tienes un problema y pues, si yo en ves de sacarte ayuda para ayudarte a*

Relajo is when you are—in other words you are not taking things seriously. In other words, it's to like—um, lift the spirits. For example, if you have a problem, right? An example, you have a problem and, well, if I instead of giving you help, to help you to get

salir—que tú olvides un poco tu problema, te distraigas. . . . El relajo se trata de que tú sonrías, de que, te despegues—tu mente se despeje un momento. Que no estés atada a lo de siempre. Eso es, eso es el relajo para nosotros.

rid of it—you forget your problem for a while, you distract yourself. . . . *Relajo* is meant to make you smile, to get you away—to clear your mind for a moment. So that you are not tied to the everyday. That is, that is *relajo* for us.

Within this social network *relajo* occurs in mixed-gender settings, but it also occurs in all-male and all-female settings. The best performances by women, however, occur in all-female settings: this is where the verbally wittier women shine and where the younger females watch and eventually practice rhetorical skills themselves, as a way of learning this particular sociolinguistic role. Given an all-female context, women are freer to break the rules that normally constrain their (especially verbal) behavior. Another young woman noted (in English):

Judith: When we're a lot of women and we joke around on heavy stuff. . . . We say very heavy things—

Marcia: Heavy? Means serious?

Judith: Serious—no, not serious, you know like I mean, bad, you know. *Relajo* is like ah, like when we're like women only and we're joking around laughing, it's like joking around. We do it a lot, all the time.

Relajo varies across nationality and gender. For example, Lauria (1964) claims that Puerto Rican *relajo* can consist of a joking game or a less frequent—and much riskier—joking contest. It can remain verbal play that no one takes seriously or become "a full-blown contest of defamation, a ritual of degradation whose players are aggressively engaged in scoring points against each other, in seeing how far they can go and still retain the superficial consensus of amiability" (Lauria 1964, 61). The goal both as Lauria describes *relajo* and as these rancheros practice it is to maintain one's composure, not showing feelings of embarrassment, hurt, or anger. Whereas Lauria claims that *relajo* among Puerto Rican men can (infrequently) result in fighting and violence, members of the social network in this study, especially the women, say that this is an unlikely outcome of their *relajo*, which usually resembles Lauria's joking game rather than his joking contest.

Although the women refer to a "heavier" version of *relajo* as *desmadres* (as described below), "heavier" means being more irreverent (for example, women might swear or tell sexual jokes), not being more competitive and potentially violent. The Mexican male verbal game of *albures* (see Cintron 1997; Roth 1995), often played in cantinas and other male gathering places, is competitive, like Lauria's description of male Puerto Rican *relajo* as joking contest as well as the African American verbal game of "playing the dozens" and other verbal dueling games among men in a variety of cultures. One woman alluded to this potential for conflict and violence in her comment that among men, especially when they are drinking, *relajo* can sometimes result in fighting:

Beatriz: *Depende en como se usan, ¿verdad? Porque muchas personas se pelean. Como los homb—hay hombres que ya echan bronca y que esto y que lo otro, pero no no no, yo para mí no. Pero también verdad hacen de—cuando destruyen cosas, este, buscan pleito, toman mucho.*	It depends on how it's used, right? Because many people fight. For example, men—there are men who pick fights and this and that, but no no no, for me, no. But also truly they—when they destroy things, um, they are looking for a fight, they're drinking a lot.

One significant instance of (mixed-gender) *relajo* recorded on audiotape did go awry, ending in hurt feelings on the part of someone who was unable to take the teasing lightly (she "lost" in Lauria's terms because she showed vulnerability and anger). But all other taped instances stayed within the joking frame, whether they were created by mixed-gender, all-female, or all-male groups. Most of the taping was done inside homes, however, where the all-male joking that might get out of hand and turn violent would be less likely to occur. I did not follow men to male gathering places such as cantinas, where more heavy-duty joking and joking contests such as *albures* are likely to occur. Not only were the home-based instances of *relajo* generally purely playful, but many of them served to bring the participants closer together, even when they were based on focused teasing of particular people.

As with Puerto Rican *relajo,* the occurrence of *relajo* within this social network is based on a feeling of *confianza* among participants in the first place (Lauria 1964, 62). *Relajo* builds community, incorporating (sometimes new) individuals into the group. When I commented to Ramón, a young man in the rancho, that someone in Chicago was shy, he responded, "¿No le gusta relajo?" (Doesn't he like *relajo?*), effectively equating being part of the group with the ability to defend and assert oneself during *relajo.* Thus although there can be a fine line between *relajo* and offense, in this study, at least, that line was almost never crossed.

The poetics of *relajo,* then, yield aesthetic pleasure for participants. Yet at a deeper level *relajo* is more than a pleasurable verbal pastime. Mexican philosopher Jorge Portilla addresses the meaning of this way of speaking in *Fenomenología del relajo* (The Phenomenology of *Relajo*):

> The significance or meaning of *relajo* is to suspend seriousness. That is to say, to suspend the subject's usual attachment to a value which limits his or her liberty. . . . *Relajo* has a certain relation to the comical, but it is not merely the comical: there are comical situations that do not involve relajo. (Portilla 1966, 18; my translation)

Thus, although *relajo* always is comical, the comical is not always *relajo. Relajo* carries a deeper moral significance: to free oneself temporarily from particular values that, in ordinary daily life, one believes in and lives by. *Relajo* is related to the verb *relajar* (to relax), but it does not simply mean relaxation in the ordinary sense. Rather, it connotes relaxation of the usual discipline that keeps behavior within appropriate bounds.

Relajo begins when someone invites others to *echar relajo* by inserting into the ongoing conversation a humorous remark that might be considered inappropriate without a humorous or play frame. Others signal the acceptance of this invitation by contributing their own such remarks or by laughing appreciatively; or they do not accept the invitation, in which case the remark stands alone (although it may occasion mild laughter), and extended *relajo* does not ensue. That is, for people to be fully *echando relajo,* such remarks are made repeatedly, and everyone joins in. The repetition of one irreverent remark after another and the complicity in creating an often noisy, disorderly atmosphere of liberating chaos build to a kind of vertigo or hilarity. Goffman (1974, 33) points out that loss of control is in fact an important part of such humor in the "special context [of] play."

In one instance on tape, a slightly inebriated man inserted such invitations to *echar relajo* during a religious ceremony (*el levantamiento,* when the baby Jesus symbolized by a doll is picked up from his place in the manger and put away for another year; see Farr 1994c) at his home. As his quite religious sister-in-law read a prayer aloud, he inserted brief comical objections that repeated and questioned some of her words. The rest of the participants' reactions to him varied from rolling eyes to slight giggles to directives that he keep quiet. *Relajo* as an invitation to sow disorder was suggested by him but rejected by other participants as inappropriate, so he eventually quieted down, and the ceremony proceeded. In other contexts, in contrast, the invitation to *echar relajo* is accepted with alacrity.

In my fieldwork, and as noted by Portillo (1966), three or more people must be present to create this sociolinguistic context; it does not emerge between only two people. In fact, on occasion the arrival of a third person by itself triggers this verbal play frame. *Relajo* emerges spontaneously and can be relatively light or heavy, simply "fooling around" in a lighter vein or "very heavy joking around" (*hacer desmadres*). This latter phrase indexes the connection between mothers and propriety by suggesting behavior without the constraint of mothers and "their" rules (*des madres,* without mothers).

A young man who still lives in this rancho (he has not yet successfully crossed the border in order to work in Chicago) talked about *relajo* as a way for people to connect as a group. To enter into *relajo* one can't be *tímido,* but participating in it connects the individual firmly to the social, with all the support—and demands—that this entails. As noted earlier, the teasing that often goes on during *relajo* leads targeted individuals to defend themselves (*defenderse*) with quick retorts. Those who learn to retort with humor, thus entertaining the others present and saving face, are valued members of the group. Thus *relajo* is simultaneously a context for individuation and for group affirmation. In this regard, it parallels both *franqueza* and *respeto:* all three verbal styles facilitate both of these ends, rather than one or the other. *Relajo,* however, provides a privileged site for critical perspectives on social life (Bauman and Briggs 1990; Briggs and Bauman 1992), relying heavily on critical "talk about talk" or metapragmatics (Philips 2000).

Metapragmatics: Talk about Talk

A unique property of language, as opposed to other cultural symbol systems, is its reflexive capacity (Jakobson 1995 [1957]; Lucy 1993; Silverstein 1976). That is, language can be used to talk about itself. In fact, as Mikhail Bakhtin and others have noted, a great deal of human speech consists of talk about previous talk. Such talk about talk is termed metalanguage, which focuses on (other) language as an object in itself. When such metalanguage focuses on object language in its pragmatic aspects (with meanings derived from context) it is metapragmatic (Silverstein 1976), as distinguished from metasemantic language, which focuses on the referential (semantic) meaning of other talk.

Metapragmatic discourse alternates metalanguage with object language (i.e., the previous speech event that is the current object for reflection). For example, when quoting someone in a story, the narrator often alternates between metalanguage (usually verbs of speaking, e.g., *dijo,* he said) and object language (the speech being quoted); alternatively, the metalanguage can be implicit, as when no verb of speaking is used (other devices such as intonation make it clear that the words represent a direct quote, even without using "he said"). A narrator can quote someone else or can quote himself or herself; in both cases, however, the quotations are part of previous speech events being brought into the present speech event. In the following example, a woman quotes herself from a previous *relajo;* her metalanguage is in boldface and the object language (the quotation) is in regular type, within quotation marks:

> *Y luego este* ***le digo yo, le digo a Carmen,*** *"Ay, Carmencita de mi alma, aunque sea una cama, aunque—" yo tendría que si me caiga no me daba recio, está de alta así.*
> And then, uh, **I say, I say to Carmen,** "Oh, little Carmen of my soul, at least a bed, at least—" I figured that if I fell I would not hit myself hard, it's only so high.

A third type of language, called "ordinary" language (Lucy 1993), is language that does not report on previous speech; instead, it is directed entirely to participants in the current context. The narrator's comment "I figured that if I fell I would not hit myself hard, it's only so high" is ordinary language. The rapid alternation between metalanguage and object language, and between such metapragmatic discourse and ordinary language, demonstrates complex rhetorical skills that can be used to persuade listeners of whatever perspective the rhetor or narrator is promoting. The attitudes and values that inevitably permeate the reported speech (e.g., through intonation and other linguistic devices) are conveyed implicitly and thus are particularly persuasive. For example, here the narrator quotes her own previous speech with exaggerated intonation, a diminutive suffix (*-cita* after the name), and a hyperfeminine phrase (*Carmencita de mi alma,* little Carmen of my soul) to convey a parody of ideal femininity. The exaggeration signals that her true attitude is critical of such gender ideology, with its emphasis on female weakness and dependence.

In the analysis of taped instances of *relajo* in this chapter, this kind of critique is evident, especially among the women. Precisely because *relajo* is not to be taken seriously (on the surface), serious concerns can be brought up in face-saving ways—people can always back off and claim the prerogatives of *relajo:* that they were only teasing, implying that the recipient of this teasing should maintain his or her composure and take the teasing lightly. Moreover, *relajo* can be used by people to try out new (challenging of the status quo) identities and voices while gaining the support of other participants, facilitating the actualization of new identities in other domains.

To explore the counterdiscursive capacity of *relajo,* I analyze two instances, one all-male and one all-female. Before moving to this analysis, however, I first examine the notable parallels between *relajo* and fiesta or carnival, as a ritual event in which the status quo is turned upside down. Drawing out the parallels between *relajo* and fiesta reveals the deeply embedded critical potential of both of these events. Bakhtin traces this aspect of carnival to the origins of festival in medieval Europe: festival emerged, he claims, in the separation between "serious official, ecclesiastical, feudal, and political cult forms and ceremonials" and "the second life of the people," who, during unofficial feasts in which laughter reigned supreme,

> . . . for a time entered the utopian realm of community, freedom, equality, and abundance. . . . As opposed to the official feast, one might say that carnival celebrated temporary liberation from the prevailing truth and from the established order; it marked the suspension of all hierarchical rank, privileges, norms, and prohibitions. (Bakhtin 1994 [1965], 197–198)

Like fiesta, *relajo* celebrates a temporary liberation from prevailing norms and established social hierarchies, by allowing, even promoting, verbal disorder. In terms of language use itself, Bakhtin (1994 [1965], 220) notes that "abuses, curses, profanities, and improprieties are the unofficial elements of speech" inasmuch as they breach etiquette and conventional verbal norms in a democratic leveling of social relations. This kind of speech is typical of fiesta and is prevalent in *relajo* as well (as is evident in the taped instances analyzed later in this chapter).

Relajo and Fiesta

As a site for critical reflexivity, *relajo* functions much like fiesta or carnival.[1] Fiestas are the site *par excellence* for a "licensed relaxation of norms and rules, a negation of the social order" (Stoeltje 1992, 270). Fiestas, like *relajo,* are playful, but they are not merely playful; they too carry a larger cultural significance. According to Roberto Da Matta (1991, 62), in his study of Brazilian carnival (Brazil's version of Mexican fiesta):

> Carnival creates its own social space . . . in direct opposition (as an inverted image) to daily life, [and] under normal conditions it merely reinforces the everyday world. But normal conditions are very relative. . . . Carnival styles seem to be very important as an alternative mode of collective behavior [in which] . . . we experiment with new avenues of social relationship that lie dormant or are considered to be utopias from the perspective of everyday life. . . .
>
> Carnival reproduces the world; but . . . this reproduction is neither direct nor automatic. The reproduction is dialectical, with many self-reflections, circuits, niches, dimensions, and levels. That is precisely why society can change and why there can be, after all, hope for the world.

Recent work on Mexican fiesta (Beezley et al. 1994) also describes this event as a space for "rituals of resistance." Just as *relajo* allows participants to free themselves temporarily from normal, everyday constraints on their freedom, so does fiesta provide opportunities for participants to resist the control of the state. The two events share an emphasis on disorder and resistance, as opposed to order and rule. *Relajo,* then, can be considered a microfiesta, a smaller, more local social practice that occurs in daily conversation within social networks of people and that shares many of the functions of the larger, community-level fiesta. Four of these important functions are discussed below (Stoeltje 1992).

Connecting the Individual to the Social

Both *relajo* and fiesta are events that connect the individual to the social world. *Relajo* is a social practice that occurs at the social network level, whereas fiesta is a social practice that occurs at the community level. Despite these differing levels, both events emphasize the participation of everyone. Stoeltje (1992, 263) notes that festival is distinguished from other large-scale ceremonial events by actively engaging participants, whose concentrated attention "heightens consciousness, creating an intersection of individual performance and social reflexivity." *Relajo* similarly pulls people into a common endeavor. Although language plays a larger role in *relajo* than in fiesta, and *relajo* is an entirely verbal event, both events rely on the active participation of people. Neither event, in fact, could happen at all were it not for such active participation.

Fiesta "works by fusing the positive emotions of symbols and events with social and moral demands on the subject" (Beezley et al. 1994, xv). One particular kind of fiesta, the patriotic fiesta, constitutes for Mexicans an "alternative civic religion" that relies not only on "ritual pageantry, but also on primary education and public monuments to symbolize social cohesion or membership in groups" (Beezley et al. 1994, xix). For example, Mary Kay Vaughan (1994, 216) argues that in Tecamachalco, Puebla, patriotic fiestas in the first part of the twentieth century effectively aroused people to participate in nation-building.

Relajo similarly emerges through a mobilization of people. As noted above, it often begins within informal conversation when one person throws out a remark that invites others to participate in a common endeavor to make *relajo* (Portilla 1966). If this invitation is accepted, others join in, and the communicative event is constructed jointly. *Relajo,* like fiesta, compels a concentration of attention from participants, which heightens consciousness, primarily through the aesthetic pleasures derived from individual performances. Thus in both events individuals are pulled together in a pleasurable social practice that serves multiple functions, although in *relajo* the emphasis is on ritual disorder, whereas fiesta, at least in Mexico, encompasses both order (e.g., nation-building) and disorder (resistance to control by the state). Even so, there is order and group identity in the construction of shared, ritual disorder, as I note below.

Affirming Group Identity

A second important function of both *relajo* and fiesta is affirming group identity. First, individuals are mobilized to participate; and then, by participating, the unity of the group is affirmed. Both events are richer in symbolic communication than is everyday life (i.e., communication is carried through an excess of symbols). In fiesta group identity is reflected in such symbols as food, clothing, rhetorical performances, music, dancing, and visual displays such as parades and flags. In *relajo* group identity is affirmed almost entirely through language and its accompanying communicative devices of gesture, facial expression, and body movement. *Echando relajo* among the families in this study affirms their Mexican identity and transforms places into Mexican spaces, even in Chicago.

Although *echando relajo* as a Mexican way of speaking affirms group identity, other symbols not related to language that are often part of this speech event (for example, food) contribute to this function as well. Stoeltje (1992, 265) notes that food in fiestas, especially food that "embod[ies] the [ethnic] identity of the group . . . emphasizes the *social* act of eating." *Relajo,* as a microfiesta, often features food and particularly the sharing of food. In my fieldwork both in Chicago and in Michoacán, *relajo* has often occurred during meal preparation, especially when it takes up the better part of a day. My first experience with *relajo* among the women in this network of families, in fact, occurred during the making of *uchepos* (Michoacán-style tamales) in the kitchen of one family's Chicago home. Other instances of *relajo* frequently occur in one kitchen or another, on both sides of the border. Often mixed-gender *relajo* spontaneously follows a meal, whether an ordinary, daily meal or after eating at a festive *matanza* (a celebration in which a pig is killed and cooked). Such *matanzas* also occur in Chicago, where the killed pig (purchased whole) is cooked over a fire in the backyard or, more riskily, in the basement on a concrete floor. At other times, only snacking accompanies *relajo,* whether the physical setting is a kitchen or a traveling van rolling down the highway from Chicago to Michoacán (see Chapter 5). But the food, whether a full meal or *antojitos* (appetizers, snacks), is as Mexican as the *relajo.*

Providing for Performances of Highly Valued Skills and Talents

Another way to express group identity is through performances of highly valued skills or talents, and providing such performances is a third important function of both *relajo* and fiesta. In fiestas performances can include verbal rhetoric, music, dance, or other displays, whereas in *relajo* the focus is on verbal performances. The Spaniards used public performative language and ceremony to justify their right to rule, especially in "the ceremonial *requerimiento* (a document, read aloud, that supposedly justified the imposition of Spanish sovereignty) to establish authority over persons, not property or trade" (Beezley et al. 1994, xiii). Such public verbal performances were a part of holiday celebrations that ultimately synthesized Spanish, Mexican indigenous, and some African symbols and images. Both the larger celebration and the verbal performances within it involved a "major shift from the frames of everyday life that focus attention on subsistence, routine, and production to frames that foster the transformative, reciprocal, and reflexive dimensions of social life" (Stoeltje 1992, 263). Likewise in *relajo* there is a shift in frame from ordinary conversation to the heightened emotional experience of joking and misbehaving with language.

Using what John Gumperz (1982) called contextualization cues (e.g., a smile to accompany a remark that is to be understood as playful rather than serious), participants signal a shift in frame. With a shift in frame to *relajo,* talk becomes playful, with bantering back and forth, and someone takes the floor to relate a humorous story. Narratives are told expressively, with abrupt and marked changes in pitch to represent the voices of different persons and to re-create dialogues from previous conversations. Performances within *relajo*, in fact, are heavily characterized by the frequent use of reported speech (see Behar 1993 for another example of this dialogue-rich narrative style) as well as much irony and humor and often include body movements and gestures accompanying the words. Audiences are attentive and appreciative, especially when older, more experienced and verbally skillful people have the floor. Within one *relajo* session, informal performances by different participants can be interspersed with casual conversation, gossip, and rounds of bantering with teasing remarks; these shifts from one kind of talk to another are often modulated by interruptions from people arriving and leaving or from children wanting attention. Thus verbal performances can be spaced out over time or can ensue one after the other, building to a climax of hilarity.

Verbal performances within *relajo*, like those during fiesta, illustrate the verbal skills and talents (i.e., rhetorical competence) highly valued by participants. The creation of *relajo* by a group of people allows individuals who excel at telling jokes and funny stories to demonstrate their verbal expertise to others in the network, and it affirms group identity for all participants by actualizing a shared and highly valued oral tradition.

Providing Experiences of Transformation for Participants

A fourth function of both *relajo* and fiesta, perhaps the most important, is the provision of transformative experiences for participants. According to Stoeltje (1992, 270), "the licensed relaxation of norms and rules . . . opens doors of risk and confronts destruction and re-creation . . . lead[ing] participants to experience transformation and regeneration. This may take many forms: personal affirmation, political action, courtship and marriage, social revitalization, and so on." Just how do such experiences, in either fiesta or *relajo*, become transformative? Stoeltje argues that it is the shift in frame from ordinary to playful that accounts for this, but all playfulness is not transformative. The shift in frame, then, must move beyond playful to "transpose . . . reality so that intuition, inversion, risk, and symbolic expression reign" (Stoeltje 1992, 263). Moreover, the playful frame in *relajo* is heightened even further with performances of verbal art: that is, the emotional and aesthetic satisfaction from such performances transforms ordinary, daily reality into something special (Bauman 1984 [1977]). In other words, the poetics of *relajo*—the focus on aesthetic pleasure derived from verbal art (Tannen 1989)—are persuasive and potentially transforming. Also adding to this transformative power is the joking during *relajo*, which by its very nature turns the social order upside down.

As Mary Douglas (1968) notes about joking in general, pressures to conform to moral codes and standards of propriety are temporarily relieved in jokes which seem to undermine them. She argues that jokes are double-edged: they appear to challenge the status quo, while they ultimately affirm it; that is, because they allow people to "let off steam," jokes do not ultimately change things. Limón (1982) contests this argument, contending that jokes can be and often are used to change reality by constructing an alternative within the joke realm. Briggs (1988, 182) similarly argues that jokes, as they critique the status quo, can contribute to social change, especially as they provide "a ludic vantage point from which the community and its workings can be critically examined."

Much of the joking during *relajo* by the people in this study can be interpreted as a criticism of the customary code of propriety or *respeto.* Much female joking, for example, relies for its humor on an understanding of the marked differences for women between traditional rural Mexican gender roles and those of modern urban society. One joke (unfortunately not on tape), for example, gave a humorous account of a woman who, upon arrival in Chicago with her husband, announced that he should turn over his paycheck to her. When her husband objected, she simply replied, "Well, we're here now. In Mexico it may be different, but here the women take the paychecks." Much hilarious laughter ensued from the all-female audience attending the baby shower that was the setting for this joke, which inverted the sanctioned attitude of *respeto* on the part of a wife toward her husband.

Other joking during *relajo* uses the principle of juxtaposition to transform reality. For example, when *relajo* turns to "heavy fooling around" (*hacer desmadres*), the topic is often sex, talked about graphically though indirectly through *doble sentido* (double meaning). With *doble sentido,* of course, utterances can be understood in two ways, depending on whether the words are interpreted within a sexual or a nonsexual frame. The two interpretive frames are juxtaposed, which transforms ordinary language into transgressive language. The fact that this topic is even treated at all, although usually only in single-gender *relajo* or in very intimate family settings, highlights by way of contrast the traditional and strict moral code by which these families live, both as conservative, practicing Catholics and as disciplined, responsible adults.

As explained in Chapter 7, part of this normal code restricts respectable women to the private space of the home in contrast to the public space of the street (Da Matta 1991; Rouse 1992), where they might encounter other men and, potentially, danger and/or soiled reputations. The street, of course, is a prime space for rebellion from social norms, whether through speech or involving music and dance. Sergio Rivera

Ayala (1994), for example, describes the "lewd songs and dances" from the streets of eighteenth-century New Spain that were prohibited by religious authorities. One such song, the "Pan de Jarabe," uses images which elicit laughter, "the best expression of popular language [which] overcomes the solemnity of religious discourse" (Rivera Ayala 1994, 36). In spite of their prohibition, such popular music and dance continued to defy the authorities, especially during fiestas.

These inversions of the usual social order, during fiestas or *relajo,* not only allow relief from daily tensions but also provide a space within which alternative meanings can be explored. Play in general serves this function; but, as many have noted, there is nothing as subversive and perhaps as regenerative as laughter. Because both *relajo* and fiesta provide a pleasurable, playful respite from ordinary constraints, they revitalize people. But they also revitalize culture by providing a space and time within which people can try out new modes of being, speaking, and acting, often asserting themselves in ways not usually possible in ordinary life. Thus both fiesta and *relajo,* by fostering risk-taking within the safe frame of "play" as well as within a supportive social network, allow for the emergence of new ways of being, especially among the women of this network.

In sum, *relajo*'s emphasis on rhetorical skill in storytelling and joking enables participants regularly to enjoy ways of using language that they highly value. A woman or man's ability to verbally perform during *relajo* is one measure of her or his status within the extended family. Poetic uses of language occur in other ways of speaking as well, but poetic structures and patterns contribute a certain forcefulness to the stories told during *relajo.* As Tannen (1989) and others have pointed out, through devices such as repetition (on multiple linguistic levels: the phonological, syntactic, and semantic) and constructed dialogue, words are made particularly pleasurable and thus particularly effective and persuasive. Therefore this speech activity is a prime site for addressing and resolving ongoing tensions within these families. As these tensions are dealt with during *relajo,* power relations are transformed, both in the immediate context and, over the long term, in their lives. Because *relajo* and fiesta allow people to assert themselves within a play frame, both events function not just to relieve normative pressures temporarily but also to facilitate a creative process that creates, re-creates, transmits, and sometimes transforms both culture and language use. Such a process is particularly evident in the treatment of gender during *relajo,* especially as *relajo* promotes the inversion of normal social order. That is, much of the gender-focused talk during *relajo* disrupts the normal binaries of house and street, female and male. Such inversion is evident in the analysis of actual instances of *relajo* below, but it is particularly evident in the all-female *relajo.*

Male *Relajo*

The first excerpt (of all-male *relajo*) is part of a larger session of storytelling in a Chicago living room in which three participants tell humorous stories. These three men vary in their rhetorical competence (i.e., their abilities to perform informal verbal art such as stories and jokes). Two of the men, in fact, are much better storytellers than the third, whose story elicits only weak laughter. The man telling the story below is the most skillful of the three, evidenced by the howls of laughter greeting his telling of stories. This is especially the case with the story that he recounts below, which in itself recounts a previous telling in Mexico of an even earlier incident in Mexico. That is, the excerpt presents the telling of a story-within-a-story; as such, it is a multilayered metapragmatic speech event (Silverstein 1993).

Overview of the Story-within-a-Story

The skilled storyteller recounts for two of his *compadres* in the living room of his home in Chicago a familiar story from the rancho that celebrates what these rancheros consider manly qualities. There are three participants in the storytelling event in Chicago, two in the previous storytelling in Mexico (a young man and his father), and two in the original incident (the young man and an old man whom he had unsuccessfully attempted to tease). After the original incident the son went to his father to complain about the old man; this narrating event was recounted in turn by the man in Chicago, who in fact is the animator (Goffman 1974) of the entire excerpt below. As animator, he enriches his multilayered story with constructed dialogue at two levels: first, with the quoted words of the angry young man and his father discussing what happened in the confrontation between the young man and the old man; and, second, with the self-quoted words of the son (narrating the confrontation to his father) that presumably were part of the original incident.

In the story the young man went to his father and complained angrily, swearing at the old man in absentia. The father responded firmly by telling his son to "calm his mouth" and not use such disrespectful words to refer to an older man. The son persisted in his anger at the old man, however, and then, to justify his anger, told the story-within-the-story: he recounted how, when he tried to scare the old man, he was surprised that the old man did not scare but instead yelled out, threw a "six-pack," and grabbed the young man by the neck so hard that the young man could not extricate himself. This behavior, while infuriating to the son, was greeted with loud, delighted, approving laughter by the men hearing the story as evidence of manliness, particularly since it was something of a surprise, given the advanced age of the old man in question. Two external evaluations (Labov 1972a) then follow the story-within-a-story; first, the young man who was grabbed provides an evaluation of the story he tells his father in line 8: *Pensé espantarlo, y el hijo de la chingada me puso un putazo y hizo que ¡me espantara YO! ¡Ya no hallaba cómo quitármelo!* (I wanted to frighten him, and the son of a bitch gave me a punch and made ME scared! I couldn't find a way to get loose!). The Chicago storyteller's own evaluation, however, is no longer quoted from others: he comments on how the man is incredibly large and strong even in old age and how he can still physically control a younger man. The retelling in Chicago follows.

1. Zenaido: *¿No se acuerda una vez que vino Tamboras, pero Tamboras el grande, el papá de ellos?*	Don't you remember one time when Tamboras came, but Tamboras the elder, their father?
2. *Dijo ese [the son], " 'APÁ," dijo, " 'PÁ," dijo, "ESE VIEJÓN* [*whispers*] *¡hijo de su re-chingada madre!"*	That one [the son] said, "PA," he said, "PA," he said, "THAT OLD MAN [*whispers*], son of a bitch!"
3. Father: [*lowers pitch, draws out syllables*] *"Hi:jo, no: le digas así a Ca:llo, es de mi eda:', respé:talo al seño:r."*	[*lowers pitch, draws out syllables*] "So:n, do:n't call Ca:llo that, he's my a:ge, respe:ct the ma:n."
[*laughter*]	[*laughter*]
4. Son: *"Es un hijo de su chingada madre," decía.*	"He's a son of bitch," he said.
5. Father: *"N'ho:mbre, José:, ca:lma esa bo:ca."*	"No, ma:n, José:, ca:lm that mou:th."
6. Son: *"¿Que crees que me pasó con el güey un día, 'apá?"*	"What do you think happened to me with the bastard one day, Pa?"
7. Father: *"¡No le digas así: aquel seño:r!"*	"Don't call that ma:n tha:t!"
8. Son: *"¡Pos hombre!" dijo, "olía medio feo y pensé asu'ta'lo." Dijo, "Viejón, te 'chas un tiro hijo de la chingada, ¿o qué?" Dijo, "Que avienta el* six-pack, *pá, y que pega un grito feo, un putasón aquí, dijo allá— [laughter*	"Well, man!" he said, "he smelled somewhat bad and I thought of scaring him." He said, "Old man, are you gonna fight, you son of a bitch, or what?" He said, "He throws the six-pack, Pa, and he lets out an ugly

throughout the following] *la chingada,* [*pause*] *pensé espantarlo," dijo, "y el hijo de la chingada me puso un putazo y hizo que ¡me espantara YO! ¡Ya no hallaba cómo quitármelo!"*	scream, a punch here, said there—[*laughter throughout the following*] the fucker, [*pause*] I wanted to frighten him," he said, "and the son of a bitch gave me a punch and made ME scared! I couldn't find a way to get loose!"
9. [*laughter*] *Es un señor que tiene como setenta años, está grandote y manudo. Tiene unos dedotes, 'ira, no se acaba ese hombre. Y el Tamboras pensó espantarlo, n'hombre que lo brinca aquel y que lo pesca del cuello.* [*laughter*] *Ya no, ya no hallaba como chingados soltarsele del pescuezo.*	[*laughter*] He is a man that is about seventy, is really big and has big hands. He has big fingers, look, that man doesn't wear out. And Tamboras thought of scaring him, no way, the other one jumped him and caught him by the neck. [*laughter*] He couldn't, he couldn't find a fuckin' way to get his neck loose.

This excerpt, like much *relajo,* is saturated with metapragmatic discourse or talk about previous talk. As Lucy (1993, 12) notes, "there can be higher order metalanguages about a first order metalanguage"; sometimes one form can be both metalanguage and object language—that is, these categories can be either overlapping or discrete. This example includes four embedded, discrete levels of metalanguage, distinguished as Current Narrating Event (level four), Past Narrating Event (level three), Narrated Event (the original core incident, level two), and the Reported Speech quoted from the original event (level one). The story includes two narrating events (one in Chicago and a previous one in Mexico) and two narrated events (both in Mexico), but the middle event is both a narrating and a narrated event: a narrating event in Mexico becomes the narrated event in Chicago.

The broadest level of metalanguage here (number 4 in Figure 8.1) is the narrating event in Chicago, represented by the entire transcribed excerpt above. Level three is a narrating event in Mexico (lines 2–8), in which a son tells his father about a previous incident in which he was involved. This *narrating* event at level three then becomes the *narrated* event at level four later in Chicago. The original core incident, represented in lines 6 to 8, is the "narrated matter" (level two), which is reported on at the narrating event in Mexico (level three), which itself is reported on in the narrating event in Chicago (level four). Both narrating events, moreover, are replete with constructed dialogue, perhaps

Figure 8.1. Four levels of metalanguage in story-within-a-story

the most explicit form of metapragmatic discourse, which constitutes a kind of primary metalanguage within the original incident (level one).

What functions does this multileveled metapragmatic discourse serve? First, it is a persuasive rhetorical device that attempts to convince listeners of a particular perspective or point of view. Second, in an overall pattern of what Gumperz (1982, 1992) calls "contextualization cues," it signals participants in the ongoing speech event how to interpret this activity; or, in Goffman's (1974) terms, it frames the discourse as a particular kind of speech activity, thus unifying the discourse into a coherent whole. Third, it constructs social reality by mirroring the social situation in which it is situated; that is, the overall structure and use of the language in the storytelling parallel—in fact help to construct or transform—the social context in which the genre (here the story) is performed. Each of these functions is explained in turn.

Constructed Dialogue as Rhetorical Strategy: Direct Quotations of Previous Talk

As already noted, much speech is full of the talk of others; but the representation of previous speech can take various forms, including direct and indirect quotation. Direct quotation purports to quote previous speech exactly, although it is actually a present creation, what Tannen (1989) calls constructed dialogue, rather than a verbatim record of past speech. Thus the storyteller above constructs a dialogue between a father and son in which he ostensibly quotes directly the father's response to his son's complaint about the old man:

Hijo, no le digas así a Callo, es de mi eda', respétalo al señor.
Son, don't call Callo that, he's my age, respect the man.

The narrator does not use indirect quotation as he constructs his story (i.e., he does not say, "The father told his son not to call Callo bad names, but to respect him, since he's the same age as the father"). Although this would convey the same referential information, it lacks the dramatic tension and flavor of constructed dialogue. Such direct quotation brings the voices of others more definitively into our present talk and often is perceived as more authoritative than indirect quotation, because someone who can quote another's words verbatim would seem to have true and unbiased information. Given the importance of straightforward, authoritative speech (*franqueza:* see Chapter 6) among rancheros, it is not surprising that their discourse is so generously spiced with reported speech in the form of direct quotations. Such direct quotation takes the perspective of the narrated event that occurred in the past and emphasizes details of form (exact speech) more than the content of what someone said. In contrast, indirect quotation, as in my hypothetical example above, takes the perspective of the current narrating event and emphasizes content and reason over form (Lucy 1993). As such, it emphasizes the point of view of the present speaker, who presumably has digested the content of someone else's past speech and now recounts it in his own words in the present, rather than the point of view of the quoted speaker, as direct speech seems to do.

Although indirect quotation is more explicit about emphasizing the point of view of the current speaker, direct quotation, because it does this implicitly, is more powerful in this regard. The use of direct quotation in a narrative subtly fuses the communication of information with the expressiveness of the narrator. So even though reported speech—especially when it occurs without an explicit *verbum dicendi* or verb of speaking (e.g., *dijo* or *decía,* he said)—seems to represent only the voice of a previous speaker, it inevitably also expresses, through intonation and other devices, the attitude of the present speaker as well.

The emphasis on form in reported speech often takes a poetic shape (Farr 1994b). Poetic devices in oral narrative make that narrative vivid, believable, and aesthetically pleasing. For these rancheros, such *sabor* (flavor) is a valued quality of speech (Farr 1993). Work on oral poetic forms in a variety of cultures has noted the ubiquity of repetition and parallelism (Jakobson 1960; Tannen 1989). Here the storyteller initiates his story-within-a-story with a direct quotation of the son (line 2), the first two lines of which show repetition and parallelism in both semantic content and intonation patterns. Moreover, the entire direct quotation can be parsed into lines according to a rhythmic pacing of pauses and pitch changes:

'APÁ, dijo,	PA, he said,
'PÁ, dijo,	PA, he said,
ESE VIEJÓN,	THAT OLD MAN,
¡hijo de su re-chingada madre!	son of a bitch!

At the end of each line the narrator pauses slightly. Within the first two lines he alternates higher and lower pitch levels (*APÁ* and *PÁ* are said with higher pitch and more stress, while *dijo* in both lines is said with lower pitch and less stress). This alternation in pitch and stress produces a rhythmic quality that culminates in a climax in the last two lines *ESE VIEJÓN* (THAT OLD MAN) and a final *¡hijo de su re-chingada madre!* (son of a bitch!). The last comment, said with a lowered but intense voice, communicates implicitly the frustration and anger of the son toward the old man; and the contrast in pitch and stress between the third and fourth lines, paralleling the contrast within the first and second lines, yields a stretch of speech that is balanced and artful. In other words, the storyteller, like all good narrators, enacts his story dramatically, building suspense with poetic devices that transform the simple telling of a story into an enhanced experience for all participants (Bauman 1984 [1977]).

A similar parallelism structures the father's words, which the storyteller quotes next in line 3, into equivalent phrases separated by pauses and modulated rhythmically:

Hijo,	Son,
no le digas así a Callo,	don't call Callo that,
es de mi eda',	he's my age,
respétalo al señor.	respect the man.

The narrator thus juxtaposes two voices, the father's and the son's, from the narrating of the original incident in Mexico. This juxtaposition of two voices parallels the two voices from the original incident, the son's and the old man's (although the old man does not speak words but only yells out and grabs the son by the neck). At the broadest level of metalanguage, the Chicago narrator's own voice—while not explicitly in the story anywhere—nevertheless colors the entire story, as he imitates the other voices in particular ways. What we have, then, are multiple voices from the social world of these rancheros, voices that invoke social positions and ideologies (Bakhtin 1981; Hill 1995; Wortham 2001). A patriarchal ideology is invoked, and affirmed, here with the representation of a son's rebellious voice toward an old man and toward his own father and, especially, with the disciplining of that younger voice (the son) by the older voice (the father).

But the narrator does not simply invoke these voices; nor does he simply affirm a patriarchal social order by telling a story in which an old man triumphs over a young man. That is, it is not just semantic content that communicates the message here. The narrator evaluates all these voices implicitly with devices such as intonation patterns that signal irony and parody. Here he uses pitch variation to present the son as practically squealing in the old man's grasp and to present the father as the (deep and calm) voice of reason and authority. Thus a direct quotation is "double voiced," in Bakhtin's (1981) terms, by expressing the son's (or father's) voice and at the same time expressing the Chicago narrator's. Moreover, by juxtaposing these voices with his own—for example when he uses ordinary (not object) language and says *dijo* (he said)—he makes it clear that he is authoring the narrative by presenting his own voice through a kind of ventriloquation as he represents the voices of others (Bakhtin 1981; Wortham 2001). That is, by positioning himself with respect to others, as represented by their voices in his story, the narrator or author speaks indirectly.

Shifting between various voices highlights the contrast between the self (the narrator) and various others. For example, a narrator can present a particular voice as closer to or more distant from his own (Lucy 1993). As noted above, intonation can parody a voice and emphasize qualities such as fear or weakness (e.g., the son's voice saying that he could not get loose from the old man in line 8). Another means for distancing a character's voice from one's own as narrator involves the relative frequency of verbs of speaking, here *dijo* (he said) and *decía* (he was saying). Here the narrator uses frequent verbs of speaking in presenting the son's voice in contrast to using none when presenting the father's voice. *Dijo* is used three times in the first direct quotation of the son in line 2, whereas it is not used at all in the first direct quotation of the father which follows in line 3. In line 4, when the son speaks again, the narrator uses *decía.* In the lines that follow, both the father's and the son's voices are represented without any verbs of speaking, as the story builds to a climax and direct quotations are hurled back and forth between the father and the son. Yet when the son speaks at length again, in line 8, the narrator uses *dijo* no fewer than five times, interspersing these *dijo*s throughout the son's entire brief final monologue. Overall, then, there is a striking contrast between the very frequent use of *dijo* (and one *decía*) when the son is speaking and no such words at all when the father is speaking.

This notable contrast is unlikely to be accidental, especially since the narrator's voice qualities and the direct juxtaposition of different voices make it clear who is speaking when. And yet the narrator keeps interspersing the son's comments with frequent *dijos*, as if to say (indirectly), "This is what HE said, not me." In other words, using verbs of speaking distances the narrator's voice from that of his character by anchoring the discourse in the current narrating event. In this sense, the narrator's frequent use of "he said" is a constant reminder that brings participants back to the current context in Chicago, away from the previous speech event in Mexico. The narrator here distances himself, then, from the son but not from the father. He positions himself much closer to the father, and thus to patriarchal ideology, than to the son, who by trying to scare an old man attempted to challenge a patriarchal order based on age as well as gender. In the contest over superior masculinity the son loses this round, and the old man, the father, and the narrator win it. The enthusiastic, whooping laughter that follows the story shows that the other participants in this storytelling, the listeners who are for the moment the audience, not only affirm patriarchy but affirm the superior masculinity (for the moment) of the narrator, their *compadre.*

Framing (Stories within) *Relajo*

How do participants coordinate their behavior so that they can make *relajo* together? How do they know at a given point in time who is to be performer and who audience? In most conversations these things fall relatively easily into structured events, which tells us that participants somehow signal each other with subtle cues that may be picked up and responded to unconsciously. If so, what are these signals? A pattern of such cues embedded in this discourse signals that this is *relajo* rather than serious talk and that a humorous story is coming. One of these cues is the opening statement by the storyteller in line 1:

> *¿No se acuerda una vez que vino Tamboras, pero Tamboras el grande, el papá de ellos?*
> Don't you remember one time when Tamboras came, but Tamboras the elder, their father?

This comment signals the listeners to become the audience for the storyteller's performance. Such shifting in roles occurs repeatedly throughout the longer *relajo* session of which this excerpt is a part, as each of the three men takes the floor to tell a story and the other two settle in as audience until the next shift in roles. Although this cue is relatively explicit, other cues are more embedded and implicit (e.g., facial expressions, intonation contours, a switch in language, the use of dialect features or taboo words). Because such cues emerge spontaneously in narrative performances, what happens as these narratives unfold cannot be predicted, and therein lies the creativity at the heart of such performances of verbal art. Both traditional resources and individual creativity are "brought to parity . . . in a dialectic played out within the context of situated action, a kind of praxis" (Bauman 1986, 4).

The opening cue above functions as the preface to the story itself (Jefferson 1978; Wortham 2001), which then emerges as a monologic narrative told by one participant. This cue itself is metapragmatic; that is, it is language that refers to other talk-in-context, in this case a favored story of a confrontation in Mexico. This metapragmatic language frames the discourse as a story, within the larger frame of *relajo* as a verbal activity. This frame helps the story to cohere, as does the pattern of poetic devices described above. As a coherent text, the story has its own implicit metapragmatic force, as a kind of textual icon (Lucy 1993; Parmentier 1997; Silverstein 1976; Wortham 2001) for the interaction in the immediate storytelling context. The storytelling, then, is an informal ritual that parallels or mirrors the context in which it unfolds. Just as the son and the old man, and then the son and his father, engage in a struggle over domination, so do the participants in this *relajo,* as they compete to tell the best story and thus control the floor. In achieving this, a narrator enacts his own superior masculinity while at the same time his story expresses a parallel struggle resolved by domination.

Indexing and Enacting Gender

Because of the emergent, interactive nature of such talk, as well as a focus on conflict talk, *relajo* is a key site for emergent cultural practices that create, re-create, or transform culture and social relations. When such talk is performative and replete with verbal art, this creative capacity is especially powerful. Because such metalanguage typically includes multiple voices from our social worlds and, unavoidably, attitudes or evaluations of those voices, such discourse reveals with acuity the language-culture nexus (Sherzer 1987). Language, then, is social action, actively constructing and reconstructing social relations and cultural ideologies. The male *relajo* in which the excerpt above occurred can be interpreted as a struggle over superior masculinity in a patriarchal system. As explicated in Chapter 7, patriarchy relies on both age and gender in organizing hierarchical relations (Stern 1995), and the challenge here from a young man to an old one is an inherent tension in patriarchal relations. (The challenge of women to men is taken up in the all-female *relajo* excerpt that follows this discussion of male *relajo*.)

This age-based challenge to patriarchy is a potential inversion of the social order. Ultimately, however, the storytelling, especially the response of the present audience to valued masculine traits in the story, affirms traditionally masculine gender ideologies. It also socializes younger members within earshot (both male and female) into these ideologies. The old man is admired for not being scared, for having the highly valued qualities of a ranchero in spite of his advanced age. The validation of physical prowess, self-assertion, and even domination affirms the men's own (superior masculine) position in an age- and gender-based hierarchy. The entire *relajo* session of which this excerpt is a part is a struggle to establish a status hierarchy, as the men compete to tell the funniest or most outrageous stories more and less successfully. One rather mild-mannered and quiet man tells a story that receives only modest laughter, while another is quite successful in generating hilarity, as is the teller of this excerpt. This teller is so successful, in fact, that he recycles the story, telling it again a little later in the session and getting just as much laughter the second time around.

Thus such storytelling not only indexes superior masculinity but enacts it as well, transforming the current context. In this way the performance of verbal art "is a form of creative linguistic play with the power to affect social reality" (Lucy 1993, 21). The context is transformed hierarchically in terms of who dominates the talk, and it is transformed from a formerly neutral space (a living room in Chicago) into a male one. This is evidenced in the brief appearance of the host's daughter, who approaches the group asking if anyone wants to eat. She stops midsentence, however, and is not responded to or heard from again during the session. She quickly leaves the living room, suggesting that she knows it is inappropriate for her to stay, that this is male space for the moment.

In terms of linguistic form, as opposed to content, the swear words in this story also construct masculinity, by indexing it indirectly (Ochs 1992). Swearing is tough and coarse, as men are ideally presumed to be; whereas men are expected to swear, women are not, especially in the presence of men or children. Even the male storyteller here lowers his voice (see line 2) the first time he swears, presumably so that nearby children or women do not overhear. As the story builds, however, he uses swear words with more abandon (see lines 4, 8).

Since swearing is associated with masculinity, women are negatively evaluated if they swear or, similarly, talk about sex in front of children.[2] In spite of such restrictions, however, this is exactly what the women do in much all-female *relajo.* Moreover, particular women swear quite frequently; and even those who swear less frequently nevertheless laugh uproariously when the more frequent swearers wax eloquent. If swearing indexes masculinity within all-male *relajo,* what does it index within all-female *relajo?* Clearly, it still is associated with masculinity, but among females who are *echando relajo* it is an appropriation of masculine discourse forms put to their own ends. By swearing and talking about sex, and indexing masculinity, women challenge the social order. Men are supposed to be the ones swearing, shooting guns, and accepting no offenses. When women do these things, they are refusing to construct themselves as deferential females. It could be argued that as long as these tougher stances are kept within the verbal borders of *relajo* they do not threaten the status quo. Yet what happens in *relajo* tends to leak into other domains, especially since other forces, including the women themselves, are pressuring for change as well.

Female *Relajo*

In what follows I explore an instance of storytelling embedded in all-female *relajo* in a kitchen in Chicago. The narrator, a widow, tells her close friend a personal anecdote about what happened to her in a recent visit to the rancho. A middle-aged unmarried man with much land in the rancho, who is often the subject of female joking (one young woman once said that she would marry him to save him, since men must marry to go to heaven), is the foil in this story. As in the all-male *relajo,* this *relajo* includes talk about previous talk in Mexico. Here, however, the story that is retold was part of a previous *relajo* in Mexico. In this story two middle-aged sisters tease the unmarried man, called Jorge here, about marrying the widow, who has both legal papers and a well-paying job in Chicago. The man does turn his eye to the widow but ultimately seems to be afraid of marriage and so only "casts his eyes" at her from time to time. Toward the end of the story another man, pounding his fist on the table, vehemently denies that Jorge will ever marry.

The widow meanwhile, put perhaps in an awkward position, responds by becoming outrageous (within the relatively safe verbal frame of *relajo*). She commits several sins verbally within this frame: in her story she quotes herself swearing profusely, talking about sex, and generally challenging the code of *respeto* that would make her deferential to men. Being a widow is not insignificant in this regard; she is able to be especially daring during *relajo* (other women also challenge gender norms, but not as extremely) because she has no husband that she might potentially shame. The original *relajo* in Mexico included both genders at least partly, as Jorge is teased and later is within hearing distance of the widow when she rises to the challenge of her friends (the two sisters). The *relajo* in Chicago, however, consists entirely of women—three middle-aged mothers (called here Ramona, Irma, and Flora) and several teenaged daughters of Ramona and Irma (Rosita is the only daughter who speaks in this excerpt). The only exception is a young son of about six (called Juanito here) who is told as the story is about to begin (line 3) to shut the door (presumably so that the men in the living room cannot hear the women's talk) and then, as the story builds, is told to sit down and be quiet while the widow recounts her adventures (line 21).

Overview of the Story

Immediately before this excerpt, the context for the story is explained in conversation. A recent visit to Mexico by the widow is mentioned, then references are made to Jorge. The story itself is triggered by Ramona in line 1, who says that the widow Irma was romancing Jorge while she was in Mexico, and by Irma herself, whose preface to the story in line 4 says, "What do you think that woman said?" The story is launched while the tape is turned over, and it begins in earnest in line 6. The following excerpt is rather long, but I include it all here to illustrate the more intensely dialogic nature of the women's *relajo* in contrast to the men's. There is more back-and-forth talk, more sharing of the floor, more supportive questions (e.g., in line 10 Flora asks what Irma was "thinking and thinking," and in line 11 Ramona exclaims about them not getting together at all).

The core of the story is narrated by Irma in lines 6–8, 18, 20, 23–24, 26–28, and 31–32. In these monologues Irma tells how the teasing started, with Jorge looking at her and giggling and her friend Magdalena telling him to get a passport and travel with Irma all over the world (line 7). Then Irma tells how Jorge came to Magdalena's house the next day to say that he could not marry Irma because they were relatives, to which Irma responds, "What an idiot, what does he remember that for?" (line 9). After politely refusing a chair offered to her by Rosita (the teenaged daughter of Ramona) and telling the young boy Juanito not to screw around while she is telling her adventures, she launches into the best parts of the story.

In this core of the story Irma reports her own speech to the women in the rancho, enacting a parody of a deferential hyperfemininity that contrasts strikingly with the content of what she says: that she would put up with Jorge's hard bed of boards with a hole in the middle located in the house at the bottom of his orchard, but only if he put the land in her name right away, in time for the guayabas to bear fruit (line 23). At this point she says that the two sisters are dying of laughter (at her open exhibition of self-assertion and talk about sex), in line 24. She then tells Jorge to forget that they are relatives and tells the women in his presence that from now on no one can say, "Let's go to the guayabas at Jorge's," but instead they will say, "Let's go to the guayabas at Irma's" (line 26). She pushes the envelope even further by declaring that she will go to the orchard with a borrowed shotgun to blast the bastard who dares to go into the guayabas, so they know that the orchard is hers now. She caps this by extending her warning about the guayabas to the chiles in the orchard: "Nor the peppers, no one is going to cut my peppers!"—the climax of the story.

After the laughter dies down, Irma extends her control of the floor by recounting what happened after her outrageous joking in Mexico: she parodies the drunken man who, pounding his fist on the table, insisted that Jorge would never marry (line 32). She moves the story along with the first of two external evaluations (Labov 1972a). Two other evaluations begin to draw the entire story to a close, although they alternate with comments and laughter from the other women as well as with more storytelling. An embedded evaluation reports how Irma felt during the *relajo* in Mexico: "And I felt the urge to, ooh I don't know what, because of the laughing" (line 29). This is followed by an aside about the two sisters who drew her into this. The final evaluation is, like the first one, external to the story itself: "Look, I had so much fun!" Finally, she signals that the story is over with a coda (Labov 1972a), a concluding exclamation and yell, "Oh dear girl of mine! aay-AAY!" The excerpt follows.

1. Ramona: *Ay se andaba enamorando a Jorge.*	She was romancing Jorge.
2. Irma: [*whispering*]	[*whispering*]
3. Ramona: *Cierra la puerta, Juanito.*	Close the door, Juanito.
4. Irma: *¿Qué crees que dice aquella . . . ?*	What do you think that woman said . . . ?
5. [*break in recording to turn tape over*]	[*break in recording to turn tape over*]
6. Irma: *Y luego voltea Jorge, y me pone cuidado como . . .* [*laughter, comments, and shrieks*] *. . . y no la puse,*	And then Jorge turns around, and he keeps an eye on me like . . . [*laughter, comments, and shrieks*] . . .

y, y yo, y yo este muy seria, ¿no?, yo muy seria acá y luego de, y luego este, "Je-je." El no más se reía, "Je-je-je, je-je-je, je-je." [*women laugh delightedly*]

and I didn't pay, and, and I, and I uh was very serious, right? I was very serious over here, and then uh—and then uh, "Heh-heh." He just laughed, "Heh-heh-heh, heh-heh-heh, heh-heh." [*women laugh delightedly*]

7. *Dice la pinche de, de esta—¿cómo se llama?—Magdalena* [*lowers voice, lengthens syllables, builds to climax*] *"Sa:ca un pa:sa:po:rte, Jorge, y se va:, y se va con Irma pa' todo el mundo." Saca la pasapo:rte—* [*women laugh raucously, make comments, cry out Ay! then fall silent*]

She says, that damn uh, uh—what's her name?—Magdalena [*lowers voice, lengthens syllables, builds to climax*] "Ge:t a pa:ssport, Jorge, and go:, and go with Irma all over the world." Get a pa:sspo:rt—[*women laugh raucously, make comments, cry out Ay! then fall silent*]

8. *Oye, Flora, el, el, luego, yo creo que este Jorge, le entró lo pendejo, ¿no?* [*lowers voice, lengthens syllables, increasing speed to climax*] *Se rían la pi:nche Carmen y Magda d' él hasta tomando—Otro día temprano viene a deci'le, "O:ye, mucha:cha, Ma:gda, yo no me puedo casar con Irma porque ¡es mi pa:ri:e:nte!"* [*laughs*]

Hey, Flora, the, then, uh, Jorge . . . I think that he got stupid, right? [*lowers voice, lengthens syllables, increasing speed to climax*] That da:mn Carmen and Magda laughed at him until drinking—Early the next day he comes over to tell her, "Li:sten, girl, Ma:gda, I can't marry Irma because she's my re:la:tive!" [*laughs*]

9. [*returns to own voice*] *Y yo diciendo, "Qué pendejo, y ¿pa' qué se acuerda de eso?"*

[*returns to own voice*] And I'm saying, "What an idiot, what does he remember that for?"

10. Flora: *¡Ay Irma! Y a ver dimi luego que tú piensi y piensi.* [*women cry out*]

Ay Irma! And tell me, after you were thinking and thinking. [*women cry out*]

11. Ramona: *¿Cómo no?—juntaba y ¡Díos mio!, ¡sin nada!*

How did he not—together, and, my God, with nothing!

12. Irma: *El no, él no, ¡él ni siquiera se fijaba!* [*laughter*]

Him no, him no, he didn't even notice! [*laughter*]

13. Flora: *¿Y qué dijiste, que era tu hermano?*

And what did you say, that he was your brother?

14. Ramona: *O que hubiera dicho—*

Or you could have said that—

15. Irma: *Yo le 'biera dicho que era mi compadre.* [*laughter*]

I would have said he was my *compadre.* [*laughter*]

16. Ramona: *Oye, tu tía Irma, y tu tía*

Listen, your aunt Irma, and your

Magdalena y tu Ma, ¡ay Dios mío! [*addressed to various daughters*]

aunt Magdalena and your Ma, oh my God! [*addressed to various daughters*]

17. Rosita: *Oye, traiga la silla a Irma.*

Listen, take the chair to Irma.

18. Irma: *Y luego—no, no, no, yo no, yo 'toy muy bien aquí. Y luego, 'ira, allá tam'ién, tiene una casita a la bajada de la huerta, ¿no?*

And then—no no no, me no, I'm fine right here. And then, look, over there he also has a house at the low side of the orchard, right?

19. Ramona: *Umjum. Sí.*

Uh huh. Yes.

20. Irma: *Y tenía una cama, de puras tablas, ¿no? Un abujero en medio de este corte—*

And he had a bed, of boards only, right? A hole of this size in the middle—

21. [*to child*] *Juanito, ahí se me sienta ahí, Juanito. Hijo, 'orita no chingues. Estoy hablando las aventuras.*

[*to child*] Juanito, sit yourself right there for me, Juanito. Son, don't screw around right now. I'm telling my adventures.

22. Ramona: *Ah bueno, enton's cállese.*

All right, then be quiet.

23. Irma: *Y luego este le digo yo, le digo a Carmen,* [*high-pitched, hyperfeminine voice*] *"Ay:, Carmenci:ta de mi a:lma, aunque sea una ca:ma, aunque—"* [*back to ordinary voice*] *yo tendría que si me caiga no me daba recio, ¡está de alta así!* [*laughter*] *Le digo, "Yo me agua:nta:ba así, pero sólo que me escrituraran la huerta, pos enseguida, ¡pa' aguantar las guayabas si no!"* [*laughter*]

And then, um, I say, I say to Carmen, [*high-pitched, hyperfeminine voice*] "Oh:, little Carmen of my sou:l, at least a be:d, at least—" [*back to ordinary voice*] I figured that if I fell I would not hit myself hard, it's only so high! [*laughter*] I tell her, "I would pu:t u:p with that but only if he put the ranch in my name, right away, to wait for the guayabas at least!" [*laughter*]

24. *Ay no, no, no, pero es rete ocupado [que no escucha] y luego ellas que se morían de la risa.*

Oh, no, no, but he is so busy [he does not hear] and then they wanted to die laughing.

25. Ramona: *No, ya me las imagino.*

No, I [can] imagine them.

26. Irma: *Yo porque ya estoy—hasta le dije, "No oye, olvídate que eres pariente de—" Y luego, mira, les digo yo, ahí estaba él ve'da', y les digo yo, "No, de aquí pa' delante no, na:die va a decir 'vamos a las guayabas con Jorge,' si no van a decir 'vamos a las guayabas con Irma.'*

Because I'm already—I even told him, "No, listen, forget that you're a relative—" And then, look, I tell them, he was there, right? And I tell them, "No, from now on, no: no: one can say, 'Let's go to the guayabas at Jorge's,' but instead you're going to say, 'Let's go to the guayabas at Irma's.'

27. *Y allá me voy a ir yo con la retro-*

And I will go there with Pelón's shot

carga de Pelón y el cabrón que entre a las guayabas y le suelto un guamazo pa' que sepan que ya ¡la huerta es mía! Ni a los chiles, ¡naiden me va a cortar chiles!" [*laughter and comments*]	gun and the bastard that goes into the guayabas I'm going to blast, so that they know that now the orchard is mine! Nor the peppers, no one is going to cut my peppers!" [*laughter and comments*]
28. *No, y me aventaba ojitos de ves en cuando.* [*laughter and comments*]	No, and he would check me out once in a while. [*laughter and comments*]
29. *Y yo que sentía ganas de aay, yo no sé qué hacer de risa* [*hushed emphatic tone*] *pero mira, Carmen y Magdalena, las dos son tan cabronas.*	And I felt the urge to, ooh I don't know what, because of the laughing, [*hushed emphatic tone*] but look, Carmen and Magdalena, they are both such bitches.
30. Ramona: *Ay, sí, sí, yo sé, yo sé. Aay.*	Oh yes, yes, I know, I know. Aay.
31. Irma: *Y dice un borrachito de lo que le están haciendo burla . . . con el borrachito, con el, con la hermana del borrachito, le están haciendo— y luego que se levanta el borrachito de allá de 'onde estaba sentado y dice,* [*slows speech*]	And a drunk says, about what they were making fun of . . . with the drunk, with the, with the drunk's sister, they were making—and then the drunk gets up from over there where he was sitting and says, [*slows speech*]
32. *"Mi:ri, con mu:ncho respe:to le voy a decir, perdone y respeto pues que,"* [*woman giggles*] *dice, "Pero yo le voy a decir una cosa," dice,* [*deep, raspy voice*], *"Jorge, Jorge, oiga, ¡ni con cua:tro lumbra:das por acá:, ya no se casa!"* [*pounds on table*] [*laughter*]	"Loo:k, with a:ll due resp:ect I am going to say, excuse me and with respect," [*woman giggles*] he says, "But I am going to tell you something," he says [*deep, raspy voice*], "Listen, Jorge, Jorge, not even with fou:r bon:fires over he:re [*at his backside*], will he get married!" [*pounds on table*] [*laughter*]
33. *'Ira, yo me divertía tanto que—* [*comments and cries by women*] *¡Ay hijita de mi vida! ¡aay-AAY!* [*laughter*]	Look, I had so much fun that—[*comments and cries by women*] Oh dear girl of mine! aay-AAY! [*laughter*]

Structure of Excerpt

This excerpt of female *relajo* differs notably from the male *relajo* discussed previously. First, it is much longer, although the core stories are roughly the same in length. The story in the female *relajo*, however, is more spread out; it is told in spurts, interspersed with comments and questions from other participants and asides to children. This partly reflects the conditions of the women's lives, juggling responsibility for children and their homes while they amuse themselves *echando relajo.* The men in the male *relajo,* in contrast, are not interrupted at all (except briefly by a daughter who asks if anyone wants to eat, who is not answered verbally and quickly leaves them alone). In addition to the interruptions, the women themselves participate more actively as audience; the narrator/performer does not simply tell an entertaining story, she draws listeners in, sometimes directing specific comments to particular people (e.g., "Hey, Flora" in line 8, and the hushed comment directed to Ramona in line 29 about the women in Mexico being such bitches, having put her on the spot by instigating the teasing with Jorge). In other words, the women place more emphasis on the current narrating event and on the interaction among its participants than do the men. Irma does tell her story, and she tells its core events dramatically and effectively, as is evidenced by the laughter it evokes. Yet the structural elements of the story are scattered throughout the entire conversation, making the boundaries of the story more permeable and the story itself less compact.

Relajo among the women in this social network, in fact, is typically organized in this fashion, and the buildup of tension as stories gradually evolve adds to the pleasure of this activity. Because this excerpt is longer and the focal story's parts more spread out, I provide below an abstracted structure of the story's important elements (in capitals), using the narrative analysis in Jefferson (1978) and Labov (1972a). I include the asides to children and comments from participants to indicate how embedded the story's elements are in the ongoing conversation (line numbers are included in parentheses).

ABSTRACT by listener (1): She was romancing Jorge [while in Mexico].
Aside by listener to child (3): Close the door [to keep men in living room from hearing].
PREFACE by narrator (4): What do you think that woman said?
COMPLICATING ACTION by narrator (6–7): Irma serious; Jorge giggles; Magdalena teases Jorge about getting a passport and traveling with Irma all over the world.
Commentary by participants (6–7): Exclamations, questions, comments by all.
Aside by listener to daughters present (16): Just listen to your aunts and your mother!
Aside by teenaged daughter to narrator (17): Give Irma a chair.
Response of narrator (18): Politely refuses chair.

ORIENTATION by narrator (18 and 20): Jorge has a little house at the end of his orchard; the house has a wooden bed, with a hole in the middle.
Asides to child (21, 22): Sit down there. Don't fool around while I'm telling my adventures. Keep quiet.
RESOLUTION #1 by narrator (23): Will put up with hard bed [at least there's a bed!], but only if land is put in her name right away, at least until guayabas bear fruit.
EXTERNAL EVALUATION #1 by narrator (24): They [two sisters] wanted to die laughing.
Supportive comment by listener (25): I can imagine.
Resolution #1 continued by narrator (26–27): I told Jorge, forget you're a relative! Then I tell them [two sisters] in his presence that from now on the guayabas will be mine. And I will use a shotgun to blast anyone who comes into my orchard. Nor will anyone take my chiles!
EMBEDDED EVALUATION by narrator (29): And I felt like, I don't know what because of all the laughing.
Aside by narrator to listener (29): But look, those two sisters are such bitches!
Response from listener to narrator (30): Oh yes, I know.
RESOLUTION #2 by narrator (32): The next day a drunk says, not even with four fires on his backside will Jorge ever marry!
EXTERNAL EVALUATION #2 by narrator (33): Look, I had so much fun!
CODA by narrator (33): Oh, dear girl of mine! aay-AAY!

All the structural elements of narrative structure proposed in various studies (see Mishler 1995 for a review) are here, but they are scattered and interspersed with many asides and commentary from listeners. External and internal boundaries of the story are not as clear as they were in the male *relajo.* The focal story is told in several short monologues, with responses by participants interspersed, in contrast to the male *relajo,* in which the story is not divided by such comments. Instead male narrators take turns telling stories; and as each one takes the floor, those who become the audience are quiet while the narrator narrates, until someone else takes the floor to tell his story. Moreover, among the women, some elements (e.g., the abstract) are provided not by the narrator but by one of the listeners. The narrator extends the story in response to appreciative laughter, as is evidenced by three separate evaluations and a coda uttered by the narrator as laughter tapers off as well as a postscript story about the drunk who comes the next day to insist that Jorge will never marry.

Many previous studies of narrative structure thus seem to be based on bounded monologues performed without interruptions. These women, however, must fit their verbal pleasures in the interstices of hectic daily life, and they do so collaboratively, as do women in other studies (Eckert 1990). In contrast to the male *relajo*, this *relajo* contains more evidence of explicit bids for audience involvement (e.g., comments directed at specific listeners). In addition, various poetic devices increase both the aesthetic enjoyment of the talk and audience involvement in it. The next section focuses on these aesthetic pleasures, primarily in the dramatic enactment of reported speech. Like most *relajo*, much of these women's talk consists of reports of other talk; here, as in the male *relajo* above, a woman recounts a previous speech event. Thus the pleasures that are so evident in this and other instances of *relajo* depend to a large extent on metapragmatic discourse.

Metapragmatic Discourse: Meaning beyond Semantic Content

The above excerpt is replete with metapragmatic discourse, as the widow Irma talks about a previous speech-event-in-context, the *relajo* in Mexico during her recent visit there. She primarily reports her own (humorous) speech in that previous *relajo*. If pragmatics involves the meaning of language that can only be understood by reference to the context in which the language occurs, then metapragmatics involves language that focuses on this kind of meaning in previous language. The meaning of Irma's self-quotations, the object language she reflects on here, is necessarily tied to the context in which they were presumably uttered (i.e., during *relajo* in a woman's home in the rancho in which Magdalena teased Jorge about marrying Irma). To make her story comprehensible in Chicago, Irma re-creates some of the previous context in the current narrating event with the orientation (Jorge has a little house in his orchard) and complicating action (her friend began to tease Jorge about getting together with her, while she was "very serious over here" and thus innocent of the teasing). The full meaning of her response to the teasing initiated by Magdalena ("Get a passport, Jorge, and go, and go with Irma all over the world" in line 7) requires contextual information already understood by her listeners in Chicago: Jorge's reputation as an unmarried man with much (coveted) land, the frequent teasing of unmarried people (including the widow) about getting married, and the restrictions on women to be deferential and submissive to men. Because all this contextual information is presupposed by her listeners, she does not re-create it in her story.

As in the all-male *relajo* above, reported speech enlivens the story; but here the narrator reports her own speech, constructing a dialogue in which she is the main character. As she quotes herself, she simultaneously expresses her attitudes toward and evaluations of some presupposed contextual information. These attitudes are expressed implicitly through such linguistic devices as intonation that departs from that expected for ordinary conversation. Listeners perceive that the narrator intends to communicate something special, since a device is being used in a marked (not usual) way. Here a high girlish pitch and lengthened vowels as she says (in line 23) *Ay, Carmencita de mi alma, aunque sea una cama, aunque—* (Oh, little Carmen of my soul, at least a bed, at least—) signal that these words are to be taken ironically, that they are a parody of a dependent, male-flattering femininity in which Irma is grateful for a broken-down bed without a mattress if she could only have Jorge in marriage, critiquing the implicit assumption that women are to be deferential and submissive to men. These words also signal, through *doble sentido,* a sexual innuendo regarding how such a hole might be used by a bachelor. Then she abruptly switches from object language to ordinary language, from a self-quotation anchored in the narrated event (the *relajo* in Mexico) to a comment anchored in the narrating event in Chicago: "I figured that if I fell I would not hit myself hard, it's only so high" (line 23). These words are uttered straightforwardly, a bit of *franqueza* in the midst of *relajo;* as such, they evoke images of Irma as independent and strategic, looking out for herself, images that contrast strikingly with the idealized femininity of a dependent, deferential woman represented in the semantic content of the immediately preceding words.

The core parts of her story are told in chunks of continuous discourse (visible in the excerpt as contiguous lines of transcription). These core parts of the retelling, even though monologues, alternate and overlap with comments from her audience. Within her monologues themselves, Irma shifts back and forth between metalanguage, using a verb of speaking (*digo,* I say), and object language (reported speech, here her own):

METALANGUAGE: *Y luego este le digo yo, le digo a Carmen,*
And then, um, I say, I say to Carmen,
OBJECT LANGUAGE: *"Ay:, Carmenci:ta de mi a:lma, aunque sea una ca:ma, aunque—"*
"Oh:, little Carmen of my sou:l, at least a be:d, at least—"

Although *digo* is in the present tense, it refers to the past, so here it functions as the historical present (e.g., as in English, "So I say to the guy . . ." to recount a past event). The use of metalanguage (*digo*) anchors the discourse in the narrating event, whereas the use of the object language (the reported speech) takes hearers back to the narrated event, the *relajo* in Mexico. The term "narrating event" refers to an ongoing process of storytelling, whereas the term "narrated event" (or narrated matter) refers to the event recounted in the story being told (Bauman 1986; Jakobson 1995 [1957]; Wortham 2001). Because the reported speech is being brought into the present from the past, however, it also functions to fuse the narrating event with the narrated event (Bauman 1986), making the retelling an aesthetically pleasing whole.

The rhetorical skill involved in such shifts is notable, although it is something speakers take for granted and seem to do without much conscious awareness. There are significant differences in such rhetorical competence among individuals, however, and people clearly are aware of who are the best *habladores* (persons with the ability to speak entertainingly). The verbal performance of such rhetorical competence is highly valued among these rancheros; and Irma, like the narrator in the male *relajo* analyzed previously, is known for this ability as well as for being particularly humorous and forthright. *Relajo,* then, abounds in performances of verbal art in which participants delight. Here the most performative and aesthetically pleasing parts of Irma's story are found at the climax in lines 26–27, especially in her last comment, as she quotes herself (from the previous *relajo*) as having declared that when people know the land is hers, no one will cut her peppers:

"No, de aquí pa' delante no, na:die va a decir	"No, from now on, no, no: one can say,
'vamos a las guayabas con Jorge,'	'Let's go to the guayabas at Jorge's,'
si no van a decir	but instead you're going to say,
'vamos a las guayabas con Irma.'	'Let's go to the guayabas at Irma's.'
Y allá me voy a ir yo con la retrocarga de Pelón	And I will go there with Pelón's shotgun
y el cabrón que entre a las guayabas	and the bastard that goes into the guayabas
y le suelto un guamazo	I'm going to blast,
pa' que sepan que ya ¡la huerta es mía!	so that they know that now the orchard is mine!
Ni a los chiles, ¡naiden me va a cortar chiles!"	Nor the peppers, no one is going to cut my peppers!"

Irma builds to this climax of her story with increasing volume, and she articulates "No one is going to cut my peppers!" with a voice that is tough and quite self-assertive. This comment, again through *doble sentido,* insinuates a sexual meaning: asserting herself like a man, no one is going to cut her balls off! With Jorge being teased about marrying her, but very reluctant to marry, Irma uses her rhetorical skills to perform her way out of a potentially uncomfortable spot. She has to *defenderse* spontaneously, using her considerable abilities to create language with *sabor* (flavor, spice) that makes everyone laugh, both in the original *relajo* in Mexico and in the retelling of it in the *relajo* in Chicago.

Several poetic qualities of the lines above increase audience involvement and the aesthetic pleasure they experience in hearing them (Tannen 1989). First, the rhythmic tempo with which Irma delivers these lines is balanced and deliberate; she does not rush the words but carefully enunciates each phrase, pausing slightly at the end of each line above and pausing slightly longer before the final phrase about the peppers, which makes it somewhat distinct. Second, she uses repetition and parallelism, a widespread feature of oral poetry (Jakobson 1960), not just to convey information in her words but to delight her listeners with artful language:

No, de aquí pa' delante no, nadie va a decir	No, from now on, no: no one can say,
'vamos a las guayabas con Jorge,'	'Let's go to the guayabas at Jorge's,'
si no van a decir	but instead you're going to say,
'vamos a las guayabas con Irma.'	'Let's go to the guayabas at Irma's.'

The repetition of *vamos a las guayabas con* and the echoing of *nadie va a decir* with *no van a decir* (a repetition with some variation) structures her language into an artful whole. Note that the *vamos* phrases are quotations within quotations: she quotes herself as having said that people will say, "Let's go to Irma's [not Jorge's] guayabas." She could have communicated the same referential information without poetic devices, and much ranchero speech does just this (see Chapter 6 on *franqueza*). During *relajo,* however, such poetic language is appreciated and appropriate, especially in narrative performances.

Gender Ideologies and Indexicals

Gender, as diametrically opposed masculinity and femininity, is both enacted and challenged in this story via linguistic form, not content. Certain forms function as indexicals (Silverstein 1976, 12), linguistic signs that point to context-specific meanings. Indexes contrast with symbols, signs that have general meaning (usually construed as semantics) apart from particular contexts (Mertz 1985, 4). Indexicality, then, mediates between the linguistic sign and an object (to which the sign refers), but that object can range from concrete entities in the context such as doors to sociological meanings such as hierarchies of gender, class, or race/ ethnicity. In between these two extremes are indexical signs that do both: they refer to concrete entities (e.g., the pronoun "you" refers to the hearer), but they also (in languages in which there is a choice of "you" pronouns) construct power relations of deference and dominance. For example, when the son in the male *relajo* story uses the familiar second person singular to the old man (*Viejón, te 'chas un tiro hijo de la chingada, ¿o qué?;* Old man, are you gonna fight, you son of a bitch, or what?), he does not follow the norms for *respeto* (see Chapter 7) that call for the deferential form. That is, instead of *te [e]chas,* he should have used (were he to say this at all, including calling him a son of a bitch) *se echa;* and his father reprimands him regarding his inappropriate language: "Son, don't call Callo that, he's my age, respect the man" and later, "Don't call that man that!"

Early in the female *relajo* excerpt, one of the listeners issues a directive to her young son: *Cierra la puerta, Juanito* (Close the door, Juanito). The indexical phrase "the door" refers to the door in the current context. It is the door between the kitchen, where women are gathered, and the living room, where men are gathered, so it is understood that the women do not want the men to hear what they are about to say. Thus the indexical refers to a concrete object in the context, but it also invokes culturally specific meaning. The use of this linguistic sign, then, transforms the presumably neutral space of the kitchen into a cultural place that is gendered female. It is not just the presence of the women in that space but their use of specific language that creates spatial boundaries that exclude men. In this case, a linguistic directive enforces a spatial boundary between men and women.

Somewhat later in the story, more comments are directed at the young son, whose physical movements apparently are disturbing the women. The narrator says, *Juanito, ahí se me sienta ahí, Juanito* (Juanito, sit yourself right there for me, Juanito), and follows this with *Hijo, 'orita no chingues. Estoy hablando las aventuras* (Son, don't screw around right now. I'm telling my adventures). Then the mother ends this set of asides with *Ah bueno, enton's cállese* (All right, then be quiet). These conversational asides from the story elements further engender the space as female by indicating to the young son that he is not old enough to be a part of such *relajo* but he is still a young-enough male to be allowed to overhear—that is, he is not yet fully male (and thus is not in the male domain, the living room). When the narrator tells the boy to "sit right there," the indexical "right there" makes this clear: it exists close by, within the kitchen. She does not say, for example, "Go to your room," or "What do you think of what we're doing?"

Irma does direct the latter comment to the daughters of the women, whom she tries to involve in the female *relajo: Oye, tu tía Irma, y tu tía Magdalena y tu Ma, ¡ay Dios mío!* (Listen, your aunt Irma, and your aunt Magdalena and your Ma, oh my God!). This bit of metapragmatic language calls attention to all-female *relajo* as a linguistic and cultural practice in which women challenge strict traditional gender norms. It attempts to bring younger females into the activity, if only peripherally in this instance, to socialize them into this adult female practice. As such, it is a teaching strategy. The effect of this comment is shown by one daughter's entrance into the conversation: she immediately suggests offering the narrator a chair, which is politely refused. The peripheral participation of younger women in adult female *relajo* (here mostly as laughter and cries of "Ay!") allows them (and the children within earshot) gradually to learn about sex, as well as approved norms regarding sex and gender and how these norms are challenged during *relajo.* Younger females frequently watch and listen intently around the edges of a group of adult women *echando relajo* and then, as they marry, have children, and form families of their own, move to the center of this verbal activity.

So far I have shown how linguistic indexicals have engendered the space in which the narrating event is taking place (i.e., how the kitchen becomes female space). Next I show how women within this space use indexicals indirectly to assert themselves against traditional norms and values that emphasize their deference and submissiveness to men. In this story Irma enacts herself both as a parody of deferential femininity and as a self-assertive woman who can do whatever men do. Her parody of a hyperfeminine voice (*Ay, Carmencita de mi alma, aunque sea una cama, aunque—;* Oh, little Carmen of my soul, at least a bed, at least—) makes fun of idealized femininity as dependent and deferential. This language, using politeness features such as the diminutive *-ita* ending and the phrase of adornment *de mi alma* (of my soul), contrasts sharply with her masculine voice of blunt, direct statements with no such verbal frills. Her language use throughout this story is extremely self-assertive; such *franqueza* constructs her as independent, self-assertive, and willing to defend herself, evoking ranchero values of *valentía* (daring) and *coraje* (courage). She enacts a masculine voice more specifically through indirect indexical references to masculinity, by appropriating traditionally masculine practices: swearing, owning land, and shooting a gun:

Y allá me voy a ir yo con la retrocarga de Pelón	And I will go there with Pelón's shotgun

y el cabrón que entre a las guayabas	and the bastard that goes into the guayabas
y le suelto un guamazo	I'm going to blast,
pa' que sepan que ya ¡la huerta es mía!	so that they know that now the orchard is mine!
Ni a los chiles, ¡naiden me va a cortar chiles!	Nor the peppers, no one is going to cut my peppers!

First, Irma directly expresses her desire to own land (marrying Jorge only if the land is put in her name right away). Working one's own land, going to *el labor* (the fields), is closely tied to masculinity and honor among rancheros in Mexico. Men who work their fields and thus support their families are honorable and are owed deference. Yet here a woman claims this kind of privilege (in fact, when she retired to Mexico she did buy her own land). Second, she threatens to shoot a gun at anyone who trespasses on her land. Although many rancheras of the older generations learned to use guns, they are nevertheless associated more closely with men than with women. Finally, she behaves like a man linguistically: in addition to the male-inflected *franqueza* direct speech style, she swears freely (*cabrón,* bastard; *cabronas,* bitches) and makes open references to sex (putting up with the bare bed with the hole in the middle, which is perhaps used by the bachelor himself).

Although women do use *franqueza,* swear, and talk about sex, such behavior does not fit dominant notions of ideal femininity that promote linguistic respectability. Notions of ideal masculinity, in contrast, rely heavily on such linguistic practices; in other words, these are unmarked behaviors for men, but marked behaviors for women (Ochs 1992, 343). When a woman enacts herself in these ways, then, she can be said to be appropriating a male voice and thus male status and power. She is thus indirectly indexing gender: using linguistic resources to enact a stance (self-assertive dominance) and activities (shooting a gun, swearing, owning land) that are unmarked (considered usual) for men (Ochs 1992, 342). By indirectly indexing the gender that is not her own, she turns the normal gender order upside down, putting herself in the dominant position, which is usually occupied by men.

Conclusion

This chapter has explored *relajo,* and the narratives that occur within its verbal frame, in terms of both poetics and politics. As a pleasurable verbal activity, ongoing discourse framed as *relajo* prompts the performance of oral narratives by participants who alternate between the roles of performer and audience. Many of these narratives are characterized by poetic devices (such as repetition and parallelism) that make them aesthetically pleasing and thus rhetorically persuasive. These narratives are saturated with ranchero cultural values, attitudes, and beliefs, including those that constitute gender ideologies. Since "every text works" (Poovey 1988, 17), these narratives, as oral texts, are implicated in the production and transformation of ideology. Although Mary Poovey (1988) focuses on written texts and the gender representations they constructed and challenged, the oral texts that emerge in everyday language practices like *relajo* similarly construct social relations and subjectivities.

The analysis of two narratives that emerged during *relajo* reveals how gender ideologies that support a patriarchal system, as an age and gender-based hierarchy, are both constructed and challenged. In the first narrative from an all-male *relajo,* superior masculinity is affirmed in the face of challenges to it: an old man in the rancho successfully fights off a challenge from a young man in a story recounted and enjoyed by middle-aged men from the rancho living in Chicago. Here male anxiety about patriarchy is enacted in a story that focuses on a challenge to age-based hierarchy. Because the narrative ultimately affirms notions of superior masculinity and age-based patriarchy, it can be seen as a metaphorical affirmation of gender-based hierarchy as well, especially in light of the ongoing changes in gender relations in this transnational community.

In the second narrative a widow in Chicago recounts her own performance in a previous *relajo* in the rancho, in which she humorously talks of marrying a man with much land, but only in order to get title to the land, which she will defend with a shotgun. In this all-female *relajo* the text inverts the normal patriarchal social order, becoming a microfiesta in which a woman appropriates practices that indirectly index masculinity (owning land, shooting guns, swearing, talking openly about sex). *Relajo,* especially female *relajo,* has "the potential to expose the artificiality of the binary logic" (Poovey 1988, 12). Because *relajo* functions like fiesta or carnival in that it facilitates the inversion of the social order, it is a fertile site for constructions and reconstructions of gender ideologies. That is, in their daily linguistic practices these ranchero men and women construct themselves as gendered beings in an ongoing process of identity shaping. As they struggle with increasing conflict between the reality of their changing lives and a dominant binary logic regarding ideal masculinity and femininity, men and especially women use language during *relajo* to play with and either affirm or challenge traditional gender norms. Women in particular use this space to critique the constraints imposed on them by norms of ideal femininity and to garner support from other women for this critique. In other words, women use tactics, in Michel de Certeau's (1988) sense, to undermine the masculine/feminine dichotomy by bringing the male street into the female house via *relajo.*

This chapter also demonstrates the importance of linguistic form, not just content, in understanding the construction of gender identities. Most literary and sociological studies of gender and other aspects of identity, if they examine language at all, rely on content analysis. That is, they address images, metaphors, and other representations in texts, but they do not generally address the significance of linguistic form in constructing such meanings. A close examination of how individual people narrate a story, for example, in addition to what they narrate, reveals a rich array of attitudes and beliefs that are communicated implicitly via such everyday linguistic devices as intonation patterns, pronoun choices, and reported speech.

NINE

Conclusion

In this chapter I summarize key understandings that emerged throughout my years of involvement with this particular community, focusing especially on insights that can better inform teachers and other community workers who interact with ranchero-origin Mexican students and families. Several themes stand out: rancheros as a relatively unrecognized subgroup of Mexicans, the importance of both individualism and familism in ranchero culture, and changes in gender relations. The last theme is linked to the dramatic rise in schooling among females and is abundantly evident in female discourse, either during *relajo* or when commenting explicitly on this topic. I then reflect on the lessons learned during the research process, in terms of both sociolinguistic analysis and the personal, and reflexive, nature of ethnographic work. I end the chapter with the implications of this research for education and other sites of cross-cultural communication in U.S. society.

Emergent Themes

I argue in Chapters 1 and 2 that rancheros, as one distinct rural Mexican population, have been largely unexplored in both U.S. and Mexican research on campesinos. I attribute this to a research bias that privileges (and sometimes romanticizes) indigenous groups as more "authentic" subjects for study as well as to the Mexican national "cosmic race" ideology that emphasizes and celebrates the Indian past of all Mexicans. I show in Chapters 5 and 6 that this widely known ideology is not generally shared within ranchero society, as evidenced in their daily language use. A history of this microregion, provided in Chapter 4, reveals the impact of heavy eighteenth-century migration from northern Spain, with its cattle-raising and dairy production practices.[1] The lack of attention to this subpopulation of rural Mexicans is especially important in the United States because of the potentially heavy representation of rancheros among migrants (Barragán 1997). In Chicago this ranchero presence is multiply evident in language, music, and clothing styles as well as in entrepreneurial and home-buying practices. These practices support a characteristically ranchero emphasis on *el progreso,* or moving forward toward improvement in life.

This study contributes to the scant research on rancheros by presenting a detailed ethnolinguistic portrait of one ranchero transnational community that emphasizes meanings as constructed from inside the group. Rancheros as presented here are not defined primarily by their social organization but by their self-constructed identities. This portrait illustrates how these rancheros construct their identities through daily speech practices or ways of speaking. Three prominent ways of speaking particularly important to ranchero identity are explored here: *franqueza,* their primary framework for most speech; *respeto,* the verbal glue of social cohesion through age and gender hierarchies; and *relajo,* the antistructural joking activity that allows people to play with, and challenge, normal *respeto* and the status quo.

A second intended contribution of this book is to provide (primarily in Chapters 2 and 3) English syntheses of Spanish-language materials on rancheros and to underscore the diversity within Mexican-origin people in the United States. This is obvious but important, because it disrupts stereotypes based on media-generated negative metaphors used to refer to Mexicans (Santa Ana 2002). Inasmuch as both liberals and conservatives use these metaphors (although to make different arguments), they are especially potent in forming widely shared attitudes, crucially among those in positions of power to affect Mexican children and their families.[2]

A second theme that emerged in this study, the importance of both individualism and familism among rancheros, disrupts another stereotype based on the commonly perceived dichotomy between (U.S.) individualism and (Mexican) familism. Chapter 6 shows how an ideology of liberal individualism underlies and supports the use of *franqueza* among these rancheros. Using Spanish research critiques of sociolinguistic politeness theory, I show how the people in this study use *franqueza* simultaneously to establish themselves as unique individuals able to defend themselves and to cement their place within the (familial) group. Interestingly, as Chapter 8 demonstrates, *relajo* as a way of speaking works similarly to distinguish the individual and simultaneously to affirm the individual's place within the group as well as to address, and potentially resolve, tensions within the group. Speaking with *respeto,* in contrast, affirms the social order of the group and the well-socialized individual's place within an age and gender hierarchy, as explained in Chapter 7.

The unexamined stereotype of Mexicans as communal (and even

worse as submissive) likely derives from generalizing all campesinos as Indian and, in turn, from generalizing (and romanticizing) Indians as communally oriented or, more importantly, as different from "us." This stereotype thus is ideologically similar to the research bias toward Indian subjects in rural Mexico. In contrast, the individualism described in other studies of ranchero societies, especially those of northwest Michoacán, was abundantly evident throughout my fieldwork, even as I came to appreciate how these rancheros were at the same time deeply embedded in family (and family-like groups). Although such individualism was noted by Taylor in the early 1930s (Taylor 1933, 1987 [1932]) and in Mexican published materials as long ago as the mid-1850s (see Chapter 2), these descriptions confront deeply entrenched ideologies in both Mexico and the United States and thus are less salient than studies that affirm the ideologies. Stereotypes that emphasize only the "communal" aspect of Mexicans (as the binary opposite of U.S. "individualism") are not only inaccurate but patronizing.

But what of variation among ranchero Mexicans? If Hispanics are diverse, and Mexicans are diverse, rancheros are diverse as well. As noted in Chapter 1, the internal variation within any cultural group (around differences in gender, age, class, region, etc.) can be the basis for conflict. Yet such conflict is addressed through a shared means of argument. Thus shared ways of speaking are used to express and even construct differences within the group: both *franqueza* and *relajo* promote the individuation of group members, and *relajo* provides a relatively safe frame in which to "argue" about such differences. The ways of speaking described in this book, then, may be rather widely shared among ranchero-origin Mexicans, even as they may differ in other ways.

A third theme that emerged in this study—tensions around gender relations—evidences one such variation within this group of rancheros. Gender is a subtheme woven throughout a number of chapters that explicitly focus on other topics. Gender appears significant in the dramatic rise in schooling across the generations (as described in Chapter 4). Such increased schooling is tied to increased opportunity, both in the United States and in Mexico; but it is even more closely tied to gender, because males even in Chicago (where there are more opportunities for formal schooling) do not avail themselves of these opportunities nearly as much as do their wives, sisters, and female cousins. I attribute this at least partly to the centrality of work (as opposed to school) in the construction of masculinity, but it also emerges from female agency.

Economic and social conditions both in the United States and in Mexico have facilitated such female agency, notably: (1) migrating males who leave their wives as heads of households in Mexico, and (2) females who work outside the home in rancho packing plants and Chicago factories and thus contribute economically to the household. In both of these cases women assume traditional male responsibilities and, sometimes, authority. The characteristic ranchero stance of self-assertion for both men and women (see Chapter 6) provides a way of speaking and being that facilitates the assumption of female authority in changing gender relations. Female agency around gender emerges frequently in all-female *relajo,* providing a space for such changes to be tried out and support built for them. Chapter 7 describes how traditional social relations are affirmed through *respeto;* and Chapter 8 shows how they are treated during *relajo,* with men affirming them and women challenging them. Thus although gender is not a primary focus of this study, its presence throughout the analysis evidences its importance as an ongoing arena of change in this transnational community.

Reflections on the Research Process

As argued in Chapter 1, ethnographic studies that include microlevel discourse analysis are strengthened in interpretive power. Supporting interpretations drawn from participant-observation with analyses of the participants' discourse makes the researcher's arguments even more convincing. Especially since so much daily discourse is unconsciously generated, it can speak volumes about stances, ideologies, and agency. Such discourse analysis, moreover, must attend to details of form, not just content, because how people say something communicates as much as, and sometimes more than, what they say. Although this is commonly understood in the fields of sociolinguistics and linguistic anthropology, it is not always so well understood in (nonlinguistic) anthropological, sociological, educational, or literary studies. This point is illustrated throughout the discourse analyses in Chapters 5–8.

As I finish writing this study, I gain perspective on the research and my long-term involvement with this social network of families. This perspective allows me to see what I could not always see in the midst of fieldwork and intense personal involvement. Ethnography itself is a reflexive process, whether acknowledged or not. That is, the research process itself involves interpersonal relationships that yield the researcher's understandings; and these interpersonal relationships not only render the insights of the study but also generate reciprocal influences on both the researcher and the researched.

As a researcher and friend I was transformed by the experience of this ethnography,[3] as I indicated in Chapter 1 and in notes for other chapters. I learned to enjoy, even crave, the *unión* of being part of a close group and to assert myself within it. Surprisingly, Spanish became for me a language of intimacy and connection with others (on occasion even within my own family, where it is understood and spoken to some degree). Yet as much as I was changed, I also affected people in this network. My ability to drive (even standard shift!) was noted with alarm by a man in the rancho. Driving my own car (in Chicago but also in Mexico) gave me mobility that few other women had, a difference so important that it cannot be overemphasized. In addition to having the independence derived from such mobility, my advanced education distinguished me, potentially inspiring my women friends and discomfiting some of the men. Although I cannot take credit for the dramatic rise in educational levels from first- to second-generation women, my engagement with particular women as an equal and friend has no doubt influenced their perceptions of the possible in their own lives.

Thus my very presence (usually without husband or children) sometimes disturbed the scenes in which I was a participant-observer. In spite of this, I was most often only one person in a large group that had multiple ties of kinship, friendship, and proximity; and the effect of my presence most often was overwhelmed by ongoing group norms and practices. Even when I was simply one person among many, however, I was nevertheless a particular kind of person, that is, an Anglo-American educated woman (and mother and wife) very interested in the life of the group.[4] In every interaction I was who I am (*Soy quien soy*). Thus the effect that my identity, especially my gender, had on this research cannot be overemphasized, inasmuch as it made some people much more comfortable with me (generally women, but also some men) than others. In my view, such reflexivity is unavoidable in ethnography, whether or not the ethnographer acknowledges it in the published study. Ethnographic research inevitably is carried out from a particular perspective grounded in researcher identity, which may constrain but does not invalidate the insights gained through such research. Ultimately, field-based research with an ethnographic perspective is the best way to derive valid understandings of life "on the ground" among particular groups of people.

Implications of the Study

The historical and ethnographic description of the transnational social network featured in this study and the analyses of their discourse via three characteristic ways of speaking contribute to a detailed understanding of one community of ranchero-origin Mexicans. Without this kind of knowledge, teachers and other community workers who interact regularly with Mexicans (e.g., police, health clinicians, social workers, and government clerics) often function with "general" knowledge frequently consisting of stereotypes and personal biases. Ideally, such stereotypes can be replaced by more accurate awareness of the sociolinguistic and other resources which students and their families bring with them to schools and other institutions. Given detailed understandings of such resources, especially linguistic abilities, educators can teach in ways that take into account the styles of language that students implicitly know as well as the ideologies and identities that these styles of discourse index. As González (2001, 185) argues, teachers must not only accept such linguistic diversity in their students but should learn from it, changing themselves in the process and thus allowing for change in the pedagogical status quo.

Such awareness of the linguistic practices of Mexicans, and the identities they index, is especially crucial in microlevel interactions between people in institutional positions of power in U.S. society and Mexican (in this study ranchero Mexican) individuals. Police officers, social workers, heath clinicians, and government workers, in addition to teachers and school administrators, are among those who exert considerable power over the lives of transnational migrants and their families. If such people's "general" information and attitudes were fed by studies such as this one, rather than by commonly accepted stereotypes and media discourse, their responses in these microinteractions might be respectful rather than disdainful or critical. Without the benefit of such research-based knowledge, even those who do not respond disdainfully or critically but attempt to be positive and helpful can mistakenly patronize those that they try to help. In schools, especially given the socialization in *respeto* within Mexican homes, fleeting comments by teachers or other school personnel can have long-lasting devastating, or inspiring, effects on children (Weinstein 2002). Teachers especially need to understand their power in this respect.

Ultimately, this study argues for the worth of oral skills of particular cultural groups. A perceived literacy crisis in the United States has led to an undervaluing of oral language, especially considering two dichotomies in the public mind: literacy/illiteracy and literacy/orality. Thus does illiteracy shadow orality, imbuing it with negative connotations. Yet oral language is the basis for the acquisition of literacy (Heath 1983). Studies of oral rhetoric clearly are relevant to literacy issues, because school literacy itself is defined by a particular rhetoric (Farr 1993; Lindquist 2001).

Not only are oral language practices interesting and valuable in their own right, but they provide evidence of the communicative competence of students. Moreover, detailed understandings of favored discourse styles or ways of speaking, such as those described in this study, can inform the creation of more sensitive and appropriate pedagogies for teaching the kinds of language (oral and written) that will enable students to be successful both in school and beyond it. If particular ways of speaking are intimately familiar to students, learning about them widens and deepens perceptions of these students as skilled users of language in places other than the classroom. In addition, attention to culturally embedded oral discourse styles reveals school literacy itself as a particular tradition of language use grounded in history and culture and opens the possibility of more flexibility in approved writing styles.

Finally, viewing literacy novices as people with rhetorical skills, albeit not the same as those of formal schooling, is a fundamentally different attitude from viewing them as deficient language users, a widespread current attitude. In fact, many Mexican-origin students are exceptionally skilled linguistically, being bilingual and sometimes biliterate as well. The range of such abilities among such students raises a host of other issues (see González 2001; Zentella 1997); but in all cases viewing these abilities positively facilitates student development of skills in both Spanish and English and helps them use familiar oral language practices in Spanish (and/or English) to acquire literacy, ideally in both languages. The ways of speaking featured in this book, whether expressed in Spanish or in English (second-generation Mexican students sometimes use English for *echando relajo*), illustrate linguistic abilities, not deficiencies.

Notes

Chapter 1

1. I use the word "rancheros" to include both genders. When specifically referring to women, I use the word "rancheras."

2. I have become so close to some of these women, their families, and their ways of living that I had difficulty writing from an academic identity as I attempted to begin this book. Realizing that the problem was a lack of perspective (what Spradley [1980, 35] called the need for climbing to the top of a very tall tree), I eventually reoriented myself to a broad interdisciplinary audience, a process that required some painful (albeit temporary) distancing. Without this distance, I could not communicate effectively to a broad audience what I have learned, a commitment I intend to keep.

3. I thank Guadalupe Valdés for providing me with this example.

4. This section is a revised version of part of the introductory chapter by Farr and Rachel Reynolds in Farr (2004).

5. One man in the rancho took his wife and me to see a nearby hacienda and then to interview a *viejito* (elderly man) nearby to find out about the history of the area. I taped this interview but never had a chance to conduct it: my friend took over, first developing *confianza* with the elderly man by establishing distant connections through kin who knew each other then proceeding to act as the interviewer. This man was not hired by me, like the young women in Chicago, but simply wanted to encourage my interest in their life and rancho and on this occasion assumed a locally appropriate gender role. The resulting interview was much more natural and informative than it would have been had I conducted it myself.

6. Sociolinguistic interviews were done with a portable (six- by nine-inch) Marantz tape recorder. For the first year, this is what we used for language use recordings as well. Then I switched to a palm-sized, high-quality Sanyo recorder for carrying ease and less obtrusiveness.

7. This use of verbal "style" should be distinguished from its use in sociolinguistic research to refer to a continuum of formal to informal language use.

8. This distinction, which tends to essentialize Indians as Others, is voiced more frequently by members of older generations. Members of younger generations acknowledge that Indians form a separate group from themselves and maintain different traditions, but some of them protest against the injustice of treating Indians as inferiors.

9. For example, on our visit to the defunct nearby hacienda mentioned in note 5,

the wife humorously portrayed herself as the mistress of the hacienda, shaking an imaginary bell to summon the servants. Certainly humor can be ambiguous, but in this instance it was clear that she considered herself potentially elite.

10. After the attack on the World Trade Center in New York on September 11, 2001, border crossing became more difficult and time-consuming. Nevertheless, people from the rancho without papers continue to arrive in Chicago.

Chapter 2

1. Like rodeos, half-sport and half-fiesta, *jaripeos* involve skill in bull-riding. They take place in small villages on fiesta days in Michoacán.

2. According to Barragán (1997), these films were a critique of the progressive agrarian reform policies of President Lázaro Cárdenas, which may explain why rancheros as a group, as extensions of the "rancheros of the screen," are sometimes viewed as reactionaries. It is also the case, however, that many rancheros are in fact fiercely opposed to such agrarian reform, maintaining that property should only be gained honorably, through one's own labor, and to do otherwise makes one's ownership of the land illegitimate.

3. For example, milk is not eaten with meat, even though people cannot explain why they follow this practice, saying only, *Bueno, no se, dice que se hace daño* (Well, I don't know; they say it's bad for you); also, a small piece of masa (tortilla dough) is put up on a shelf before the rest of the dough is made into tortillas.

Chapter 3

1. When I joked during a visit to the rancho that it seemed to be a suburb of Chicago, my remark was taken seriously. I was told, "Well, yes, it's about a 45-hour drive."

2. Such references were especially frequent during the period when Michael Jordan and the Bulls made all Chicagoans proud of their city.

3. Luckily for me, Zamora is also the home of El Colegio de Michoacán, with which my husband and I were affiliated during academic year 1995–1996 on Fulbright fellowships. Not having teaching responsibilities, I used my Fulbright to do research in and on the rancho.

4. In 2003 I was told that berries are now being grown there instead of sugarcane, since the market for Mexican sugar has declined.

5. It snowed there on Christmas Day of 1995, while we celebrated in Zamora, which was cool but by no means cold.

6. This history is an English synthesis of a final narrative report written in Spanish by María Teresa Fernández Aceves while a research assistant for this study and a Ph.D. candidate in history at the University of Illinois at Chicago. Teresa searched Mexican archives for relevant information, and she and I carried out oral history interviews in the microregion of the rancho, primarily during June 1997.

7. El Archivo General de las Notarias de Michoacán (hereafter AGNM), Tierras y Aguas, "Títulos de tierras de los naturales de Tacátzcuaro," 1758, vol. 11, leg. 6, exp. 10, fs. 122–145v; "Títulos de la hacienda Ayumba," 1709, vol. 10, t. 2, leg. 5, exp. 82;

"Tierras de Francisco de Alcazar," 1709, vol. 23, t. 3, leg. 9, 2nd part, exp. 99; "Solicitud de títulos del Rancho Guáscuaro," 1758, vol. 17, t. 2, leg. 8, no. 57, fs. 20–34.

8. Oral tradition holds that these ancestors came from a villa bearing their own last name in the northern province of Asturias. Alfonso Carabez (the name Cárabes is sometimes spelled Carabez), a researcher at the Universidad Nacional Autónoma de México (UNAM), showed me this villa on a map of Spain during an interview in Mexico City in June 2000; his information was based on research done by his late father in tracing the family's origins. I visited this village in July 2004 (see Chapter 9, note 1).

9. Various laws during the War of Reform were intended to promote a rural middle class of small property owners (rancheros) by targeting "unused" church and Indian community properties. Although some growth in small landowners occurred, the hacienda system was also inadvertently fortified (Keen 1996).

10. Interview with Tito Castillo Pulido, June 29, 1998.

11. AGNM, Protocolización de Escrituras de La Magdalena, May 11, 1880.

12. AGNM, Transacción de La Magdalena, December 17, 1880.

13. AGNM, Testamento, December 30, 1880.

14. Archivo General e Histórico del Poder Ejecutivo de Michoacán (AGHPEM), Hijuelas, 1899.

15. Dependent ranches were located around an hacienda and were part of its economy. Independent ranches were the property of small landowners.

16. AGHPEM, Ley de División Territorial, 1906.

17. Interviews with Aurora Cárabes Zepeda and Carlos Cárabes González, June 30, 1998. Although a first name for General Zepeda was not used in these interviews, Purnell (1999, 170) notes that the Puntada bandit gang, led by "an ex-villista named Eliseo Zepeda . . . concentrated their attacks on the wealthier rancheros" of northwestern Michoacán.

18. Interview with José Alvarez Corona, June 29, 1998.

19. Interview with Aurora Cárabes Zepeda, June 30, 1998.

20. A family from the rancho that migrated to Kansas in the 1920s accumulated enough wealth to donate land for the construction of the chapel in the rancho.

21. Mexican-Polish and Mexican-Italian marriages have been fairly common in Chicago. A recent superintendent of the Chicago Police Department with a Mexican last name, in fact, had a Polish mother and spoke only Polish, not Spanish, in addition to English. In the network in this study, outmarriages have been to two Italian Americans and one Pole.

22. In a recent ethnographic dissertation located in South Chicago (Cohen 2003), the (white ethnic) uncles in one family teased their half-Mexican niece about being a "spic," because she chose to identify as Mexican in her high school populated entirely by Mexicans and African Americans (and where an African American teacher referred to the Mexican students as "the white kids").

23. Although this seems an impressive figure, Germans (first and second generation) represented 29 percent of Chicago's population in 1900, the result of massive waves of migration during the second half of the nineteenth century (Holli 1995 [1977]). Mostly artisans, they had the fortune of fitting into an industrializing economy. They participated in labor struggles, as well as struggles to maintain their language and culture, but eventually assimilated.

24. Marie Bousfield, director of the Department of Planning and Development

for the City of Chicago, provided me with the numbers of Mexicans, Puerto Ricans, Cubans, Central Americans, and South Americans, as well as non-Latinos, for each census tract in the city. These figures yielded the numbers cited in this chapter for the three neighborhoods of Pilsen, Little Village, and Gage Park.

25. This situation was summed up humorously by a young man in the network who has built a successful mortgage business in Chicago. As we stood in front of his father's home in the rancho during a recent visit (he drove his Mercedes down from Chicago), he said in English, "We move in, and the Poles move out. The blacks move in, and we move out!"

Chapter 4

1. An attempt to represent *compadrazgo* (fictive kin) relations across the network resulted in so many crossing lines that the entire figure became unreadable.

2. My husband had a Fulbright there during the fall semester but returned to Chicago in the spring.

3. One man who worked as a cook for years eventually opened his own restaurant and subsequently catered family parties. A trio of three female cousins set up a business providing special clothing for *quinceañera* celebrations, baptisms, and so forth.

4. Elizabeth Juárez of the Colegio de Michoacán conducted this survey as my research assistant while completing her doctoral work.

5. As described in Chapter 2, this rebellion was a grassroots revolution against the anticlerical postrevolutionary government. Although the Cristero Rebellion was deeply rooted in the historical conflict between church and state in Mexico, Meyer (1976) insists that it was actually about religion, so strong was the commitment to Catholicism in this part of Mexico.

6. My having been baptized as a Catholic significantly facilitated my acceptance within this group. See Chapter 6 for an illustration of this, when I was interrogated about my religion in the rancho.

7. Such repeated sound patterns become visible when the tape-recorded speech is digitized and viewed as a speech wave form. We used the software Cool Edit Pro for this.

8. Although people in this network say that they can identify Indians by the way in which they speak Spanish ("not well" or "with a certain tone"), they do not articulate exactly what features of speech distinguish Indians from themselves. Since I would anticipate linguistic manifestations of the continuously maintained divide between these two social identities, it would be interesting to explore how "Indian" Spanish differs from ranchero Spanish in this part of Mexico.

9. *Mochos* is a colloquial word which refers here to uneducated rancheros who are said to "cut off their words" inappropriately and thus to speak improperly.

Chapter 5

1. The term *indígena* (indigenous) is used in Mexico to refer to those who are native to Mexico. "Indian" (*indio*), although it is sometimes used in the rancho, is

considered less polite. *Güare* or the diminutive *güarecita* is a name used in the rancho to refer to indigenous women.

2. Malinche is the indigenous woman who became the mistress of the conquistador Cortés; her name is used here to mean any indigenous woman.

3. This house now has three bedrooms (the newer two bedrooms and bathroom having been built with money from Chicago). Like others of their generation, these parents, in their fifties, have seven children, ranging in age from the late teens to the early thirties. The parents use one bedroom (a luxury not shared by all in the rancho), the female offspring use another, and the male offspring use a third. When more people are "home" from Chicago (including not only the two eldest daughters but cousins and guests), females share the two double beds and extra mattresses put on the floor in the "female" bedroom. The father has remarked that it is all right for women to sleep all over each other, but not for men; so he plans to build more rooms onto the house.

4. Interview with Salvador Zambrano, February 5, 1996.

5. Because of this I was relatively inconspicuous during my fieldwork in the rancho. On several occasions while visiting in other ranchos with an entire family except for the wife, I was assumed to be the wife and mother. Conversely, on occasions when others visited the family that I was staying with, I sometimes was assumed to be a relative until it was pointed out, to the visitors' surprise, that I was from the United States.

6. Until recently public representations and most studies ignored another complexity in the racial history of Mexico: the presence of Africans. Gonzalo Aguirre Beltrán (1972) pioneered the study of Africans in Mexico; but until recently most have assumed that the presence of Africans was limited primarily to coastal areas. Highland Michoacán, however, including the microregion of the present study, had significant numbers of Africans, who were brought to Mexico as slaves to work in households, in mines, and on sugar plantations (Chávez Carbajal 1995; Esquivel Vega 1985). This "third root" of Mexico has not been studied until recent decades because the historical awareness of African presence was buried as Africans assimilated, as individuals, into the population. Lomnitz-Adler (1992) explains that, whereas colonial policy allowed Indians a group identity within a hierarchical "Indian nation," Africans were not allowed to form groups that promoted a separate African identity. Slavery was justified as a transitory condition that enabled the Spaniards to convert individuals whose nations of origin rejected the Catholic faith. Thus individual Africans, but entire Indian nations, were the focus of the church's efforts toward "redemption" and conversion to Catholicism.

7. In the 2000 census, people were able to identify either as one race or as more than one. Although this is more reflective of contemporary reality, it still perpetuates the notion that a "race" is biologically real.

8. Even today in some isolated ranchos in western Mexico people practice apparently "Jewish" customs such as not eating milk with meat, although they are unaware of why they do this, as noted in Chapter 2. Guillermo de la Peña (1984, 218) also notes that, according to oral tradition, many of these isolated ranchos were Jewish in origin (when Jews escaped the Inquisition in Mexico) and describes a social organization in each rancho that was headed by a "bearded patriarch."

9. Anyone from the United States is initially presumed to be *güera güera* (really white), as one woman in the rancho once described me, due to the stereotypical

image of the tall, blond, slim, white North American. Nevertheless, over time, as I was assimilated into their social life, I was recast in their own terms: *blanca* but not *güera*, as some of them are. The phrase *güera güera* shows the use of reduplication in Mexican Spanish as an intensifier.

10. In Mexico *prieto* usually refers to darker skin than *moreno*, which refers to skin of a light brown color (Lara Ramos 1996), but local usage of these terms sometimes differs from this. They are often used interchangeably simply to mean nonwhite, and sometimes they are reversed: *moreno* is darker than *prieto*. Thus the terms are quite fluid and relative. Experience in the United States may have affected this descriptive color code: since African Americans are politely referred to as *morenos*, *prieto* is now frequently used by those who have been to the United States to mean "darker," while *moreno* (or less politely, *negro*) is used for African Americans.

11. This interview was carried out by Teresa Fernández Aceves and me in June 1998 in the home of the woman in a neighboring indigenous village.

12. Many second-generation members living in the rancho continue to make clear distinctions between themselves and those they perceive as indigenous, in spite of the school-taught message. This is illustrated by an incident recorded in my field notes, after three of us (the woman I usually stay with, her nephew, and I) had walked to a nearby indigenous hamlet to buy *güanengas* (handmade embroidered blouses for women). On the return trip, I asked the nephew, who was in his early twenties at the time and *güero* (with white sunburned skin, freckles, light brown hair, and blue eyes), if any P'urhepecha had migrated to Chicago. Because they did not wear their distinctive clothing there, I asked how one would know if a particular Mexican was P'urhepecha or not. He looked at me with incredulity and exclaimed, "¡Por el color!" (By the color!). His tone made it quite clear that he thought I had missed a fundamental point.

13. As already noted, this phrase is commonly used to mean that people appear to be native to Mexico (i.e., they look Indian).

Chapter 6

1. Of course, these young people may be trying to avoid offending their Mexican elders, who might not approve of such intimacy without a formal commitment (being *novios* or engaged to be married).

2. See note 5 for Chapter 1.

3. The Indians that the Namiquipans fought, and contrasted themselves with, were said not to work—or at least the men were characterized thus. The male Apaches were said to be nomadic (rather than property owning) and lazy, leaving all the work to their women. In this study, in contrast, although work and owning property are central values of ranchero identity, the contrast with the local P'urhepecha Indians revolves not around work but around the owning of individual rather than communal property and around the idea of progress.

4. Juan Guerra was at the time a Ph.D. student and co-ethnographer in the first phase of the study.

5. One young woman provided me with an example of this, saying, "It took me some time to get my husband to understand" why she could not keep the house as perfectly clean and tidy as they both would like after working a full day outside

the home. Her husband ultimately responded to this discussion with a back rub to ease her tension and a comment not to worry about the house, that she was more important to him than a neat house.

6. Instead of using literal translations of taboo words and phrases, I attempt to match the level of offensiveness in Spanish with appropriate English phrases, because how taboo they are considered to be is different from one language and culture to another.

Chapter 7

1. When I watched children while parents were not at home in the rancho, I was told quite firmly to hit the children if they misbehaved, both by the father as he left and by a middle son in reference to his younger sister who became embroiled in a verbal fight with her age-mate cousin: "¡Pégalas!" (Hit them!), he urged me.

2. See note 2, Chapter 5.

3. Early in my fieldwork I inadvertently stayed too long watching the men cook a pig in oil (over a fire in a basement in Chicago!) and was pulled from this male context by two women.

Chapter 8

1. This section is a revised version of Farr (1998), "El relajo como microfiesta" (*Relajo* as Microfiesta).

2. Many instances in my field notes evidence this. In one case in Mexico, after we left the house of relatives in a nearby rancho one evening, a man scolded his wife for joking about sex (she had teased her brother-in-law about having had five children) in front of the relatives, which included many children. Although this seemed to me to be a rather mild, indirect reference to sex, their Chicago-born and raised teenaged son joined in the father's criticism: "Ma! You don't DO that!"

Chapter 9

1. During a trip to northern Spain in July 2004, I located the natal village of the ancestors of the central families in this network, in the mountains of eastern Asturias. I was struck on this trip by the similarities in architecture between northern Spain and northwest Michoacán and the emphasis on dairy products. Northern Spain, and especially Asturias, is the primary source of dairy products for the rest of Spain.

2. A recent program on National Public Radio (NPR) interviewed Mexican workers at ski resorts in Colorado. Because they were willing to work under conditions, and for pay, not acceptable to U.S. workers (whom NPR also interviewed for this program) the reporter kept using the word "submissive" to describe the Mexican workers, although he, like the radio station, was clearly progressive and sympathetic toward the workers.

3. Once at a gathering in someone's Chicago home, the woman on my right (a friend of someone in the family) turned to me and asked, with *franqueza,* "Who are

you?!" Before I had a chance to answer, the woman on my left (a member of the family and a friend) responded heartily, "She's a friend of the family, the WHOLE family!"

4. A woman in the rancho noted to me that many people from the United States come to Mexico, *pero tú aprecias* (but you appreciate). Her husband added that I was *muy sencilla* (very unpretentious) for a person with so much education. These comments and others indicate that my very interest in their lives engendered a sense of respect sadly lacking on the part of many people from the United States.

Glossary

agrarista: agrarian reformer
bracero: laborer, specifically a Mexican worker in the United States under the Bracero Program
campesino: peasant, someone who works in the fields (*campos*)
casta: someone from one of a number of mixed-race categories
catrines: city people viewed as effete dandies by rancheros
comadre: co-parent (female)
compadrazgo: fictive kinship, akin to godparenthood, but with a more substantive connection to both child and parents
compadre: co-parent (male)
confianza: relationship of trust between people
dicho: common saying, phrase, or expression
echar relajo: to engage in antistructural joking
ejidatario: co-owner of an *ejido*
ejidos: agricultural cooperatives that resulted from land reform after the Mexican Revolution of 1910–1920
encomendero: Spaniard granted power of the Crown over the encomienda
encomienda: estates created after the Spanish conquest which gave rights over the tribute and labor of Indians
estancia: cattle-raising ranch
franqueza: frank, direct, candid, even earthy, verbal style
güero/a: white or blond person
hacendado: owner of hacienda
hacer desmadres: to engage in antistructural joking that is more intense than *relajo*
hacienda: large plantation (organized for profit through the production of rice, sugar, etc.)
indígena: indigenous (Indian) Mexican
ingenio: sugar-processing plant
maldiciones: taboo language, swearing
Meseta Tarasca: Tarascan Tableland, the highlands in which Tarascan villages predominate
mestizaje: race mixture
mestizo/a: someone of mixed Indian and Spanish descent
mulato/a: someone of mixed African and Spanish descent
P'urhepecha: group of indigenous Mexicans who live in northwest Michoacán (and their language)

quinceañera: celebration for a girl (the *quinceañera*) who turns fifteen
ranchería: very small rancho
ranchero/a: person from a rancho; clothing, food, music related to ranchos or the people who inhabit them
rancho: rural hamlet
respeto: code of respect involving roles based on age and gender
tarasco: Spanish word for *p'urhépecha*

References

Aguirre Beltrán, G. 1972. *Problemas de la población indígena de la cuenca del Tepalcatepec.* Mexico City: Ediciones del INI.

Aiton, A. S. 1994 [1940]. Latin-American Frontiers. In *Where Cultures Meet: Frontiers in Latin American History,* edited by D. J. Weber and J. M. Rausch, pp. 19–25. Wilmington, DE: Scholarly Resources.

Alonso, A. M. 1995. *Thread of Blood: Colonialism, Revolution and Gender on Mexico's Northern Frontier.* Tucson: University of Arizona Press.

American Anthropological Association. Executive Board. 1998. Statement on "Race." May 17, 1998. Available from http://www.aaanet.org/stmts/racepp.htm.

American Association of Physical Anthropologists (AAPA). 1996. Statement on Biological Aspects of Race. Available from http://www.physanth.org/positions/race.html.

Appadurai, A. 1996. *Modernity at Large: Cultural Dimensions of Globalization.* Minneapolis: University of Minnesota Press.

Arias, P. 1996. *Los vecinos de la sierra: Microhistoria de Pueblo Nuevo.* Guadalajara: University of Guadalajara.

Bakhtin, M. M. 1981. *The Dialogic Imagination: Four Essays.* Edited by M. Holquist. Translated by C. Emerson and M. Holquist. Austin: University of Texas Press, 1981.

———. 1986. *Speech Genres and Other Late Essays.* Austin: University of Texas Press.

———. 1994 [1965]. Carnival Ambivalence: Folk Humour and Carnival Laughter. In *The Bakhtin Reader,* edited by P. Morris, pp. 206–225. New York: Arnold.

Barkin, D., and T. King. 1970. *Regional Economic Development: The River Basin Approach in Mexico.* London: Cambridge University Press.

Barragán, E. 1990a. Identidad ranchera: Apreciaciones desde la sierra "Jalmichana" en el occidente de México. *Relaciones: Estudios de Historia y Sociedad* 43 (Summer 1990): 75–106.

———. 1990b. *Más allá de los caminos.* Zamora, Mexico: El Colegio de Michoacán.

———. 1997. *Con un pie en el estribo: Formación y deslizamientos de las sociedades rancheras en la construcción del México moderno.* Zamora, Mexico: El Colegio de México.

Barragán, E., O. Hoffmann, T. Linck, and D. Skerritt. 1994. *Rancheros y sociedades rancheras.* Zamora, Mexico: El Colegio de Michoacán.

Barragán, E., and T. Linck. 1994. Los rincones rancheros de México: Cartografía de sociedades relegadas. In *Rancheros y sociedades rancheras,* edited by E. Barragán, O. Hoffmann, T. Linck, and D. Skerritt, pp. 57–80. Zamora, Mexico: El Colegio de Michoacán.

Barrett, E. M. 1975. La Cuenca del Tepalcatepec. *SepSetentas* 2:177–178.

Barth, F. 1969. *Ethnic Groups and Boundaries: The Social Organization of Culture Difference.* Boston: Little, Brown, and Co.

Basch, L., S. N. Glick, and C. Blanc-Szanton. 1994. *Nations Unbound: Transnational Projects, Postcolonial Predicaments, and Deterritorialized Nation-States.* Amsterdam: Gordon and Breach.

Bateson, G. 1972. *Steps to an Ecology of Mind.* New York: Ballantine Books.

Bauman, R. 1984 [1977]. *Verbal Art as Performance.* Prospect Heights, IL: Waveland Press.

———. 1986. *Story, Performance, and Event: Contextual Studies of Oral Narrative.* Cambridge: Cambridge University Press.

———. 1997. Mediational Performance, Traditionalization, and the Authorization of Discourse. Paper read at Conference on Aesthetic Forms of Communication, University of Konstanz.

Bauman, R., and C. Briggs. 1990. Poetics and Performance as Critical Perspectives on Language and Social Life. *Annual Review of Anthropology* 19:59–88.

Becker, M. 1995. *Setting the Virgin on Fire: Lázaro Cárdenas, Michoacán Peasants, and the Redemption of the Mexican Revolution.* Berkeley: University of California Press.

Beezley, W. H., C. E. Martin, and W. E. French, eds. 1994. *Rituals of Rule, Rituals of Resistance: Public Celebrations and Popular Culture in Mexico.* Wilmington, DE: Scholarly Resources, Inc.

Behar, R. 1993. *Translated Woman: Crossing the Border with Esperanza's Story.* Boston, MA: Beacon Press.

Berg, C. R. 1992. *Cinema of Solitude: A Critical Study of Mexican Film, 1967–1983.* Austin: University of Texas Press.

Besnier, N. 1995. *Literacy, Emotion and Authority: Reading and Writing on a Polynesian Atoll.* Cambridge: Cambridge University Press.

Blas Arroyo, J. L. 1994–1995. *Tú* y *usted:* Dos pronombres de cortesía en el español actual—Datos de una comunidad peninsular. *Estudios de Lingüística de la Universidad de Alicante* 10:21–44.

Boas, F. 1911. Introduction. In *Handbook of American Indian Languages,* edited by F. Boas. BAE-B 40, Part I. Washington, D.C.: Smithsonian Institution.

Bonfil Batalla, G. 1996. *México Profundo: Reclaiming a Civilization.* Austin: University of Texas Press.

Borah, W. 1954. Race and Class in Mexico. *Pacific Historical Review* 23:331–342.

Bourdieu, P. 1977. *Outline of a Theory of Practice.* Cambridge: Cambridge University Press.

Bousfield, M. 2001. The Population of Chicago in the Year 2000. Presentation made to the Chicago Board of Health, September 19.

Boyarin, J., ed. 1992. *The Ethnography of Reading.* Berkeley: University of California Press.

Boyer, C. R. 1998. Old Loves, New Loyalties: Agrarismo in Michoacán, 1920–1928. *Hispanic American Historical Review* 78:3. Durham, NC: Duke University Press

Brading, D. A. 1978. *Haciendas and Ranchos in the Mexican Bajío: León, 1700–1860.* Cambridge: Cambridge University Press.

———. 1991. *The First America: The Spanish Monarchy, Creole Patriots, and the Liberal State, 1492–1867.* Cambridge: Cambridge University Press.

———. 1994. Epilogue: A 25 años del encuentro con "rancheros." In *Rancheros y sociedades rancheras,* edited by E. Barragán, O. Hoffmann, T. Linck, and D. Skerritt, pp. 329–334. Zamora, Mexico: El Colegio de Michoacán.
Brantz, M. 1853. *Mexico: Aztec, Spanish and Republican.* Hartford: S. Drake and Co.
Bravo, D. 1996. *La risa en el regateo: Estudio sobre el estilo comunicativo de negociadores españoles y suecos.* Stockholm: Institutionen för Spanska och Portugisiska.
Briggs, C. 1986. *Learning How to Ask: A Sociolinguistic Appraisal of the Role of the Interview in Social Science Research.* Cambridge: Cambridge University Press.
———. 1988. *Competence in Performance: The Creativity of Tradition in Mexicano Verbal Art.* Philadelphia: University of Pennsylvania Press.
Briggs, C., and R. Bauman. 1992. Genre, Intertextuality, and Social Power. *Journal of Linguistic Anthropology* 2 (2):131–172.
Brown, P., and S. Levinson. 1987. *Politeness: Some Universals in Language Usage.* Cambridge: Cambridge University Press.
Cabrales Barajas, L. F. 1994. Los rancheros y la engorda de las tierras flacas. In *Rancheros y sociedades rancheras,* edited by E. Barragán, O. Hoffmann, T. Linck, and D. Skerritt, pp. 301–315. Zamora, Mexico: El Colegio de Michoacán.
Cameron, R. 2000. Language Change or Changing Selves?: Direct Quotation Strategies in the Spanish of San Juan, Puerto Rico. *Diachronica* 2 (17):249–292.
Capps, L., and E. Ochs. 1995. Out of Place: Narrative Insights into Agoraphobia. *Discourse Processes* 19:407–439.
Cárdenas, N. D. 1967. *El español de Jalisco: Contribución a la geografía lingüística hispanoamericana. Revista de Filología Española,* Supplement 85.
Cardoso, L. 1980. *Mexican Emigration to the United States, 1897–1931.* Tucson: University of Arizona Press.
Caro Baroja, J. 1966. Honour and Shame: A Historical Account of Several Conflicts. In *Honour and Shame: The Values of Mediterranean Society,* edited by J. G. Peristiany, pp. 79–137. Chicago: University of Chicago Press.
Carricaburo, N. 1997. *Las fórmulas de tratamiento en el español actual.* Madrid: Arco Libros.
Casuso, J., and E. Camacho. 1995. Latino Chicago. In *Ethnic Chicago: A Multicultural Portrait,* edited by M. G. Holli and P. d.'A. Jones, pp. 346–377. Grand Rapids, MI: William B. Eerdmans Publishing Company.
Cazden, C. 1988. *Classroom Discourse: The Language of Teaching and Learning.* Portsmouth, NH: Heinemann.
Chávez, O. 1993. *La charrería: Tradición mexicana.* Mexico City: Casa Pedro Domecq.
Chávez Carbajal, M. G. 1995. *El rostro colectivo de la nación mexicana.* Encuentro de afromexicanistas (5). Morelia, Mexico.
———. 1997. *El rostro colectivo de la nación mexicana.* Morelia, Mexico: Universidad Michoacana de San Nicolás de Hildalgo.
Chávez Torres, M. 1994. Uno es la de todo. In *Rancheros y sociedades rancheras,* edited by E. Barragán, O. Hoffmann, T. Linck, and D. Skerritt, pp. 109–124. Zamora, Mexico: El Colegio de Michoacán.
———. 1998. *Mujeres de rancho, de metate y de corral.* Zamora, Mexico: El Colegio de Michoacán.
Chevalier, F. 1982. Acerca de los orígenes de la pequeña propiedad en el occidente de México: Historia comparada. In *Después de los latifundios (la desintegración de la gran propiedad en México),* edited by H. Moreno, pp. 3–8. Mexico City: El Colegio de Michoacán.

———. 1985 [1956]. *La formación de los latifundios en México.* Mexico City: Fondo de Cultura Económica.

Chicago, City of. Department of Planning and Development. 2001. *Hispanic or Latin by Specific Origin by Community Area: 2000.* Report based on 2000 Census of Population and Housing, June 29.

Chicago Fact Book Corsortium. 1995. *Local Community Fact Book: Chicago Metropolitan Area 1990.* Chicago: University of Illinois at Chicago.

Chodorowska, M. 1997. On the Polite Function of *¿me entiendes?* in Spanish. *Journal of Pragmatics* 28:355–371.

Chodorowska-Pilch, M. 1998. Encoding of Politeness in Spanish and Polish: A Cross-Linguistic Study. Ph.D. dissertation, Hispanic Linguistics, University of Southern California.

Cintron, R. 1997. *Angel's Town: Chero Ways, Gang Life, and Rhetorics of the Everyday.* Boston: Beacon Press.

Clifford, J. 1988. *The Predicament of Culture: Twentieth-Century Ethnography, Literature, and Art.* Cambridge, MA: Harvard University Press.

Cochet, H. 1991. *Alambradas en la sierra: Un sistema agrario en México.* Zamora, Mexico: El Colegio de Michoacán.

Cockcroft, J. D. 1986. *Outlaws in the Promised Land: Mexican Immigrant Workers and America's Future.* New York: Grove Press.

Cohen, J. 2003. Creativity within Constraints: Language, Identity, and U.S.-Born Mexican Girls in Southeast Chicago. Ph.D. dissertation, University of Illinois at Chicago.

Collins, J., and R. Blot. 2003. *Literacy and Literacies: Texts, Power, and Identity.* Cambridge: Cambridge University Press.

Correa-Uribe, F. 1995. El discurso oral del chicano como nueva perspectiva de análisis de la segunda personal singular. *Lenguas Modernas* 22:167–179.

Cosío Villegas, D., I. Bernal, A. Moreno Toscano, L. González, E. Blanquel, and L. Meyer. 1995. *A Compact History of Mexico.* Mexico City: El Colegio de México.

Craig, A. 1983. *The First Agraristas: An Oral History of a Mexican Agrarian Reform Movement.* Berkeley: University of California Press.

Cross, H. E., and J. A. Sandos. 1981. *Across the Border: Rural Development and Recent Migration to the United States.* Berkeley: University of California, Institute of Governmental Studies.

Da Matta, R. 1991. *Carnivals, Rogues, and Heroes: An Interpretation of the Brazilian Dilemma.* Notre Dame, IN: University of Notre Dame Press.

Damien de Surgy, J., K. Rocío Martinez, and M. Thierry Linck. 1988. El auge del aguacate: ¿Hacia que tipo de desarrollo? (Municipio de Atapan). In *Paisajes agrarios de Michoacán,* edited by H. Cochet, E. Leonard, and J. Damien de Surgy, pp. 350–395. Zamora, Mexico: El Colegio de Michoacán.

de Certeau, M. 1988. *The Practice of Everyday Life.* Berkeley: University of California Press.

DeGenova, N. 1998. Race, Space, and the Re-invention of Latin America in Mexican Chicago. *Latin American Perspectives* 25 (5):87–116.

de la Peña, G. 1984. Ideology and Practice in Southern Jalisco: Peasants, Rancheros, and Urban Entrepreneurs. In *Kinship Ideology and Practice in Latin America,* edited by R. T. Smith, pp. 204–234. Chapel Hill: University of North Carolina Press.

de la Vega Alfaro, E. 1995. Origins, Development and Crisis of the Sound Cinema

(1929–1964). In *Mexican Cinema*, edited by P. A. Paranaguá, pp. 79–93. London: British Film Institute.

Delgado-Gaitán, C. 1993. Parenting in Two Generations of Mexican American Families. *International Journal of Behavioral Development* 16 (3):409–427.

Del Paso y Troncoso, F. 1945. *Papeles de Nueva España, Segunda serie: Geografía y estadística, Tomo VII, Suplemento, Relaciones geográficas de Michoacán, Instrucción relaciones: Chocandirán, Tarecuato.* Mexico City: Editor Vargas Rea.

Denton, N. A., and D. Massey. 1989. Racial Identity among Caribbean Hispanics: The Effect of Double Minority Status on Residential Segregation. *American Sociological Review* 54:790–808.

Dickerson, M. 2004. Funds Sent to Mexico Hit Record. *Los Angeles Times*, July 30.

Dinerman, I. R. 1982. *Migrants and Stay-at-Homes: A Comparative Study of Rural Migration from Michoacán, Mexico.* Monograph series 5. San Diego: Center for U.S.-Mexican Studies, University of California, San Diego.

Domínguez Barajas, E. 2002. Reconciling Cognitive Universals and Cultural Particulars: A Mexican Social Network's Use of Proverbs. Ph.D dissertation, University of Illinois at Chicago.

———. 2005. Socio-cognitive Aspects of Proverb Use in a Mexican Transnational Social Network. In *Latino Language and Literacy in Ethnolinguistic Chicago*, edited by M. Farr, pp. 67–95. Hillsdale, NJ: Erlbaum.

Douglas, M. 1968. The Social Control of Cognition: Some Factors in Joke Perception. *Man* (3):361–376.

Dow, J. 1981. The Image of Limited Production: Envy and the Domestic Mode of Production in Peasant Society. *Human Organization* 40:360–363.

Duranti, A. 1997. *Linguistic Anthropology.* Cambridge: Cambridge University Press.

Eckert, P. 1990. Cooperative Competition in Adolescent Girl Talk. *Discourse Processes* 13:92–122.

———. 2000. *Linguistic Variation as Social Practice.* Oxford: Blackwell.

Elías-Olivares, L. 1979. Language Use in a Chicano Community: A Sociolinguistic Approach. In *Sociolinguistic Aspects of Language Learning and Teaching*, edited by J. B. Pride, pp. 120–134. Oxford: Oxford University Press.

Elías-Olivares, L., and M. Farr. 1991. Final Report: Sociolinguistic Analysis of Mexican-American Patterns of Non-response to Census Questionnaires, July. Report to the U.S. Bureau of the Census, Washington, D.C.

Elliott, J. H. 1987. Spain and America before 1700. In *Colonial Spanish America*, edited by L. Bethell, pp. 59–111. Cambridge: Cambridge University Press.

Espinosa, V. 1998. *El dilema del retorno: Migración, género y pertenencia en un contexto transnacional.* Zamora, Mexico: El Colegio de Michoacán.

Esquivel Vega, E. 1985. *Peribán y su antigua jurisdicción: Los Reyes, Tingüindín, Charapan, San Francisco de Peribán—Metamorfosis de un pueblo.* Guadalajara, Mexico: Castro Impresores.

Esteva-Fabregat, C. 1995. *Mestizaje in Ibero-America.* Tucson: University of Arizona Press.

Farr, M. 1990. Dialects, Culture, and Teaching the English Language Arts: A Review of Research. In *Handbook of Research on Teaching the English Language Arts*, edited by J. Jensen, J. Flood, D. Lapp, and J. Squire, pp. 365–371. New York: Macmillan.

———. 1993. Essayist Literacy and Other Verbal Performances. *Written Communication* 10 (1):4–38.

———. 1994a. Biliteracy in the Home: Practices among Mexicano Families in

Chicago. In *Adult Biliteracy in the United States,* edited by D. Spener, pp. 89–110. McHenry, IL, and Washington, DC: Delta Systems and Center for Applied Linguistics.

———. 1994b. *Echando relajo:* Verbal Art and Gender among Mexicanas in Chicago. In *Cultural Performances: Proceedings of the Third Berkeley Women and Language Conference,* edited by Mary Bucholtz et al., pp. 168–186. Berkeley: University of California Press.

———. 1994c. *En los dos idiomas:* Literacy Practices among Mexicano Families in Chicago. In *Literacy across Communities,* edited by B. Moss, pp. 9–47. Cresskill, NJ: Hampton Press.

———. 1998. El relajo como microfiesta. In *México en fiesta,* edited by H. Pérez, pp. 457–470. Zamora, Mexico: El Colegio de Michoacán.

———. 2000. Literacy and Religion: Reading, Writing, and Gender among Mexican Women in Chicago. In *Language in Action: New Studies of Language in Society,* edited by J. K. Peyton, P. Griffin, W. Wolfram, and R. Fasold, pp. 139–154. Cresskill, NJ: Hampton Press.

———, ed. 2004. *Ethnolinguistic Chicago: Language and Literacy in the City's Neighborhoods.* Hillsdale: NJ: Erlbaum.

———, ed. 2005. *Latino Language and Literacy in Ethnolinguistic Chicago.* Hillsdale, NJ: Erlbaum.

Farr, M., and A. Ball. 1999. Standard English and Educational Policy. In *Concise Encyclopedia of Educational Linguistics,* edited by B. Spolsky, pp. 205–208. Oxford: Elsevier.

Farr, M., and J. Guerra. 1995. Literacy in the Community: A Study of *Mexicano* Families in Chicago. *Discourse Processes Special Issue: Literacy among Latinos* 19 (1):7–19.

Farr, M., and R. Reynolds. 2004. Introduction: Language and Identity in a Global City. In *Ethnolinguistic Chicago: Language and Literacy in the City's Neighborhoods,* edited by M. Farr, pp. 3–32. Mahwah, NJ: Erlbaum.

Field, L. 1998. Post-Sandinista Ethnic Identities in Western Nicaragua. *American Anthropologist* 100 (2):431–443.

Finnegan, R. 1988. *Literacy and Orality: Studies in the Technology of Communication.* Oxford: Blackwell.

Florescano, E. 1987. The Hacienda in New Spain. In *Colonial Spanish America,* edited by L. Bethell, pp. 250–285. Cambridge: Cambridge University Press.

Flores-González, N. 1999. Puerto Rican High Achievers: An Example of Ethnic and Academic Identity Compatibility. *Anthropology and Education Quarterly* 30 (3):343–362.

Foster, G. M. 1988 [1967]. *Tzintzuntzan: Mexican Peasants in a Changing World.* Prospect Heights, IL: Waveland Press.

Fraser, B. 1980. Conversational Mitigation. *Journal of Pragmatics* 4:341–350.

Friedrich, P. 1971. Dialectal Variation in Tarascan Phonology. *International Journal of American Linguistics* 37 (3):164–187.

———. 1977. *Agrarian Revolt in a Mexican Village.* Chicago: University of Chicago Press.

———. 1986. *The Princes of Naranja: An Essay in Anthrohistorical Method.* Austin: University of Texas Press.

Frye, D. 1996. *Indians into Mexicans: History and Identity in a Mexican Town.* Austin: University of Texas Press.

Galetto, M. V. 1999. Aguacate y migradólares: Un estudio sobre la migración a Estados Unidos y la transformación de la economía agrícola de San Juanico, Michoacán. Master's thesis, Social Anthropology, Universidad Iberoamericana, Mexico City.

Galindo, L. 1992. Dispelling the Male-Only Myth: Chicanas and Caló. *Bilingual Review/La Revista Bilingüe* 17 (1):3–35.

Galindo, L., and M. D. Gonzales. 1999. *Speaking Chicana: Voice, Power, and Identity.* Tucson: University of Arizona Press.

García, J. 1996. *Mexicans in the Midwest: 1900–1932.* Tucson: University of Arizona Press.

García Riera, E. 1995. The Impact of Rancho Grande. In *Mexican Cinema,* edited by P. A. Paranaguá, pp. 128–132. London: British Film Institute.

García y Griego, M. 1996. The Importation of Mexican Contract Laborers to the United States, 1942–1964. In *Between Two Worlds: Mexican Immigrants in the United States,* edited by D. G. Gutiérrez, pp. 45–85. Wilmington, DE: Scholarly Resources, Inc.

Gibson, C. 1987. Indian Society under Spanish Rule. In *Colonial Spanish America,* edited by L. Bethell, pp. 361–399. Cambridge: Cambridge University Press.

Gledhill, J. 1991. *Casi Nada: A Study of Agrarian Reform in the Homeland of Cardenismo.* Austin: University of Texas Press.

Goffman, E. 1967. *Interaction Ritual: Essays on Face-to-Face Behavior.* New York: Anchor Books.

———. 1974. *Frame Analysis: An Essay on the Organization of Experience.* New York: Harper and Row.

Gonzales, M. G. 1999. *Mexicanos: A History of Mexicans in the United States.* Bloomington: University of Indiana Press.

González, L. 1968. *Pueblo en vilo: Microhistoria de San José de Gracia.* Mexico City: El Colegio de México.

———. 1974. *San José de Gracia: Mexican Village in Transition.* Austin: University of Texas Press.

———. 1991. Del hombre a caballo y la cultura ranchera. *Tierra Adentro* 52:3–7.

———. 1995. A Century of Enlightenment. In *A Compact History of Mexico,* edited by D. Cosío Villegas, I. Bernal, A. Moreno Toscano, L. González, E. Blanquel, and L. Meyer, pp. 65–102. Mexico City: El Colegio de México.

González, N. 2001. *I Am My Language: Discourses of Women and Children in the Borderlands.* Tucson: University of Arizona Press.

González de la Vara, M. 1994. Rancheros en las ciudades: La organización productiva de los heladeros en Mexticacán y Tocumbo. In *Rancheros y sociedades rancheras,* edited by E. Barragán, O. Hoffmann, T. Linck, and D. Skerritt, pp. 287–300. Zamora, Mexico: El Colegio de Michoacán.

González Méndez, V., and H. Ortiz Ybarra. 1980. *Los Reyes, Tingüindín, Tancítaro, Tocumbo y Peribán: Centro occidental de Michoacán.* Monografía Municipal del Estado de Michoacán. Morelia, Mexico: Gobierno del Estado de Michoacán.

Goody, J. 1968. *Literacy in Traditional Societies.* Cambridge: Cambridge University Press (1st paperback ed. 1975).

———, ed. 1977. *The Domestication of the Savage Mind.* Cambridge: Cambridge University Press.

Griswold del Castillo, R., and A. De León. 1996. *North to Aztlán: A History of Mexican Americans in the United States.* New York: Twayne Publishers.

Guerra, J. 1998. *Close to Home: Oral and Literate Practices in a Transnational Mexicano Community.* New York: Teachers College Press.

Guerra, J., and M. Farr. 2002. Writing on the Margins: Spiritual and Autobiographical Discourse among Mexicanas in Chicago. In *School's Out!: Literacy at Work and in the Community,* edited by G. Hull and K. Schultz, pp. 96–123. New York: Teachers College Press.

Gumperz, J. 1982. *Discourse Strategies.* Cambridge: Cambridge University Press.

———. 1992. Contextualization and Understanding. In *Rethinking Context: Language as an Interactive Phenomenon,* edited by A. Duranti and C. Goodwin, pp. 229–252. Cambridge: Cambridge University Press.

Gutiérrez, R. 1991. *When Jesus Came, the Corn Mothers Went Away: Marriage, Sexuality and Power in New Mexico, 1500–1846.* Stanford, CA: Stanford University Press.

Gutmann, M. C. 1996. *The Meanings of Macho: Being a Man in Mexico City.* Berkeley: University of California Press.

Haverkate, H. 1994. *La cortesía verbal: Estudio pragmalingüístico.* Madrid: Editorial Gredos.

Heath, S. B. 1972. *Telling Tongues: Language Policy in Mexico, Colony to Nation.* New York: Teachers College Press.

———. 1983. *Ways with Words: Language, Life, and Work in Communities and Classrooms.* Cambridge: Cambridge University Press.

Herguth, R. C. 2002. Archer Heights Popular with Newly Arrived Poles. *Chicago Sun-Times,* August 21.

Hernández-Flores, N. 1999. Politeness Ideology in Spanish Colloquial Conversations: The Case of Advice. *Pragmatics* 9 (1):37–49.

Hernández Galvan, M. 1926. Psicología ranchera. *Mexican Folkways* 8 (August–September): 8–10.

Herrera-Sobek, M. 1990. *Mexican Corrido: A Feminist Analysis.* Bloomington: Indiana University Press.

———. 1993. *Northward Bound: The Mexican Immigrant Experience in Ballad and Song.* Bloomington: Indiana University Press.

Hewitt de Alcántara, C. 1976. *Modernizing Mexican Agriculture: Socioeconomic Implications of Technological Change, 1940–1970.* Geneva: United Nations Research Institute for Social Development.

Hill, J. H. 1995. The Voice of Don Gabriel: Responsibility and Self in a Modern Mexicano Narrative. In *The Dialogic Emergence of Culture,* edited by D. Tedlock and B. Mannheim, pp. 97–147. Urbana: University of Illinois Press.

Hill, J. H., and K. C. Hill. 1986. *Speaking Mexicano: Dynamics of Syncretic Language in Central Mexico.* Tucson: University of Arizona Press.

Hirsch, J. S. 1999. *En el norte la mujer manda:* Gender, Generation, and Geography in a Mexican Transnational Community. *American Behavioral Scientist* 42 (9):1332–1349.

Hirsch, S. F. 1998. *Pronouncing and Persevering: Gender and the Discourse of Disputing in an African Islamic Court.* Chicago: University of Chicago Press.

Hoffmann, O. 1994. Rancheros y notables en Veracruz: Su actuación política en las sociedades locales. In *Rancheros y sociedades rancheras,* edited by E. Barragán, O. Hoffmann, T. Linck, and D. Skerritt, pp. 219–236. Zamora, Mexico: El Colegio de Michoacán.

Holli, M. G. 1995 [1977]. German American Ethnic and Cultural Identity from 1890 Onward. In *Ethnic Chicago*, edited by M. G. Holli and P. d'A. Jones, pp. 93–109. Grand Rapids, MI: Eerdmans.

Holli, M. G., and P. d'A. Jones, eds. 1995 [1977]. *Ethnic Chicago*. Grand Rapids, MI: Eerdmans.

Hondagneu-Sotelo, P. 1994. *Gendered Transitions: Mexican Experience of Migration*. Berkeley: University of California Press.

Hurtig, J. 1998. Gender Lessons: Schooling and the Reproduction of Patriarchy in a Venezuelan Town. Ph.D. dissertation, University of Michigan.

Hymes, D. 1972. On Communicative Competence. In *Sociolinguistics*, edited by J. B. Pride and J. Homes, pp. 269–293. Harmondsworth: Penguin.

———. 1974a. *Sociolinguistics: An Ethnographic Approach*. Philadelphia: University of Pennsylvania Press.

———. 1974b. Ways of Speaking. In *Explorations in the Ethnography of Speaking*, edited by R. Bauman and J. Sherzer, pp. 433–451. Cambridge: Cambridge University Press.

———. 1975. Breakthrough into Performance. In *Folklore: Performance and Communication*, edited by D. Ben-Amos and K. S. Goldstein, pp. 11–74. The Hague: Mouton.

———. 1981. *"In Vain I Tried to Tell You": Essays in Native American Ethnopoetics*. Philadelphia: University of Pennsylvania Press.

———. 2002. Problems of Translation. *Anthropology News* 43 (5):23.

Ingham, J. M. 1986. *Mary, Michael, and Lucifer: Folk Catholicism in Central Mexico*. Austin: University of Texas Press.

Jacobs, I. 1982. *Ranchero Revolt: The Mexican Revolution in Guerrero*. Austin: University of Texas Press.

Jakobson, R. 1960. Closing Statement: Linguistics and Poetics. In *Style in Language*, edited by T. Sebeok, pp. 350–434. New York: John Wiley.

———. 1995 [1957]. Shifters and Verbal Categories. In *On Language: Ramon Jakobson*, edited by L. R. Waugh and M. Monville-Burston, pp. 386–392. Cambridge: Harvard University Press.

Jefferson, G. 1978. Sequential Aspects of Storytelling in Conversation. In *Studies in the Organization of Conversational Interaction*, edited by J. Schenkein, pp. 219–248. New York: Academic Press.

Jones, O. L. 1979. *Los Paisanos*. Norman: University of Oklahoma Press.

Kamphoefner, W. D., W. Helbich, and U. Sommer. 1991. *News from the Land of Freedom: German Immigrants Write Home*. Ithaca, NY: Cornell University Press.

Keen, B. 1996. *A History of Latin America*. Boston: Houghton Mifflin.

Keesing, R. M. 1974. Theories of Culture. *Annual Review of Anthropology* 3:73–97.

Kerr, L. A. N. 1976. The Chicano Experience in Chicago: 1920 to 1970. Ph.D. dissertation. Department of History, University of Illinois at Chicago.

———. 1977. Mexican Chicago: Chicano Assimilation Aborted, 1939–54. In *Ethnic Chicago*, edited by M. G. Holli and P. d'A. Jones, pp. 270–298. Grand Rapids, MI: William B. Eerdmans Publishing Co.

———. 1984. Mexican Chicago: Chicano Assimilation Aborted, 1939–54. In *Ethnic Chicago*, edited by M. Holli and P. d'A. Jones, pp. 270–298. Grand Rapids, MI: Eerdmans Publishing Co.

Knight, A. 1990. Racism, Revolution, and Indigenismo: Mexico, 1910–1940. In *The*

Idea of Race in Latin America, 1870–1940, edited by R. Graham, pp. 71–113. Austin: University of Texas Press.

Kroskrity, P., ed. 2000. *Regimes of Language*. Santa Fe, NM: School of American Research Press.

Kuper, A. 1999. *Culture: The Anthropologists' Account*. Cambridge, MA: Harvard University Press.

Labov, W. 1972a. *Language in the Inner City: Studies in the Black English Vernacular*. Philadelphia: University of Pennsylvania Press.

———. 1972b. *Sociolinguistic Patterns*. Philadelphia: University of Pennsylvania Press.

———. 1994. *Principles of Linguistic Change: Internal Factors*. Oxford: Basil Blackwell.

Lane, J. B., and E. J. Escobar. 1987. *Forging a Community: The Latino Experience in Northwest Indiana, 1919–1975*. Chicago: Cattails Press.

Lara Ramos, L. F., ed. 1996. *Diccionario del español usual en México*. Mexico City: El Colegio de México.

Lauria, A. 1964. "Respeto," "Relajo," and Inter-personal Relations in Puerto Rico. *Anthropological Quarterly* 37 (1):53–67.

Lawrence, D. H. 1986/1927. *Mornings in Mexico*. New York: Viking Penguin.

LeVine, R. A., and M. I. White. 1986. *Human Conditions: The Cultural Basis of Educational Development*. New York: Routledge.

Levinson, B. 2001. *We Are All Equal: Student Culture and Identity at a Mexican Secondary School: 1988–1998*. Durham: Duke University Press.

Limón, J. 1982. History, Chicano Joking, and the Varieties of Higher Education: Tradition and Performance as Critical Symbolic Action. *Journal of the Folklore Institute* 19:141–166.

———. 1992. *Mexican Ballads, Chicano Poems: History and Influence in Mexican-American Social Poetry*. Berkeley: University of California Press.

———. 1994. *Dancing with the Devil: Society and Cultural Poetics in Mexican-American South Texas*. Madison: University of Wisconsin Press.

Lindquist, J. 1999. Class Ethos and the Politics of Inquiry: What the Barroom Can Teach Us about the Classroom. *College Composition and Communication* 51 (2):225–247.

———. 2001. Hoods in the Polis. *Pedagogy: Critical Approaches to Teaching Literature, Language, Composition, and Culture* 1 (2):261–274.

Lipski, J. 1994. *Latin American Spanish*. New York: Longman.

Lloyd, J. D. 1988. Desarrollo histórico del ranchero y rancheros y revolucionarios en Chihuahua. In *Historia de la cuestión agraria mexicana*. Vol. 3: *Campesinos, terratenientes y revolucionarios, 1910–1920*, edited by O. Betanzo et al., pp. 60–106. Mexico City: Siglo XXI/CEHAM.

Lomnitz-Adler, C. 1992. *Exits from the Labyrinth: Culture and Ideology in the Mexican National Space*. Berkeley: University of California Press.

López, G. 1995. *El Río Bravo es charco*. Zamora, Mexico: El Colegio de Michoacán.

Lucy, J. A. 1993. *Reflexive Language: Reported Speech and Metapragmatics*. Cambridge: Cambridge University Press.

Malkin, E. 2004. Loan Office in New York Looks to Tap Mexican Market. *New York Times*, March 4.

Massey, D. S. 1981. Hispanic Residential Segregation: A Comparison of Mexicans, Cubans, and Puerto Ricans. *Sociology and Social Research* 65:311–322.

———. 1997. *Worlds in Motion: International Migration at Century's End.* Oxford: Oxford University Press.

———. n.d. March of Folly: U.S. Immigration Policy under NAFTA. Undated MS. Population Studies Center, University of Pennsylvania.

Massey, D. S., R. Alarcón, J. Durand, and H. González. 1987. *Return to Aztlán: The Social Process of International Migration from Western Mexico.* Berkeley: University of California Press.

Massey, D. S., and N. A. Denton. 1989. Residential Segregation of Mexicans, Puerto Ricans, and Cubans in Selected U.S. Metropolitan Areas. *Sociology and Social Research* 73 (2):73–83.

———. 1993. *American Apartheid: Segregation and the Making of the Underclass.* Cambridge, MA: Harvard University Press.

Mauss, M. 1990 [1950]. *The Gift: The Form and Reason for Exchange in Archaic Societies.* Translated by W. D. Halls. London: Routledge.

McBride, G. M. 1923. *Land Systems of Mexico.* New York: American Geographical Society.

Medina de la Serna, R. 1995. Sorrows and Glories of Comedy. In *Mexican Cinema,* edited by P. A. Paranaguá, pp. 163–170. London: British Film Institute.

Melhuus, M. 1996. Power, Value, and the Ambiguous Meanings of Gender. In *Machos, Mistresses, Madonnas: Contesting the Power of Latin American Gender Imagery,* edited by M. Melhuus and K. A. Stølen, pp. 159–183. New York: Verso.

Mertz, E. 1985. Beyond Symbolic Anthropology: Introducing Semiotic Mediation. In *Semiotic Mediation: Sociocultural and Psychological Perspectives,* edited by E. Mertz and R. J. Parmentier, pp. 1–19. New York: Academic Press.

Meyer, J. 1976. *The Cristero Rebellion: The Mexican People between Church and State, 1926–1929.* Cambridge: Cambridge University Press.

Miller, P. 1994. Narrative Practices: Their Role in Socialization. In *The Remembering Self: Construction and Accuracy in the Self-Narrative,* edited by U. Neisser and R. Fivush, pp. 158–179. Cambridge: Cambridge University Press.

Milroy, L. 1987. *Language and Social Networks.* 2nd ed. Oxford: Blackwell.

Mishler, G. E. 1995. Models of Narrative Analysis: A Typology. *Journal of Narrative and Life History* 5 (2):87–123.

Moliner, M. 1998. *Diccionario de uso del español.* Madrid: Editorial Gredos.

Montsiváis, C. 1995. Mythologies. In *Mexican Cinema,* edited by P. A. Paranaguá, pp. 117–127. London: British Film Institute.

Mora, C. 1982. *Mexican Cinema: Reflection of a Society, 1896–1980.* Berkeley: University of California Press.

Moreno de Alba, J. 1994. *El español en América.* Mexico City: Fondo de Cultura Económica.

Mörner, M. 1987. Rural Economy and Society in Spanish South America. In *Colonial Spanish America,* edited by L. Bethell, pp. 286–314. Cambridge: Cambridge University Press.

Morse, R. 1987. Urban Development. In *Colonial Spanish America,* edited by L. Bethell, pp. 165–202. Cambridge: Cambridge University Press.

Mummert, G. 1994. From *Metate* to *Despate:* Rural Mexican Women's Salaried Labor and the Redefinition of Gendered Spaces and Roles. In *Women of the Mexican Countryside, 1850–1990,* edited by H. Fowler-Salamini and M. K. Vaughan, pp. 192–209. Tucson: University of Arizona Press.

Nelson, C., and M. Tienda. 1997. The Structuring of Hispanic Ethnicity: Historical and Contemporary Perspectives. In *Challenging Fronteras: Structuring Latina and Latino Lives in the U.S.*, edited by M. Romero, P. Hondagneu-Sotelo, and V. Ortiz, pp. 7–29. New York: Routledge.

Newbart, D. 2003. Immigrants Enjoy Life in "Burbs." *Chicago Sun Times*, June 16.

Northeastern Illinois Planning Commission. 2005. Census 2000 Demographic Profiles. Available from http://www.nipc.org/forecasting/GDP4-counties/gdp4-counties.htm.

Nugent, D., and A. M. Alonso. 1994. Multiple Selective Traditions in Agrarian Reform and Agrarian Struggle: Popular Culture and State Formation in the *Ejido* of Namiquipa, Chihuahua. In *Everyday Forms of State Formation: Revolution and the Negotiation of Rule in Modern Mexico*, edited by G. M. Joseph and D. Nugent, pp. 209–246. Chapel Hill, NC: Duke University Press.

Oboler, S. 1995. *Ethnic Labels, Latino Lives: Identity and the Politics of (Re)presentation in the United States*. Minneapolis: University of Minnesota Press.

Ochs, E. 1990. Indexicality and Socialization. In *Cultural Psychology: Essays on Comparative Perspective*, edited by G. Herdt, R. Schweder, and J. Stigler, pp. 287–308. Cambridge: Cambridge University Press.

———. 1992. Indexing Gender. In *Rethinking Context: Language as an Interactive Phenomenon*, edited by A. D. C. Goodwin, pp. 335–358. Cambridge: Cambridge University Press.

Olson, D. 1977. From Utterance to Text: The Bias of Language in Speech and Writing. *Harvard Educational Review* 41:257–281.

———. 1994. *The World on Paper: The Conceptual and Cognitive Implications of Writing and Reading*. New York: Cambridge University Press.

Omi, M., and H. Winant. 1994. *Racial Formation in the United States from the 1960s to the 1990s*. New York: Routledge.

Ong, W. J. 1982. *Orality and Literacy: The Technologizing of the Word*. New York: Methuen.

Ortner, S. B. 1996. *Making Gender: The Politics and Erotics of Culture*. Boston, MA: Beacon Press.

Ortner, S. B., and H. Whitehead. 1981. *Sexual Meanings: The Cultural Construction of Gender and Sexuality*. Cambridge: Cambridge University Press.

Padilla, F. M. 1985. *Latino Ethnic Consciousness: The Case of Mexicans and Puerto Ricans in Chicago*. Notre Dame: University of Notre Dame Press.

Pardo Pulido, R. 1957. *La Villa de Tingüindín de Argandar*. Zamora, Mexico: Ramirus Vargas Cacho.

Paredes, A. 1993. *Folklore and Culture on the Texas-Mexican Border*. Edited by R. Bauman. Austin: University of Texas Press.

Parmentier, R. J. 1997. The Pragmatic Semiotics of Cultures. *Semiotica* 116 (1):1–115.

Parodi, C. 1995. *Orígenes del español americano, I: Reconstrucción de la pronunciación*. Mexico City: Universidad Nacional Autónoma de México.

Peñalosa, F. 1995. Toward an Operational Definition of the Mexican American. In *Latinos in the United States: History, Law and Perspective, Volume I, Historical Themes and Identities: Mestizaje and Labels*, edited by A. Sedillo López, pp. 411–422. New York: Garland.

Pérez, H. 1994. El vocablo rancho y sus derivados: Génesis, evolución y usos. In *Rancheros y sociedades rancheras*, edited by E. Barragán, O. Hoffmann, T. Linck, and D. Skerritt, pp. 33–56. Zamora, Mexico: El Colegio de Michoacán.

———, ed. 1998. *México en fiesta*. Zamora, Mexico: El Colegio de Michoacán.

Philips, S. U. 2000. Constructing a Tongan Nation State through Language Ideology in the Courtroom. In *Regimes of Language*, edited by P. V. Kroskrity, pp. 229–257. Santa Fe, NM: School of American Research Press.

Pitt-Rivers, J. A. 1966. Honour and Social Status. In *Honour and Shame: The Values of Mediterranean Society*, edited by J. G. Peristiany, pp. 19–38. Chicago: University of Chicago Press.

———. 1971 [1954]. *The People of the Sierra*. Chicago: University of Chicago Press.

Poovey, M. 1988. *Uneven Developments: The Ideological Work of Gender in Mid-Victorian England*. Chicago: University of Chicago.

Portilla, J. 1966. *Fenomenología del relajo*. Mexico City: Ediciones Era, S.A.

Pratt, M. L. 1991. Arts of the Contact Zone. *Profession* 91:33–40.

Purnell, J. 1999. *Popular Movements and State Formation in Revolutionary Mexico: The Agraristas and Cristeros of Michoacán*. Durham, NC: Duke University Press.

Quinones, S. 2001. *True Tales from Another Mexico: The Lynch Mob, the Popsicle Kings, Chalino, and the Bronx*. Albuquerque: University of New Mexico Press.

Reisler, M. 1976. *By the Sweat of Their Brow: Mexican Immigrant Labor in the United States, 1900–1940*. Westport, CT: Greenwood Press.

Rivera, J. M. 1855. El ranchero. In *Los mexicanos pintados por sí mismos*, edited by various authors, pp. 201–215. Mexico City: Casa de M. Murguia.

Rivera Ayala, S. 1994. Lewd Songs and Dances from the Streets of Eighteenth-Century New Spain. In *Rituals of Rule, Rituals of Resistance: Public Celebrations and Popular Culture in Mexico*, edited by W. H. Beezley, C. E. Martin, and W. E. French, pp. 27–46. Wilmington, DE: Scholarly Resources.

Rockwell, E. 1991. Palabra escrita, interpretación oral: Los libros de texto en la clase. *Infancia y Aprendizaje* 55:29–43.

Rodríguez, C. E. 2000. *Changing Race: Latinos, the Census, and the History of Ethnicity in the United States*. New York: New York University Press.

Rodríguez, C. E., and H. Cordero-Guzman. 1992. Placing Race in Context. *Ethnic and Racial Studies* 15 (4):523–541.

Rodríguez, V. M. 1997. The Racialization of Puerto Rican Ethnicity in the United States. In *Ethnicity, Race and Nationality in the Caribbean*, edited by J. M. Carrion, pp. 233–273. Rio Pedras: Institute of Caribbean Studies.

Rogers, S. C. 1975. Female Forms of Power and the Myth of Male Dominance: A Model of Female/Male Interaction in Present Society. *American Ethnologist* 2:727–756.

Romero Flores, J. 1960. *Diccionario michoacano de historia y geografía*. Ed. del Gobierno del Estado. Morelia, Mexico: Talleres Tipográficos de la Escuela Técnica Industrial "Alvaro Obregón."

Rosales, F. A. 1995. The Regional Origins of Mexicano Immigrants to Chicago during the 1920s. In *Latinos in the United States: Historical Themes and Identity, Volume One: Mestizaje and Labels*, edited by A. S. López, pp. 247–307. New York: Garland.

Rosales, F. A., and D. T. Simon. 1987 [1981]. Mexican Immigrant Experience in the Urban Midwest: East Chicago, Indiana, 1919–1945. In *Forging a Community: The Latino Experience in Northwest Indiana*, edited by J. B. Lane and E. J. Escobar, pp. 137–160. Chicago: Cattails Press.

Roth, A. 1995. La categoría "popular" y los debates sobre "lo mexicano": El caso de las chingaderas. In *El verbo popular*, edited by A. Roth and J. Lameiras, pp. 47–65. Zamora, Mexico: El Colegio de Michoacán.

Rouse, R. 1988. Migración al suroeste de Michoacán durante el Porfiriato: El caso de

Aguililla. In *Movimientos de población en el occidente de México,* edited by T. Calvo and G. López, pp. 231–250. Zamora, Mexico: El Colegio de Michoacán.

———. 1989. Mexican Migration to the United States: Family Relations in the Development of a Transnational Migrant Circuit. Ph.D. dissertation, Department of Anthropology, Stanford University.

———. 1991. Mexican Migration and the Social Space of Postmodernism. *Diaspora* 1 (1):8–23.

———. 1992. Making Sense of Settlement: Class Transformation, Cultural Struggle, and Transnationalism among Mexican Migrants in the United States. In *Towards a Transnational Perspective on Migration,* edited by N. Glick Schiller, L. Basch, and C. Blanc-Szanton, pp. 25–52. New York: New York Academy of Sciences.

Sabean, D. W. 1984. *Power in the Blood: Popular Culture and Village Discourse in Early Modern Germany.* New York: Cambridge University Press.

Sanders, R. 1978. *Lost Tribes and Promised Lands: The Origins of American Racism.* New York: Harper Perennial.

Santa Ana, O. 2002. *Brown Tide Rising: Metaphors of Latinos in Contemporary American Public Discourse.* Austin: University of Texas Press.

Santa Ana, O., and C. Parodi. 1998. Modeling the Speech Community: Configuration and Variable Types in the Mexican Spanish Setting. *Language in Society* 27 (1):23–51.

Saucedo Ramos, C. L. 1998. *Expresiones genéricas de los adolescentes en el contexto sociocultural de un Conalep.* Mexico City: Centro de Investigación y de Estudios Avanzados del Instituto Politécnico Nacional.

Saville-Troike, M. 1989. *The Ethnography of Communication.* London: Basil Blackwell.

Scarano, F. 1996. The *Jíbaro* Masquerade and the Subaltern Politics of Creole Identity Formation in Puerto Rico, 1745–1823. *American Historical Review* 101 (5):1398–1431.

Schieffelin, B., and E. Ochs. 1986. *Language Socialization across Cultures.* Cambridge: Cambridge University Press.

Schieffelin, B., K. A. Woolard, and P. Kroskrity, eds. 1998. *Language Ideologies: Practice and Theory.* New York: Oxford University Press.

Schiller, N. G., L. Basch, and C. Blanc-Szanton. 1992. *Transnationalism: A New Analytic Framework for Understanding Migration.* New York: New York Academy of Sciences.

Schryer, F. J. 1980. *The Rancheros of Pisaflores: The History of a Peasant Bourgeoisie in Twentieth-Century Mexico.* Toronto/Buffalo/London: University of Toronto Press.

Scott, J. 1990. *Domination and the Arts of Resistance: Hidden Transcripts.* New Haven: Yale University Press.

Shadow, R. D., and M. Rodríguez-Shadow. 1994. Clase y etnicidad entre los rancheros mexicanos del norte de Nuevo México. In *Rancheros y sociedades rancheras,* edited by E. B. López, O. Hoffmann, T. Linck, and D. Skerrit, pp. 153–172. Zamora, Mexico: El Colegio de Michoacán.

Sherzer, J. 1983. *Kuna Ways of Speaking: An Ethnographic Perspective.* Austin: University of Texas Press.

———. 1987. A Discourse-Centered Approach to Language and Culture. *American Anthropologist* 89 (2):295–309.

———. 1990. *Verbal Art in San Blas: Kuna Culture through Its Discourse.* Cambridge: Cambridge University Press.

———. 2002. *Speech Play and Verbal Art.* Austin: University of Texas Press.

Sigüenza-Ortiz, C. 1996. Social Deixis in a Los Angeles Spanish-English Bilingual Community: *Tú* and *Usted* Patterns of Address. Ph.D. dissertation, University of Southern California.

Silva-Corvalán, C. 1994. *Language Contact and Change: Spanish in Los Angeles.* Oxford: Oxford University Press.

Silverstein, M. 1976. Shifters, Linguistic Categories, and Cultural Description. In *Meaning in Anthropology,* edited by K. H. Basso and J. H. A. Selby, pp. 11–55. Albuquerque: University of New Mexico Press.

———. 1993. Metapragmatic Discourse and Metapragmatic Function. In *Reflexive Language: Reported Speech and Metapragmatics,* edited by J. A. Lucy, pp. 33–58. New York: Cambridge University Press.

Silverstein, M., and G. Urban, eds. 1996. *Natural Histories of Discourse.* Chicago: University of Chicago Press.

Skerry, P. 1993. *Mexican Americans: The Ambivalent Minority.* Cambridge, MA: Harvard University Press.

Skertic, M., and C. Lawrence. 2002. Ethnics Disappearing: European Groups Don't Dominate. *Chicago Sun-Times,* August 21.

Slatta, R. W. 1990. *Cowboys of the Americas.* New Haven: Yale University Press.

———. 1992 [1983]. *Gauchos and the Vanishing Frontier.* Lincoln: University of Nebraska Press.

Spicer-Escalante, M. 2005. Writing in Two Languages/Living in Two Worlds: A Rhetorical Analysis of Mexican-American Written Discourse. In *Latino Language and Literacy in Ethnolinguistic Chicago,* edited by M. Farr, pp. 217–244. Mahwah, NJ: Erlbaum.

Spradley, J. P. 1980. *Participant Observation.* New York: Holt, Rinehart and Winston.

Stern, S. 1995. *The Secret History of Gender: Women, Men, and Power in Late Colonial Mexico.* Chapel Hill: University of North Carolina Press.

Stoeltje, B. J. 1992. Festival. In *Folklore, Cultural Performances, and Popular Entertainments,* edited by R. Bauman, pp. 261–271. Oxford: Oxford University Press.

Street, B. 1984. *Literacy in Theory and Practice.* Cambridge: Cambridge University Press.

———, ed. 1993. *Cross-cultural Approaches to Literacy.* Cambridge: Cambridge University Press.

Sullivan, T. R. 1990. *Cowboys and Caudillos: Frontier Ideology of the Americas.* Bowling Green, OH: Bowling Green State University Popular Press.

Szwed, J. 1981. The Ethnography of Literacy. In *Writing: Functional and Linguistic-Cultural Variation,* edited by M. Farr Whiteman, pp. 13–23. Hillsdale, NJ: Erlbaum.

Tannen, D. 1989. *Talking Voices: Repetition, Dialogue, and Imagery in Conversational Discourse.* New York: Cambridge University Press.

Taussig, M. 1979. *The Devil and Commodity Fetishism in Latin America.* Chapel Hill: University of North Carolina Press.

Taylor, P. S. 1933. *A Spanish-Mexican Peasant Community: Arandas in Jalisco, Mexico.* Berkeley: University of California Press.

———. 1987 [1932]. Mexican Labor in the Calumet Region. In *Forging a Community: The Latino Experience in Northwest Indiana, 1919–1975,* edited by J. B. Lane and E. J. Escobar, pp. 33–79. Chicago: Cattails Press.

Taylor, W. B. 1979. *Drinking, Homicide and Rebellion in Colonial Mexican Villages.* Stanford, CA: Stanford University Press.

Tedlock, D. 1983. *The Spoken Word and the Work of Interpretation.* Philadelphia: University of Pennsylvania Press.

Tedlock, D., and B. Mannheim. 1995. *The Dialogic Emergence of Culture.* Urbana: University of Illinois Press.

Telles, E. E., and E. Murguia. 1990. Phenotypic Discrimination and Income Differences among Mexican Americans. *Social Science Quarterly* 71 (4):682–696.

Thompson, G. 2003. A Surge in Money Sent Home by Mexicans. *New York Times,* October 28.

Tompkins, J. 1992. *West of Everything: The Inner Life of Westerns.* New York: Oxford University Press.

Turner, F. J. 1994 [1893]. The Significance of the Frontier in American History. In *Where Cultures Meet: Frontiers in Latin American History,* edited by D. J. Weber and J. M. Rausch, pp. 1–18. Wilmington, DE: Scholarly Resources.

Valdés, D. N. 1991. *Al Norte: Agricultural Workers in the Great Lakes Region, 1917–1970.* Austin: University of Texas Press.

———. 2000. *Barrios Norteños: St. Paul and Midwestern Mexican Communities in the Twentieth Century.* Austin: University of Texas Press.

Valdés, G. 1996. *Con Respeto: Bridging the Distances between Culturally Diverse Families and Schools: An Ethnographic Portrait.* New York: Teachers College Press.

Valdés, L. M., and M. T. Menéndez. 1987. *Dinámica de la población de habla indígena (1900–1980).* Mexico City: Instituto Nacional de Antropología e Historia.

Vargas, Z. 1993. *Proletarians of the North: A History of Mexican Industrial Workers in Detroit and the Midwest, 1917–1933.* Berkeley: University of California Press.

Vaughan, M. K. 1994. The Construction of the Patriotic Festival in Tecamachalco, Puebla, 1900–1946. In *Rituals of Rule, Rituals of Resistance: Public Celebrations and Popular Culture in Mexico,* edited by W. H. Beezley, C. E. Martin, and W. E. French, pp. 213–245. Wilmington, DE: Scholarly Resources, Inc.

———. 1997. *Cultural Politics in Revolution: Teachers, Peasants, and Schools in Mexico, 1930–1940.* Tucson: University of Arizona Press.

Warman, A. 1982. *We Come to Object.* Baltimore: John Hopkins University Press.

Warren, B. 1985. *The Conquest of Michoacán.* Norman: University of Oklahoma Press.

Weber, D. J., and J. M. Rausch. 1994. *Where Cultures Meet: Frontiers in Latin American History.* Wilmington, DE: Scholarly Resources, Inc.

Weinstein, R. S. 2002. *Reaching Higher: The Power of Expectations in Schooling.* Cambridge, MA: Harvard University Press.

West, R. C. 1973. *Cultural Geography of the Modern Tarascan Area.* Westport, CT: Greenwood Press.

Wexman, V. W. 1993. *Creating the Couple: Love, Marriage, and Hollywood Performance.* Princeton, NJ: Princeton University Press.

Wierzbicka, A. 1991. *Cross-cultural Pragmatics: The Semantics of Human Interaction.* Berlin: Mouton de Gruyter.

Williams, R. 1977. *Marxism and Literature.* Cambridge: Cambridge University Press.

Wolfram, W., and N. Schilling-Estes. 1998. *American English.* Oxford: Blackwell.

Woolard, K. A. 1998. Introduction: Language Ideology as a Field of Inquiry. In *Language Ideologies: Practice and Theory,* edited by B. B. Schieffelin, K. A. Woolard, and P. Kroskrity, pp. 3–47. Oxford: Oxford University Press.

Wortham, S. 2001. *Narratives in Action: A Strategy for Research and Analysis.* New York: Teachers College Press.

Zavala, S. 1994 [1965]. The Frontiers of Hispanic America. In *Where Cultures Meet: Frontiers in Latin American History,* edited by D. J. Weber and J. M. Rausch, pp. 42–50. Wilmington, DE: Scholarly Resources.

Zentella, A. C. 1997. *Growing Up Bilingual: Puerto Rican Children in New York.* Oxford: Blackwell.

Index

Page numbers in italics refer to figures and tables.